D0850595

Expressive Forms in Brahms's Instrumental Music

MUSICAL MEANING AND INTERPRETATION
Robert S. Hatten, editor

PETER H. SMITH, *P. H.*

Expressive Forms
in Brahms's
Instrumental Music,

Structure and Meaning
in His *Werther* Quartet

INDIANA UNIVERSITY PRESS
Bloomington and Indianapolis

Chapter 4 is a revised version of "Brahms and Schenker: A Mutual Response to Sonata Form," © 1994 by the Society for Music Theory, Inc., reprinted from *Music Theory Spectrum* 16, no. 1, by permission of the publisher, University of California Press.

Example 2.10 is from Charles J. Smith, "Musical Form and Fundamental Structure: An Investigation of Schenker's *Formenlehre*," *Music Analysis* 15 (1996): 263, by permission of the publisher, Blackwell Publishing.

Example 2.16 is from Carl Schachter, "The First Movement of Brahms's Second Symphony: The Opening Theme and Its Consequences," *Music Analysis* 2 (1983): 62 and 64, by permission of the publisher, Blackwell Publishing.

Example 5.11 is reproduced from Maury Yeston, ed., *Readings in Schenkerian Analysis and Other Approaches*, by permission of the publisher, Yale University Press.

This book is a publication of

Indiana University Press
601 North Morton Street
Bloomington, IN 47404-3797 USA

http://iupress.indiana.edu

Telephone orders   800-842-6796
Fax orders   812-855-7931
Orders by e-mail   iuporder@indiana.edu

Library of Congress Cataloging-in-Publication Data

Smith, Peter Howard.
   Expressive forms in Brahms's instrumental music : structure and meaning in his Werther quartet / Peter H. Smith.
      p. cm. — (Musical meaning and interpretation)
   Includes bibliographical references (p.) and index.
   ISBN 0-253-34483-2 (cloth : alk. paper)
   1. Brahms, Johannes, 1833-1897. Quartets, piano, strings, no. 3, op. 60, C minor. 2. Brahms, Johannes, 1833-1897—Criticism and interpretation. I. Title. II. Series.
   MT145.B72S65 2005
   785'.28194—dc22   2004017942

1 2 3 4 5 10 09 08 07 06 05

To the memory of my mother,

Carol Ruth Carlin

1933–2003

Contents

Acknowledgments

It would be difficult given limitations of space and memory to acknowledge each and every individual who assisted in the completion of this book. I nevertheless would like to recognize those who were at the forefront in helping me develop the book's intellectual substance and sustaining me through the inevitable ups and downs of authorship. My interest in the dialectic of articulation and continuity in nineteenth-century music was first sparked by the teaching of Robert Morgan of Yale University. Professor Morgan was kind enough to accept me as a dissertation advisee at a time at which my application of his insights to the music of Brahms was in its most formative stages. It is a testament to his powerful influence as a teacher and musician that the ideas that he helped me develop then still stand at the core not just of this book but of my work in general.

The idea for a monograph focusing on intersections of structure and expression in the C-minor Piano Quartet, op. 60, grew out of a long series of discussions of the work with Professor Michael Friedmann, also of Yale University. Professor Friedmann's passion for music in general and Brahms in particular has been an ongoing source of inspiration. The three professors who have served as departmental chair during my years on the faculty of the University of Notre Dame—Ethan Haimo, Susan Youens, and Paul Johnson—have each in their own separate ways provided professional accommodation and personal support. Without their help I would have had a much more difficult time maintaining the proper balance among research, teaching, and service necessary to see me through to the completion of this book.

I also would like to thank Robert Hatten of Indiana University for his immediate interest when I first brought my ideas for a book to him and for his careful reading and editing of the completed manuscript. Gayle Sherwood and the staff of Indiana University Press deserve credit for their professionalism in handling all aspects of the book's production. Ken Froelich provided expert note-processing of the music examples, whose preparation was made possible by a generous grant from the Institute for Scholarship in the Liberal Arts, College of Arts and Letters, University of Notre Dame.

Finally I owe my deepest gratitude to my family. My wife, Lumi, and my son, Manny, have an uncanny ability to take me away from the struggles and frustrations of academia, providing a joyous home life that allows me to put all else in perspective. Over the years my parents and stepfather have provided not only unconditional love but also all the support for a musical career that any son could wish for, starting with viola lessons in the third grade and continuing on through graduate school and beyond. It will always hearten me to recall the sudden brightness in my mother's voice as she responded to my report that my book had been accepted for publication, even as she was struggling with the later stages of the cancer that was to take her life.

Introduction

1   Quintessential Brahms and the Paradox of the C-Minor Piano Quartet: A Representative yet Exceptional Work

"Imagine a man who is about to shoot himself, and for whom there is no other way out." So suggested Johannes Brahms to his friend Hermann Deiters upon showing him a version of the first movement of his C-Minor Piano Quartet, op. 60, in the summer of 1868.[1] As advice for music appreciation, this certainly stands out as one of the most unusual suggestions ever offered by a composer. Brahms nevertheless continued to associate the quartet with images of suicide through the work's completion in 1873–74. He wrote to another friend, Theodore Billroth, to explain that he was presenting him the final version of the quartet "purely as a curiosity! An illustration, as it were, to the last chapter of the man in a blue swallow-tail coat and yellow waistcoat."[2] This sartorial description is an obvious reference to the famous dress of Werther, the central character in Goethe's *Die Leiden des jungen Werthers* (The Sorrows of Young Werther), a novella about the emotional agony and eventual suicide of a young man in love with the wife of an admired older friend.[3]

What could it possibly mean to suggest that an abstract instrumental work, by of all composers Brahms, illustrates an act of suicide? The quartet is a piece, after all, that like so many of Brahms's instrumental cycles unfolds in four movements, in a standard fast-fast-slow-fast pattern. Moreover, as is typical for Brahms, each movement follows conventions of the Classical forms traditionally associated with its position in the cycle: sonata form for the first and last movements, an ABA' ternary pattern for the scherzo, and for the Andante a sonata-ternary hybrid characteristic for Brahms and in no way unprecedented in the Viennese tradition. In genre, instrumentation, form, tonal language, and motivic process, the quartet hardly appears to stand apart from Brahms's other chamber works in a manner that would justify associations with something as disturbing as the image of a man about to commit suicide.

Yet the crucial phrase here is "hardly appears." For, as we all know, appearances can be deceiving, especially when considered superficially. The connection Brahms suggested between the quartet and Goethe's *Werther*—and by extension with his relationship to Robert and Clara Schumann—has often been cited in the Brahms literature. One nevertheless searches in vain for sustained exploration of specifically *how* the musical processes of this amazing composition could possibly correlate with the agony of an individual about to commit suicide. My intention is to fill this gaping lacuna in Brahms studies.

Music theory—at least in its contemporary guise as a postwar academic discipline—has tended to pursue issues of structure rather than expression. This in part is a consequence of the historical context in which the seeds for postwar, Anglo-American theory were first planted. In carving out a place for a new discipline, musicians such as Milton Babbitt and Allen Forte presented their approach as an alternative to what they saw as the unselfconscious analytic habits of musicology, as well as to that discipline's focus on historical context. Theory was to correct these deficits, replace impressionistic discussions of expression with objective engagement with structure, and develop tools for understanding the music of the twentieth century.[4] The technical orientation of theorists in turn led musicologists to criticize the interpretive context of the emerging subdiscipline as too narrow.[5] The theory community's focus on structure notwithstanding, there existed from the outset a minority voice dedicated to broader concerns. Edward T. Cone, for example, wrote essays in a humanistic vein that eventually led to a theory of dramatic personification, while Leonard B. Meyer addressed concepts of emotion and meaning as well as style development.[6]

More recently some of music theory's basic premises—the idea of structural unity and the autonomous artwork and, indeed, the very possibility for analytical objectivity—have been called into question. Characteristics that made theory seem fresh in an earlier era had come to make it appear outdated in the eyes of some feminist and postmodernist critics.[7] Although many theorists today no longer insist on a scientific model for their work—with discussions of expression mocked as the all-too-subjective ramblings of dilettantes, critics, and program annotators—a scarcity of studies directed at the intersection of structure and expression persists. Theory and analysis nevertheless retain their relevance to broader concerns, as the recent books on style and expression by V. Kofi Agawu and Robert S. Hatten demonstrate. Their engagement with theory as a tool for a comprehensive understanding of music represents a more fruitful approach than a postmodern rejection of structural analysis.[8]

This outlook forms the basis for my investigation of intersections of structure and expression in the C-minor piano quartet. My intention is to engage the quartet as a case study for how it might be possible to steer a middle course between the old music theory, which tends to be purely analytical and formalist, and the new musicology, which often denies itself the insights of careful musical analysis in the pursuit of critical interpretation. Now that the theory community has developed and disseminated sophisticated analytical tools, the time is ripe to explore how our work can contribute still further to insight into expressive content. Brahms's quartet constitutes an ideal context in which to counter claims that a theoretical approach is inimical to broader understandings of music. The work's idiosyncratic characteristics allow it to function as a test case for development of a generalized analytical approach that engages close technical analysis not as an end in itself, but as a means of pursuing questions of expression. Moreover, the same idiosyncratic characteristics make the quartet fertile ground for a reappraisal of signature elements of Brahmsian style.

My approach resists the impulse to close off dialogue by either rejecting the potential insights of theory on the one hand, or insisting on a pseudo-scientific, self-referential vision of music on the other. Rather, I embark on a substantial work of technical analysis that also engages questions of expression. My intention is to promote an analytic program of general applicability that respects the traditions and working methods of theory but likewise takes seriously the need to extend the analytical enterprise into the expressive realm. Indeed, theory and analysis are necessary tools in this regard: they have the capacity to bring us closer to the individuality of an artwork and thus to its particular expressive profile.

At first glance, Brahms and his C-minor quartet might seem to be unlikely choices for such an undertaking. During his lifetime and even to this day, Brahms has been associated with the idea of absolute music perhaps more than any other composer. Moreover, the quartet, like his other chamber works, represents the branch of his oeuvre most at odds with the nineteenth-century trend toward program music. His vocal works and even his symphonies—a large and public genre—would appear to be more likely candidates for discussion of musical expression. Yet it is precisely the absence of a text or program that forces engagement with relationships revealed through structural analysis as primary sources for expressive content. The analysis will not be able to focus on verbal or literary components in the pursuit of an expressive interpretation; structural characteristics will have to stand at the forefront.

This is not to say that I will avoid reference to extra-musical materials. Indeed, one reason the quartet is an apt choice is the aforementioned association with Goethe's *Werther*. The connection suggests the great personal significance of the quartet for Brahms based on the parallelism between Werther's love for Charlotte despite her marriage to Albert and Brahms's love for Clara Schumann despite her marriage to Robert. Indeed, an earlier C♯-minor version of the final work of 1875 dates from the mid-1850s, the height of Brahms's emotional entanglements with the Schumanns. Part of my argument is that the quartet's highly idiosyncratic structural characteristics find their motivation in the personal aspect of the composer's expressive aims and the fact that, as an expression of suicidal despair, the work stands at an emotional extreme relative to other pieces by Brahms.

Another reason the quartet stands as an apt choice for extended study is the crucial role it played in Brahms's artistic development. Along with the First Symphony—not coincidentally, another C-minor work begun many years before completion—it forms a bridge from his "first maturity" in the early 1860s to the new stage of composition he seems to have entered in the 1870s.[9] The *Alto Rhapsody* (1870) and the *Schicksalslied* (1871) of the intervening years and the C-Minor String Quartet, op. 51, no. 1, of 1873 join the symphony to form a comparative context for exploration of structure and expression in the quartet. All of these pieces exploit the key character and intertextual resonance of C-minor tonality in the service of tragic expression. Yet the differences among the works are as telling as the similarities. A comparison with compositional strategies in these pieces will highlight the unusual expressive consequences of Brahms's idiosyncratic approach in the piano quartet. I will eventually broaden out to consider aspects of Brahms's overall approach to tragic expression, not only in C minor but also in other keys, as well as connections with the approaches of his Viennese precursors.

In addition to issues of artistic development, biographical significance, and intersections of structure and expression, a focus on the quartet easily radiates outward to a reexamination of signature elements of Brahmsian style. At first glance, one piece might seem to constitute too narrow a context to yield insight into the overall achievement of a major figure like Brahms. Part of my argument, however, is that close and methodologically self-conscious analysis is a necessary step toward insight into broader concerns like expression, historical significance, and style. The quartet is an appropriate choice for several reasons. On the one hand, it is in many respects unique in Brahms's oeuvre. Yet it achieves its special status through intensification of standard Brahmsian strategies. In other words, the work is governed by a paradox: it represents a prototype of Brahms's core compositional concerns, while at the same time it stands apart in both structural organization and expressive content.

It is true that to a certain degree each of Brahms's works is governed by its own set of structural and expressive characteristics, while simultaneously reflecting at least some of the proclivities that define his style. Yet the piano quartet does appear to be a special case—perhaps not the only special case, but a work that is highly idiosyncratic nevertheless. Although many of its compositional strategies appear in other works by Brahms, a combination of so many unusual attributes is rare. Moreover, the most characteristically Brahmsian features appear in extreme form. The quartet encapsulates the essence of Brahms's language and, what is more, concentrates that essence to such a degree that the composition could be said to represent quintessential Brahms. Illumination of the quartet's special features profitably merges into reflection on Brahms's overall approach to composition as well as the ubiquitous question of his relationship to tradition.

A focus on the quartet also has a strong critical intention. Normally when musicians speak of the greatest of Brahms's chamber pieces, works such as the G-Major Viola Quintet, op. 111, the A-Minor Clarinet Trio, op. 114, or the B-Minor Clarinet Quintet, op. 115, first come to mind. Even among the three piano quartets, the C-minor quartet is perhaps the least often performed. The quartet has also been slighted—unintentionally, I believe, given its quality—in a number of the most influential studies of Brahms's instrumental works. James Webster forgoes discussion of the opening sonata form in his seminal study of Schubert's influence on Brahms's first maturity, even though documentary evidence supports a connection between the completed first movement of 1875 and the C♯-minor version of the mid-1850s. Logically enough, Webster cites the Allegro's unique form and the fact that it is impossible to know the precise relationship between the two versions as reasons why the completed movement falls beyond the purview of his essay.[10] Walter Frisch likewise does not discuss the quartet at all in his well-known monograph on Brahms and Schoenberg's concept of developing variation.[11] Here

I champion the quartet as a work on a par with any of his instrumental masterpieces and therefore deserving of the attention these other pieces have received in the scholarly literature. Indeed, I regard the quartet as Brahms's crowning achievement as a composer of instrumental music.

At the core of my approach rests the idea that a complex interaction of musical dimensions characterizes Brahms's style. Although a layering of structural parameters—or *dimensional counterpoint*—typifies music of the tonal tradition, Brahms was especially adept at extending the degree to which individual strands of the total musical fabric might function quasi-independently to yield multiple interpretive possibilities. He often creates discrepancies among locations of different types of critical events in the tonal plan, the beginning and ending points of thematic sections, changes in patterns of accompaniment and/or instrumentation, and large-scale instances of rhythmic-metric articulation. This structural noncongruence results in both multivalence with regard to the meaning of standard musical gestures and a formal process in which tension and instability extend across enormous stretches of time.[12] Attention to discrepancies among dimensions is important not only for aesthetic appreciation, but also because flexible interaction among parameters is one of the chief means through which Brahms sustains the vitality of traditional procedures in a late nineteenth-century historical context.

A vision of Brahms that stresses the idea of dimensional counterpoint requires diverse theoretical tools to communicate its insights. My analytic practice draws on a variety of approaches from historical and contemporary music theory to respond to the complex tapestry of relationships that Brahms weaves into his compositions. In addition to its advantages for illumination of Brahmsian style, the strategy serves as a corrective to the tendency for music theorists to pursue the concerns of a given analytical approach in a single-minded manner. Over the years commitments to isolated theoretical frameworks have helped the field reach a point of refinement and sophistication. Yet by now music theorists have enough understanding of individual methodologies so that an approach dedicated to multiple perspectives can enrich, rather than confuse, discourse on musical structure. Moreover, in the process of exploring Brahms's dimensional counterpoint via a counterpoint of analytical methods, the need for further refinements of those very methods emerges. The present work thus has a powerful metatheoretic component.

The topically focused chapters of Part I will place idiosyncrasies of the quartet in the context of standard Brahmsian practice. This approach has two main advantages: first, it will ensure that the paradoxical character of the quartet—its status as a highly idiosyncratic yet representative work—will remain in the forefront; and second, it will guarantee that the concerns of the book extend well beyond the single opus to engage the larger topic of style in Brahms's instrumental works. In addition, these chapters will throw light on ways in which Brahms reimagines conventions of the Viennese tradition to conform with late nineteenth-century practice. The perspective on style is appropriately complex and engages both norms and deviations from those norms in Brahms's own works, nineteenth-century repertoires, and the Classical tradition.

Throughout, the theoretical concepts of Heinrich Schenker will play a central role. Arnold Schoenberg's profound insight into Brahms's musical language, although less omnipresent in the foreground, will also inspire some of the crucial large-scale developments in my analysis. The emphasis is logical given both the historical proximity of these musicians to Brahms in late nineteenth-century Vienna, as well as their overwhelming importance for developments in music theory. The idea is to combine their contrasting perspectives with more recent approaches, to uncover the multifarious means of organization that undergird Brahms's sensuous surface. A varied analytic practice also provides an opportunity to critique the strengths and limitations of existing methodologies. The strategy adopts the sort of sympathetic yet critical attitude toward underlying premises that is essential for progress in any field—but above all in one dominated by powerful seminal figures like Schenker and Schoenberg. Instead of discounting this or that perspective in favor of another, the book explores the insights of multiple viewpoints as a means of illuminating different strands of the Brahmsian structural tapestry. The result is not a wishy-washy "on the one hand, on the other hand" approach, but rather a methodology in which conclusions are based on an appropriately rich analytical database.

The payoff for the attention to structural detail in Part I arrives in Part II with chapters that explore expressive motivations for the stylistic deviations revealed in the topically focused sections. In addition to a tendency toward dimensional non-congruence, a hallmark of Brahms's approach to composition was his ability to merge genuine qualities of structure building with deep powers of emotional communication. This is one reason why he has earned the admiration of composers and scholars as well as performers and the general concert audience alike. A healthy trend in Brahms scholarship has been a move away from treatment of the composer's language merely as abstract technical achievement. Instead recent years have shown a marked increase in research dedicated to exploring expressive motivations for his motivic processes, formal innovations, and intertextual allusions.[13] Following this trend, my exploration of the quartet marshals structural analysis in the service of a larger hermeneutic enterprise.

My approach to issues of expression avoids the tendency in music theory to focus exclusively on the work in-and-of-itself. Instead I take as my point of departure the notion that biographical information can assist analysis and interpretation. Indeed, a theme running throughout is that the quartet's high degree of structural idiosyncrasy is a consequence of Brahms's unusual expressive aims, as they relate to the connection of the work with his experience with the Schumanns. The quartet is a composition in which extreme stylistic deviations contribute to an uncommonly bleak form of tragic expression. Many of its characteristics stretch beyond what is required on purely structural grounds and suggest a sense of profound frustration that resonates with the idea of suicidal despair. This is true throughout the work, both in detail and with respect to global organization.

The overall tragic tone of the quartet is apparent from the outset, as announced by the ominous octave C's that set the work in motion. Brahms himself hinted at an unusual intensity of expression with his aforementioned statements associating the work with images of suicide. If the inevitability of death through old age rep-resents a basic form of tragedy—human connections must eventually be severed no matter how strong the bonds—then premature death through illness or in-jury stands as an intensification of this fundamentally negative aspect of the hu-man condition. Yet suicide and especially the kind of youthful suicide depicted in Goethe's *Werther* extends into its own unique category of response to human struggle. The taking of one's own life is both absolute and irreversible in ways that no other human act can be, and as such reflects a singular expression of complete and utter hopelessness. The emotions involved would have to be among the most highly charged, whether they involve some combination of anger, frustration, de-spair, despondency, angst, disappointment, or any other manifestation of negative feeling.

Brahms's instrumental cycles that deal with themes of fate rarely suggest any-thing as emotionally bleak as suicide. Quite the contrary, his minor-mode works typically close with some elements of hope and consolation, if not outright tri-umph. It is in this context that we can begin to survey some of the quartet's eccen-tricities. These extreme, even at times bizarre, characteristics help to stir fateful energies that are excessive compared to other Brahms works and that are traceable to the quartet's special affective motivations as an expression of suicidal despair. The intention at this stage is not to engage in detailed interpretation, but rather to whet the reader's appetite for the analysis and interpretation to come.

The first factor to consider is perhaps the most basic: Brahms's choice of tonality. Originally he intended to set the work in C♯ minor, a key he otherwise avoided as an overriding tonality in his chamber and symphonic output. C minor, on the other hand, was a key he elsewhere turned to as a resource for tragic expression, most famously in the First Symphony but also in the op. 51, no. 1, string quartet and the C-Minor Piano Trio, op. 101. Brahms had yet to compose the piano trio when, after long gestation, he finally finished the piano quartet in 1873–74. He had, however, been at work on the symphony and string quartet for some time and likewise fin-ished them in the early to mid-1870s. He also already had three other scherzo-type movements in C minor in his list of published works: the fast middle movements of the G-Minor Piano Quartet, op. 25, and the F-Minor Piano Quintet, op. 34, and the scherzo he contributed to the *FAE* Sonata. All three of these movements share the compound meter and at least some of the motoric intensity of the piano quartet's scherzo. C minor is likewise Brahms's key of choice for engagement with issues of despair and human frailty in the *Alto Rhapsody* and *Schicksalslied*, works roughly contemporaneous with the symphony, string quartet, and piano quartet, as already noted.

In addition to creating an association with these works, Brahms's decision to shift the quartet down a half step also put it firmly in line with a long composi-tional tradition. Musicians generally accept the notion that C minor was a key of special expressive significance for Beethoven, especially for pieces that engage ques-tions of fate.[14] The same can be said for Haydn, Mozart, and Schubert, who also reserved the key for some of their most darkly expressive essays, for example,

Haydn's C-Minor *London* Symphony, no. 95, Mozart's C-Minor Piano Concerto, K. 491, and Schubert's *Quartettsatz*. C♯ minor by contrast has very little precedent as a tonality for complete multimovement cycles, with the notable exceptions of Beethoven's *Moonlight* Sonata and C♯-Minor String Quartet, op. 131. The intertextual connections that arise from Brahms's decision to shift the quartet into C♯ minor will prove crucial to interpretation of expressive content in Part II.

The second global factor to consider is the theme of relentless C-minor despair that pervades the cycle. The quartet's overarching tragic sweep overwhelms even those areas that typically afford opportunities for relief in minor-mode cycles. Any glimmers of hope that Brahms allows to emerge, he ultimately undercuts. This occurs on a number of different levels of musical organization and throughout the four movements. We shall see that even in the rare passages in which Brahms seems to suggest the potential for an escape from anguish, he nevertheless hints at the ultimate impossibility of transcendence.

On the most basic level, the quartet's bitter pessimism arises out of its failure to transform its C-minor tonic into the kind of transcendent C major that became a hallmark for nineteenth-century works following Beethoven's Fifth Symphony. The recapitulation of the first movement's secondary material in the unique key of the major dominant (mm. 236–87.1) instead of the tonic—arguably the quartet's most striking feature—crystallizes this aspect of the work's catastrophic tendencies. What kind of sonata principle could possibly motivate tonicization of major V in the very area of form normally dedicated to reconciliation of material with the home key? The exposition certainly does nothing to prepare for this startling divergence from formal convention. It modulates to the conventional key of E♭ major and articulates the mediant at m. 70 via the kind of arresting lyrical material characteristic for nineteenth-century sonata forms.

The exposition's conventional path holds out hope for the recapitulation to respond in kind with transposition of the lyrical material into C major. Instead Brahms willfully transforms this area of apparent relaxation into a section marked by an intense form of tragic irony. Through transposition into G major at m. 236, he reinterprets the lyrical material's outward sense of repose as an element of literal meaning completely at odds with what is actually being expressed. G major sounds peaceful on the surface, but as major dominant it is a tonal area predestined to collapse into C-minor despair. Indeed, when G does eventually resolve in the coda at m. 313, it is not to just any C minor, but to a C minor articulated by a return of the foreboding octaves from which the struggles of the movement began. That Brahms creates this devastating close via one of his most daring experiments with large-scale tonal organization—indeed, an unprecedented recapitulatory tonicization of the major dominant—and following one of his most extensively recomposed returns of primary material encapsulates the unique status of the quartet in his oeuvre.[15]

A similar instance of willful resistance to the possibility for C-major transcendence occurs in the recapitulation of the closing idea in the finale. Once again a conventional tonal path in the exposition suggests the potential for a C-major return. Although the recapitulation does restate the secondary material in the major tonic in mm. 271–310, it scarcely fulfills any promise of emotional healing. Rather, as we shall see, C major enters only to fail catastrophically as a potential source of consolation.

A common factor to note with respect to the secondary material in both the first and last movements is their unusual thematic character. For although the initial arrival of lyrical material in the first movement appears to follow convention as noted above, Brahms crafts the body of the secondary area as a set of variations on his eight-measure subordinate theme. The finale similarly sets the closing idea of mm. 75–95 off from the composer's range of typical procedures in its identity as a chorale. Brahms, of course, was a composer fully engaged in the great tradition of variation writing. The piano quartet, however, is the single case in which he adopts the technique as the basis for an entire secondary area, rather than for an independent movement. Likewise, although Brahms was fond of incorporating chorale-style passages into his symphonic music, the quartet is one of the few occasions in which he absorbs this particular religious topic into a chamber context.[16]

In the first movement the expository version of the second theme seemingly provides one of the quartet's only islands of stability. Yet even here, close analysis in later chapters will reveal seepage of the tonic area's C-minor foreboding into the secondary material. For its part we will see that the finale's chorale enters on the heels of a passage characterized by a stubborn conflict between transitional and second-theme functions (mm. 55–74), all introduced by one of Brahms's most peculiar moments of formal articulation in mm. 51–54. As seen in Example 1.1, the absence of a preparatory dominant and the $^6_3$ position of the local E♭ tonic together prevent articulation of a structural mediant *Stufe* at this point in the form. Thus although second-theme rhetoric begins to emerge, the exposition struggles to make a decisive move away from the fateful home key. In both the first and last movements the mediant falls under the shadow of despondent C minor.

Brahms sustains the idea of both tonal delay and formal duality across the chorale, which articulates its own conflict between second- and closing-theme functions. The mixed formal signals of the two sections of this second group reflect a larger tendency toward formal bivalence that permeates the quartet. Avoidance of repose grows from the fact that through abrupt shifts in dynamics, registration, and texture at m. 75, the chorale fails to resolve its preparatory V/E♭. Annotations in Example 1.2 highlight these elements of disjunction through which Brahms continues to hold in abeyance the idea of a resolution to E♭. It is as if the rug has been pulled out from under the potential point of arrival. Close reading in later chapters will show that the chorale thereby further delays articulation of the exposition's tonal goal until the latest possible moment (m. 95). That this occurs not simply across a closing idea—one level of formal contradiction—but also by means of music of a religious topic presents yet another multilayered irony characteristic of the quartet's expression of despair.

The extensive delay of this expository mediant reflects the same tendency toward frustration that we have just seen in the recapitulation of secondary material in the first movement. In both cases an area that easily could have provided a break from C-minor angst instead creates a musical correlation for the kind of profound

Example 1.1. First Attempt at E♭ Articulation

Example 1.2. Second Attempt at E♭ Articulation

disappointment that could lead to suicidal despondency. The finale's recapitulation follows through in a similar vain. There the secondary material returns in C major at m. 271, but Brahms nevertheless retains the same characteristics that created the tonal delay in the exposition. The result is that we are left waiting in vain for a decisive C-major tonic even as the restatement of the chorale merges into the coda at m. 311. The most Brahms provides is the newly composed yet crushingly brittle climax formed by the piano's statement of the chorale theme shown in Example 1.3.

The forced and hollow character of this false climax provides another example of the quartet's catastrophic failure to achieve a transcendent C major, at the very formal moment when it would seem to be most called for. It would be hard to imagine a starker contrast to the function of chorale material in other works of

Example 1.3. False Climax on Chorale Theme

Brahms's such as the First Symphony and the *Alto Rhapsody*. In the symphony multiple passages of chorale-style music—not only in the finale's tonic area but also in its slow introduction—famously contribute to the victory of C major, following rather than negating the model of Beethoven's Fifth Symphony. It is true that we would hardly expect this kind of universal expression of transcendence in the more intimate context of a chamber work. Yet the piano quartet nevertheless avoids even the kind of more personal and consolatory resolution that chorale material provides in the concluding C-major section of the *Alto Rhapsody*.[17] Indeed, through the failed climax at the coda, the quartet explicitly negates this conventional function for chorale music.

An even more straightforward example of C-minor relentlessness can be found in the quartet's scherzo—one of Brahms's most terse and demonic inventions. The movement's A and A′ sections of mm. 1–71 and 159–234 are almost entirely oriented around the home key with only two brief passages providing the barest minimum of contrast. This secondary material of mm. 23–33 and 177–87 again falls in the dominant key, yet now in *both* the opening A and returning A′ formal sections. In each case the secondary idea immediately collapses back into the minor tonic, thereby providing a foreground echo of the G-major to C-minor middleground progression across the recapitulation of the first movement. The omnipresence of C minor in relation to the suddenly attenuated dominant has the effect of tightening the grip of C-minor despair applied by the first movement's coda.

On the level of the entire movement, Brahms similarly resists any challenge to C minor's dominance. His B section eschews not only the customary contrast normally provided by a secondary key but even the simpler scoring or reduced tensions of a conventional trio section. Instead the B material (mm. 72–158) provides little tonal or thematic relief and culminates in one of Brahms's longest and most agonizingly tense retransitions.

Also significant to the unyielding despondency of the quartet is the fact that when Brahms does provide breaks from intensity, he distances them from the work's main line of argument. The E♭-major key of the Andante, for instance, holds the movement at a tonal remove from the overriding C minor. This tonal distance complements the sharp affective contrast created by the movement's dreamlike thematic character. The strategy again stands somewhat at odds with Brahms's more typical procedures, in this case a tendency toward reliance on closely related keys for his middle movements. (The key choice does, however, provide a further link with his First Symphony as well as to the tragic C-minor tradition via the precedent of Beethoven's Third Piano Concerto.)

Similarly, the calm of the secondary area in the exposition of the first movement stands at arm's length from the formal extremes articulated by the two main sections of the tonic area—extremes that themselves likewise contribute to the idiosyncratic character of the quartet. Although it is not unusual for Brahms to begin a sonata form with some tension between elements of initiation and preparation, the opening thirty-one measures of the quartet present one of his most frank and extended evocations of slow introductory character within a section that nevertheless turns out to be part of the exposition. At the other end of the formal spectrum stands the counterstatement (mm. 32–41.1), which corrects the tonal wandering and rhythmic starts and stops of the quasi introduction with a relentless focus on the tonic anchored by an obsessive C pedal. Following these abrupt shifts in character, a long transition carries the movement far away to the golden glow of the E♭ theme and variations. The distance of the lyrical second theme from the material that prepares it stands in parallel relation to the distance that separates the Andante from the other three movements. As we shall see, this multileveled relationship with respect to breaks in relentlessness has enormous consequences for the bitterly tragic outcome of the cycle.

The introductory character of the tonic area's first section provides an ideal opportunity to segue from consideration of some of the quartet's striking global-level features, to a selective survey of idiosyncrasies in compositional detail. As our analytical lens zooms in for a close-up view, the quartet continues to serve up a concentration of peculiar characteristics. The quasi introduction immediately estab-

Example 1.4. *Pizzicato* E♮'s

lishes a tone of foreboding through sustained C's in the piano as a call to order for the opening phrase. This in itself is not an unusual use of texture in a minor-mode work. It does, however, become part of the extreme idiosyncrasy of the quartet when Brahms intensifies the uncertainty with a sequential statement on B♭ in m. 11.

The creation of foreboding through seemingly foreign and abrupt tonal moves continues with the work's most notorious gesture, the *pizzicato* E♮'s in mm. 28–30. These E♮'s are not only tonally bizarre, as is often remarked, but also timbrally isolated from their immediate context, as seen in Example 1.4. All four movements, in fact, begin with some type of striking characteristic in compositional detail. This is true not only with respect to pitch structure but in terms of rhythm as well. The Andante and finale even expand the idiosyncrasy to include elements of instrumentation. The eccentricities of the initial gestures set the stage for what follows in each movement and help to establish an overall 2 + 2 grouping of those movements within a cycle otherwise marked by relentless continuity of motion and drama.

The first two movements are linked by parallel presentation of initial unison ideas in the piano marked *forte*. The last two movements, by contrast, both begin with extended passages in solo-sonata texture at moderate dynamic levels. In terms of affective meaning, this intimacy of texture draws attention to the individual as the locus for suffering. A similar relationship between solo texture and personification plays a crucial role in the secondary material in the first movement, where the piano and viola briefly step to the forefront, in the exposition and recapitulation, respectively (mm. 70–77, 236–43, and 252–69). That solo texture plays an important role both in this secondary material and in the Andante—the closest Brahms gets to allowing a reprieve of relentlessness—is certainly no coincidence.

Example 1.5. I–iv–I Tonic Expansion with C♮ and Augmented Triad

The focus on the individual adds poignancy to the dilemma these passages face as they attempt to sustain themselves in the face of C minor's unyielding despair.

In addition to aspects of texture, the openings of the Andante and finale are linked by transformation of a striking motivic detail. Like the quasi introduction in the first movement, the Andante's main theme incorporates a foreign chromatic element, in this case the prominent lowered 6̂ that is highlighted in Example 1.5. The C♮ is part of a I–iv⁶₅–I expansion of the tonic in mm. 1–2—a type of plagal progression of which Brahms was fond. The effect is not nearly as jarring as the first movement's *pizzicato* E♮'s: the E♮'s signal the *Unheimliches* as an important component of the quartet overall while the C♮'s endow the Andante's main theme with a bittersweet character. The lowered 6̂ nevertheless stands out in an otherwise diatonic E-major framework. The C♮ detail thus underscores the distance of E major from the cycle's overriding C♮ tonality.

In expressive terms the quartet is able to enter into an area of tranquility only in an E-major dream world in which the principal representative of tragic reality—the C♮ tonic pitch—functions as a foreign element. The *pizzicato* E♮'s similarly function as strikingly foreign elements in the first movement's C-minor context. C♮ and E♮—the two pitches that would need to come together to form a transcendent major tonic—seem always to be at odds. Any attempt to bring them into unity creates the feeling of resistance one gets when trying to force the wrong ends of two magnets together. When one pushes forward, the other is repelled.

Also noteworthy is the way the cello highlights C♮ as part of an augmented triad embedded within its melody in descending thirds. The augmented triad plays an important role on various levels of formal and motivic organization throughout

Example 1.6. Augmented Triad at Beginning of (a) Andante and (b) Finale

the quartet. One ingenious example is the unusual three-stage sequence that forms a retransition to the return of the opening material at the beginning of the A′ section later in the Andante (mm. 68–78). The augmented triad also solidifies the relationship between the opening sections of the Andante and the finale, where Brahms again embeds the idea within a pattern of descending thirds—the motivic transformation mentioned above. Example 1.6 highlights the connection. The motivic repetition helps to underline the affective shift from the individual, in the form of the solo cello, experiencing (or perhaps looking back on) a time of warmth and tranquility in the Andante, to the despair that person/violin feels in the face of the finale's tragic destiny.

Themes of despair likewise resonate strongly with details in the opening of the scherzo. Here, however, additional aspects of disorientation and instability create a connection with the first movement. The bond between the Allegro and scherzo complements the connection between the last two movements to form the aforementioned 2 + 2 subdivision within the cycle. An immediate tone of despondency in the scherzo grows from the character of the linear descent from $\hat{5}$ to $\hat{1}$ that the movement articulates as part of its brief introductory segment. As Example 1.7a indicates, Brahms inexplicably breaks off the line at $\hat{3}$, so that the arrival of $\hat{1}$ in the bass of the main theme at m. 5 enters within a passage that creates an odd sense of frustration rather than fulfillment. The disappointment is heightened by the *decrescendo* that accompanies the arrested stepwise descent. A normalized version appears only at the recapitulation, where the material participates in the climactic double return of main theme and tonic shown in Example 1.7b.

A sense of disorientation, on the other hand, arises from a rhythmic oddity: the durational pattern of the introduction's opening $\hat{5}$–$\hat{6}$ outburst, a scream of anguish that is virtually impossible to pin down metrically. Only in retrospect can it be understood as a strange kind of augmentation of the central rhythmic germ of the main theme, as annotations demonstrate in Example 1.7a. Likewise, the first movement's main theme begins with a quarter-note motive that teeters uneasily between strong-weak and weak-strong metric identities—a characteristic that becomes a source for compositional development at crucial formal moments, most notably just after the beginning of the recapitulation and in the coda (mm. 208–12.1 and

Example 1.7. Linear Descent at (a) Beginning and (b) Reprise of Scherzo

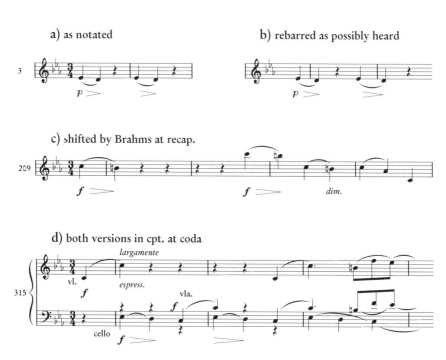

Example 1.8. Quarter-Note Motive and Its Metric Development

313–17, respectively). Example 1.8 identifies the original metric ambiguity and traces its development at these two areas of formal return.

The first two movements are also linked by issues of large-scale tonal organization. It is not simply a matter of balance, with the scherzo focusing attention almost exclusively on the tonic, after all the time away from C minor in the first movement. (Recall that the first movement not only spends considerable time in the mediant in the exposition, but also devotes the body of the recapitulation to tonicization of the major dominant.) It is also the sense that the scherzo tightens the grip of fate applied by the delayed return of the tonic in the coda of the first, as previously mentioned.

The preparation for this coda contains yet another passage of willful denial in which Brahms seems to be reaching beyond structural requirements to create a sense of despair, similar to the effect of the missing $\hat{2}$ at the outset of the scherzo. The material appears in Example 1.9. After the enormous delay of tonic return across the first movement's recapitulation, Brahms finally leads to a cadential dominant at the dramatic apex of m. 307. Yet despite more-than-adequate preparation, he refuses to allow the dominant finally to resolve at m. 308. Instead the tonic enters *fortissimo* but with G nevertheless still in the bass. Brahms thereby pushes a strategy of delay that already extends across the entire recapitulation to its bitter end, withholding a structural tonic until the final phrase of the movement (m. 313). It is with this type of stubborn resistance, in the face of a compositional

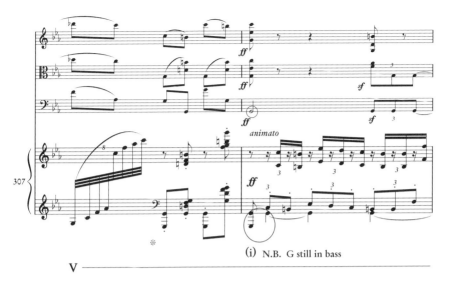

Example 1.9. Climactic Dominant and Thwarted Resolution

strategy that has already been taken to an extreme, as well as with other idiosyncratic if not downright bizarre characteristics—be they *pizzicato* E♮'s, sequences on ♭vii, failed climaxes on chorale material, theme and variation secondary areas, embedded augmented triads, recapitulations in the dominant key, and so forth—that the work points to its unusual affective motivations as an expression of suicidal despair.

Bizarre structural characteristics and their expressive corollaries are not all that mark the quartet as a special case. Several additional and related attributes that have already been mentioned set the work apart as worthy of focused attention. The first two points to consider are the quartet's long compositional gestation and chronological position within Brahms's oeuvre, the third, the composer's frank statements associating it with Goethe's *Werther* and, by extension, with his experiences in the Schumann household during the 1850s.

The quartet joins the First Symphony and the C-minor string quartet as pivotal works that form a bridge from Brahms's first maturity to the masterpieces of his later years. As a young composer he had difficulty completing emotionally charged minor-mode works, especially works in C minor. The first movement of the symphony dates from at least as far back as 1862, and the string quartet seems to have been completed in some fashion in the mid-1860s.[18] Both did not reach their final forms until the early to mid-1870s, as has already been noted. The pressure Brahms felt to live up to the standards set for him in these genres by his Viennese precursors was a likely source for the long gestation period. An additional difficulty, as James Webster has suggested, was Brahms's search for "a deeper level of integration of a multimovement work than was possible by thematic-motivic links alone." As Webster sees it, Brahms struggled to find appropriate means to create a sense of psychological progression across the whole of a work, especially a work in C minor.[19]

Less extreme but nevertheless noteworthy examples of compositional struggle include Brahms's efforts to complete the F-minor piano quintet and the D-Minor Piano Concerto, op. 15. Brahms was nevertheless able to finish these works in a much more timely fashion than his C-minor essays. This supports Webster's thesis that C minor itself posed a special challenge for Brahms. Although anxiety associated with the symphonic genre seems to have played a role in the case of the concerto, the main difficulty with it and the quintet centered around challenges of instrumentation and Brahms's indecision regarding the relationship between musical materials and the appropriate performing body. The quintet went through several adjustments in instrumentation alone, while the concerto began its life as a symphony and was also finished only after much tinkering and hesitation.

The piano quartet was a much safer genre for Brahms compared to the symphony and string quartet and perhaps even the concerto. There was not nearly as much tradition to live up to, and he had already completed two compositions in this scoring as well as in the related scoring of the piano quintet. The long gestation of the C-minor piano quartet thus demonstrates that it was not the weight of the musical past alone that prevented him from completing *Sturm und Drang* works in a timely fashion early in his career. In addition to the challenge of confronting the C-minor-to-C-major topos in the shadow of Beethoven, the more specific connection of the quartet with his experiences with the Schumanns also would seem to have played a role.

As is well known, Brahms generally kept both the technical genesis of his works and their relation to his emotional world out of reach for study by contemporaries or future generations. He closed the door to his compositional workshop through his notorious practice of destroying sketch material and draft copies of his published works. The same was true for youthful efforts or pieces that he considered unworthy of completion or publication. Information about the personal significance of his works also remains scant. His correspondence, as well as markings on his manuscripts and personal copies of published works, only occasionally provides hints about such issues.

As with questions of musical structure, information about the genesis and personal significance of the op. 60 piano quartet show it to be both representative of the standard situation with Brahms yet exceptional in certain telling respects. The surviving evidence about the C♯-minor version is characteristically slight yet somewhat more revealing than is normally the case. The same is true for revelations regarding the work's personal significance. Brahms's references to Goethe's *Werther* raise a red flag, while at the same time they scarcely go beyond the composer's characteristic terseness on these matters.

There is solid evidence that a draft of a three-movement precursor to the op. 60 quartet dates from the mid-1850s. Scholars disagree only on whether the precise date of composition falls in November of 1856 or earlier in 1855. References to the quartet emerge in Brahms's correspondence with Joseph Joachim in letters that were left undated. Andreas Moser's edition of the Brahms-Joachim correspondence places the two letters with an exchange of April 1856, a time when Brahms and Joachim were discussing their mutual study of counterpoint.[20] James Webster, however, has convincingly redated them to the last week of November 1856.[21]

Webster concludes, from this redating and other evidence, that although the first movement of the C#-minor version may have originated in 1855, the draft of all three movements was probably complete only in the fall of 1856. David Brodbeck, on the other hand, is more trusting of evidence put forward by Max Kalbeck in favor of an earlier dating. Brodbeck cites both a letter of Clara Schumann to Joachim in March of 1855, in which she describes "a magnificent first movement of a piano quartet," and Kalbeck's report of Albert Dietrich's "recollection from the y[ear] 1855 of the beginnings of a very somber piano quartet and of a very melodic and expressive second theme, which my friend Dr. H[ermann] Deiters also recognized again later in the Third Piano Quartet (C minor)."[22]

Part of Brodbeck's disagreement with Webster would appear to stem from a misunderstanding. Webster does not argue that *all* of the C#-minor version was composed in 1856, simply that a draft of the whole was probably completed only in late November of that year. Indeed, he cites both an entry in Clara's diary and a letter from Brahms to her as evidence that Clara already knew the first movement, as well as the slow middle movement, before the end of November.[23] Thus Brodbeck's argument for origins of the work in 1855 does not really contradict Webster, even though he presents it as if it does. The evidence Brodbeck cites for his earlier dating, for example, makes explicit reference to the first movement only. In the final analysis, moreover, it is not clear that it makes any difference. Neither Webster nor Brodbeck establish the significance that a slight adjustment in dating might make as we interpret the op. 60 quartet today. The main point—and on this no one disagrees—is that the work that eventually became the C-minor piano quartet originates in an earlier version that Brahms was working on at the height of his involvement with the Schumanns.

Webster crosses more significant ground when he moves from the question of a precise dating of the draft, to the relationship of content between the discarded C#-minor version and the later mature work. The following discussion of possible connections between the two versions summarizes arguments offered by Webster. The telling evidence again comes from the exchange between Brahms and Joachim. Joachim's letter refers to three movements: a first marked by austere seriousness, a deeply felt Andante, and a concise finale of terse passion. Clara also mentions a first movement and a slow middle movement, as we have already seen, although she identifies the tempo for the latter as Adagio rather than Andante.

Brahms and Joachim both describe characteristics of the C#-minor first movement that clearly found their way into the final C-minor version. A connection between the two is therefore unquestionable. It is also clear that the op. 60 finale—the one movement of either version that survives in autograph—dates from the winter of 1873–74. Brahms tells us as much in his own handwritten manuscript catalog of his works.[24] The real mystery therefore surrounds the question of what, if anything, from the earlier slow movement and finale survives in op. 60. Scholars have tended to assume, following Kalbeck's lead, that the Andante of the C-minor quartet takes its "form and key" from the 1856 version, although even Kalbeck acknowledges the likelihood that alterations probably took place in the transfer.[25] In this scenario a direct relationship exists between the first and third movements of op. 60 and their counterparts in the C♯-minor version. Brahms inserted a scherzo between them and discarded the original finale in favor of a newly composed movement.

Yet as Webster points out, there is not enough information in the Brahms-Joachim exchange or in any of the other letters to draw a safe conclusion about a connection between the two slow movements. This is true not only with respect to content but even with respect to the E-major tonality of the later Andante. Moreover, Brahms's manuscript catalog explicitly states that the slow movement was newly composed along with the finale in 1873–74. A letter of 1875 from Clara to Albert Dietrich confirms Brahms's recollection. She tells Dietrich that Brahms "had already written the first two movements earlier," and that "now the last two are also entirely works of genius."[26] As Webster notes, her specific identification of the second movement as a scherzo rules out the possibility that the Andante originally followed the first movement in the cycle, only later to be moved by Brahms to the third position.

It nevertheless remains tempting to adopt Kalbeck's general line of thought, if not the specifics of his argument, regarding the Andante. This is the case not only because of the proximity of E major to C♯ minor and its distance from C minor. It is also due to the character of the Andante, which Kalbeck wants to see as a secret expression of Brahms's love for Clara. Even if the content of the slow movement had been newly composed—as Brahms and Clara indicate—it seems likely that E major would have suggested itself to the composer based on his many years thinking about the quartet in terms of C♯ minor. Moreover, the affective gulf between the glow of the Andante and the grim despair of the surrounding movements suggests a parallel with Brahms's feelings for Clara in the 1850s and the psychological conflicts they must have caused him in the highly charged emotional context of the Schumann household. It would be shortsighted to deny this connection simply because the specific musical materials of the slow movement apparently date from the 1870s. By reconceiving the quartet in C minor while retaining the relative major key from the earlier version, Brahms heightens the chasm between the work's overall anguish and the dream world of the Andante.

Questions about the relationship between the middle movements of the two versions do not end with the lack of evidence pertaining to the Andante. Further difficulty arises from the fact that, in 1875, both Brahms and Clara identified the scherzo as originating earlier. This would seem to contradict the absence of any mention of a scherzo in the letters of the 1850s, but instead references to a finale. One dubious explanation, which was offered some time ago, was that the op. 60 scherzo perhaps had its origins in the scherzo Brahms composed for the *FAE* Sonata.[27] The *FAE* scherzo is also set in C minor with a $^6_8$ time signature and shares a driving intensity with the op. 60 movement. The emphasis on E♮—both in the middle section of the *FAE* movement and, more emphatically, in the top of the violin's final quadruple stops—makes for a suggestive connection to op. 60's *pizzicato* E♮'s and the tonality of the Andante. Nevertheless, the relationships between the two scherzi are otherwise far too generic to suggest that the *FAE* movement represents the earlier version to which Brahms and Clara refer. Indeed, Webster notes that this thesis was taken seriously only around 1900, during a time when the *FAE* scherzo was lost.[28]

Webster puts forward the alternative explanation that the op. 60 scherzo perhaps revises material from the *finale* of the C♯-minor version. It is true, as Webster points out, that Joachim describes the C♯ finale as terse, passionate, and concise—adjectives that apply equally to the scherzo. Furthermore, the scherzo's "⁶₈ motor rhythm, if not the themes in their present form, could be associated with a finale; and its middle section is not a true trio, but an episode growing seamlessly out of the main section and returning as smoothly to the *da capo*."[29] Webster also notes that Joachim, in his only reference to the specific musical content of the C♯ finale, mentions a passage in ²₄ that to Joachim suggests a parody for two bassoons. Webster speculates that the idea of parody material might refer to a passage that eventually became the second theme in the op. 60 scherzo. Joachim's specific reference to a ²₄ measure suggests a change in meter and indicates that the C♯ finale may have stood in ⁶₈ or ³₄—meters appropriate for a scherzo-like character.

Suggestive as these connections may be, any relationship between either middle movement of op. 60 and the C♯-minor quartet must remain speculative, as Webster emphasizes. The first movement, however, is an entirely different matter. The Brahms-Joachim correspondence alone establishes clear connections between the two versions. Not surprisingly many of the characteristics that Brahms and Joachim corresponded about are the same features that remain striking today. The implication is not merely that bizarre idiosyncrasies seem to have been part of the original conception of the first movement. An additional point is that the affective motivations for these eccentricities appear to date back to a time when Brahms was actively struggling with his relationship with the Schumanns. The composer's later comments associating the work with Goethe's *Werther* thus cannot be taken merely as references to musical expression divorced from personal experience. Rather, they seem in a very real sense to point to the exceptional significance of the work for Brahms and by extension to its special place within his oeuvre.

The exchange begins fittingly with Brahms's defense of a *pizzicato* E♮, a characteristic that Joachim initially found bothersome but that he came to accept, as his letter in response indicates. (Here and throughout, I transpose Brahms's and Joachim's references to tonal material down a half step to facilitate comparison with the final version.) The context Brahms describes for the E♮—a long cadence to the dominant followed by a lack of activity—matches the circumstances in mm. 27–30 of op. 60 precisely. Joachim's reference, both to the location of E♮ at the beginning and to a low G bass in the piano, clinches the connection.

Further evidence that the basic materials of the first movement were present in the C♯-minor version comes in the form of a musical excerpt that Joachim uses to illustrate a suggested revision. The passage Joachim proposes appears in Example 1.10. The bulk of the excerpt is based on material that eventually found its way into

pp [3]

[3] [♮] [♮] etc.

Example 1.10. Joachim's Suggested Revision (Original in C♯ Minor)

the secondary area of op. 60. This particular transformation matches the form of the second theme that Brahms first presents in m. 87. Furthermore, Joachim's excerpt culminates in the arrival of two measures of sustained C, similar to the delayed arrival of the tonic in the coda of op. 60 (m. 313)—itself a return of the piano's octave C's from the opening measures of the movement.

These connections are solidified by the fact that Joachim offers his excerpt as an example of the kind of continuation he would like to see Brahms add in order to "linger a while longer on C, when one is finally at home after so long on G." Whether this refers to a tonic return at the beginning of the recapitulation or perhaps in the coda is not specified. In both formal locations of this movement in op. 60 (mm. 199 and 313, respectively), Brahms spends very little time on C following considerable emphasis on the dominant. Webster finds both explanations plausible but favors the first due to details in Joachim's references to page numbers of the manuscript. Either way, what is clear is that the quartet of the 1850s already included the idea of an extended passage oriented around the dominant as a means of creating a tonal delay, as well as a sustained C as part of the resolution.

But this is not all. Joachim's excerpt also contains a final measure that quotes the basic idea of the main theme. Moreover, it does so at the ♭VII level. This matches almost exactly the sequential restatement of the motive in m. 13 of the 1875 version, notwithstanding Brahms's emphasis on B♭ minor as opposed to Joachim's B♭ major. In addition, Joachim refers to a B♭-major entry that he finds "Lisztisch," as well as to two measures on B♭ that Brahms apparently had deleted in the manuscript. Clearly, emphasis on ♭VII was part of the original conception of the quartet, even if Brahms reworked the specifics in the final version. Prominent thematic statements on B♭ survive not only in the opening of the first movement but also in the main theme of the scherzo (mm. 9–10).

The final bit of evidence of a connection between the two versions is Joachim's mention of a section in contrasting timbres for strings and piano. He suggests that the passage would be improved if Brahms were to give the viola double stops, so that the strings and the piano would each independently present complete harmonies. As Webster suggests, the material may well have found its counterpart in the ostentatious transformation of the main theme at the heart of the development of op. 60 (mm. 142 and 164), with its prominent double stops in the viola.

To summarize: it seems that the primary and secondary themes of the exposition, the basic form and structure of the opening quasi introduction, the peculiarities of *pizzicato* E♮'s and entrances on B♭, the idea and some details of an extended tonal delay later in the movement, and perhaps even the thematic transformation that stands at the heart of the development were all present in some form in the C♯-minor version. These connections aside, it is likely that the first movement underwent considerable revision before finding its way into op. 60. The example of the B-Major Piano Trio, op. 8, demonstrates that Brahms could create very different movements from the same primary thematic material.

Yet the two versions of the op. 60 Allegro seem to have shared more than just their opening themes. Moreover, the first version of the piano trio had already been published, and thus had been put aside as a finished work before Brahms recomposed it some thirty-five years later. The C♯-minor version of the piano quartet was never officially completed. The work remained on the back burner, and Brahms did not wait quite as long to return to it. That many of the same basic materials remained compelling for him nearly twenty years later testifies to their provocative character and potential for compositional development. Further insight into the structural function of these idiosyncrasies must await detailed analysis. This in turn will lead to an exploration of their impact on tragic expression. First, however, it is necessary to outline the basics of an analytic method up to the task of interpreting quintessential Brahms.

Part One

2 Analytical Preliminaries: Brahms's Sonata Forms and the Idea of Dimensional Counterpoint

Before starting in-depth exploration of the quartet, it will be helpful to describe the theoretical framework that forms the basis for subsequent analytical discussion. My approach to the quartet focuses primarily on musical form as a road leading to the intersection of structure and expression. Form, however, is conceived from a perspective that is more inclusive than is often the case in either theoretical or musicological studies. A movement's form consists of the total structure that emerges through a *counterpoint of musical dimensions*.[1] These dimensions can include virtually any aspect of a piece's sound world, but for convenience they can be reduced to three main categories: thematic design, key scheme, and tonal structure.

Thematic design refers to patterns of melodic ideas organized into phrases, phrase groups, and so forth up to the largest sections of a piece. Key scheme indicates the succession of harmonic areas that are tonicized across the main sections of the form. Tonal structure encapsulates contrapuntal and harmonic relationships revealed through Schenkerian analysis. It is important to note from the outset that, although it is convenient to speak of these three parameters as distinct, any given musical dimension can never be completely isolated from the others. To evaluate the function of thematic components, an analysis must at minimum attend to aspects of key scheme, if not also to articulations provided by tonal structure. It would be impossible, for instance, to group the melodic ideas of a sonata into first- and second-theme groups without the guiding hand of the exposition's modulatory trajectory. At the same time, evaluation of the significance of a tonicization depends on information provided by the thematic dimension: a modulation to the dominant cannot normally achieve the status of a key area until it is articulated into a section by thematic components. Similarly, a convincing account of tonal structure requires sensitivity to all aspects of the foreground, not least thematic, motivic, and rhythmic-metric characteristics.

The interaction of thematic design and key scheme produces patterns of organization associated with traditional form theory—binary forms, ternary forms, sonata and rondo forms, and so forth. A source of great musical interest in Brahms emerges from the counterpoint of these dimensions with tonal structure. Among other insights, a Schenkerian perspective provides a basis to distinguish between a formal section's tonal center and its main prolonged harmony or controlling *Stufe*. Although traditional discussions of form often conflate key scheme and large-scale harmonic progression, these dimensions are not necessarily coextensive.

It is crucial to recognize that keys are relational networks, not sounding entities. A tonal center is formed by functional relationships between chords, not by any single chord. This is what makes it possible for a passage to be in a key without necessarily articulating the key's local tonic. Thus metaphors of motion such as "the form progresses from the opening tonic to the dominant of the secondary area" are better suited to harmonies than to keys.[2] It is true that the governing harmony for a section is typically its tonic, but this is by no means the only possibility. A local tonic may not appear until well within a formal section or even until the section's point of closure. In other cases the tonic might not appear as a structural harmony in root position, but instead may be represented by an inversion. And in extreme situations, it might not surface in any form. For Brahms as well as his Classical forebears, the multiple possibilities are available not only in developmental passages but also in expositions, as alternatives to more conventional coordination of key scheme and *Stufengang*. This is one reason why it is important to draw a distinction between a work's key scheme and its tonal structure: the progression of *Stufen* provides an important component of musical form distinct from a movement's key scheme.

A brief yet beautiful passage from Mozart—the beginning of the second key area in the slow movement of his F-Major Piano Sonata, K. 280—illustrates all of these points (Example 2.1a). The passage encapsulates the essence of dimensional counterpoint on a small scale and thus lays bare the issues involved. It also demonstrates that considerations of dimensional interaction are crucial not only for interpretation of Brahms's music, but also for the great tonal tradition of which he was a part. From the perspective of conventional formal analysis, the simultaneous entrance of a new thematic idea and a shift in key orientation from F minor to A♭ major articulate the movement's secondary area at m. 9. In other words, the thematic and key scheme dimensions come together at this point to announce the beginning of a new formal section.

Yet, as the graph of Example 2.1b highlights, the $^6_4$ position of the opening A♭ sonority participates in a dominant rather than tonic prolongation. Indeed, Mozart delays the root-position A♭ *Stufe* that more conventionally would enter at the outset of a secondary area all the way until the point of closure for the exposition (m. 21). Annotations beneath the graph highlight the lack of coordination between a traditional formal parsing based on theme and key and the middleground progression from i to III. A further layer of artistry arises out of the fact that the $^6_4$ chords throughout the beginning of the section project a double meaning. Because they contain the pitches of the tonic, they hint at the presence of the very harmony they participate in delaying.

An analytic method sensitive to distinctions between key scheme and structural harmonic progression allows for greater responsiveness to the complexity of a passage like the Mozart sonata's. We can at once observe ways in which the secondary area follows convention in the thematic and key-scheme dimensions, while also responding to the element of delay in the tonal structure—a crucial component of our aesthetic experience of the passage. Another advantage of drawing the scheme/

a) Second Key Area

Example 2.1. Mozart, Piano Sonata in F Major, K. 280, II
(a) Second Key Area

structure distinction is that it allows for evaluation of the main harmonies of the key pattern according to their function in a large-scale tonal-contrapuntal framework. The middleground mediant at m. 21 in the Mozart sonata, for example, forms a stepping stone on the way from the tonic point of departure to the dominant that arrives toward the end of the development. Example 2.2 illustrates the coordination of this *Bassbrechung* with the movement's sonata design.

Although traditional formal analysis tends to treat tonicized harmonies as main pillars, a Schenkerian perspective dictates that not all tonicized chords are necessarily structural harmonies, and that not all structural harmonies are necessarily tonicized chords.[3] Even if a tonicized chord is the main harmony for a formal section, it nevertheless may be subsidiary to other chords that form the pillars for a

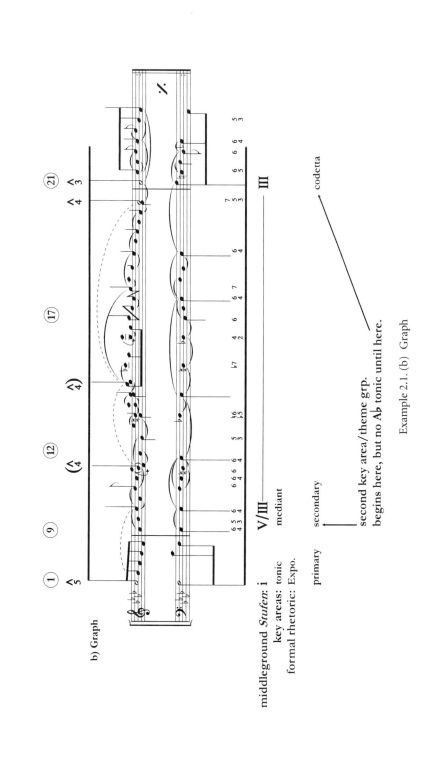

b) Graph

middleground *Stufen*: i V/III——— III

key areas: tonic   mediant

formal rhetoric: Expo.

primary   secondary

second key area/theme grp.
begins here, but no A♭ tonic until here.

codetta

Example 2.1. (b) Graph

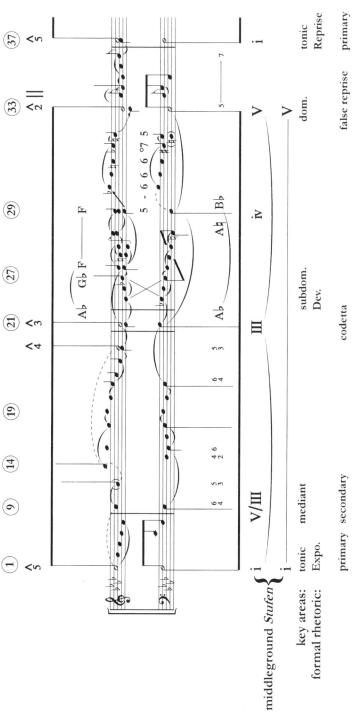

Example 2.2. Mozart, K. 280, Middleground Graph

structural progression. This is the case in the Mozart movement, where the tonic and dominant have a deeper structural significance than the mediant, even though III governs a key area.

Mozart emphasizes the dominant in this particular movement via tonicization at the false reprise of m. 33. Yet even if the dominant were never tonicized, it could participate in a high-ranking i–V progression. Because this point has been cause for concern among critics of Schenker's approach, I will return to it later. For now, it suffices to say that the concept of dimensional counterpoint affords the opportunity to acknowledge the importance of key-scheme characteristics while still leaving room for the possibility of a *Stufengang* distinct from a succession of tonicized chords. An analysis thereby can respond both to a pattern of keys and to specific details of harmony and counterpoint through which a key scheme is articulated.

The importance of viewing Brahms's forms through the interaction of thematic design, key scheme, and tonal structure is most easily demonstrated through a look at some actual music. My approach in this preliminary discussion will be to compare the first and last movements of the piano quartet with the first movements from the First Symphony and the C-minor string quartet. In addition to illustrating my analytical approach, the discussion will begin to present a formal overview of the piano quartet, as well as of two related works that we will return to in later chapters. The symphony and string quartet movements provide an appropriate context not merely because they are also C-minor sonata forms, or even because of the complex mix of similarities and differences among them and the piano quartet. They also, as already noted, share important expressive and biographical connections with op. 60: all three works wrestle with tragic themes and were completed in the early to mid-1870s after long compositional gestation. These connections will prove important when the discussion in later chapters shifts from a focus on abstract musical organization to a consideration of expressive meaning.

A good place to begin is with thematic design and key scheme in the expositions from the four movements. Example 2.3 provides a summary of the main characteristics in these dimensions. All the expositions share a i–III key scheme, with closure in the mediant at the end of the secondary area. The movements also begin their secondary areas in the mediant at approximately the midpoint of the exposition; there are no examples of the kind of three-key exposition in which an intervening area sits between the tonic and the goal key.[4] With the exception of the finale from the piano quartet, a big dominant arrival at the end of a modulatory transition prepares the entrance of each E♭ area.

All these features, of course, are highly conventional. Indeed, the key-scheme dimension is an area in which Brahms tended, at least in sonata expositions, to adhere closely to tradition. Even when he does choose a path independent of eighteenth-century conventions, he opts for tonal plans with precedents in Beethoven and Schubert.[5] Brahms's contemporaries undoubtedly had their ears trained on this aspect of his style, among others, when they leveled their charges of epigonism. We shall see, however, that the specific contrapuntal and harmonic details through which Brahms articulates these traditional key patterns belie the charge of epigo-

Example 2.3. Summary of Expository Characteristics

Movement	E♭ Key Area	Preparation for E♭ via Its Dominant	Immediate Articulation of E♭ Tonic	Formal Rhetoric of Secondary Material	Closure in E♭
C-minor piano quartet, I	Yes: mm. 70–121	Yes: mm. 52–69 prolong V/E♭	Yes: m. 70	Lyrical second theme (with variations!)	Yes: m. 118
C-minor string quartet, I	Yes: mm. 32–78.1	Yes: mm. 31–32	No: Root position only at m. 75	Nearly continuous *Fortspinnung*	Yes: m. 75
C-minor piano quartet, IV	Yes: mm. 55–95	No: Not until mm. 73–74	No: E♭$^6_3$ chord at m. 55. Root position at m. 75 but weakly articulated.	Two-part: Appassionata theme (mm. 55–74) and chorale (mm. 75–95)	Yes: m. 95
First Symphony	Yes: mm. 121–84.1	Yes: mm. 97–120 prolong V/E♭	No: E♭$^6_3$ chord at m. 121	Two-part: Continued development of material from tonic area with shift from E♭ major to E♭ minor at m. 157	Yes: m. 185

nism. Rather than adhere to a formulaic conception of sonata form, he engages in a highly inventive play between middleground structure and the dimensions of theme and key.

As we have already seen in our Mozart example, this type of flexible interaction among structural parameters—or dimensional counterpoint—typifies music of the tonal tradition. Brahms nevertheless tends to exploit the possibilities of dimensional noncongruence to an exceptional degree. Thus although any two of his movements might fall into the same formal category, the location of deep middleground harmonies in the formal plan may vary considerably. His engagement with sonata form in the symphony and quartet movements involves at least above average, if not indeed extreme, degrees of noncongruence among locations of the following aspects of formal articulation: different types of critical events in the realm of key scheme, middleground harmony, and large-scale voice leading; the boundaries created by patterns of thematic articulation; breaks in continuity provided by shifts in accompanimental patterns, instrumentation, and/or dynamics; and moments of large-scale rhythmic-metric arrival.[6]

These movements demonstrate that dimensional noncongruence functions as one of the chief means through which Brahms satisfies his proclivity for extended tension and instability as well as for formal multivalence. Yet attention to discrepancies among structural parameters is crucial not only for insight into this aspect of Brahms's style. It is also important because dimensional noncongruence was one means through which Brahms reinvigorated eighteenth-century formal conventions at a time in which traditional approaches to composition were under fire from "progressive" musical circles.[7]

A good example of Brahms's formal diversity is found in the arrival of E♭ at the beginning of each secondary area. Among the four movements, the opening Allegro of the piano quartet most closely follows convention: its transitional dominant resolves to an E♭ tonic at the entrance of the second theme (m. 70). As Example 2.4a outlines, this resolution articulates a middleground shift from tonic to mediant, and the remainder of the section expands III. (Although in this general sense the exposition follows convention, closer study in Chapter 5 will reveal ways in which the secondary area represents a departure from norms in Brahms's approach to sonata form.) The other three works delay the arrival of a middleground III until the closing material at the end of the exposition. Brahms conflates arrival and closure into a single entity, in a quintessential reflection of his compositional economy.

The graphs in Example 2.4 summarize the large-scale tonal trajectory of each exposition. In the first movement of the string quartet the process of delay centers on an enormous prolongation of V/E♭ across the body of the secondary area. In the symphony and in the finale of the piano quartet, it involves the entrance of E♭$^{6}_{3}$ chords at crucial points of thematic articulation. A traditional formal analysis might regard this emphasis on $^{6}_{3}$ chords simply as a minor deviation from the norm. Indeed, there is Classical precedent for departure from a first-inversion tonic instead of root position at the beginning of the secondary area. The strategy is common enough in sonata and other contexts for Schenker to have developed a category of voice-leading transformation—the auxiliary cadence—to model it.[8]

Yet upon closer inspection, it turns out that neither $^{6}_{3}$ chord initiates an auxiliary cadence. In fact, only the symphony even articulates a structural connection between the $^{6}_{3}$ chord and the goal E♭ *Stufe*. In other words, the idiosyncrasy of these secondary areas extends beyond the simple fact of departure from a $^{6}_{3}$ chord. In pointing out the structural diversity, I do not wish to disavow a relationship between the movements; quite the contrary. Moreover, it would be a mistake, in evaluating the finale, to deny the possibility for the $^{6}_{3}$ chord at m. 55 to call to mind the goal E♭ *Stufe,* even though the connection is associative rather than structural. The advantage of dimensional counterpoint is that it allows for observation of shared characteristics while also affording an opportunity to explore distinctions in the function of the $^{6}_{3}$ chords. This, of course, is in addition to the means dimensional counterpoint provides for highlighting differences among these two sonata forms and the first movements from the string quartet and piano quartet. A relationship, in the finale, between the $^{6}_{3}$ chord and the more solid arrival of the mediant key occurs in the key-scheme dimension. In the symphony the connection penetrates into the tonal structure as well—a difference with possible ramifications for expressive as well as structural analysis. The distinction is essential not because one type of connection is more legitimate; they are both important. Rather, it is a matter of clarity in analytical discourse.

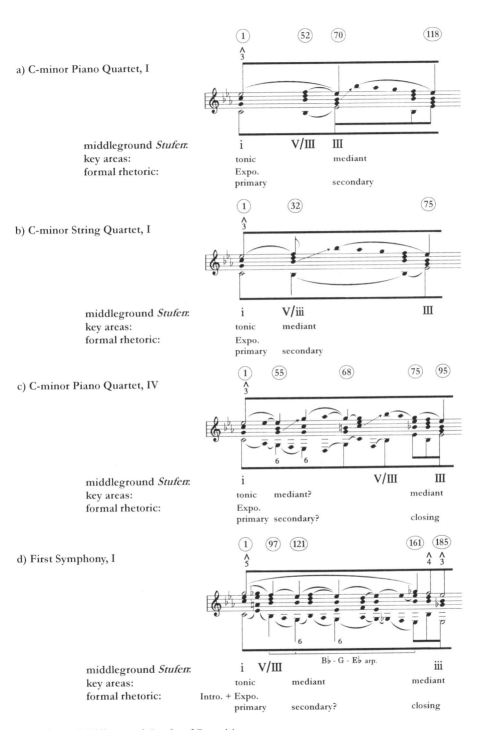

Example 2.4. Middleground Graphs of Expositions
(a) C-Minor Piano Quartet, I
(b) C-Minor String Quartet, I
(c) C-Minor Piano Quartet, IV
(d) First Symphony, I

Instead of initiating an auxiliary cadence, the E♭$^{6}_{3}$ at m. 121 in the symphony forms part of a descending arpeggiation in the bass. As Example 2.4d shows, the $^{6}_{3}$ chord divides the motion from the B♭ dominant to the root-position E♭ tonic. The graph indicates that the prolongational structure shifts to an E♭ orientation at m. 121, despite the absence of a new thematic entrance. The continued emphasis on fragments from the tonic area notwithstanding, a number of recent commentators identify this point as the beginning of the secondary area, confirming the intuition that E♭ takes control here.[9]

An expressive characteristic of the passage, however, is the possibility also to hear continued prolongation of the dominant until the E♭$^{6}_{3}$ chord of either m. 138 or m. 148. The possibility for further prolongation of V arises out of the potential to hear a link between the dominant in mm. 117–20 and the arrival back on $\hat{2}$/V at m. 130. In this interpretation the combination of the $^{6}_{3}$ position of the tonic at m. 121 and the absence of a new second theme prevent a satisfactory resolution of the first dominant. Instead, V remains available for a connection with the second big dominant arrival. The fact that the second dominant does finally lead into a fresh thematic idea strengthens the continuity. The second articulation picks up where the formal process previously left off, as it were, poised on a large-scale dominant arrival. Yet now the passage moves ahead by following through with the kind of new thematic material that Brahms withheld at the previous formal moment.

Yet even here the material lacks both the full-blown melodic distinctiveness and tonal stability of a proper second theme. Rather than coalesce around a decisive point of articulation, the formal rhetoric centers on a series of failed attempts to resolve the transitional V. The first attempt provides a tonic $^{6}_{3}$ chord yet no new theme; the second provides somewhat more in the way of a thematic articulation but no tonic. The result is an interpretation in which the dominants join together as part of a larger prolongation that leads to a still later resolution.

Later in this chapter I will return to this passage as a means of introducing another aspect of my analytic method. For now, the main point is that the shift to an expanded $^{6}_{3}$ chord, regardless of precisely where it occurs, functions as an anticipation of the E♭$^{6}_{3}$ that governs the closing material beginning at m. 161. In that sense it takes on structural significance as part of an expansion of the mediant *Stufe*. Recognizing this structural connection is important in part for the distinction it creates with the $^{6}_{3}$ articulation in the finale. Although the $^{6}_{3}$ chord there points ahead to the E♭ arrival yet to come, it does not, as already mentioned, form a prolongational connection with the mediant *Stufe*. Rather, it remains trapped within an expansion of the opening C tonic.

Interpretation of the secondary area in the finale represents one of the greatest challenges among the four movements. This is due to the complex relationship between formal signals in the three main dimensions of thematic design, key scheme, and tonal structure. Chapter 5 will explore the situation in considerable detail. For the purposes of the present discussion the salient characteristic is the ambivalent function of the material in mm. 55–74. On the one hand, the passage begins in the key of E♭ with the entrance of a new theme. It also follows a section in which thematic content has been liquidated to the point that the only remaining substance is the A♭ accompanimental pattern in mm. 51–54. The liquidation has a dual function: it endows the preceding passage with a transitional character and helps to articulate the E♭ theme as the beginning of a new section as well. All these features point to m. 55 as the onset of the secondary area. Yet despite the transitional liquidation, the brief bridgelike passage fails to leave the tonic key. Until the C–C♭ motion in mm. 52–53, the A♭ harmony functions as VI of C. Furthermore, in addition to the new theme's failure to articulate a root-position E♭ harmony, the apparent secondary idea merges into an unstable sequential passage that leads to a climactic arrival back on the dominant of the home key in m. 68.

From a Schenkerian perspective, this home G dominant functions as a back-relating V chord, as seen in Example 2.4c. Only after the return to the home key does the tonal structure make a decisive move to the mediant via its own dominant at m. 73. In other words, the tonic *Stufe* remains in effect all the way up to the repetition of the G dominant in m. 70. This would imply that the E♭$^6_3$ theme is part of the bridge and that the secondary area arrives only with the entrance of the chorale at m. 75. Yet even this second arrival of E♭ is not without multiple meanings. The chorale enters late in the exposition and has the simplicity and compactness of a closing theme. In terms of location and thematic rhetoric, the earlier E♭ idea perhaps more closely follows conventions for second-theme function.

The conclusion we can draw is that the secondary area ultimately resists a single, unambiguous interpretation. The result of all the mixed signals is a formal overlap: the material at m. 55 begins to initiate the E♭ key area that takes over at m. 75, while C minor lingers in the shadows until it is reawakened by the G dominant at m. 68. The chorale theme partly confirms both aspects of the overlap. Its closing character supports the notion that the secondary area begins at m. 55, while its articulation of E♭ highlights the inadequacy of the preceding passage as an area of key definition.

In summary, the four expositions present a complex blend of similarities and differences. All share the same key scheme and initiate the mediant area at the midpoint of their expositions. In addition, three of the four prepare E♭ with a big dominant arrival. And even though the finale avoids V/E♭ before its first tentative shift to the mediant, it does incorporate some of the textural and thematic characteristics of a second-key articulation at m. 55. By contrast, the movements' thematic and tonal structures represent a continuum of possibilities. The thematic possibilities range from the full-blown thematicism of the E♭ material in the first movement of the piano quartet, through the less thematically distinct materials in the symphony and finale, to the virtually continuous *Fortspinnung* in the string quartet.

With respect to tonal structure, the first movement of the piano quartet represents one extreme with its articulation of a root-position E♭ *Stufe* at the outset of its secondary area. On the other end of the continuum stands the string quartet, which continues to expand the transitional dominant across the secondary area until the closing material. The symphony and the finale again fall between these extremes. Both signal the arrival of the new E♭ tonic via E♭$^6_3$ chords. The symphony, however, is closer to the end of the continuum represented by the first movement of the piano quartet in the sense that its $^6_3$ chord is a prolongational offshoot of the

Eb *Stufe.* Eb, in other words, has a structural presence at the outset of the secondary area. The finale is somewhat more like the first movement of the string quartet in withholding a structural Eb harmony until the closing idea.

Up to this point, the idea of dimensional counterpoint has served as a means of responding to diverse formal signals. It has made it possible to include multiple conclusions about form by segregating these conclusions according to the dimension of structure that supports them. What is true from the perspective of one dimension need not be true from the perspective of another, provided that we give up the idea that any single parameter must dominate all others in formal evaluation. What is an effective response, however, to situations in which multiple interpretations seem possible within a single dimension? This brings us back to the previous debate about the resolution of the retransitional dominant in the symphony. Recall that my analysis of the symphony's secondary area revealed the possibility to hear a shift from the transitional dominant to an expansion of an $E\flat^{\flat6}_3$ chord at one of three places. To remain focused on the main issues at hand, it was assumed that the $E\flat^{\flat6}_3$ takes control at m. 121. Continued prolongation of the dominant, until either m. 138 or m. 148, however, was suggested as an alternative.

One way to deal with such passages is to pay special attention to the temporal perspectives from which various interpretive statements are rendered. Conflicts, in other words, can arise from differences of chronological viewpoint, that is, from differences in what is initially perceived on the one hand, and what is eventually understood on the other. The idea is that a listener can hear a resolution to $E\flat^{\flat6}_3$ at m. 121, from the vantage point of that formal moment. Subsequently, however, the initial perception may be canceled in favor of the dominant, at the return of $\hat{2}/V$ in m. 130. Example 2.5a outlines this possibility. It is important to note that the later perception does not erase the earlier perception, but rather subsumes it in an accumulation of interpretive data. The return to dominant prolongation is colored by the fact that it enters as a reversal of a previous prolongational shift.

Similarly, the subsequent return to $E\flat^{\flat6}_3$ at m. 138 can be heard to reawaken an $E\flat^{\flat6}_3$ prolongation that was itself previously thought to have ended. Example 2.5b illustrates this interpretation. Once again, the second perception does not cancel the idea of a shift in favor of the dominant at m. 130, which in turn does not cancel the even earlier perception of resolution at m. 121. Rather, the analysis depicts a series of structural reversals in response to a passage characterized by quintessentially Brahmsian ambivalence. The interpretation remains logical because it never claims that we hear both continued dominant prolongation and resolution to $E\flat^{\flat6}_3$ *at the same time.* Just as we need not favor tonal structure over theme and key in formal analysis, neither do we need to deny localized perceptions in favor of interpretation from a synoptic perspective. Both viewpoints can and should be included in discussions of musical form.[10]

Although I have not yet described them in these terms, one way to think about the mediant articulations in the Brahms movements is in relation to the concept of a structural downbeat. In the first movement of the piano quartet, Brahms follows formal convention and allows the second key area to begin with the arrival of

a)

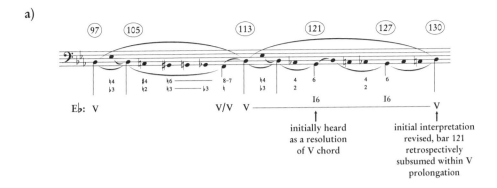

b)

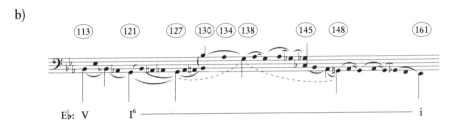

Example 2.5. Alternative Interpretations of First Symphony

the mediant *Stufe* at a point of large-scale rhythmic accent.[11] In the other three movements he withholds a stable point of initiation and transforms the entire secondary area into an enormous anacrusis to a point of resolution toward the very end of the exposition. He delays the arrival of the structural downbeat, in other words.

A similar structural delay occurs across the entire recapitulation of two of the four movements. Because the idea of a delayed structural downbeat depends on some degree of misalignment among parameters, the recapitulations allow for further exploration of dimensional counterpoint, as an essential component of Brahms's style. The recapitulations also afford an opportunity to confront issues surrounding the potential for nontonicized chords—in particular, retransitional dominants—to function as structural harmonies. The topic is important not only because of its relevance to the Brahms movements, but also because it has been an aspect of Schenker's approach that has attracted skepticism, as previously mentioned.

The recapitulations of all four sonata forms, like their expositions, exhibit a blend of similarities and differences in key scheme, thematicism, and large-scale voice leading. Once again, the greatest similarities occur in the key-scheme dimension. Example 2.6 summarizes salient characteristics of theme and key for the recapitulations of all four movements. All four present the return of the main-theme group in the tonic key, and all but the string quartet prepare this return with an expansion of the home dominant at the end of the development. Similarly all the recapitulations, with the exception of the first movement from the piano quartet, transpose the secondary material into C.

Brahms's treatment of the thematic dimension also follows sonata conventions in three of the four movements. Although there are small but significant alterations in the main-theme groups and transitions, each recapitulation closely parallels its exposition, with the exception of the reprise in the piano quartet's first movement. The return of the secondary material, in particular, matches the template formed by the exposition, in the symphony, quartet, and finale. This is a reflection of Brahms's fidelity to the sonata principle—the idea that "important statements made in a key other than the tonic must either be restated in the tonic, or brought into a closer relation with the tonic, before the movement ends."[12] By contrast, Brahms radically recomposes the tonic area and transition in the first movement of the piano quartet. Moreover, the secondary material returns fully in the key of the major dominant—a singular strategy about which I will have much to say in later chapters.

The first movement notwithstanding, the perspective of theme and key again appears to ratify the image of Brahms as conservative. It also seems to reveal a conformity to similar formal procedures among the other three movements. Once tonal structure is taken into account, however, a different picture emerges. Not surprisingly, the recapitulation of the first movement of the piano quartet exhibits the most atypical middleground, while the symphony and finale most closely follow sonata paradigms. Yet although the string quartet shares many conventional recapitulatory features with the symphony and finale, it reconceives aspects of recapitulation in a manner similar to the situation in the first movement of the piano quartet. Put otherwise, the recapitulation of the string quartet unfolds like the symphony and finale in terms of theme and key, while in terms of middleground harmony it follows a path more like the piano quartet's first movement.

In order to respond to this difference, an analytic method must be able to draw distinctions between key centers and prolonged harmonies, and, by extension, between the segmentations of traditional formal analysis and Schenkerian tonal structure. Example 2.7 presents graphic analyses of large-scale structure for all four sonata forms. The symphony and finale follow Schenker's concept of interruption as a basis for sonata form.[13] A large-scale i–III–V *Bassbrechung* spans the exposition and development. This tonal motion, however, remains incomplete: the recapitulation rearticulates the *Kopfton* before the initial *Urlinie* descent can progress from $\hat{2}$/V to $\hat{1}$/i. It is only in a second descent that the *Urlinie* reaches its ultimate goal, as the structure traverses a complete i–V–i progression across the recapitulation.

By contrast, in the first movements of both the string and piano quartets, the return to material from the opening does not initiate a structural rebeginning. In the piano quartet the retransitional dominant discharges onto a climactic A♭ (mm. 196–200) that flows across what otherwise might have been a return of the tonic. As it stands, the new context for the main theme transforms its C-minor chords into apparent rather than structural tonics.[14] Although the recapitulation returns to the home key—or more precisely, continues the focus on the home key initiated by the retransition—the retransitional dominant remains the prolonged harmony.

Example 2.6. Summary of Recapitulatory Characteristics

Movement	Main Theme and Bridge in Tonic Key	Preparation for Recap. via Home Dominant	Immediate Rearticulation of C Tonic	Tonal Orientation of Secondary Material	Closure
C-minor piano quartet, I	Main Theme: Yes (mm. 199–226) Bridge: No (mm. 227–35 modulate to G)	Yes: mm. 176–97 prolong V	No: Continues dominant prolongation of retransition. C tonic only at m. 313.	In G major (!) (mm. 236–77)	m. 313
C-minor string quartet, I	Yes: mm. 135–73 (with subdominant emphasis at m. 164)	No	No: Introduces home dominant as controlling *Stufe* at m. 143. C tonic only at m. 216.	In C-minor, but prolongs dominant (mm. 173–215)	m. 216
C-minor piano quartet, IV	Yes: mm. 217–70	Yes: mm. 173–216 prolong V	Yes: But m. 217 anticipates more solid articulation at m. 225	C major (mm. 271–327)	m. 351
First Symphony	Yes: mm. 343–93	Yes: mm. 273–342 prolong V	Yes: m. 343	C with shift from major of m. 394 to minor at m. 428 and back again at final tonic in coda	m. 458

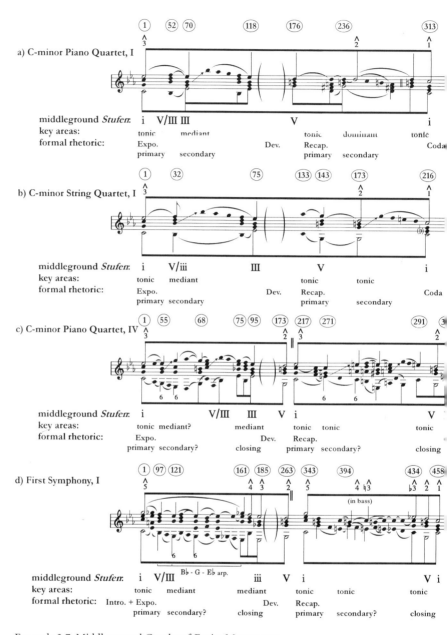

Example 2.7. Middleground Graphs of Entire Movements
(a) C-Minor Piano Quartet, I
(b) C-Minor String Quartet, I
(c) C-Minor Piano Quartet, IV
(d) First Symphony, I

Example 2.8. A♭ at Reprise in C-Minor String Quartet

The string quartet similarly bypasses a structural rebeginning at the return of the main theme in mm. 133–44. In this case Brahms withholds the dominant until after the thematic restatement enters. Once again, the addition of A♭ to what had been a tonic point of departure for the theme plays a crucial role, as Example 2.8 highlights. In both recapitulations the remainder of the main-theme group continues to focus on dominant harmony. In the piano quartet the new orientation involves radical recomposition, while in the string quartet the changes are less extensive. Example 2.9 summarizes the relationship between exposition and recapitulation for the tonic area of both movements.

The tendency toward a closer thematic parallelism in the string quartet continues in the reprise of its secondary material. What had been an enormous expansion of V/E♭ across the second group in the exposition becomes an enormous expansion of the home dominant when the material is transposed to the tonic in the recapitulation. The result is that the dominant introduced by the return of the main theme continues to extend across the body of the recapitulation.

In the piano quartet the recomposition centers around the theme and variations form of the secondary area: Brahms composes a new set of variations on his expository idea. This is a logical solution to the problem of redundancy posed by recapitulation of a section based on variation principles. The extraordinary change occurs in the tonal dimension: the theme and variations now appear in the key of

Example 2.9. Recapitulatory Recomposition for Tonic Areas

C-Minor Piano Quartet

Exposition	Recapitulation
mm. 1–10: Phrase 1, i to V	mm. 199–205: Phrase 1, continued prolongation of retransitional V
—	mm. 206–12.1: New material with metric displacement of head motive, expands V
mm. 11–20: Phrase 2, ♭vii	—
mm. 21–31.1: Descending 5–6 sequence, expands V	mm. 213–16: Material from transition, pt. 1, expands V
mm. 32–41.1: Counterstatement, i–V–i	—
mm. 42–51.1: Transition, pt. 1, i to V/E♭	mm. 217–26: Descending 5–6 sequence, expands V
—	mm. 227–35.1: 5–6 sequence extended, to V/G
mm. 52–69.1: Transition, pt. 2, expands V/E♭	—

C-Minor String Quartet

Exposition	Recapitulation
(A) mm. 1–8: Phrase 1, i to V	(A) mm. 135–44: Phrase 1 (with augmentation of head motive), $C^{(5-)6}$ to V
mm. 9–10: Sequential extension, V/B♭	mm. 145–50: Partially sequential extension, tonicizes B♮ and G
(B) mm. 11–22.1: Middle section, expands V	(B) mm. 151–63.1: Middle section, expands V
(A′) mm. 23–32: Counterstatement merges into transition, i to V/E♭	(A′) mm. 164–73: Counterstatement merges into transition, iv to V

the major dominant. On the one hand, this feature distinguishes the movement from our other three examples. Yet on the other hand, it can be understood as a more extreme form of the strategy that is also at work in the string quartet. With respect to tonal structure, both movements pick up the dominant either extended across or introduced by the return of the main theme, and continue to prolong it throughout the body of the secondary material. One involves tonicization of G, while the other remains in the home key. Both nevertheless result in a continuous tonal structure that stretches across the parallel thematic design of sonata form. Brahms withholds the structural downbeat that typically occurs at the beginning of the recapitulation and delays its arrival all the way to the end of both movements.[15]

In pointing out this similarity, again I must emphasize that my intention is not to minimize differences between the string and piano quartets. Rather, my goal is to respond fully to both the flexibility of Brahms's tonal language and the breadth of expressive resources in the Viennese sonata tradition. There is no question that a tonicization of the major dominant has a different effect than an expansion of V within the tonic key. Moreover, aesthetic distinctions aside, the emphasis on G in the recapitulation of the piano quartet is unprecedented in the Viennese sonata tradition. (But see note 15 in Chapter 1.) Prolongation of the dominant across part or all of a recapitulation that stands in the tonic key is a procedure that Brahms adopts fairly often. It is also a strategy that Brahms's precursors, most notably Beethoven, would indulge in on occasion.[16] Recall also that we have already looked at a Mozart second key area in which the local dominant rather than tonic provides the main tonal focus all the way to the point of closure for the exposition.

Although Brahms was especially adept at weaving complex tapestries of dimensional counterpoint, his tendencies in this regard are a matter of intensification rather than outright innovation. The same type of flexible relationship between thematic design, key scheme, and tonal structure characterizes the sonata style, as reflected in Beethoven's dominant-oriented recapitulations and the passage from Mozart. It is for this very reason that a defense of traditional methods of formal analysis cannot simply isolate Brahms's strategies as idiosyncratic special cases. A formal analysis that ignores middleground tonal structure is as inadequate a response to Haydn, Mozart, and Beethoven as it is to Brahms. Likewise, a Schenkerian approach that pays insufficient attention to issues of thematic design and key scheme similarly falls short.

The different forms of emphasis on the dominant in the piano and string quartets raise important questions about how a V *Stufe* might relate to thematic design and key scheme. One criticism of my analyses might be that the main harmonies of my graphs do not always correspond with harmonies emphasized in the key scheme and thematic dimensions. Charles Smith, for example, in what is to date the most comprehensive critique of Schenkerian views on form, questions the practice of privileging "functional harmony" as opposed to "formal harmony," as an analysis moves from the level of phrases and small sections on to global organization. As Smith and others see it, functional relationships give way to a progression of large-scale harmonic areas at higher levels of form. These large-scale harmonic progressions may or may not follow conventions of chord succession that are in effect on more local levels.[17]

By contrast, Schenkerian theory proposes that principles governing harmony and counterpoint are essentially the same at all levels. One consequence is that tonic-dominant frameworks recur throughout the different levels of tonal structure, as exemplified by the priority I assign to i and V in my graphs. What is objectionable about this to some theorists is that dominant harmonies that are not tonicized, like the retransitional V chords in the symphony and finale, often achieve structural significance. Moreover, intermediate harmonies that do govern a key area, like the mediant in these movements, may reside on lower levels.

Smith, in fact, takes exception not only to this aspect of Schenker's theory. He also objects to the idea that different pieces of the same formal type, like our Brahms movements, might articulate diverse relationships between deep middleground structure and formal design. Central to his critique of Schenker's *Formenlehre* is Smith's observation that Schenker sorts pieces with similar forms into radically different categories. For example, in the final chapter of *Free Composition*, Schenker identifies some three-section open forms as one-part, some as two-part, and yet others as three-part. This is because, as Smith puts it, Schenker allows the structural tail to wag the formal dog. He defines formal parts by prolongational spans and the technique of interruption and not always by the segmentations of traditional form theory.

Smith's critique is valuable for the information it provides on the relationship between formal categorization and analysis of tonal structure in *Free Composition*. Yet although Smith is justified in taking issue with inconsistencies in Schenker's methods of formal categorization, I differ with him on the best remedy for the situation. Smith's proposals center on a fixed repertoire of structural paradigms intended to correspond with traditional formal types. His approach focuses on predetermined ways in which form should provide access to fundamental structure with respect to harmony. For example, he puts forward the idea that whatever harmony appears as goal at the end of the first part of an open form should make it to the background regardless of whether it is the dominant, mediant, submediant, subdominant, or indeed—in the case of Chopin's *Revolutionary* Etude—the subtonic.[18] In addition, he also suggests that formal identification should function as the crucial variable leading to choice of *Kopfton* and location of *Urlinie* constituents. If a sonata form is set in a major key, for instance, then $\hat{3}$ should function as *Kopfton;* if it is minor, the analyst should choose $\hat{5}$.[19]

The problem with this approach is that it ties the analyst's hands, forcing him or her into interpretations that may not be confirmed by details of individual works. Smith trades one canine scenario for another: instead of the structural tail wagging the formal dog, he would have the formal tail wagging the structural dog. My view is that both perspectives fall short. A theory of form must allow room to acknowledge traditional formal types, such as the shared sonata identity of our four Brahms movements. But it also must leave space to explore the diversity of interaction between theme, key, and structure that Brahms and other composers create.

The first point to consider is Smith's idea that tonic-dominant-oriented functional harmony should give way to progressions of formal harmony at deeper levels of structure. Schenker's view of the standard situation in minor-mode sonata form, as exemplified by the symphony and the finale, provides a prototypical example of the distinction between the two types of harmonic orientation. In major, no discrepancy between functional and formal harmony arises because Schenker can locate a structural dominant in the second key area. In minor, however, a large-scale V usually appears only in the retransition. Schenker's solution is to allow retransitional dominants, like the V chords at the end of the development in the symphony and finale, to function as structural harmonies. One reason Smith and others find this solution unsatisfactory is that it seems unresponsive to the similarity of treatment of dominant and mediant key areas. In both situations Brahms and other composers similarly emphasize V and III and respond by bringing the nontonic material back in the home key in the recapitulation. Why, therefore, should the tonic of the secondary key be a structural harmony in one case, while it is a stepping stone on the way from tonic to dominant in the other?

In defense of Schenker, one might respond that, although composers tend to treat dominant and mediant key areas similarly, the tonal contexts in which they function are not identical. Schenker's interpretation attempts to capture an important difference between sonata form in major and minor. In major, the retransition manifests a return to a structural harmony already achieved by the end of the exposition. In minor, the tonal trajectory does in fact continue onward from the mediant to the dominant.

But although this may be true, the question remains: Why should an unstable retransitional V achieve superior structural status, when it is the mediant that governs a key area? Smith's solution, as seen in Example 2.10, is to include retransitional dominants at deeper levels, but to depict them as lower-ranking connectives between mediant and tonic pillars.[20] Implicit in this reformulation, however, is a somewhat narrow conception of what constitutes formal emphasis. It is true that control over a formal section may endow a tonicized harmony with structural weight. Nevertheless, the position of a harmony at the dramatic apex for a development section can also mark it for consciousness. Even though a retransitional dominant appears in the home key, it nevertheless is typically the main goal to which a development is directed. In terms of *formal* hierarchy, therefore, it can be thought to reside on as high a level as the mediant: both harmonies function as goal for one of the three main sections of the sonata structure. There are, in other words, multiple ways in which a structural harmony can gain salience. Emphasis through tonicization is one; standing as the culmination point for a section that is typically the most tension-generating of sonata form is another. Moreover, phenomenal emphasis and structural significance are not necessarily coextensive in tonal music. Few analysts would dispute this statement as it applies to the foreground. Why should it not apply to larger levels of structure as well?

Discussion of the mediant key area in the four movements has demonstrated the limitations of an approach that equates large-scale tonal structure with formal harmony. The expositions likewise highlight the possibility for diverse relationships between structure and design even within movements that share a number of conventional formal characteristics. The articulation of deep-level dominants in the movements reinforces these two points. The recapitulation of the piano quartet

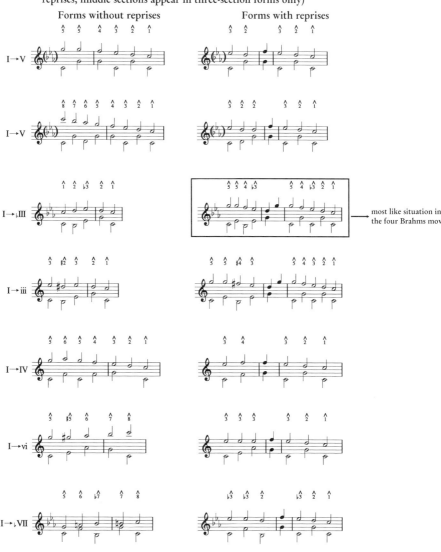

Ex. 38 Repertoire of background structures for open forms (in forms with reprises, middle sections appear in three-section forms only)

Example 2.10. Charles Smith's Proposed Background Structures for Open Forms

represents the one case in which V is tonicized across a formal section and therefore achieves the status of a formal harmony. Yet can we safely say that the dominant plays a role in deep-middleground structure only in the quartet's first movement? In the symphony and finale Brahms places enormous emphasis on V in the movements' retransitions. It seems at least possible, if not mandatory, to hear these dominants as part of large-scale i–V structural progressions.

Moreover, an analysis that denies structural significance for the dominant in the recapitulation of the string quartet would have to opt for the tonic, since the entire reprise is in the home key. Yet such an approach would force structural status onto tonic articulations that clearly lack the resolving power to initiate middleground tonal control. This highlights another problem with an approach that equates formal harmony with tonal structure: What do we do in cases in which a key area delays the arrival of its tonic or even withholds it entirely?[21] Still another shortcoming is an inability to depict a relationship between the string quartet and the first movement of the piano quartet. Both are pieces in which Brahms requires the listener to wait across the entire recapitulation for the type of structural downbeat that occurs at the beginning of the reprise in the symphony and finale. Brahms's formal genius compels us to confront the diverse means by which a movement can carve out a special role for the dominant. Rather than limit a structural role for cases in which the dominant governs a key area, a more responsive approach explores multifarious ways in which V *Stufen* may interact with thematic design and key scheme.

One final objection to Smith's stance regarding structural dominants has to do with the consistency with which he follows his principles of analysis. For although he criticizes Schenker's commitment to functional harmony, some of his reformulated middlegrounds include nontonicized dominants as structural harmonies.[22] This is the case, for example, in the first part of his paradigm for sonata form in minor with 5̂ as *Kopfton,* as shown in a box in Example 2.10. Notice that the V/E♭ within the first formal section makes its way to Smith's background. What this means in practice is that Smith would allow the transitional V/E♭ in the exposition of the First Symphony to reach a deeper level of structure than the movement's retransitional home dominant. Similarly, Smith includes not one, but two home dominant harmonies as part of the background for the reprise, even though neither would normally constitute a formal harmony.

The contradiction in Smith's argument is especially glaring when this type of V chord is compared to a retransitional dominant in terms of relationship to formal hierarchy. A retransitional dominant, like the V *Stufe* in mm. 263–342 of the symphony, typically resides on a higher formal level in the sense that it usually functions as the governing harmony for the entire development. Smith's graphs demonstrate as much with their exclusive focus on V for the middle section of all of his models for reprise forms. The dominants he includes within exposition and reprise, by contrast, will virtually always turn out to be either transitional or cadential harmonies. In the symphony, for example, the closing tonic is preceded by a structural dominant that appears on the musical surface only as a cadential harmony. (This is the case regardless of whether one hears the structural close at the V–i progression that initiates the coda at m. 458 or at the later V–I motion that articulates the shift to C major at m. 495.) Assigning deep-level status to a cadential V chord is not in itself necessarily untenable. Schenker's middleground V *Stufen* also often correspond with cadential harmonies, although it is true that the practice has been a point of contention among critics of Schenkerian analysis. My point is that this aspect of Smith's approach is inconsistent with a theory that otherwise denies the possibility of structural status for retransitional dominants. In the end, Smith seems to have a special prejudice against retransitional dominants. Why this should be so, he never explains.

Although my focus up to this point has been on harmonic issues, an approach that uses formal classification to determine tonal structure encounters similar problems with respect to decisions about *Kopfton* choice and location of *Urlinie* constituents. Schenkerians have long recognized that Schenker tended to choose $\hat{3}$ as *Kopfton* for his analyses of major-mode sonata forms and $\hat{5}$ for minor-mode examples. This, however, should not lead us to the conclusion that all such movements should be analyzed in this way, as Smith suggests.[23] The issue again centers on the potential for conflicts between analytical prejudgment and details of individual works.

As Example 2.7 (p. 46) shows, I believe that middleground and foreground characteristics support interpretation of $\hat{3}$ as *Kopfton* for three of the four Brahms movements. In the case of the first movement of the piano quartet, for instance, it would require great willfulness to hear $\hat{5}$ as the main top-voice pitch in face of the overwhelming emphasis on $\hat{3}$. There simply are no articulations of G as main top-voice pitch within the tonic area, as the foreground sketch of Example 2.11 highlights. E♭ initiates the melodic activity in the opening phrase; reenters as resolution of an F seventh at the counterstatement of m. 32; shifts to E♮ at the point of articulation at m. 38; and returns one last time—again as resolution of an F seventh—above the tonic that initiates the transition at m. 42. G, by contrast, enters only as the goal of what is clearly a motion into an inner voice in the opening phrase and as a pitch that covers the structurally more significant E♭ at the beginning of the transition. (This final E♭ achieves superior structural status because it connects to the previous top-voice articulations of E♭.) Would it be analytically convincing to force G somehow to function as *Kopfton* in the face of these foreground characteristics, simply because $\hat{5}$ often serves in this capacity in minor-mode sonata movements?

On the other hand, a straightforward major-mode example like the first movement of Mozart's Piano Sonata in B♭ Major, K. 333, articulates $\hat{5}$ as main pitch, as shown in Example 2.12a. In this case an argument in favor of $\hat{5}$ grows from the saturation of the main theme with two basic motives: a G–F neighbor figure (X) and a descending stepwise motion from $\hat{5}$ to $\hat{1}$ (Y). The intimate rapport between structural levels that Schenker's organicism led him to seek here arises through replication of the fundamental voice leading in the motivic details of the foreground.[24] A brief digression to look yet further at the Mozart movement demonstrates other ways in which its form fails to predict structural characteristics. It thus provides additional evidence that the flexible relationships between form and structure that we have observed in Brahms may also be found in earlier music.

A fruitful place to begin is with middleground relationships in the exposition. Like the tonic area, Mozart's dominant material focuses on its own local $\hat{5}$ in the top voice, as highlighted in Example 2.12b. Here again we see motivic justification for *Kopfton* choice: the second theme, like the first, teems with repetitions of neighbor motion around the local $\hat{5}$ and descending motions from $\hat{5}$ to $\hat{1}$.[25] The analysis

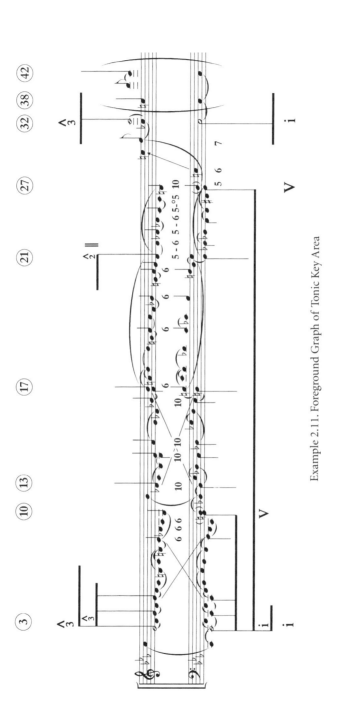

Example 2.11. Foreground Graph of Tonic Key Area

a) Main Theme and Graph

Example 2.12. Mozart, Piano Sonata in B♭ Major, K. 333, I
(a) Main Theme and Graph

highlights these aspects of motivic unification, which counterbalance the contrast between primary and secondary material. As is usually the case in a major-mode sonata, this local $\hat{5}$ functions as a large-scale $\hat{2}$. Yet in K. 333, an analyst will struggle in vain to find a $\hat{4}$–$\hat{3}$ motion to connect the $\hat{5}$ of the tonic area to the $\hat{2}$ of the second group. According to Smith's guidelines, we would have already given up the idea of $\hat{5}$ as *Kopfton,* so the problem would not even arise. Yet although a choice of $\hat{3}$ would

b) **Second Theme and Graph**

Example 2.12. Mozart, Piano Sonata in B♭ Major, K. 333, I
(b) Second Theme and Graph

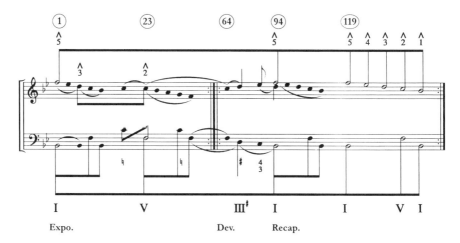

Example 2.13. Mozart K. 333, Middleground Graph (after Oster)

provide a stepwise connection with the $\hat{2}$ of the secondary area, it would result in an unconvincing response to details of the main theme.

A more productive approach begins with the notion that certain middleground structures are more common in some formal contexts than others, yet keeps open the possibility for idiosyncrasy in the particular work at hand. Ernst Oster's suggestion for dealing with sonata forms like the Mozart movement has the advantage of remaining responsive to foreground details of the main theme, although as we will see it too has problems of its own. As illustrated in Example 2.13, he proposes $\hat{5}$ as *Kopfton* in cases like this, but suggests that the $\hat{2}$ of the secondary area enters via stepwise motion from $\hat{3}$, *in an inner voice.*[26]

His solution might be acceptable for the exposition, but when we consider the consequences for the entire movement, it is not difficult to anticipate Smith's objections. One consequence of the proposed $\hat{3}$–$\hat{2}$ inner-voice motion is that $\hat{5}$ remains active in the top voice across the exposition and into the development. This means that when the main theme reenters at the beginning of the recapitulation, its $\hat{5}$/I does not interrupt the $\hat{2}$, but instead connects with the opening $\hat{5}$, as shown in Example 2.13. In other words, this sonata form projects a continuous tonal structure across the thematic parallelism of exposition and recapitulation.

Yet why should the structure of K. 333 be uninterrupted when the entrance of the recapitulation falls well within the bounds of standard sonata practice? This is not a case like the first movement of our Brahms op. 60 piano quartet or op. 51, no. 1, string quartet in which the beginning of the reprise is recomposed to create an overlap with the end of the development. A problem with Oster's solution, in other words, is that, while it responds to foreground details in the exposition, it makes the movement overall look exceptional, despite its conventional formal characteristics. A Schenkerian might respond that the emphasis on the inner voice $\hat{2}$, followed by the return to $\hat{5}$ at the reprise, creates the effect of interruption, without actually constituting interruption. This, however, would strike critics of Schenker as an argument motivated by an ideological commitment to protect Schenker's theory; indeed, it strikes me that way.

Another solution might be to accept that the exposition articulates a gapped top-voice motion—$\hat{5}$-($\hat{4}$)-($\hat{3}$)-$\hat{2}\|$—which is answered by a complete stepwise descent to $\hat{1}$ in the recapitulation. Indeed, Smith explores the possibility for disjunct top-voice structures toward the end of his study of Schenkerian *Formenlehre*.[27] Yet although the exposition appears to articulate a disjunct top voice, such a structure is difficult to reconcile with Schenker's principle of stepwise melodic fluency. One could well wonder under what conditions, beyond K. 333, is it acceptable to give up the requirement for stepwise motion? An answer to this question falls well beyond the scope of this chapter. My intent here is not to solve the analytic quandary posed by the otherwise innocent K. 333 movement, but rather to point out another problem with Smith's notion that form alone provides reliable access to deep levels of structure.

Up to this point I have presented the idea of dimensional counterpoint partly as a fruitful approach to Brahms and partly as a response to criticisms leveled against Schenkerian analysis. The discussion has perhaps given the impression both that I accept Schenker's theory without reservation and that dimensional counterpoint reflects his ideas on form. Neither conclusion is entirely correct. Since Smith aims his criticism specifically at the "new theory of form" laid out in the final section of *Free Composition*, it is necessary to clarify how the perspective outlined in this chapter relates to what Schenker says there.[28] It will also be helpful to place my approach in the context of more recent trends in Schenkerian theory, which likewise represent a departure from the chapter on form in *Free Composition*.

Although distinctions between thematic design, key scheme, and tonal structure are essential to Schenkerian analysis, dimensional counterpoint per se is not the main thrust of Schenker's *Formenlehre*. Rather, as Smith observes, Schenker bases his categorization of formal types on two main criteria: a vaguely defined notion of parts or sections deduced from tonal structure, and tacit recourse to traditional formal types that otherwise are the target of Schenker's scorn. Smith points out some of the shortcomings of this approach. As previously mentioned, he highlights the fact that Schenker groups into different categories movements that a more traditional approach would regard as representatives of the same formal type.

The best course of action, in my view, is to give up both Schenker's idea that fundamental structure can form the basis for a new *Formenlehre* and Smith's belief that form provides direct access to fundamental structure. Identification of a movement's formal type is usually unproblematic provided it need not depend on parts as defined by prolongational spans and the technique of interruption. Schenker's achievement was to open our ears to whole new dimensions of structure—dimensions that contribute to form, to be sure, but that do not by themselves define it. Nor, despite Smith's efforts, can formal identification be made to determine large-scale tonal organization, even though certain middleground structures tend to correspond with certain formal types.

A more productive approach extracts from these form/structure correspondences the idea of default middleground options that may need to be overridden once an analysis engages the details of a particular movement. When first confronting a major-mode sonata form, for example, it is certainly helpful to be aware that many such movements focus on $\hat{3}$ as *Kopfton,* present descending fifth progressions from $\hat{2}$ as the content for their dominant key areas, articulate an interruption through structural rebeginning at the reprise, and so forth. But it is another matter entirely to assume that every major-mode sonata form will or should unfold with these characteristics, as our brief look at the first movement of Mozart's K. 333 sonata has demonstrated.

We also have seen, in just four Brahms movements, three different ways in which the dominant *Stufe* can relate to formal design and two possibilities for *Kopfton* choice, in minor-mode contexts. The examples have also demonstrated that an interruption pattern is hardly essential to sonata form, Schenker's insistence to the contrary notwithstanding. Smith might counter that these are exceptional cases and, in any case, reflect the practice of a late nineteenth-century composer, not the Classical style to which a theory of form must first apply. Yet even a cursory glance through the Schenkerian literature reveals a similar flexibility in the relationship of structure and design in eighteenth-century music. To repeat a point made earlier: the difference between Brahms and his Classical forebears is one of degree, not kind. To map a fixed set of middleground structures onto traditional formal types would be to deny the flexibility that characterizes the relationship between formal archetypes and tonal structure. It would replace one type of Schenkerian dogmatism with another.

The advantage of dimensional counterpoint over Smith's approach is that it provides a means to respond to characteristics of theme, key, and formal harmony, while also addressing the potential diversity of middleground structure. Although it contradicts some of Schenker's more extreme statements about the significance of the thematic dimension, about the possibility for authentic key change within a tonally unified work, and indeed about the exclusive generative power of the *Ursatz,* this should not trouble us too much. Schenker made all sorts of extreme statements about musical structure, not to mention society and politics, that we in the United States of the early twenty-first century do not subscribe to, while we nevertheless reap insights from his analytic approach. Moreover, although it differs from the approach to form that he lays out in the final section of *Free Composition,* the idea of dimensional counterpoint is implicit in many of Schenker's own analyses. Examples 2.14 and 2.15 provide several instances that clearly show Schenker incorporating standard letter designations or descriptive labels into his analyses even as these markings interact in diverse ways with middleground voice leading.

In the *Appassionata* analysis of Example 2.14a, Schenker responds to Beethoven's dimensional counterpoint by allowing the retransitional dominant to extend across the beginning of the thematic reprise at m. 135. Note that he acknowledges the partial independence of the thematic dimension by marking "Recap." under m. 135. Contrast this with Schenker's more conventional default option for minor-mode sonata form, here reproduced in Example 2.14b, in which rearticulation of $\hat{5}/i$ corresponds with the entrance of the recapitulation.

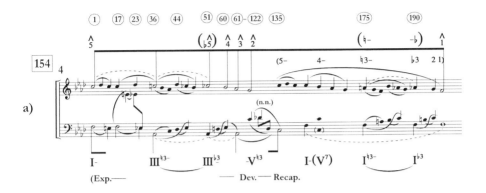

a)

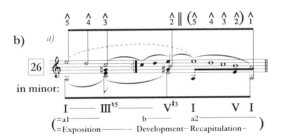

b)

Example 2.14. Schenker's Graph of the *Appassionata* Sonata

Similarly, the analyses in Example 2.15 show Schenker acknowledging the mutual three-part form of both the minuet and trio sections of the second movement from Mozart's Piano Sonata in A Major, K. 331. He does so via the standard a1–b–a2 letter designations beneath both graphs. Yet Schenker simultaneously responds to an important difference between the two ternary forms. The interruption that he hears in the minuet (2.15b) reflects the literal restatement of opening material at its reprise. Schenker applies a default-option structural paradigm in response to a conventional formal situation.

By contrast, the continuous tonal structure in his graph of the trio (2.15a) results from changes of emphasis that arise through Mozart's recomposition of his primary material. Schenker highlights the prominence of $\hat{8}$ in the opening statement of the main theme, on the one hand, and the recapitulatory shift to $\hat{5}$ for the recomposed return, on the other. He acknowledges the thematic rebeginning and thus the three-part design via his a1 and a2 labels. Yet he also responds to the possibility of hearing a structural continuity across the reprise as a consequence of

Three section open form but no interruption: responds to emphasis both on $\hat{8}$ at beginning of a1 and on $\hat{5}$ when the material is recomposed at a2. Cf. graph below where interruption responds to literal restatement at a2.

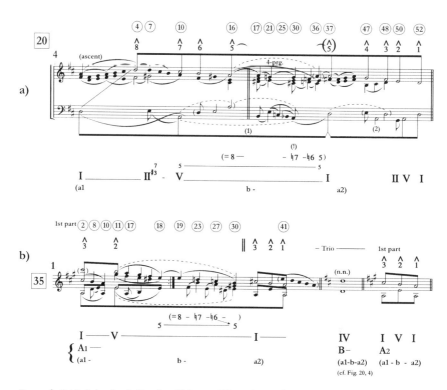

Example 2.15. Schenker's Graph of Mozart, Piano Sonata in A Major, K. 331, II

Mozart's reworking of his main theme. The default analysis is adjusted to respond to idiosyncrasies of the individual case.[29]

Dimensional counterpoint has also formed the basis for more recent Schenkerian writings that address formal issues. Although the authors of these studies do not use the term to describe their approach, their analyses focus attention on flexible relationships between form and middleground structure. David Beach has explicitly laid out an analytic method based on the interaction of thematic design, formal design, and tonal structure as a means of exploring some of Schubert's formal innovations.[30] Eric McKee applies the related concepts of inner and outer form, borrowed from William Rothstein, to analyses of auxiliary cadences as sources of conflict between tonal structure and phrase structure.[31] Lauri Suurpää likewise has shown that categorization of Classical expositions as two-part or continuous hinges not on distinctions of middleground structure, but on aspects of articulation provided by traditional formal dimensions.[32] Perhaps most relevant to the current context is Carl Schachter's penetrating

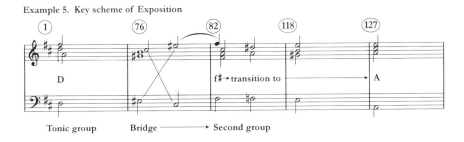

Example 5. Key scheme of Exposition

Tonic group   Bridge ⟶ Second group

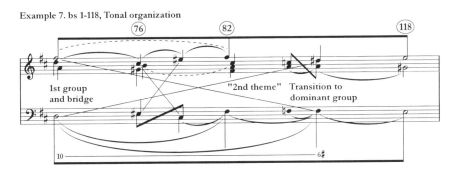

Example 7. bs 1-118, Tonal organization

Example 2.16. Schachter's Graph of Exposition from Brahms's Second Symphony, I

study of the first movement of Brahms's Second Symphony.[33] Among other insights, Schachter proposes that the F♯-minor middle key of the exposition's three-key layout is subsidiary to a large-scale voice exchange. Example 2.16 reproduces Schachter's graph of this voice-leading structure, beneath his summary of the exposition's key scheme.[34] The voice exchange connects the overriding 3̂/I of the tonic area to an augmented-sixth chord, which in turn resolves to V/V. Schachter points out that the F♯ articulation corresponds with the arrival of the second theme; in terms of thematic design and key scheme this represents a turning point in the form. Yet his analysis also responds to both the tonal instability of the F♯ section and the enormous textural emphasis on the later arrival of the E dominant. In terms of middleground structure, a deep-level move away from the tonic *Stufe* occurs only after the augmented-sixth chord resolves to V/V. Although Schachter does not use the term *dimensional counterpoint* to describe his analytic method, his analysis highlights the possibility for flexible interaction among parameters in a sonata context. He demonstrates that the dimensions of theme and key divide the exposition at the arrival of F♯ minor, while the tonal structure provides its main point of articulation only later.

Schachter's analysis drives home two points that were made in reference to previous examples. First, unstable tonal constituents, like the augmented-sixth and V/V chords, can have greater structural significance than chords articulated through tonicization and thematic stability, like the F♯ harmony. The other point that reemerges relates to the impossibility of isolating completely any of the dimensions of form. For although theme and key seem to favor the arrival of F♯, other aspects of design—accumulation of dramatic tension, registration, orchestration, and indeed the entrance of new thematic material—give enormous emphasis to the arrival of V/V. In other words, some design components support the importance of the F♯ arrival, while other competing design factors highlight the superior structural weight of the motion to V/V. It would be incorrect, therefore, to say that design supports the idea of the F♯ articulation as a turning point while factors of voice-leading and large-scale tonal structure, in isolation, point to the entrance of V/V. Both moments are marked for consciousness, similar to the arrival of expository mediants and retransitional dominants in the minor-mode movements of Brahms discussed earlier. It is the difficulty of weighing these types of competing signals that often makes evaluation of the relationship between tonal structure and form difficult. Tonicization and thematic stability constitute only one type of formal emphasis. It would be a damaging oversimplification to deny the possibility for a harmony to be emphasized through other means, such as the dramatic articulation of either V/V in the Second Symphony or the retransitional dominant in the First.

Neither Schachter nor any of the other authors just cited present their ideas as major revisions of Schenkerian theory. This is because, although the idea of dimensional counterpoint differs from Schenker's theoretical statements on form, its basics are compatible with his analytic practice. A multidimensional perspective involves a change in emphasis and conceptualization rather than a fundamental recasting of Schenker's theory. Schenker's ideas on tonal structure can remain intact; we need only apply them somewhat differently to questions of form. This is what I have done in my brief look at four Brahms movements, and it is what Beach, McKee, Suurpää, and Schachter have done in their own separate ways in the essays cited above.

Recognizing the roots of dimensional counterpoint in Schenker's approach is important to the present study because it allows us to see a mutual response to Classical form in Brahms's music and Schenker's analyses, a result of shared historical positions, musical inclinations, and aesthetic values. Brahms and Schenker were both concerned with the perpetuation of traditional compositional procedures at a time in which untraditional approaches to composition were gaining status in musical circles. Despite the influence of Wagner and the New German School (and later, for Schenker, the even more radical changes in compositional technique in the early twentieth century), they both still regarded species counterpoint and figured bass as essential foundations for composition, were committed to traditional forms as opposed to program music, and revered the great composers of the German tradition.[35] Their kinship even has a biographical basis. Not only did both live in late nineteenth-century Vienna, but Brahms recommended the aspiring composer Schenker to his publisher, and Schenker later declared Brahms the "last master of German composition."[36]

Despite their apparent conservatism, Brahms's and Schenker's response to the music of the past has a distinct late nineteenth-century stamp. A tension between conservative and progressive yearnings is revealed in Brahms's and Schenker's attempts to reconcile the sharply articulated musical surfaces of eighteenth-century sonata style with the aesthetics of the late nineteenth century, which by contrast favored continuous motion and evolutionary formal relationships. In Brahms the result is a focus on musical processes that tend to flow across points of formal sectionalization. The composer was a master of strategies devised simultaneously to evoke and efface the boundaries of traditional formal patterns. Schenker likewise developed an analytic method dedicated to the pursuit of tonal continuity across points of articulation, from the level of the local cadence to the largest sections of form.

Composer and theorist both engaged eighteenth-century formal conventions as dynamic processes rather than as patterns in which to string together thematic ideas—as Brahms famously put it to his student Gustav Jenner.[37] One way in which they maintained the vitality of these forms was through their commitment to a flexible relationship between tonal organization and formal design. Neither of them required a predetermined correspondence between sectional articulation provided by theme and key and the beginnings and endings of prolongational spans. We have seen this both in our overview of four Brahms movements and in our exploration of the roots of dimensional counterpoint in Schenker's own analytic practice. Brahms achieved creatively the diversity of dimensional interaction that Schenker demonstrated in his analyses of Haydn, Mozart, and Beethoven. Composer and theorist both sought justification for Classical forms through their superior insight into this inherent characteristic of sonata style. For them, musical tradition was neither dead nor in need of radical reformulation. All Classical form needed was the kind of penetrating insight of which they were both capable.

A particularly resonant example of the Brahms-Schenker relationship can be found in their treatment of sonata-form recapitulation. Brahms and Schenker both strove to subsume this most significant element of division and repetition within a continuous and dynamic unfolding. While they remained committed to a historically validated formal type characterized by the restatement of large blocks of material, they refused to sacrifice the Romantic ideal of an unbroken, goal-directed flow. They both struck a compromise between a strong organicist impulse and their sensitivity to the realities of a formal type based in part on the dramatic delineation of a parallel thematic design.

The similarities, however, are more than incidental. In Chapter 4 we will see that Brahms's creative appropriation of sonata procedures gives rise to an overarching tonal structure that cuts across the parallel division, much the way Schenker attempts to derive Classical period sonata forms from a single *Ursatz*. In a select group of sonata forms, Brahms achieves creatively the specific type of organic unity that Schenker has difficulty demonstrating in his analyses of eighteenth-century music. Dimensional counterpoint will prove indispensable to our exploration of this mutual response to sonata form.

3   A Schoenbergian Perspective: Compositional Economy, Developing Recapitulation, and Large-Scale Form

Up to this point discussion of analytic matters has focused attention on insights that a Schenkerian perspective can offer when set in counterpoint with traditional views of form. Although Schenker made no secret of his deep admiration, even reverence, for Brahms, very few of his published analyses focus on works of the master. His expressions of veneration, however, were more than a matter of lip service. Recent research into Schenker's *Nachlass* has shown that Schenker was fully engaged with Brahms's music, both throughout his career and with the kind of close scrutiny that we have come to associate with his published work.[1]

Few musicians and scholars would require similar archival digging to support the depth of commitment of that other influential fin de siècle Viennese musical figure who championed Brahms. Brahms's importance to Schoenberg's musical thought has long been a mainstay of critical response to the Second Viennese School. The tradition originates with Schoenberg himself, as exemplified most famously by his essay "Brahms the Progressive."[2] Identification with Brahms was one of Schoenberg's central strategies in the defense he mounted on behalf of his own music. Those unsympathetic to Schoenberg might dismiss this identification as a self-serving ploy.[3] A more charitable view is that Schoenberg's Brahmsian affinities were based on powerful insight into the composer's musical essence. That Schoenberg expressed these insights as part of an apologia for his own approach to composition should not prevent us from benefiting from the authentic vision they reflect.

Of Schoenberg's many insights, some of the most penetrating relate to Brahms's skill in dealing with issues of repetition, development, and contrast. For Schoenberg, a composer's ability to maintain a proper balance among these elements is fundamental. Indeed, a trichotomy of repetition, development, and contrast forms the starting point for his *Formenlehre*. Following a brief discussion of the concept of motive, *Fundamentals of Musical Composition* quickly moves on to a description of two phrase types: the sentence and the period.[4] The choice not only is practical—it provides the beginner a point of departure for learning to compose in the Viennese Classical style—but also reflects a compositional philosophy.

As Schoenberg defines them, differences between the period and the sentence center not on how each phrase type begins: both commence with the statement of a basic idea. The crucial distinctions emerge from consequences of the compositional decision to repeat or to introduce contrast. The immediate introduction of a contrasting idea in the period "endangers comprehensibility" and necessitates a counterbalancing repetition. To maintain unity and to prevent a period from degenerating into a potpourri of unrelated ideas, a phrase of this type must return to its initial motive as a starting point for a consequent.

The sentence, by contrast, repeats immediately. The danger is not incoherence but redundancy: a single repetition helps to fix a basic idea in the listener's mind; a second would be unnecessary if not, in fact, tedious. A skillful composer will take advantage of the clarity provided by sentential repetition to develop a basic idea via a motivic process of fragmentation and liquidation. Although Schoenberg is often thought of as a composer who abhorred repetition, this characterization misrepresents his attitude. It is not repetition per se that Schoenberg railed against, but *needless* repetition. Indeed, to Schoenberg the fact that repetition allows for a process of development makes the sentence a more "advanced" phrase type than the period. And even the period finds a positive role for restatement as a necessary counterforce to thematic contrast.

What Schoenberg admired about Brahms was the composer's ability to maximize opportunities for development without endangering comprehensibility. The point is not that Brahms abandons repetition, but that he exploits repetition only as much as necessary to make his ideas and their rapid evolution coherent. Brahms is certainly not alone in this skill. A penchant for compositional economy characterizes the works of composers of earlier eras that Schoenberg admired. Mozart, in particular, features prominently as a model of elastic phrase construction in "Brahms the Progressive."[5] The special status Schoenberg grants Brahms grows out of a difference of degree, not kind. Schoenberg considered Brahms's concision a sign of historical progress in the development of musical language and evidence of the composer's progressivism. What Mozart and others had taken only so far due to their historical moment, Brahms took further.

Schoenberg's admiration was also a result of the contrast he perceived between Brahms and other late nineteenth-century figures who, in Schoenberg's opinion, tended toward excessive amounts of unvaried repetition. It was Brahms alone among the immediately preceding generation who was most qualified to pass the baton of compositional economy on to Schoenberg, who in turn would carry it on to yet further stages of development. Although this type of teleological view of history has fallen out of favor in more recent years, it need not diminish the power of Schoenberg's Brahmsian insights. Over fifty years after its publication, "Brahms the Progressive" remains a seminal work of criticism.

Schoenberg demonstrates his appreciation for Brahms's compositional economy largely through analysis of phrase-length passages. He does not comment at all on Brahms's approach to large-scale repetition in "Brahms the Progressive." There is another parallel here with his *Formenlehre*. The most original insights of *Fundamentals of Musical Composition* emerge in the sections devoted to phrase construction. Once Schoenberg moves on to movement-length forms, his descriptions become somewhat pedestrian. Yet there is no reason that a proper balance between repetition, development, and contrast should be any less relevant to global organization than to the sentence or period. This is especially the case for Brahms, who took care to mark his large-scale formal restatements with signs of developing variation.[6]

Brahms's developmental impulse is most obvious in his approach to sonata-form recapitulation, but it is also evident in his treatment of large-scale return in other formal types. The C-minor piano quartet reflects this fundamental affinity for developmental restatement. Its first movement includes one of Brahms's most thoroughly developmental recapitulations, while the Andante demonstrates the composer's tendency to maintain many of the same evolutionary strategies in the context of a slow middle movement. The scherzo, by contrast, presents a large-scale return that is a nearly exact repetition of the opening A section. The transparency of form in the scherzo, however, is not inconsistent with Schoenberg's view of Brahms as progressive. When considered both from the perspective of internal factors and in relation to the first movement, its large-scale restatement emerges as far from needless. Again, the point is not that Brahms abandons repetition as a compositional resource; his fidelity to traditional modes of formal organization precludes that possibility. Rather, Brahms is a master at pushing the limits of developmental possibility within a framework in which repetition still plays an essential role.

An exploration of large-scale restatement throughout the piano quartet will provide a means to reflect further on formal characteristics of the outer movements discussed in the previous chapter, as well as to begin to address the scherzo and Andante. A fruitful way to begin is to engage the first two movements as a pair, a strategy designed to highlight the paradoxical character of the work, as described in Chapter 1. That is to say, a pairing of the movements will set in relief the quartet's status as a highly idiosyncratic piece that nevertheless reflects many of Brahms's core compositional concerns. A focus on the opening Allegro and the scherzo allows for reflection on some of the quartet's unique characteristics as well as on the degree to which it exhibits compositional strategies that permeate Brahms's instrumental works. Viewing the movements as a pair will also help to engage the overall trajectory of the cycle, for as Chapter 1 noted, a 2 + 2 grouping pattern articulates the unfolding of the whole.[7]

Although both the Allegro and the scherzo stand out as special cases, they establish their individual profiles at least in part through intensification of standard Brahmsian procedures. This is the crux of the paradox that governs the work. Consider the recapitulation of the first movement. Its most remarkable feature—the return of the second theme in the key of the major dominant (m. 236)—is unique among Brahms's sonata forms (and in the history of sonata form, for that matter). Brahms's standard practice, as previously mentioned, is to follow the sonata principle: he typically reconciles important thematic statements presented outside the home key with the tonic before a movement ends.[8]

Yet as we have already seen from the example of the C-minor string quartet, this apparent fidelity to the sonata principle also often embraces a seemingly contradictory emphasis on the dominant. It is not unusual for Brahms to introduce or extend the main dominant prolongation of sonata form across the transposed re-turn of secondary material. Recall that the secondary area in the string quartet centers on V/III, not III itself. When this material returns in the tonic key, it like-wise focuses on V, not i. In major-mode sonata forms of the Classical era, this type of deep-level V normally corresponds with the tonicized dominant of the exposition—a part of the form that creates large-scale dissonance. In the minor mode, a structural dominant typically arrives in the retransition. By articulating a deep-level dominant in the recapitulation, Brahms turns the sonata principle on its head. The transposed return of secondary material, although in some respects a form of reconciliation, simultaneously prolongs the dissonant dominant pole of the large-scale form. Thus although the recapitulation in the piano quartet's first movement represents a unique case, it is unique through its degree of dominant emphasis, not through dominant emphasis per se.

Similarly, the beginning of the first movement's recapitulation (m. 199) consti-tutes one of Brahms's most thorough recompositions of a tonic key area. Both the motivations and consequences of the recomposition, however, reflect standard Brahmsian practice. It was his habit to extend developmental instabilities across the onset of the reprise. The process usually involves intensification and develop-ment of characteristic features whose implications are not fully realized in the ex-position. The repetition of the main theme thus becomes an example of developing variation on a colossal scale. Rather than present a straightforward restatement of what has already been absorbed by an astute listener, Brahms takes advantage of an opportunity to explore more remote consequences. He thereby avoids a needless repetition, in Schoenberg's terms.

Virtually any aspect of the total musical context might inspire a reinterpretation of a main theme; common sources for development include motivic details and the overall formal shape of the material. In the first movement of the piano quartet, two characteristics stand out as sources for recapitulatory reinterpretation: the *piz-zicato* E♮'s just prior to the counterstatement at m. 32 and the introductory char-acter embedded within the first part of the tonic key area (mm. 1–31.1). The E♮'s instantiate the *Unheimliches* as an indication of the harmonic and expressive range of the movement and the piece as a whole, and signal an unusual attention to that pitch globally to an extent that remains unresolved within the section or even within the movement. There will be many occasions, therefore, to address E♮'s in-fluence as the discussion unfolds. First, however, it will be helpful to explore reper-cussions of the tonic area's formal shape as it influences the character of the re-capitulation.

Example 3.1 summarizes the formal layout of the opening of the movement and compares it with the recomposition at the recapitulation. In terms of formal shape, the most obvious choice might have been for Brahms to locate a recapitulatory structural downbeat at a point analogous to the entrance of the counterstatement. Example 3.2 shows the outlines of a possible connection from the retransition to the material of mm. 31–32. Undoubtedly Brahms would have done it more artis-tically. The example nevertheless suffices to illustrate a potential compositional re-sponse to the status of m. 32 as the main point of initiation for the tonic area. A

Example 3.1. Formal Layout of Tonic Area and Recapitulatory Recomposition

Exposition	Recapitulation
mm. 1–10: Phrase 1, i to V	mm. 199–205: Phrase 1, continued prolongation of retransitional V
—	mm. 206–12.1: New material with metric displacement of head motive, expands V
mm. 11–20: Phrase 2, ♭vii	—
mm. 21–31.1: Descending 5–6 sequence, expands V	mm. 213–16: Material from transition, pt. 1, expands V
mm. 32–41.1: Counterstatement, i–V–i	—
mm. 42–51.1: Transition, pt. 1, i to V/E♭	mm. 217–26: Descending 5–6 sequence, expands V
—	mm. 227–35.1: 5–6 sequence extended, to V/G
mm. 52–69.1: Transition, pt. 2, expands V/E♭	—

strategy along the lines of Example 3.2 would coordinate a moment of harmonic resolution with a point of thematic initiation and thus would conform to traditional expectations for the entrance of the reprise. Brahms instead chooses to do something significantly more inventive and of greater consequence for the entire recapitulation.

One strategy that Brahms often exploits to create a developmental return of main-theme material is to recompose an opening paragraph so that it can be absorbed into an ongoing retransitional trajectory. This type of recomposition delays the structural downbeat that conventionally arrives at the beginning of the reprise, and pushes it ahead to a later point of articulation within the expository material. Brahms adopts this strategy in the first movements of the B♭-Major Sextet, op. 18, the G-minor piano quartet, and the F-minor piano quintet. If he were to articulate a climactic double return with the counterstatement in the C-minor piano quartet, however, he would almost certainly have had to do away with the entire opening passage, as suggested in Example 3.2. Formal exigencies would require more active material to form part of a retransitional bridge. Brahms nevertheless manages to focus the beginning of the recapitulation on the first part of the key area—the passage that he must have felt was more promising as a source for development. It is the counterstatement that he eliminates.

Here again we see the approach to composition that Schoenberg so admired. Brahms's compositional economy doesn't just compel him to take advantage of repetition as an opportunity to develop: a proclivity for concision pushes him

Example 3.2. Hypothetical Recapitulation with Material of m. 32

to explore more remote consequences of his material. Brahms eschews the obvious choice of reinterpreting the counterstatement as his recapitulatory structural downbeat—even if that choice would involve at least a degree of responsiveness to his material. Instead he bends the form yet further to accommodate the development of even more highly idiosyncratic characteristics.

The developmental potential of the opening material grows not only from its formal shape and anomalous E♮'s, but from several additional idiosyncrasies as well. The section (1) establishes a special rhythmic relationship between the E♮'s and the head motive of the main theme, (2) emphasizes the dominant as goal of two sub-phrases (mm. 9 and 27), and (3) includes a 5–6 step sequence with inherent modulatory potential (mm. 21–27). The counterstatement, by contrast, is harmonically static and avoids any type of striking chromatic detail. We will see how Brahms ingeniously builds on these characteristics. First, it will be worthwhile to present a brief comparison with the C-minor string quartet and First Symphony, as well as with the first movement of the piano quintet, in order to gain a clearer sense of the particular type of instability that characterizes the quartet's opening material.

Many main themes in Brahms begin with tension between elements of initiation and preparation. The specific anacrusic character, however, may vary considerably. The string quartet and piano quintet exhibit different degrees of instability for an opening tonic. Both begin with main themes of ABA′ form, as indicated by annotations in the score excerpts of Example 3.3. One consequence of the themes' initial anacrusic character is an enhanced significance for the tonic articulations at the beginning of their A′ sections. The A′ arrival locks in a harmonic point of departure only tentatively established at the outset. In this regard the movements resemble the first movement of op. 60, which also throws its weight of emphasis onto the tonic that initiates the counterstatement.

Despite the similarity, different idiosyncrasies of ABA′ design lead to different forms of recapitulatory reinterpretation. In the spirit of developing variation, Brahms takes advantage of large-scale repetition as an opportunity to develop nuances of his themes. The result is a process in which he balances aspects of formal convention—characteristics of repetition and articulation that Schoenberg viewed as aids to comprehensibility—with responsiveness to the developmental potential of his material. The string quartet begins with a theme in mm. 1–8 (= A) that immediately articulates a structural i chord. Indeed, it unfolds over a tonic pedal. The

Example 3.3. ABA′ Main Themes in C-Minor String Quartet and Piano Quintet
(a) C-Minor String Quartet, Op. 51, No. 1, mm. 1–26

phrase nevertheless drives urgently ahead to the half-cadential dominant at its end. The B section of mm. 11–22.1 then luxuriously expands the dominant, with the tonic reentering only at the A′ return of m. 23.

Brahms reinterprets both the end-accented shape of the A section and the harmonic orientation of the B material as part of a focus on the dominant at the beginning of the reprise. This dominant orientation is a crucial component of the continuous tonal structure that he projects across the movement, as discussed in Chapter 2. As part of the overlap, Brahms heightens emphasis on a motivic $^6_3$ chord above C, whose multidimensional appearances in the main theme are highlighted with annotations in Example 3.3a. In the original version, the $^6_3$ chord emerges via a 5–6 motion within the theme's opening structural tonic. At the reprise, the $^6_3$ chord takes over as a substitute for the tonic $^5_3$. The result is that Brahms avoids rearticu-

Example 3.3. ABA′ Main Themes in C-Minor String Quartet and Piano Quintet
(a) C-Minor String Quartet, Op. 51, No. 1, mm. 1–26

lation of a structural tonic specifically through a process of motivic development, in which characteristic features become the focus.

The quintet displays some overall similarities of formal strategy, yet Brahms adjusts his approach in response to the individuality of his material. In the quintet there is considerably less assertiveness of tonic function in the unharmonized A section of mm. 1–4. It is only with the climactic return of the material at m. 12 (= A′) that a structural tonic emerges. In contrast to the reduced tensions of the B material in the string quartet, the middle section in the quintet (mm. 5–11) is dynamically charged. The agitated character of the dominant-prolonging B material is ideally suited to reinterpretation as part of the retransition (mm. 166–72)—a formal function unavailable to the middle section of the quartet. Not only is it powerfully goal-directed, but it also leads to an emphatic structural downbeat at the expanded return of the opening phrase. Brahms thus reinterprets the first solid articulation of the tonic in the exposition (m. 12) as the point of harmonic return in the recapitulation (m. 173).[9] The process again involves development of a neighboring $\hat{6}$ motive. Annotations in Example 3.3b highlight the neighbor figure as it appears in the opening theme. At the reprise Brahms transfers the motive into the bass of mm. 165–66 and exploits it as a means to extend the retransitional dominant prolongation across the emergence of the main theme.[10]

The piano quartet, in contrast to both the string quartet and piano quintet, opens with material that evokes characteristics associated with a slow introduction. Under more conventional circumstances, a slow introduction will occur as a sec-

Example 3.3. ABA′ Main Themes in C-Minor String Quartet and Piano Quintet
(b) F-Minor Piano Quintet, Op. 34, mm. 1–16

tion distinct from the exposition, as is the case with the First Symphony. The quartet, however, embeds introductory characteristics within the tonic area. (At least in this sense, its exposition is more like the opening of the first movement of the Second Symphony.)[11] The initial paragraph of the quartet is slow-paced and fragmentary rather than dynamically charged. The dominant, instead of forming part of an agitated upbeat, itself forms a rhythmic goal, and its prolongation builds ten-

Example 3.3. ABA′ Main Themes in C-Minor String Quartet and Piano Quintet
(b) F-Minor Piano Quintet, Op. 34, mm. 1–16

sion through an absence of motion or activity. It would be difficult if not impossible to absorb this material into a retransition along the lines of the B section in
the quintet. Instead, Brahms begins the thematic reprise at m. 199 as an area of
dramatic crisis, an enormous anticlimax following the forward-driving expansion
of the dominant in the retransition.

The return of the main theme becomes part of a struggle for coherence and continuity, rather than a point of resolution or even a continuation of retransitional trajectory. Brahms transforms the slow introductory character into a kind of pregnant pause in the form. Although he provides some recapitulatory signals, his responsiveness to his material tips the balance between form and content in favor of characteristic features. Material that is not suited to a traditional recapitulatory articulation, or even the kind of straightforward formal overlap found in the piano quintet, returns nevertheless, and itself dictates a reinterpretation of formal convention.

A tight connection between form and content even extends to the manner in which Brahms evades resolution of the retransitional dominant. At first glance, the half-step shift from G to A♭ at m. 198 might not appear to have any particular motivic significance. The $\hat{5}$–$\hat{6}$ dyad, however, first enters motivically as goal for the descending melodic motion at the very outset of the movement and forms part of the figuration within the dominant harmony just prior to the counterstatement. Example 3.4 highlights these motivic occurrences. Similar to the situation in the string quartet and piano quintet, Brahms develops this $\hat{5}$–$\hat{6}$ neighbor figure to create a recapitulatory formal overlap. In addition, the development has modulated through the keys of E♭ minor, B major, and G major, at mm. 122, 142, and 164, respectively, before settling on G as home dominant in the retransition (m. 176). The shift to A♭ thus completes a large-scale iteration of an augmented-triad-plus-half-step tetrachord—an important source of unity across the entire quartet. It also establishes the $\hat{5}$–$\hat{6}$ dyad as a component of recapitulatory articulation throughout the four movements—a point that we will return to later.

In addition to its motivic significance, the motion to A♭ helps to prevent articulation of a structural tonic and thus plays a crucial role in extending the tension of the development across the return of the main theme. The octave A♭'s replace the original C octaves that initiated the overriding tonic *Stufe* for the main theme in the exposition. Although Brahms does touch on C-minor triads—note in particular the extended C bass in mm. 201–204—these chords are apparent rather than structural tonics, as the graph in Example 3.5 shows. They are part of an extension of the middleground dominant initiated by the retransition, as described in Chapter 2. This is where Brahms takes advantage of the two dominant arrivals within the first part of the tonic area in the exposition. The dominant chords at the end of the opening phrase and at the end of the 5–6 sequence become the focus of harmonic gravity at mm. 205 and 223, respectively. Without the tonic point of departure from which they originally grew, these dominants function as offshoots of the dominant expansion initiated by the retransition. They form part of an enormous prolongation of V that flows across the boundary between development and recapitulation.

The concept of an apparent tonic has a parallel in the thematic dimension at the entrance of the recapitulation: on the one hand, the essential pitches and rhythms of the main theme return at m. 199, as highlighted in Example 3.6. Yet on the other hand, reinstrumentation of the thematic idea creates continuity with the retransition, so that the effect of restatement is illusory. Central to the heightened instability of the theme is the fact that the statement and repetition of its basic idea—the

Example 3.4. A♭ Neighbor Motive in Tonic Key Area

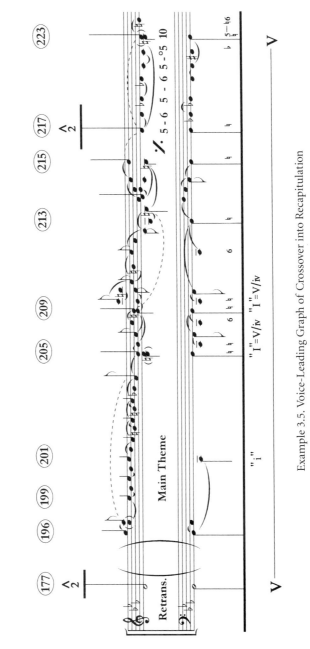

Example 3.5. Voice-Leading Graph of Crossover into Recapitulation

Example 3.6. Recapitulation of Main Theme

parts of a sentence that normally provide a clear point of departure—are split off from the main body of the phrase and presented by the piano only. The reinstrumentation creates an effect of fragmentation rather than initiation. Brahms introduces abrupt shifts in register to intensify the fragmentary character. Moreover, the thematic entrance in the piano is disguised by repetitions of the triplet motivic idea of m. 198, material that also appears scattered in multiple registers. These motivic repetitions are labeled with X's in Example 3.6. By the time the retransitional dust has settled following a rhythmically augmented version of the X motive in the cello at mm. 201–202, the main theme is already half over.

Elements of continuity with the retransition even extend to the end of the phrase (m. 205), where the A♭ within the main theme reawakens the A♭ introduced just prior to the thematic return. As Example 3.5 suggests, the expanded A♭ finally resolves to G in m. 205, followed by further repetitions of the neighbor motive in mm. 206–13. This connection confirms the motivic origins of the retransitional $\hat{5}$–$\hat{6}$ dyad in the A♭–G fragment at the end of the movement's opening phrase. The voice-leading continuity across the reemergence of the main theme is bolstered by the fact that the dominant that supports the resolution to $\hat{5}$ itself connects to the middleground dominant of the retransition, as depicted in Example 3.5. Thus although from a purely surface orientation the beginning of the reprise fulfills the idea of a double return, harmonic and thematic components are both illusory. They serve to evoke conventions associated with the onset of a recapitulation without carrying true recapitulatory function. Brahms saves an authentic double return for the coda (m. 313), where he finally gives in to a structural tonic along with a clearly articulated restatement of the main theme.

This delay of a double return until the coda represents an extreme on a continuum of possible locations for recapitulatory structural downbeats in Brahms's sonata forms. The particular form of dominant emphasis through which the delay is accomplished also contributes to the quartet's extreme position on the continuum. At one end of the range of possible locations for structural downbeats are conventional double returns, those cases in which both the character of the tonic key area and the formal trajectory of the development dictate a stable rearticulation of main theme and tonic. In movements of this type—as in examples of conventional double returns in the music of Brahms's Viennese precursors—straightforward restatement gains formal justification as a resolution of tension that has built across the development. The tendency to avoid needless repetition must be fulfilled primarily by the effectiveness of the preparation so that the return to stability is strongly motivated.

In addition, composers in the Viennese tradition often consolidate their main-theme material. This practice allows them to avoid repetitions of phrases and cadential articulations, at a point in the form in which such aids to comprehensibility are no longer necessary.[12] Similarly, recapitulatory procedures of expansion or development, such as Mozart's so-called second development sections, also can be understood to arise from a desire to avoid a slackening of momentum in what otherwise might threaten to become a dead spot in the form. In Brahms's works, conventional double returns are far less common than restatements characterized by delay and development, but they do occur. Examples include the recapitulations in the first movements of the G-Major Sextet, op. 36, and E-Minor Cello Sonata, op. 38; another is the A′ return in the scherzo of the quartet, which, although not a sonata form, adopts a sonata-like retransition and climactic double return at m. 159 as part of its ternary design.

As the continuum of recapitulation types progresses, it moves from these conventional situations toward greater and greater lengths of thematic and/or tonal delay. Brahms tends to focus his powers of motivic development on recomposition of the tonic area; in all but a few recapitulations, he restates his secondary material tonally transposed but otherwise in exact or nearly exact restatement.[13] This means that a degree of thematic resolution normally occurs at least at the arrival of the second theme, if not earlier. Other possible locations for a return to thematic stability include points of articulation within an opening phrase (First Symphony, I; G-major string quintet, I); the entrance of a counterstatement of an opening idea (piano quintet, I); the beginning of a secondary idea within the tonic area (F-Minor Clarinet Sonata, op. 120, no. 1, I); or perhaps the beginning of the transition (B♭-major sextet, I). Any of these locations might also provide a delayed rearticulation of a structural tonic.

Yet it is also the case that Brahms sometimes leaves the retransitional dominant unresolved beyond the return of the tonic area and bridge. He bypasses the possibility of a double return, for example, at the entrance of the counterstatement in the first movement of the op. 60 quartet by cutting the material, as has already been noted. The option of an unresolved dominant can have enormous consequences, as it relates to the tonal structure of secondary material. Brahms often orients his secondary material around the dominant of the local key, as previously mentioned here and in Chapter 2. This is the case in the middle section of the quartet's Andante, a passage that we will consider shortly; it is also true, as we have seen, in the first movement of the C-minor string quartet, to cite just two of many possible examples.

When a secondary area oriented around its local V returns transposed to the tonic key, it will prolong the home dominant rather than the tonic. If the beginning of the reprise has failed to rearticulate a structural tonic, then the dominant prolongation of the secondary material will continue to extend the middleground dominant left unresolved at the end of the development. Thus, on the other end of the continuum, we arrive at movements, like the first of the string quartet and piano quartet, in which Brahms merges tonic return and closure into a single and enormously powerful articulation. This conflation might occur at a final cadence of the secondary area, or it might even be delayed into the coda. The string quartet provides an example of the first option, the piano quartet an example of the second.

The characteristic that differentiates the piano quartet from other movements at this far end of the continuum is the specific manner of dominant prolongation across the return of the secondary material. (The recapitulation is also noteworthy for Brahms's recomposition of the secondary material. As has already been noted, Brahms's standard practice is to restate his secondary material intact with tonal transposition as the only significant alteration. The new set of variations he writes for the recapitulation in the quartet is a logical response to the potential for redundancy posed by the return of material based on variation principles.) The second group extends the retransitional V not through continued expansion of G as home dominant, but as a tonic in its own right. This was a central aspect of the discussion of dimensional counterpoint in Chapter 2: rather than resolve large-scale dissonance, the recapitulation introduces a large-scale dissonance.

In addition to its location in the recapitulation, the tonicization of the major dominant is noteworthy specifically in the context of a minor-mode work. Brahms himself exposes the willfulness of the strategy as an expressive device within the music itself. As the recapitulation continues, he hints at the possibility of a far less extreme continuation and resolution for the recapitulatory crisis—indeed, a solution that would be consistent with the sonata principle. At m. 213, material from the transition returns transposed from the V/E♭ level to the level of the home dominant. The transitional material allows the dominant left hanging at the end of the development to reemerge as a harmony that still signals the imminent return of the tonic. This raises hopes—in the end, false hopes—that the transitional material will follow a path of resolution to the major tonic at the arrival of the lyrical second theme. Such a scenario would result in a location of the movement at the midpoint of our recapitulatory continuum. Brahms instead chooses to travel on a significantly more consequential path.

The strategy of raising hopes only to thwart them relates to the sense of crisis or catastrophe that characterizes the entire beginning of the reprise. Aspects of thematic process and motivic development join the continued dominant prolongation to create this atmosphere of intense disquiet. Just after he completes the apparent

Example 3.7. *Appoggiatura* and *Pizzicato* Motives

rcstatement of the opening phrase, Brahms reaches a point of extreme motivic liq-uidation: the chord progression in the piano of mm. 206–12.1 is virtually devoid of thematic content. It is out of this thematic vacuum that the transitional material emerges, seemingly to provide new coherence and the promise of progress toward resolution. The abrupt dissolution at the return of the 5–6 step sequence at m. 217 thus enters not as a mere continuation of a crisis, but as a sinking back into defeat following a momentary glimmer of hope.

Another aspect of this vacillation between hope and defeat engages character-istics of metric ambivalence embedded within Brahms's motivic materials. Just prior to the entrance of the transitional material, the feeling that the form has lost its way is so intense that the fragmentary iterations of the head motive in mm. 208–12 lose their grip on the meter and slide into positions of metric dis-placement. This aspect of motivic development builds on a relationship between the head motive and the *pizzicato* E♮ motive. Both are based on the same quarter-note rhythm, but each is positioned differently in relation to the meter, as can be seen in Example 3.7. Some factors in the exposition help to delineate the distinct metric identities of the two motives. The appoggiatura character of E♭ in the head motive signals a strong/weak metric interpretation, while the low-to-high contour of the *pizzicato* figure indicates a weak/strong pattern.

Yet the metric identity of each figure is less than fully secure, in part due to the fact that they both follow metrically undifferentiated, quasi fermata-like so-norities. The head motive has some hints of weak-strong displacement, while the *pizzicato* motive leaves open the possibility of strong-weak articulation until E♮ resolves to F at the clear metric accent on the downbeat of m. 31. The rhythmic-metric ambivalence works hand-in-hand with ambiguity of tonal function. At the point of crisis at the beginning of the recapitulation, the head motive is overcome by characteristics of the tonally ambiguous E♮ (vl. and vla., mm. 208–12). What was originally centered on both the tonic and the metric downbeat becomes domi-nant oriented and displaced in a manner that associates it with the anomalous E♮. Brahms must have viewed this aspect of instability at the reprise as significant. For as we shall see, he takes care to provide both metric resolution for the head motive and tonal resolution for the *pizzicato* figure as part of the powerful articulation of the delayed structural downbeat at m. 313 of the coda.

The *pizzicato* motive stands at the heart of another aspect of development in which a latent characteristic in the exposition reaches fruition at the recapitula-tion. In the exposition the E♮ arises out of an implied 5–6 motion above a stationary G bass, as shown in Example 3.8. The resulting $^6_3$ chord functions not as an inver-sion of an E♮-minor triad, but as a by-product of linear elaboration of the control-

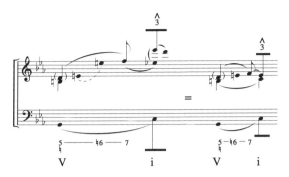

Example 3.8. E♮ as Part of Linear 5–♮6–7 Motion within Dominant

ling dominant *Stufe*. A slightly larger context confirms a contrapuntal function for E♮. As the voice leading progresses to F, the *unheimlich* E♮ reveals its identity as a passing tone that fills in the space between the (implied) fifth and the seventh of the dominant.

A contrapuntal interpretation of the E♮ sonority notwithstanding, $^6_3$ chords in Brahms that arise via 5–6 motions often do in fact achieve significance as inversions of root-position triads.[14] This is the case in the recapitulation of the quartet, where the latent harmonic significance of the $^6_3$ chord emerges to generate a tonicization of ♮iii at m. 227. Brahms in turn exploits the function of ♮iii as relative minor of G: the tonicization of E♮ becomes a link to the sharp side for the return of the second theme in the dominant key. Example 3.9 traces the voice leading for the modulation. The influence of the *pizzicato* motive thus resonates beyond expansion through tonicization to embrace the most idiosyncratic aspect of tonal structure in the recapitulation. In creating the E♮–G key succession, Brahms also takes advantage of the modulatory potential of the 5–6 step sequence. He not only recapitulates the sequential material that expands the dominant (mm. 217–23), but also returns to the 5–6 pattern at m. 230 as the means of leading from E♮ minor onward to G.

The development of latent characteristics—whether they consist of metric relationships among motives or tonal implications of an unusual chromatic inflection—demonstrates Brahms's uncanny ability to compose a recapitulation in which not much is new but all is different. An ingenious blend of repetition and development results in a kind of formal irony. Brahms seizes an opportunity at the return of the main theme to create a deliberate contrast between apparent and intended meaning: he enters into a process of recapitulation without seeming to. Or from another perspective, perhaps he only seems to have entered a process of recapitulation though he really does not.

Whichever way one chooses to view the situation, the recapitulation of the second theme at first appears to be considerably more straightforward. Yet here too Brahms stands at ironic distance from formal convention. On the one hand, the entrance of the second theme provides an element of thematic resolution; often in Brahms, thematic stability emerges in the recapitulation before tonal resolution, as

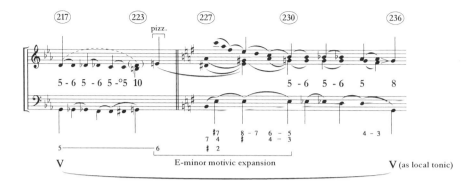

Example 3.9. Voice Leading for Modulation to G Major

already noted. Similarly the arrival of the G tonic at m. 236 offers at least a local point of harmonic resolution. Yet it is important to realize that the resolution is illusory. G major functions as a kind of impostor tonic. Although locally it provides a release of tension, it participates in a tension-building *Bassbrechung*, C–E♭–G, that spans the entire movement. Moreover, although G enters via preparation by its own D dominant, it originates in the G prolongation of the retransition and main-theme return, where its home dominant function is manifest directly on the musical surface.

The dual meaning of the G *Stufe* has a profound impact on the affective function of the secondary material. The lyrical theme only seems to break free from the catastrophe of the beginning of the recapitulation. Ultimately the thematic dimension also turns out to have an ironic meaning. The situation recalls Tovey's thoughts about the function of the return of the second theme in the tonic major in some of Beethoven's minor-mode sonata forms. In Tovey's view a recapitulatory turn to major is often a form of tragic irony in Beethoven: a glimmer of hope only heightens the tragic effect of the shift back to the grim realities of minor in Beethoven's codas.[15] In the Brahms quartet the effect is doubled: not only does the coda return to minor and material of despondent character; it also unmasks the particular major key that previously provided a ray of hope, as an impostor for the tonic. The second theme is not just one step removed from tragic fate via mode, but two steps via mode and key center. The fact that the major dominant is normally so heavily directed toward tonic resolution in the minor mode intensifies the illusory character of stability at the return of the lyrical theme. There is much more tension here then might be the case with a key related by third to the tonic.

I have already mentioned that Brahms almost always brings back his secondary material tonally transposed but otherwise in exact or nearly exact restatement. To appreciate the component of developing variation in this part of his recapitulations, it is therefore necessary to extend Schoenberg's concept of compositional economy beyond the thematic dimension. This is true even for the quartet—one of the few examples in which there is some recomposition of the secondary area.

Brahms's recapitulations usually do contain elements of thematic development, but mainly in the return of primary material. He nevertheless often reinterprets the tonal function of the secondary material so that its recapitulation also becomes an opportunity to pursue developmental possibilities. New tonal functions allow Brahms to eschew a formulaic approach to form in which conventional patterns of organization create a mold into which content is poured. Similar to the phrase level, where a focus on motivic evolution forces symmetries of grouping and meter into the background, strategies of reinterpretation on the global level help to efface the large-scale periodicity of sonata form. Brahms continues to compose in the spirit of developing variation even as he adjusts the means of evolution to accommodate both the enormous scope of the repetition and the exigencies of sonata form.

In the quartet Brahms provides three new variations as part of the theme and variations form of the secondary area. In this sense there is an element of thematic development in the restatement, as just noted. The character of the new variations contributes to the ironic meaning of the apparently stable turn to major. The first, at m. 244, transforms the theme into a delicate, almost ethereal point of imitation, whispered by each voice *pianissimo* and *molto dolce*. The second and third variations, at mm. 252 and 260, also seem to float above reality. The tension of the V/G pedal, the continual *pianissimo*, and the music-box timbre provided by the piano's high tessitura all temporarily hold the material beyond the grip of fate. Yet even here the fact that Brahms engages traditional variation procedures makes the new content distinct from material that evolves via a process of developing variation.

Even more representative of Brahms's compositional economy is the transposition of the material into the dominant key. Brahms not only sustains tension across the restatement but also consolidates points of harmonic resolution. Instead of multiple locations for tonic return—for example, at the beginning of the recapitulation and at the beginning of the second theme and each variation—Brahms merges, into a single entity, the return of the tonic and the structural close for the movement as a whole. The spirit of concision that Schoenberg admired in the motivic dimension thus resonates in the harmonic dimension as well. Just as Brahms avoids needless repetition of thematic ideas, so too does he avoid needless repetition of large-scale tonal goals.

It is also important to observe that the secondary material has a much different affective meaning based on the new context in which it occurs. In the exposition, the second theme provides an authentic area of repose following the introductory character of the opening paragraph and the agitation of the counterstatement and transition. In the recapitulation, the sense of resolution is false, or in Tovey's formulation, ironic, as already noted. The tonicization of G stabilizes a retransitional *Stufe* that already points toward tonic resolution. The exposition ends with solid closure in E♭, while in the recapitulation tragic fate dictates that G must push on to fulfill its function as dominant.

This indeed begins to occur toward the end of the secondary material, when the fifth variation restores home dominant function via the addition of F♮ at m. 279. Brahms sustains tension yet further, however, through an entirely new passage designed to create the necessary buildup to the coda. In particular, the new material leads to potential points of tonic articulation that are each undercut in favor of

Example 3.10. Failed Attempts at Resolution in Coda *Continued on next pages*

continued dominant prolongation. Example 3.10 reproduces these failed attempts at tonic return.

The first such progression does provide a tonic at m. 288. The approach, however, is from an altered dominant with Db in the bass, a much weaker progression than the standard root-position V–I. The sense of resolution in the top voice is especially tenuous because C sounds like an appoggiatura to B♮ rather than like a stable point

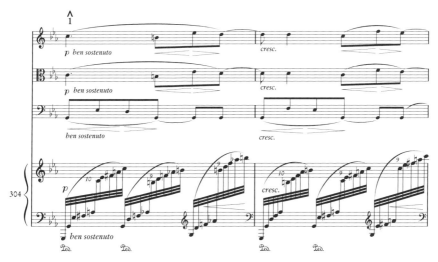

but G bass and vii^{o7}/V

Example 3.10. *Continued on next page*

of arrival—an outgrowth of the aforementioned appoggiatura character of the E♭–D head motive in m. 3. The C–B♮ motion results in momentary articulation of the motivic ♮iii chord against the sustained C in the cello. The appoggiatura character of C and the resulting emphasis on ♮iii emerges more forthrightly at m. 289. There the cello motion to E♮ supports rather than contradicts the shift away from the tonic, further disturbing any sense of resolution.

The second two progressions at mm. 304 and 308 contain straightforward dominants, but withhold a structural tonic. Of these two evaded resolutions, the second is more remarkable. The continuation at m. 304 harmonizes Î with a vii^{o7}/V chord—a conventional technique for continued dominant expansion at an evaded cadence. It also heightens the sense of cadential evasion through a *subito* shift to *piano ben sostenuto*. The articulation at m. 308 comes closer to resolution but nevertheless stubbornly frustrates the attempt at fulfillment. This is one of those moments, as described in Chapter 1, in which Brahms creates an uncommon intensity of expression by pushing an already extreme compositional strategy virtually beyond its limits. He articulates a complete tonic triad in the upper parts and arrives at the *fortissimo* goal of a *crescendo*. Yet he simultaneously denies structural resolution through continued repetition of G in the bass.

In performance the effect of denial at the evaded cadences of mm. 304 and 308 can be intensified if a slight break occurs between the dominant and the entrance of each new phrase. That is, both dominants form quasi half-cadential goals, while the material that follows functions as the point of departure for a new formal unit. It is only at the arrival of the octave C's from the opening of the movement (m. 313) that the dominant discharges onto the tonic at a phrase overlap. Brahms corrects the earlier substitution of A♭ octaves for C octaves at the beginning of the

but G bass, thus "i " $^6_4$

Example 3.10. Failed Attempts at Resolution in Coda

reprise and thereby provides a component of motivic resolution as a complement to the delayed structural downbeat. He also transforms an aspect of the tonic area that originally helped to create the effect of an embedded slow introduction into an agent of closure.

The visceral impact of the final tonic expansion is not only a result of this "bookend" transformation or its extraordinary delay, but also of a number of other aspects of resolution highlighted in Example 3.11. Brahms combines the main theme with the exposition's closing theme so that the opening material is associated with one of the only other points of closure in the movement. Moreover, the C–B♭–A♭–G tetrachord within the continuation of the theme appears in the bass of mm. 318–21—a more stereotypical location for this ancient symbol of lamentation.

Brahms also puts to rest aspects of tonal, rhythmic, and timbral idiosyncrasy in both the *pizzicato* and head motives from the tonic area. The *pizzicato* motive appears at the tonic pitch level and *arco* and thus completes a trajectory of tonal-timbral dissonance to resolution. This creates a motivic analogue to the kind of large-scale reconciliation of key areas that we expect in sonata form. There is a similar element of resolution in the rhythmic dimension, where the *pizzicato* idea now has a clear metric identity as weak-strong, in contrast to its earlier appearances where a strong-weak displacement was a possibility. In expressive terms the *pizzicato* E♮'s represent an attempt to escape the tragic C-minor necessities of the work—a theme that will emerge on a larger scale with the shift to E♮ major for the Andante. The coda dooms the E♮'s to their tragic C-minor transposition with its metric corollaries. Finally, the metric displacement and dominant orientation of the head motive at the beginning of the recapitulation are set right by the motive's rock-solid articulation of the notated meter in the context of the coda's tonic expansion.

If the first movement demonstrates Brahms's proclivity for recomposition as a means of avoiding needless repetition on global levels, then the scherzo reminds us that Brahms was also comfortable with straightforward restatement as a component of large-scale form. Again, the Schoenbergian point is not that Brahms avoids repetition, but that he avoids needless repetition. An important critical task remains to explore motivations for the clarity of form in the scherzo, in particular the clearly articulated and nearly exact restatement of the opening section (mm. 1–71) as the third part of an ABA′ form.

Tovey provides an appropriate point of departure in his observation that the scherzo's idiosyncrasies must be understood in relation to the first movement.[16] In particular, he notes the paradoxical character of the first movement's close—the idea that, on the one hand, the movement's "terrible tragic end . . . has been stated with a completeness that admits of no addition," while, on the other, it closes with "a suddenness that leaves us in suspense." Brahms's solution, Tovey suggests, is to follow with a scherzo that "furnishes the tonal balance unprovided for by the end of the first movement." In other words, part of the function of the scherzo is to further resolve the large-scale dissonance that was left only partly reconciled by the powerful return of C minor at the end of the first movement.

Tovey proposes this idea to explain not only the fact that the scherzo "throws comparatively little emphasis" on keys other than C minor, but also to account for the movement's brevity. His remarks are insightful yet characteristically terse and unelaborated. The critical view he offers can provide the basis for a deeper understanding of the scherzo's idiosyncrasies. First, however, it is important to emphasize that Tovey's idea of tonal balance refers to an issue of self-referential musical struc-

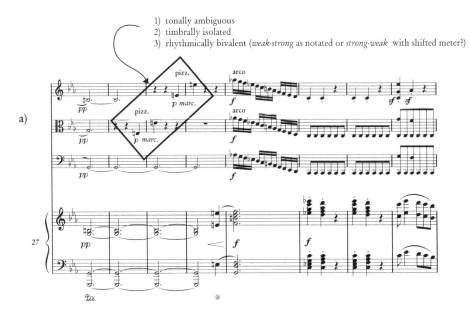

Example 3.11. Elements of Resolution in Coda

ture. Ideas of balance are helpful as far as they go, but it is also crucial to begin to evaluate the C-minor focus in light of its expressive meaning. In expressive terms the rhythmic-affective gestures of the scherzo embody relentlessness rather than resolution, or at least not resolution in its traditional technical meaning. Further emphasis on the C minor achieved at the end of the first movement provides a means of extending, in a harmonically and thematically confined field, the fatefulness of the Allegro's coda. So the scherzo may be about "resolution," but resolution in the form of the inevitability of a tragic close. This is the perspective that must be brought to bear in the context of my analysis.

To appreciate the relationship between the first two movements, we must first have a clear idea of how the scherzo compares with other fast middle movements in Brahms's chamber works. Brahms's standard practice is to organize his fast middle movements into conventional ABA′ alternations of scherzo (or minuet) and trio. The A and B sections themselves usually fall into the standard aba′ patterns of either rounded binary or sonata form. On the lower formal level, the tripartite organization tends to be expressed in the context of a two-repeat scheme: that is, within these smaller forms, there is usually a simple repeat of the [a] section and a combined repeat of the [b] and [a′] sections as a continuous unit. In all of these characteristics Brahms follows Classical convention. He does not even go so far as to experiment with the kind of extended alternation of A and B sections found in some of Beethoven's and Schumann's fast middle movements.

This does not mean that Brahms's scherzo-like movements are formulaic or that he avoids unconventional forms of organization. He sometimes puts aside conventions of aba′ form in favor of a unique mode of organization, for the big A section.

Example 3.11. Elements of Resolution in Coda

In addition to the scherzo from the piano quartet, the fast middle movements of the piano quintet and G-minor piano quartet have A sections of this type. Another option is for a fast middle movement to unfold without a contrasting trio. The third movement of the D-Minor Violin Sonata, op. 108, for example, avoids an independent B section. Or Brahms might give up the idea of a fast middle movement entirely and opt instead for one of his moderately tempoed scherzo substitutes or scherzo/slow-movement hybrid forms.

In the case of a hybrid form, Brahms combines aspects of slow and fast middle movements, by means of an alternation of sections in slow and fast tempos within a single design. This is the approach he takes in the A-Major Violin Sonata, op. 100, and the F-Major Viola Quintet, op. 88. The result is a conflation of the normal four-movement cycle into a cycle of three movements. What is at issue in the scherzo of the piano quartet then is not simply that it has an unusual form. Rather, the point is that its formal idiosyncrasies are best understood in relation to the first movement and ultimately—as is the case for all the extreme idiosyncrasies under discussion here—in relation to the quartet's special affective motivations.

The first issue to confront in the scherzo is the absence of a clear articulation of multiple levels of ternary organization. Upon closer scrutiny, it turns out that—literal restatement notwithstanding—the scherzo is not without complexity in its formal relationships. The potential for formal multivalence relates to both the scherzo's short duration and Tovey's point that the movement's brevity invites us to hear it as continued discourse on issues raised by the first movement. Example 3.12 provides an overview of the form. The relationships of neither the B section to the A sections that surround it, nor the subsections within the A sections themselves, are entirely transparent. This formal ambivalence stands out all the more in light of Brahms's standard practice in fast middle movements, where formal clarity is the norm.

The brevity of the scherzo and the lack of tonal-thematic independence for the B material give the global ternary form some of the flavor of the first part of a scherzo-trio-scherzo alternation. The absence of an internal aba' organization for the B section further contributes to the sense of formal conflation. In place of the typical rounded binary form, the B section pushes on from the statement and re-statement of a single paragraph, in invertible counterpoint, to an enormous retran-sition based on thematic ideas from the A section. This type of retransitional con-tinuity is uncommon as preparation for the return of the A section in Brahms's fast middle movements.

The idea that Brahms would omit a contrasting trio makes sense in light of Tovey's idea that the scherzo is designed to restore focus on C minor following the delayed return to the tonic at the close of the first movement. The scherzo avoids the quasi-independent tonicization of a secondary key normally articulated by a B section. The absence of an independent middle section also contributes to the con-tinuity of an ongoing tragic sweep. Brahms, like his Viennese precursors, usually fashions his trio sections as areas of relaxation. Yet in the quartet there is no break from the relentless flow of dramatic tension. The *moto perpetuo* rhythmic activity and C-minor tonality of the A section refuse to relinquish their grip.

The sense of conflation on the larger formal level is also encouraged by internal details of the A section. As can be seen in Example 3.12, the A section falls into three main parts: a main theme that modulates from tonic to dominant (mm. 1–22), a contrasting idea in the dominant (mm. 23–33), and an expanded return of the first part adjusted to close in the home key (mm. 34–71). Although it is possible to interpret the pattern as a type of aba' form, the theme in the dominant is more like a brief episode within an essentially one-part form. The A section lacks both

Example 3.12. Formal Overview of Scherzo

A Section (mm. 1–71)	B Section (mm. 72–158)	A′ Section (mm. 159–234)
a Section	*Main Section*	*a Section*
mm. 1–4: Introductory unit (on V)	mm. 72–90: Pt. 1 with no strong move away from C, but some emphasis on iv	mm. 159–76: Main theme with modulation from i to v
mm. 5–22: Main theme with modulation from i to v	mm. 91–114: Pt. 2 (invertible counterpoint of pt. 1)	
b Section	*Retransition*	*b Section*
mm. 23–33: Secondary idea with shift from v to V	mm. 115–55: Development of material from main theme of A section	mm. 177–87: Secondary idea with shift from v to V
a Section	mm. 155–58: Return of introductory unit of mm. 1–4 (on V)	*a Section*
mm. 34–61.1: Main theme (expanded) and return of i		mm. 188–215: Main theme (expanded) and return of i
mm. 62–71: Codetta		mm. 216–34: Coda

emphatic tripartite articulation and the repeat scheme that normally characterize the first part of a compound ternary form. There is no middle section to carry us back from the tonicized dominant to the home key, nor does the secondary theme return in the tonic following restatement of the opening material. The A material is in these respects more like a small-scale [a] section. It thus joins the integration of the B material to cloud the normally transparent formal relationships in a fast middle movement.

A second noteworthy feature is Brahms's treatment of the dominant material within the A section. When Brahms casts either an A or B section in rounded binary or sonata form, there is an element of tonal reconciliation in the [a′] return. In the case of rounded binary form, motion from the tonic to closure in a secondary key will be balanced by a restatement that redirects the motion to closure in the home key. The same is the case for a sonata-form A section, where the sonata principle calls for a transposed restatement of the material of the secondary area. Even in fast middle movements of unique form, Brahms tends to transpose secondary ideas when he restates them. The Intermezzo from the G-minor piano quartet, for example, has a second theme in the subdominant (m. 35). Brahms brings back this material in the tonic later in the A section (m. 74). Similarly the secondary material oriented around C and its dominant in the scherzo from the piano quintet (m. 23) returns with a new orientation around III and V/III toward the end of the A section (m. 110).

The dominant material in the scherzo, however, is noteworthy for its lack of restatement in the tonic key, or indeed of any type of tonal transposition. Brahms conspicuously avoids sonata-like reconciliation either within the A section or across the global ABA′ form. It might be argued that reconciliation is unnecessary because the dominant is not articulated as a sonata-style large-scale dissonance. This in fact is precisely the point. Brahms reawakens the tonicization of G from the first movement, but does so in a context in which its powers of tonal dissonance have been vitiated.

On the one hand, the tonicization is stable: there is a V–i cadence at the end of the transition even before the new theme has entered (mm. 21–22), and the theme itself consists of three I–IV–V–I progressions. The scherzo also shares, with the first movement, emphasis on the major form of the dominant. Brahms takes advantage of the phrase repetitions within his secondary material to provide a Schubertian shift from dominant minor to major. But here the tonicization of G major in mm. 27–33 is both lightly articulated and brief. Moreover, the immediate return to C confirms the tendency—so flagrantly violated in the first movement—for the major dominant to remain highly dependent on tonic resolution.

The nearly exact return of the entire A section later in the movement further undercuts the quasi independence that the dominant was able to achieve in the first movement. Brahms harnesses the tonicized G under the control of the tonic not once, but twice, in the scherzo. It is here that we begin to see an important justification for the straightforward repetition on the global level of the movement: the repetition is hardly needless, but forms part of a strategy of C-minor dominance following the developmental tendencies of recapitulation in the first movement.

Once we recognize some of these larger aspects of continuity between the movements, similarities of detail take on new-found significance. Emphasis on E♮ in the scherzo's dominant theme, for example, might appear to have only coincidental relationship with the E♮ motive from the first movement. But within a framework of pan-movement C control, the return of E♮ puts to rest another idiosyncrasy that was left partially hanging at the end of the first movement. It is true that the E♮ motive appears transposed to the tonic pitch level and without any metric ambivalence in the first movement's coda. But in the scherzo Brahms goes a step further and reinterprets E♮ as a straightforward neighbor note, as shown in Example 3.13. A connection with the first movement is solidified by the fact that this liquidation of E♮ occurs within a transformation of G major into a key that no longer achieves even ironic quasi independence from C minor. The brevity of the G tonicization and its immediate collapse back into C minor instead express directly and without irony the major dominant's inability to escape from C-minor despair. Furthermore, E♮ originally enters in the first movement via a motion from D and within an expansion of V. The context, in other words, is similar in the two movements, although D is implied rather than literally stated in the Allegro.

Up to this point, a relationship to the first movement has been established through discussion of formal ambivalence, tonic focus, and characteristics of the A section's dominant theme. It is also the case that the scherzo's main theme recalls characteristic features from the Allegro. Like the dominant theme, it too liquidates

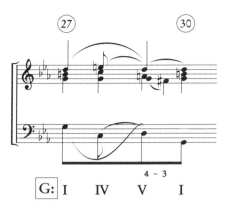

Example 3.13. E♮ as Neighbor in Scherzo

these attributes so that only a residue of idiosyncrasy remains. In particular, the main theme harkens back to details from the opening of the first movement, but places them in a context in which there is no longer a tension between elements of initiation and preparation. Put otherwise, a shift occurs in the character of C minor. At the opening of the first movement, the anacrusis shape of the tonic area and transition allow for some hope for the possibility of escape from C-minor despair. The resolution of the tonic area's turbulence into the peaceful E♭-major second theme further encourages this optimism. Yet by the time the scherzo begins, the recapitulation and coda of the first movement have dashed all hope. C minor has become an inescapable goal, a kind of tonal symbol for tragic fate.

Comparison of the openings of the two movements highlights the shift. The harmonic instability of the first movement's embedded slow introduction arises in part through the real sequence of the opening idea on the B♭ level at m. 11. The main theme of the scherzo begins in the same way, with tonic and ♭vii forms at mm. 5 and 9, respectively. The continuation even includes a subsequent turn to D♭ major, similar to the progression in the first movement (cf. mm. 15–16 of the first with mm. 11–12 of the scherzo). Yet another similarity is the mutual articulation of these local tonicizations within a descending bass motion from tonic to dominant. In the first movement, this occurs across mm. 1–21; in the scherzo, across mm. 5–22. The main theme of the scherzo, however, has an unambiguous expository function, without any suggestion of an embedded slow introduction. Thus, striking harmonic details are absorbed into a less idiosyncratic formal environment.

While it is true that the scherzo eschews the first movement's initial formal bivalence, Brahms nevertheless remains committed to the idea of an introductory passage: he begins the scherzo with an anacrusis gesture in mm. 1–4. In the spirit of clarification, however, he separates the introductory material from the main theme that follows. In this sense the formal reconciliation is similar to the treatment of the tonicized dominant and E♮ motive. Each of these idiosyncrasies returns, but in less characteristic form.

The $\hat{5}$–$\hat{6}$–$\hat{5}$ neighbor figure at the head of the anacrusis forms another important connection with the first movement. The G–A♭ shift in bare octaves recalls the evaded resolution of the retransitional dominant at the recapitulation in the first movement. In the scherzo, however, A♭ immediately resolves back to G and thus provides a motivic analogue to the reigning in of anacrusis tendencies. At the return of the A section (mm. 155–59), the sense of resolution in relation to the first movement is even more intense, since the formal location parallels the entrance of the G–A♭ shift in the recapitulation of the opening Allegro. The new context allows for expanded treatment of the A♭ neighbor. The neighbor idea is further reflected in the bass motion from augmented-sixth chord to dominant $^6_4$ in mm. 154–55. Here too $\hat{6}$ resolves to $\hat{5}$ before the double return—another way in which an agent of formal overlap becomes an agent of formal articulation.

In my analysis of the first movement, we saw that Brahms's compositional economy influences his approach to harmonic as well as thematic issues. In particular, Brahms is careful to avoid excessive articulation of large-scale tonal goals, above all in processes of recapitulation. Brahms's practice of recapitulatory recomposition tends both to reduce the frequency and to delay the arrival of tonic articulations. In the scherzo, however, he maintains the number and location of structural C-minor chords in the A and A′ sections. On the face of it, this strategy would appear to fly in the face of the concept of tonal parsimony. Yet there are actually very few tonic articulations, and those that do occur all have an essential function. In the harmonic dimension, as in the thematic dimension, it is needless repetition, not repetition per se, that Brahms avoids.

Motivation for each tonic relates to the internal structure of the scherzo, as well as its relationship to the first movement. First, it is important to observe that the A section contains only three tonic articulations, the C-minor chords in mm. 5–7, 34–36, and 62–71. The first and last are necessary as points of departure and closure, respectively. In addition, the foreground expansion of these tonics is relatively brief. The opening tonic last for only three measures before the [a] section moves—via tonicizations of B♭, D♭, and G♭/F♯—toward a modulation to the dominant. Similarly the closing tonic initiates a concise ten-measure codetta. The return of the tonic following the secondary idea (m. 34) is likewise brief and provides the only other middleground C chord within the A section. In addition to its brevity, this tonic gains justification through its role in further unmasking the major dominant as a chord that can achieve only apparent stability in the face of an overwhelming tragic C minor.

These three tonic articulations similarly assume essential harmonic function when they return in the A′ section. The reentry of the main theme at m. 159 provides a classic example of a climactic double return. This type of sonata-style articulation was known to Viennese composers and listeners alike since the late eighteenth century. Brahms nevertheless manages to maintain its vitality through both the effectiveness of its preparation and the visceral impact of its arrival. Put otherwise, the tonic at the A′ return receives formal justification through the enormous release of tension it provides following the retransition. Given the length of the buildup, the brief tonic expansion could hardly be called wasteful. Brahms pauses just long enough for a decisive resolution before he pushes on with the tonal insta-bilities of the [a] section. The harmonic parsimony of the original main theme thus allows for its reinterpretation as part of a conventional double return.

From this point on, tonic articulations have a similar function as analogous points in the A section. The return to the tonic following the secondary idea at m. 188 puts the dominant at the mercy of C minor for yet a second time, and the final tonic provides closure. Because this closing tonic has the added function of capping off the entire movement, Brahms strengthens it first through evasion at the original cadence point (m. 216), and then through expansion of the final ca-dential progression in mm. 216–34.

Brahms's approach to large-scale restatement in the Andante stands halfway be-tween the extremes of the Allegro and scherzo. Example 3.14 summarizes the main formal outlines of the movement. As the example shows, the Andante blends as-pects of binary and ternary form with a sonata component. This type of hybrid or-ganization is not unusual for Brahms. Even in his slow movements he remains com-mitted to strategies that create formal bivalence. A ternary interpretation emerges through three main factors: (1) the thematically rounded-off aba' design of the first main section of the form, (2) the strong sense of tonic closure at the end of this A material, and (3) the fact that Brahms shortens the B material when it re-turns following the reprise of the A section. Indeed, it is characteristic for Brahms to include a brief reference back to middle-section material as part of the closing passage of an ABA' form.

On the other hand, the dominant does not normally function as tonal center for the middle section of a ternary form. V is far more characteristic as the goal for the first half of a binary or sonata design. This fact has led scholars to read the Andante as well as several other of Brahms's middle movements as formally am-biguous.[17] Along with the Andante, the slow movements from the Second and Third Symphonies reflect a tendency in Brahms to blend binary and ternary char-acteristics. But in the symphonic movements Brahms forgoes reconciliation of his dominant material with the tonic, and instead closes with a return to the A section only. A ternary orientation therefore emerges in retrospect.

In the piano quartet Brahms does bring back at least part of the B section trans-posed to the tonic. He thus fulfills exigencies of a binary-sonata interpretation sig-naled by the key orientation of his secondary material. As for the abbreviation of the B section, it is important to note that composers frequently cut some material in the thematic reprise of a binary form. This is one way in which the repeat of material from the first half can be adjusted to avoid modulation, in favor of closure in the tonic. The abbreviation in the restatement of the B material thus does not in itself preclude a binary interpretation of the Andante.

Binary or ternary interpretation notwithstanding, there is a clear parallelism be-tween the initial appearance of the A and B sections and their restatement. In this sense, the strategy of recapitulation is similar to the transparency of form in the scherzo. The entire A section returns, and although some alterations occur, the changes are similar to the type of embellishment found in a theme and variations

Example 3.14. Formal Overview of Andante

PART 1 OR — PART 1	PART 2	PART 2 — A' Section	B' Section	Coda
A Section (mm. 1–34)	**B Section** (mm. 35–77)	**A' Section** (mm. 78–110)	**B' Section** (mm. 111–18.1)	*Coda* (mm. 119–22)
a Section	*Phrase 1*	*a Section*	*Phrase 1'*	Head motive from main theme returns as part of expansion of final I
mm. 1–8: Main theme with modulation from I to V	mm. 35–38.1: Continues to prolong V/B from transition	mm. 78–85: Variation of main theme with modulation from I to V	mm. 111–14 and 115–18.1: Prolongs V and leads to closing I	
b Section	*Phrase 2*	*b Section*		
mm. 9–16.1: Development of material from main theme	mm. 39–45: More expansion of V/B	mm. 86–93.1: Development of material from main theme		
a' Section	*Phrase 1'*	*a' Section*		
mm. 17–26.1: Variation of main theme with return of I and expansion of final cadence	mm. 46–51.1: Still on V/B	mm. 94–103.1: Variation of main theme with return of I and expansion of final cadence		
Codetta Merges into Transition	*Phrase 2'*	*Codetta Merges into Transition*		
mm. 27–34: Closing tonic expansion followed by motion to V/B	mm. 52–61.1: Finally leads to B but as V^7/E	mm. 104–10: Closing tonic expansion followed by motion to V		
	Retransition			
	mm. 62–67.1: Expands V^7/E			
	mm. 68–77: Sequence based on main-theme material, tonicizes C and G♯			

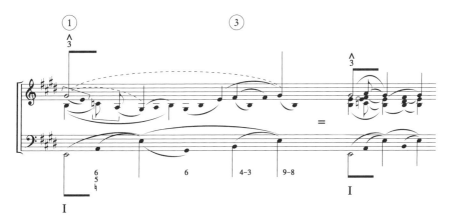

Example 3.15. C♮ as Neighbor within Tonic Expansion

movement. What returns of the B material also remains basically unchanged with the exception of transposition to the tonic key, the factor that invests the movement with its sonata component.

Yet within a basically straightforward recapitulatory framework, Brahms manages to incorporate some of the same strategies of development and delay found in the first movement. One similarity is his development of a motivic idea from the main theme as a means of creating an overlap between retransition and reprise. Once again, Brahms avoids rearticulation of a structural tonic via a process of thematic development across a formal hinge. Another similarity is that the return of material from the B section extends rather than resolves the resulting harmonic tension. Despite an apparent fidelity to the sonata principle, Brahms prolongs a middleground V *Stufe* across the B restatement and withholds tonic articulation until the coda, similar to the strategy in the first movement.

The thematic idea that Brahms develops across the beginning of the restatement originates in the head motive at the very opening of the movement. Like the *pizzicato* motive in the first movement, this opening idea projects a striking chromatic detail within an otherwise diatonic framework. As Example 3.15 shows, the head motive's foreign C♮ is part of an expansion of the tonic in which 3̂ and 5̂ are both decorated by neighbor notes. The cello's arpeggiation across the I–iv⁶̣₅–I progression articulates the neighboring C♮ as part of an augmented triad. From a strict voice-leading perspective, the G♯–E–C♮ arpeggiation is incidental to the structure. It is a by-product rather than a building block. To hear the augmented triad as a structural entity requires the listener to ignore not only voice-leading considerations, but also the parallelism between the motivic thirds marked with brackets in Example 3.15.

Yet it is not unusual for Brahms to exploit structurally incidental configurations as sources for motivic development. We have already seen an example of this practice in his treatment of the motivic ⁶₃ chord in the first movement. There, in mm. 27–31 of the exposition, a (5)–♮6–7 motion above a dominant bass gives rise

Example 3.16. E♮–C♮–G♯ Augmented Triad in Retransition

momentarily to a $^6_3$ chord with E♮ and B♮ sounding over G. But because the E♮ sixth functions as a passing tone, the triad has only apparent identity as an inversion of an E-minor harmony. It is not until the recapitulation that Brahms exploits the $^6_3$ chord to generate a tonicization of ♮iii and thus to elevate the incidental to structural status.

In the Andante the situation is similar. Brahms prepares the return of the main theme so that it occurs as the third statement in a sequential progression based on the augmented triad. The incidental pitch configuration thus emerges as a generative basis for Brahms's idiosyncratic formal strategy. The model for the sequence tonicizes C♮ major/minor in mm. 68–72; the first sequential statement transposes the material to G♯ major/minor in mm. 73–77. The return of the main theme completes the process with its articulation of E major. A connection with the original version of the augmented triad motive is solidified by repetitions of the main theme's head motive at the beginning of each sequential statement. The symmetry of the configuration allows each repetition to hold the E–G♯–C♮ form of the augmented triad invariant.

Changes among the repetitions center on two factors: the order of the pitches and the identity of the note added to the triad to complete the pattern of descending thirds. In each case, as in the original, the fourth note functions as a neighbor to the melodic point of departure. Example 3.16 outlines this neighbor-note function. The half-step connection creates a further motivic resonance. It is Brahms's tendency to include half-step inflections of the augmented triad in its different occurrences throughout the cycle. In the first movement, for example, we saw that the development spans the keys of E♭, B♮, and G before the dramatic shift to A♭ just prior to the return of the main theme. The Andante similarly avoids rearticulation of a structural tonic in favor of emphasis on a half-step connection with the augmented triad. In the case of the Andante, however, articulation of a large-scale minor second relationship occurs later in the reprise, at the arrival of the B dominant at the end of the first phrase (m. 85).

Part of what allows the B arrival to join the C♮–G♯–E augmented triad in a motivic configuration is the character of the E-major return at the beginning of the reprise. The lightness of the E articulation helps the trajectory of the sequential progression continue to the more stable arrival of B as goal. Indeed, the E chord provides another example of a recapitulatory apparent tonic. The lack of structural status for the E tonic grows from a number of factors. First and foremost, the preparation for the reprise makes E sound like VI in G♯ minor. The reinstrumentation and variation of the theme also weaken the sense of harmonic arrival. Brahms shifts the melody from the warm cello middle register to a more delicate tessitura and timbre in the piano. The new *pizzicato* accompaniment is also much lighter compared to the sustained chords of the keyboard in the original. Again, the idea is that an apparent tonic return has its analogue in the illusory character of a thematic restatement.

The formal irony of the main theme pushes the weight of emphasis forward onto the more solid arrival of the tonicized dominant at the end of the phrase. The strategy is reminiscent of Brahms's approach in the first movement in several respects. First, a dominant articulation within the main theme creates a broad middleground connection with a dominant left hanging prior to the thematic return. In the Andante the connection is with the dominant that arrives toward the end of the B section in mm. 62–69, just before the sequential retransition; in the first movement it is with the retransitional dominant itself. The graph in Example 3.17 depicts the dominant prolongation in the slow movement. Second, in both instances the overriding V *Stufe* subsumes an apparent tonic at the beginning of the reprise. Finally, in both movements overlap of retransition and return articulates large-scale statements of the augmented-triad-plus-half-step idea, as already noted. Brackets in the graph of Example 3.17 highlight the parallelism between foreground and middleground statements of the motive.

There is yet another similarity between the recapitulatory overlaps in the first and third movements. It centers around the $\hat{5}$–$\hat{6}$ neighbor motive. Indeed, the G–A♭ dyad plays an important role at the initiation of large-scale return in all four movements. The first and third movements articulate tension-generating shifts from $\hat{5}$ up to $\hat{6}$. This occurs in the context of their shared strategies of overlap at the return of opening material. The second and fourth movements resolve $\hat{6}$ down to $\hat{5}$ as part of more clearly articulated reprises. In the Andante the neighbor motive appears transposed into the key of G♯ minor and in the bass of mm. 77–78. In other words, the deceptive D♯–E bass progression has a motivic significance beyond its role in the middleground projection of the augmented triad. In addition to this transposed version of the neighbor motive, A♭ itself functions enharmonically as the main top-voice pitch at the return of the A material at m. 78 and as *Kopfton* for the entire movement.

Another connection arises out of the motivic significance of the C♮–B neighbor motive (= $\hat{6}$–$\hat{5}$) that lies just beneath the surface of the Andante's main theme, as highlighted in Example 3.15. A relationship with the first movement is solidified by the fact that the key of the Andante can be heard as a motivic consequence of the E♮ *pizzicato* figure. The recapitulatory A♭/G♯ also occurs in the same register in the top voice of both movements. Indeed, all four movements articulate A♭/G♯ at their reprises in the register two octaves above middle C.

In contrast to both the first and third movements, the scherzo allows $\hat{6}$ to resolve to $\hat{5}$ as part of an unequivocal climactic double return. The finale contains char-

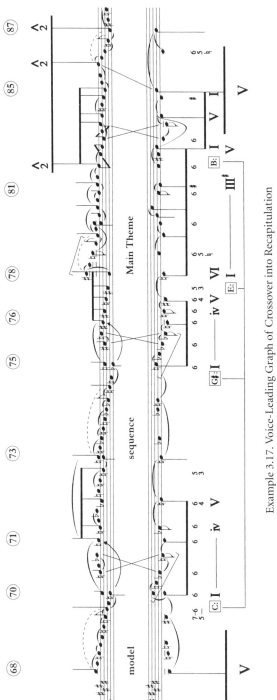

Example 3.17. Voice-Leading Graph of Crossover into Recapitulation

acteristics of both types of recapitulatory treatment. On the one hand, it resolves A♭ to G as part of a simultaneous return of main theme and structural tonic at m. 217. At the same time, the texture, accompanimental pattern, and dramatic trajectory of the development flow across this point of articulation. I will return to the duality of articulation and overlap in the finale as a topic of discussion shortly.

Although emphasis on the dominant in the second half of the Andante is reminiscent of the situation in the recapitulation of the first movement, it is important to recognize that the overall strategy is not nearly as extreme. Rather, in this sense the slow movement is somewhat more like the scherzo: there are tonic articulations within the body of the restatement, but there are few of them, and those that do occur avoid excessive emphasis on resolution. Brahms takes advantage of the original design of both the A and B sections as a means to achieve his characteristic tonal parsimony. The A material has its own aba′ ternary form, as outlined in Example 3.14. As we have already seen, Brahms extends a middleground dominant across the [a] recapitulation (m. 78) and into the transposed return of the dominant-prolonging [b] material. He does, however, allow a structural tonic to resurface at the entrance of the [a′] phrase (m. 94).

Yet although this material provides a point of resolution, it does so through a decorated version of the opening idea. The embellishment disguises the thematic entrance and, perhaps more importantly, lightens the downbeat orientation of the tonic, in favor of an anacrusic character. This is true both for the original expository version of m. 17 and for the version that falls within the large-scale restatement at m. 94. The effect, however, is especially strong in the restatement. There, in addition to the original variation in the top voice, Brahms also varies the accompaniment. The new accompanimental pattern not only avoids the stability of the half notes in the expository version: it also sustains elements of formal overlap and anacrusis character by continuing the triplet pattern that has remained constant throughout the return of the [a] and [b] phrases.[18]

Within the original A section, the lightness of the tonic articulation at the [a′] variation (m. 17) does not have a decisive effect on middleground tonal structure. The lighter tonic connects to the more forthright tonic that Brahms articulates at the outset via the original version of the [a] phrase. But in the return of the A section, the embellished version has no preceding tonic *Stufe* to attach itself to. Instead it forms a kind of quasi-structural tonic: a tonic that is in fact structural, but that initiates a formal unit directed toward more forthright articulation of its controlling middleground harmony. It is a chord, in other words, that falls into a category halfway between straightforward structural tonics and outright apparent tonics.[19]

In the Andante the more forthright articulation occurs at the entrance of the coda-like material at the end of the A′ section (m. 104). Here Brahms finally gives in to the first fully satisfactory tonic resolution in the reprise. Not coincidentally, this is also the first point at which the complete texture of the restatement matches the expository version. Yet in spite of the momentary stability, the delayed tonic arrival simultaneously initiates the transition. After only two measures, Brahms's

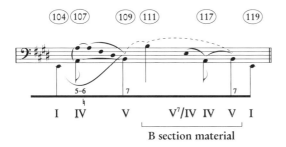

Example 3.18. Structural Bass for mm. 104–19

tonal parsimony compels him to transform the tonic into a V/IV chord as part of another progression leading to an emphatic dominant arrival at m. 109.

These elements of compositional economy notwithstanding, one cannot deny that the Andante resolves the dominant of the recapitulatory overlap prior to the transition. The first V *Stufe* does not remain available for a middleground connection with the dominant that enters at the transposed restatement of material from the B section (m. 111). In this respect the Andante differs from the more extreme first movement, as well as from the first movement of the C-minor string quartet. Recall from the discussion in Chapter 2 that the string quartet also has secondary material oriented around its local dominant.

The Andante also differs from the first movement more obviously in its orientation around V as home dominant, rather than as a tonicized chord. The spirit of the strategy, however, remains the same, as Chapter 2 argued via the example of the string quartet movement. It is just that the dominant prolongation of the B material does not penetrate as deeply into the structural hierarchy as the dominant that Brahms projects across the second theme in either the first movement or the string quartet. The B material's dominant nevertheless constitutes the middleground V *Stufe* for an overriding I–V–I progression across the second half of the form, as outlined in Example 3.18. Again Brahms partly conforms to the sonata principle yet resists one of its most basic components. Material that originally appears in the dominant key returns in the tonic. But because the secondary idea prolongs its local V, it emphasizes the home dominant in its transposed return. It thus delays rather than provides resolution. Brahms consolidates the arrival of the tonic in the secondary material and the structural close for the entire movement into a single entity, the resolution to E at the beginning of the coda (m. 119).

In comparison to either the developmental tendencies of the first and third movements or the nearly exact repetition in the scherzo, the reprise of the finale reflects a seemingly more conventional sonata practice. This, however, does not mean that the movement is without formal interest or that it stands apart from the paradoxical character of the piano quartet as a representative yet exceptional work. Example 3.19 outlines the clear parallelism between the finale's exposition and recapitulation. The main changes occur in the return of the first phrase of the tonic

Example 3.19. Formal Overview of Exposition and Recapitulation

Exposition	Recapitulation
Tonic Key Area	*Tonic Key Area*
mm. 1–20: Main theme with modulation from i to v	mm. 217–36: Main theme with modulation from i to v
mm. 21–34.1 and mm. 35–38.1: Development of material from main theme, leads back to tonic key	mm. 237–50.1 and *mm. 251–62.1* *(expanded):* Development of material from main theme, leads back to tonic key
Continuation of Tonic Area/Transition (?)	*Continuation of Tonic Area/Transition (?)*
mm. 39–54.1: Builds transitional energy but provides no modulation and continues to develop material from main theme	*mm. 263–70.1 (condensed):* Builds transitional energy but provides no modulation and continues to develop material from main theme
Bridge Theme/Secondary Material (?)	*Bridge Theme/Secondary Material (?)*
mm. 55–74: New theme in E♭ but no local tonic $^5_3$, leads to V/E♭	mm. 271–90: New theme in C major but no local tonic $^5_3$, leads to V
Secondary Material/Closing Theme (?)	*Secondary Material/Closing Theme (?)*
mm. 75–95: Chorale theme in E♭ with local tonic $^5_3$'s but weakly articulated until m. 95	mm. 291–310: Chorale theme in C major with local tonic $^5_3$'s but weakly articulated
	mm. 311–27.1: *New forte statement of chorale theme in piano* = final attempt at solid articulation of C major, which merges into transition to coda
	Coda
	mm. 328–79

area (m. 217) and in the transitional passages that begin at mm. 251 and 263. As we would expect, Brahms redirects the second transitional passage so that it leads to a recapitulation of the E♭ secondary material in the tonic key. In addition to the necessary tonal adjustments, Brahms partly expands and partly condenses the material, as Example 3.19 indicates. The effect is to heighten the intensity that builds as the bridge leads into the first part of the second group at m. 271.

A similar expressive intensification occurs in Brahms's recapitulation of the initial phrase of the tonic area (mm. 217–24.1). The melodic-harmonic structure of the passage creates a clear parallelism with the original version. Yet as has already been observed, the texture, accompanimental pattern, and dramatic trajectory of the development flow across the return of this expository material. Brahms more nearly restores the original setting only at m. 225. The elements of variation endow the material with a tone of pathos appropriate for a large-scale return of the minor tonic at this late point in a tragic work. In structural terms the surface elements of overlap between retransition and recapitulation transform the C-minor chord at the very beginning of the main theme into a quasi-structural tonic. The situation is similar to the E♭-major rearticulation at m. 94 in the Andante. Although it is an offshoot of the main deep-level tonic *Stufe* that governs the beginning of the recapitulation, the C chord at m. 217 is not assertive enough to resolve the tensions of the development. Brahms withholds a more complete sense of tonic arrival until the articulation at the counterstatement of the main theme at m. 225.

On the face of it, the recapitulation of the secondary material seems even more clear-cut in its parallelism with the exposition. The material returns in full and without substantial alteration beyond transposition into the tonic key. There is one major difference, however. Just as he is about to reach the point that would correspond to the arrival of closure in the exposition (m. 311), Brahms disrupts the clear parallelism with one final statement of the chorale's opening phrase. The material appears for the first time in the piano and *forte*. Prior to this point the strings have always been the ones to sing the chorale, and they have done so *mezza voce* and at a *piano* or *piu piano* dynamic level. The piano similarly has been limited to a cascading arpeggio figure, which derives from the accompaniment in the section that precedes the chorale. Within the chorale the piano's arpeggios have functioned as a means of punctuation at the quasi fermatas that mark the ends of each phrase.

The new chorale statement in the piano reflects Brahms's practice of merging his recapitulations into his codas without the articulation normally provided by tonal closure. In the quartet the strategy has special significance: it ushers in the piano's statement as the last opportunity the cycle has to articulate a transcendent C major. The passage represents a more overt example of the kind of overcompensation reflected in the theme and variations of the first movement, and the outcome is even more devastating: the desperate attempt falls flat. What transpires has the character of an anxious lunge rather than anything even remotely like a triumph over darker emotions. The piano crashes in, *subito forte,* but is unable to provide a sustainable C major of transcendent character.

The brittleness of the failed climax results in part from the timbral shift from the more vocal character of the strings to the percussiveness of the piano. The cascading accompanimental pattern also becomes aggressive. Compare the markings of *piano, leggiero,* and *diminuendo* to *pianissimo* for the earlier version in the piano (mm. 294–310) to the *forte, crescendo,* and *sforzandi* of the strings in the coda. Moreover, the C tonic almost immediately loses stability. It not only shifts to $^6_3$ position at m. 317 but also begins to function as V/iv, with the addition of B♭ and a painful minor ninth, D♭ (m. 320).

Following the failed climax of the chorale, the remainder of Brahms's finale maintains the major form of the tonic. The coda, however, absorbs this tonic into the surroundings of the bleak C-minor landscape in which the cycle closes. This is not a case of a conciliatory Picardy third, but rather an example of a tragic major tonic. Deeper insight into the meaning of this tragic close and, more broadly, into intersections of structure and expression in the finale hinges not so much on the present topic of large-scale repetition and development. Rather, it depends first on detailed structural analysis of the finale's secondary material.

Idiosyncrasies of the second group are best viewed in relation to a spectrum of possibilities in Brahms's sonata forms, similar to the approach to issues of recapitulation in this chapter. The topic involves, among other concerns, distinctions between (1) two-part versus continuous exposition, (2) secondary areas that form a single large-scale unit and those that contain one or more emphatic subdivisions, and (3) within these subdivided second groups, those that create a division via a mode shift within a single key and those that articulate two distinct tonal areas. Brahms's proclivity for tonal delay in relation to norms of sonata practice will also be at issue, as the summary discussion of mediant key areas in Chapter 2 has already demonstrated. Finally, the diversity of Brahms's practice with respect to secondary areas needs to be compared to precedents in the Viennese tradition. Attention to relationships with traditional approaches will afford the opportunity to explore some of the ways in which Brahms's innovations build not only on the practice of Schubert—the connection that scholars have emphasized—but also on the practices of Haydn, Mozart, and Beethoven.[20] Obviously the task is complex and requires separate treatment. This will be the focus of Chapter 5.

4 Brahms and Schenker: A Mutual Response to Sonata Form

At the end of Chapter 2, I suggested that a flexible view of relationships between thematic design, key scheme, and tonal structure is a hallmark of Brahms's and Schenker's conceptions of sonata form. This similarity of perspective is not surprising given their shared values and dedication to tradition in the face of what they both saw as a decline in musical culture. A connection between Brahms's and Schenker's musical thought, however, resides not only in their insight into broad characteristics of the Viennese tradition. They also responded in similar ways to more specific issues that they each confronted as late nineteenth-century champions of time-honored compositional strategies.

Brahms and Schenker both wrestled with a fundamental tension as they approached sonata form. On the one hand, they remained committed to a formal type characterized by a division at the deepest levels of structure. Conventions of recapitulation tend to articulate the large-scale form into two parallel parts. Yet Brahms and Schenker were equally consumed by Romantic notions of organic unity and the idea of an unbroken, goal-directed continuity as the basis for musical form. How could an element as basic to sonata form as the practice of recapitulation be made to fulfill these principles of organicist aesthetics to which Brahms and Schenker were so intensely devoted?

We have already seen that Brahms's proclivity for developing recapitulation often results in a continuous tonal trajectory, similar to Schenker's efforts to project a single *Ursatz* across the parallelism of sonata form. Close scrutiny of Schenker's interruption paradigm in this chapter, however, will reveal his difficulties in deriving sonata form from a continuous background. Yet we will see that these very difficulties evaporate when his method of analysis is applied to some of Brahms's more unusual movements, not least the opening Allegro of the piano quartet. It appears that Brahms reimagined sonata conventions in terms of the same kind of overarching tonal unity that Schenker strove to apply to works from the Classical era.

Though they represent extreme cases, these movements can be understood as a logical extension of what Schoenberg viewed as the progressive element of Brahms's style. As we have just seen in Chapter 3, a movement like the opening Allegro of the piano quartet reflects Brahms's tendency to avoid literal recapitulatory repetition in favor of continuous evolution or musical prose. As such, it provides evidence of new ways Brahms was thinking about sonata form, despite the charges of epigonism leveled against him by some of his contemporaries. It also reveals an unlikely connection between Schoenbergian notions of developing variation and Schenker's conception of sonata form.

Despite obvious differences between Schoenbergian and Schenkerian views, their contrasting philosophies highlight different ways in which a part of sonata form that might otherwise threaten to become static can be rendered dynamic. In the case of Schenker the focus is on continuous contrapuntal writing, while in Schoenberg it is on continuous motivic development. With both musicians there nevertheless appears to be a similar motivation: a desire to conceive repetition in evolutionary terms. A Schoenbergian perspective emphasizes ways in which Brahms takes advantage of recapitulation as an opportunity to explore possibilities for thematic development. A Schenkerian perspective reveals ways in which he creates an ongoing flow by means of large-scale voice-leading continuities.

More broadly, Schoenberg's view of Brahms emphasizes the degree to which the composer's focus on motivic evolution creates a proselike unfolding across periodicities of meter and phrase rhythm. Schenker likewise pursues voice-leading connections that extend across the articulations highlighted by traditional formal analysis. As he evolved his theory, Schenker was eventually able to trace these types of continuities throughout all levels of musical form. Schoenberg, on the other hand, focused his attention on motivic evolution on the phrase level. Yet as we have seen in Chapter 3, the spirit of developing variation resonates on the largest levels of Brahms's forms. Not only does he create large-scale voice-leading structures that subsume the recapitulatory parallelism of sonata form; he also exploits the motivic dimension as a resource to counterbalance large-scale formal symmetries.

The style of Brahms's music, in which virtually every repetition or articulation seems to be effaced by elements of development and continuity, simultaneously fulfills Schoenbergian and Schenkerian aesthetics. He creates intricate motivic processes that evolve in tandem with highly complex voice-leading structures, all within the context of traditional formal patterns. Through this dimensional counterpoint, he stakes his claim for the hallowed place he holds in both the Schenkerian and Schoenbergian pantheons. Brahms too was a late nineteenth-century figure looking back with reverence on the compositional tradition that Schenker and Schoenberg held so dear, and he absorbed and intensified those very characteristics that Schoenberg and Schenker responded to in earlier music.

This is why it is important to acknowledge that, the originality of Brahms's strategies notwithstanding, precedents for many of his procedures can be found in earlier music. A tension between articulation and organic continuity is part of the original fabric of the sonata idea. This is certainly the case with other nineteenth-century composers, in particular Beethoven, Schubert, and Schumann, who have long been recognized as important influences on Brahms. Haydn and Mozart also took care to invest their recapitulations with signs of developing variation, and all these composers occasionally wrote sonata forms with continuous middleground structures.[1] Rather than view the issue as a dichotomy between continuous evolution in Brahms versus large-scale parallelism in earlier music, it would be more appropriate to understand Brahms's approach as an intensification of the organicist component embedded in the sonata forms of the Viennese tradition.

One important distinction, however, can be drawn: Brahms, unlike his Viennese precursors, lived after generations of *Formenlehre* writers had codified what they took to be defining characteristics of sonata form, a practice that resulted in the fossilization of Classical conventions in the eyes of many late Romantics. Sonata-form composition was a much more self-conscious endeavor for Brahms than for his predecessors. He chose to substantiate the most prestigious of Classical forms in a late nineteenth-century historical context by investing all of its component parts with continually developing motivic content and essential harmonic function. An irony, revealed by more recent trends in analysis of eighteenth-century music, is that this approach was very much in the original spirit of the sonata style.

A similar commitment to musical tradition can be understood as a motivation for Schenker's analytic work. The result is a curious parallel between composer and theorist when they, in their own separate ways, tackle sonata form. To trace this mutual response to sonata form, it is first necessary to explore some of the shortcomings of Schenker's interruption paradigm as a model for sonata conventions. We will then be in a position to observe how Brahms creates a sonata design that articulates the specific type of tonal unity that Schenker has difficulty reconciling with eighteenth-century music.

Schenker develops the concept of interruption in an attempt to reconcile his view that all musical form derives from an undivided *Ursatz*, with formal types that display a strong element of parallelism, and thus sectionalization. In brief, interruption consists of an *Urlinie* descent to $\hat{2}$/V followed by a rebeginning and a second descent that reaches all the way to $\hat{1}$/I. Though it is not a requirement of interruption, the parallelism of *Urlinie* descents is often reinforced by thematic parallelism.[2] Through the concept of interruption, Schenker downplays the degree to which the consequent of a period is heard as a static counterweight to the antecedent, a perception that would run counter to his predilection for continuous linear evolution. Rather, for Schenker the repetition increases the goal-directedness of the second descent by creating a situation in which the arrival of a goal is implied but then delayed until a later point. This increased directionality heightens the unifying force of the *Ursatz*.[3]

When applied to sonata form, interruption has the advantage of modeling a dynamic quality of the recapitulation. Schenker's assertion that a return to the tonic at the reprise is not a resolution is compelling if the concept of resolution is defined in ultimate terms, as the structural close for a movement as a whole. Resolution, in this specific sense, can be achieved only through the progression of the *Ursatz* to its final goal. In sonata form this usually takes place across the entire recapitulation. Following resumption of the *Kopfton* at the return of the main theme, it is only the linear trajectory of transposed secondary material that carries the top voice down to $\hat{1}$/I. When viewed as the completion of a motion to $\hat{1}$/I, the restatement of the second group takes on a more dynamic function than if it is interpreted merely as a tonal transposition that, in Charles Rosen's words, resolves the large-scale dissonance of the exposition.[4]

While it is true that Rosen presents his concept of large-scale dissonance resolution as a dynamic process, Schenker attempts to pin down the nature of this dynamism in more specific terms. Yet despite this laudable attempt to respond to recapitulatory dynamism, Schenker's interruption paradigm encounters problems when scrutinized in light of the axiomatic and hierarchical basis of his theory. Problems also arise when interruption is examined from the perspective of musical intuition. In many sonata forms neither the middleground rebeginning nor the new tonal structure that results from transposition of secondary material can be derived from a single *Ursatz*. In the end, these features are often more convincingly explained in Rosen's terms, although Schenker undoubtedly would have rejected the idea of large-scale-dissonance resolution as a concept too mechanistic for music he regarded as organic.

Because Schenker claims that all musical form arises from a single *Ursatz*, the two-part middleground of interruption should derive from a continuous background structure. Yet as Allan Keiler has argued, Schenker can achieve such a derivation only by either contradicting his intuitions regarding relationships between *Urlinie* pitches across the point of interruption, or by transgressing a fundamental premise that normally governs his interpretation of tonal structure.[5] The difficulty Schenker has in accounting for the divisional aspect of many sonata forms suggests that the articulation at the reprise often remains at the deepest levels of structure. The body of the recapitulation typically functions as a hierarchically equivalent repetition that closes in the tonic through transposition of the secondary material. The tension between an organicist conceptualization and the architectonic realities of sonata form reveals that Schenker was anachronistically forcing a method of analysis based on nineteenth-century aesthetic principles onto the formal conventions of the Classical period.

In *Free Composition*, Schenker explores two possible derivations of the interruption paradigm.[6] His discussion ironically exposes some of the limitations of his theory in accounting for crucial aspects of many standard formal patterns. The difficulty arises from the need to determine which constituents of a divided middleground, particularly which of two dominants, should take on greater hierarchical significance as members of a continuous background. In his first interpretation, Schenker hears the initial *Urlinie* descent as a prolongation of the *Kopfton*. The *Kopfton* reappears following the interruption, with the result that the $\hat{2}$ in the parallel part of the structure provides the fundamental passing motion from $\hat{3}$ to $\hat{1}$. "The initial succession $\hat{3}$–$\hat{2}$ gives the impression that it is the first attempt at the complete fundamental line," and "[t]he first $\hat{3}$, which is the *primary tone* of the total fundamental line $\hat{3}$–$\hat{1}$, although not expressly retained, is taken up again by the second $\hat{3}$, as primary tone of the resumed linear progression which now leads to $\hat{1}$."[7] Although Schenker does not illustrate this derivation graphically, it could be diagrammed as in Example 4.1.

This derivation, henceforth to be referred to as the type 1 derivation, is attractive for its consistency with what Keiler identifies as "an important constituent constraint of Schenker's view of tonal coherence: harmonic progression is goal-directed in such a way that, generally, the hierarchical importance of harmonic constituents continues to increase as the piece unfolds."[8] One important reflection of this constraint is Schenker's tendency to assign background significance to the final cadential progression as support for the *Urlinie*'s descent from $\hat{2}$ to $\hat{1}$. In the case of a piece that takes $\hat{3}$ as *Kopfton*, Schenker often interprets considerable

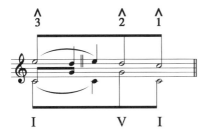

Example 4.1. Type 1 Derivation   Example 4.2. Type 2 Derivation

stretches of tonal activity prior to the structural close as prolongation of the *Kopfton* and initial tonic. Accordingly the type 1 derivation interprets the second $\hat{2}$/V as more significant than the first. The *Ursatz* does not make its fundamental motion to V until the second half of the paradigm, just as a typical phrase might prolong the tonic by means of embellishing dominants before progressing to a more significant cadential dominant.

The type 1 derivation nevertheless contains one serious drawback. It appears to suggest that the first $\hat{2}$ is a neighbor note in a $\hat{3}$–$\hat{2}$–$\hat{3}$ melodic motion. This would contradict Schenker's intuition that the $\hat{2}$ "never takes on the character of a lower neighboring note."[9] In fact, one of the reasons Schenker proposes the concept of interruption is to avoid a neighbor-note interpretation. Once an *Urlinie* has begun its descent, it cannot return to its point of origin; it can only lead on to its goal or be interrupted by a fresh departure from the *Kopfton*.

In an attempt to clarify his position, Schenker proceeds to a second interpretation, henceforth to be referred to as the type 2 derivation. In a type 2 derivation, "the first occurrence of $\hat{2}$/V is more significant than the second [and] the first $\hat{3}$–$\hat{2}$ represents a course already run; only the $\hat{1}$ is still lacking."[10] Now the paradigm appears as in Example 4.2.[11] Because it is hierarchically more significant than the second $\hat{3}$, the first $\hat{2}$ retains its downward motion as a passing tone to $\hat{1}$. It clearly cannot be confused with a lower neighbor. But to achieve greater clarity with respect to the *Urlinie*, Schenker must lower the rank of the second $\hat{2}$/V and therefore contradict the aforementioned principle that the hierarchical importance of tonal constituents tends to increase as a piece unfolds. The graph, in other words, appears precipitate in making its fundamental motion to the dominant.

Emphasis on the first V all the way through to the final close also flies in the face of the strong emphasis parallel formal constructions usually place on the tonic, both at the moment of return of opening material and throughout the body of the large-scale restatement. One need only think of the consequent of a period or the A′ section of a rounded binary form to sense the conflict between the early dominant orientation of a type 2 derivation and this tonic emphasis.

A still further problem with the type 2 derivation relates to principles of interval succession derived from species counterpoint. Species principles dictate that perfect consonances should occur at phrase beginnings and cadences, where the stability of these perfect consonances is aesthetically appropriate. Imperfect conso-

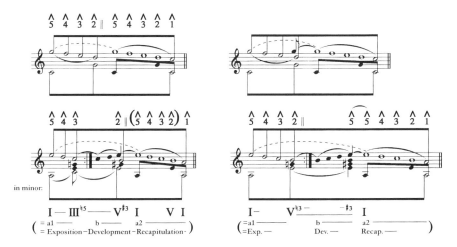

Example 4.3. *Free Composition,* Figures 24–26

nance and dissonance, on the other hand, should predominate within the body of a phrase, where forward motion is the rule. Yet in the type 2 derivation, a sonata will find itself on the closure-signaling perfect fifth, $\hat{2}$/V, already by the arrival of the secondary area in the exposition![12]

Evidence of the contradictions between the type 1 and type 2 derivations appears in the examples that accompany Schenker's introductory discussion of interruption in *Free Composition*. These graphs are reproduced in Example 4.3.[13] In each case Schenker beams the first descent to $\hat{2}$ onto the background. This implies that the second descent emerges on a lower structural level, as in the type 2 derivation. Yet in each of these figures, Schenker simultaneously connects the two statements of the *Kopfton* with a broken slur and assigns open note heads to the second descent, factors that suggest a prolongation of the *Kopfton* across the interruption, as in a type 1 derivation.[14] The presence of both alternatives within each graph reflects Schenker's ambivalence regarding the proper means of derivation.

It is important to note that, as is often the case with Schenker, the contradiction appears to have a musical motivation. He seems to want to remain sensitive to both the formal-tonal emphasis on the dominant in the exposition and the importance for closure of the structural $\hat{2}$–$\hat{1}$ motion at the end of the recapitulation. The problem is that his *Ursatz* formulation requires correspondence between the structural $\hat{2}$ and the main deep-level dominant. In sonata and other open forms characterized by large-scale return, the two do not typically coincide.[15] The main dominant emphasis falls in the exposition, while the conclusive top-voice motion to $\hat{1}$ arrives only toward the very end of a movement.

In addition to contradictions that arise in a theoretical discussion of interruption, the derivation of sonata form is also problematic when examined intuitively. In either of Schenker's solutions, an obvious element of the form is compromised in an attempt to demonstrate that the recapitulation is part of a continuous structure. When applied to sonata form, the type 1 derivation indicates that the *Kopfton* and tonic remain in effect until after the recapitulation. The slur that connects statements of the *Kopfton* responds to the strong parallelism often manifest between the beginning of the exposition and recapitulation. The drawback is that the analyst must locate the dominant of the *Ursatz* within the recapitulation. Instead of focusing on the clear emphasis on V in the exposition (or at the end of the development in the case of minor-mode movements), the analysis elevates, to background status, what usually amounts to a cadential dominant toward the end of a movement. This is the case even though the final cadential dominant is usually part of tonic prolongation on more foreground levels of structure. It is perhaps for these reasons that in many of his analyses Schenker seems to favor the type 2 derivation in which the dominant prior to the recapitulation extends across the large-scale restatement.

But the type 2 derivation is also not problem free. Its prolongation of the first dominant obscures two characteristic features of sonata form, both of which depend on emphasis on the tonic in the recapitulation: (1) the just-mentioned parallelism between the beginning of the exposition and recapitulation, and (2) the reconciliation of secondary material with the home key through tonal transposition. Instead of focusing attention on the new tonic emphasis across the entire recapitulation as a contrast to the harmonic openness of the exposition, the type 2 derivation makes the dominant seem to be the main issue. The body of the recapitulation appears to be a mere anticipation of the closing $\hat{1}/\text{I}$. In the end, neither derivation effectively addresses the formal necessity for a retraversal of the thematic path of the exposition. Schenker's desire to subsume the recapitulation within a continuous tonal structure obscures the motivation of large-scale dissonance resolution.

In defense of Schenker, one might object that the critique presented here rests on the assumption that his is indeed a hierarchical theory that requires derivation of interruption from a single *Ursatz*.[16] Is it really the case that transformation of a continuous *Ursatz* into a divided structure requires a formal mapping of the three-member background (I–V–I) onto the five-member middleground (I–V I–V–I)? But this counterargument only further supports my ultimate point: that if we attend to the implications of Schenker's theory, we are left with a divided structure for sonata form. Moreover, Schenker's introductory discussion of interruption in *Free Composition* and the visual image of many of his graphs provide evidence that it was important to him to derive parallel descents from a single *Ursatz*.[17] In the spirit of analytic pragmatism, however, we can accept the fact that the interruption paradigm is not satisfactorily reconcilable with a continuous background. Instead the *Ursatz* can function as a metaphysical connection between Schenker's chord of nature and the musical reality of a specific parallel construction. The theoretical issues do not diminish the fact that on the scale of an antecedent-consequent phrase, the interruption model produces a cogent musical interpretation.[18]

An additional inconsistency arises, however, when the interruption paradigm is applied to sonata form. Unlike the consequent of a period, the recapitulation closes in the tonic through transposition of a key area, not acceleration and completion

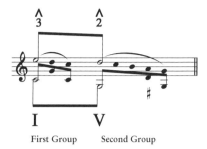

Example 4.4. Typical Tonal Structure of a Sonata Exposition

of an otherwise identical harmonic progression. The alterations between statement and restatement on the phrase level are rhythmic, while on the scale of an entire movement they are tonal. This distinction works against Schenker's interpretation of the first middleground of sonata form as analogous to the structure of a period.

Similar to the beginning of a consequent, the return of the main theme often articulates a reentry of the *Kopfton* and tonic. Since it arises out of a nontransposed restatement, this rebeginning can be graphed convincingly on the same structural level as the original constituents of the *Ursatz* in the exposition. However, in the interpretation of a common type of sonata form—a major-mode movement that takes $\hat{3}$ as its *Kopfton*[19]—the analyst is in many cases forced to cut across the hierarchical boundaries of Schenker's tonal strata to locate the $\hat{2}$/V within the second part of the form. In these situations the constituents of the recapitulation's replica *Ursatz* can no longer all derive from the same structural level, in a clear violation of the principles that normally govern Schenker's theory.

In the exposition, the $\hat{2}$/V of the interrupted descent is typically prolonged by a tonicization of the dominant in the second group, as shown in Example 4.4. In the recapitulation, the background $\hat{2}$/V must be located *within* this linear progression since the second group returns in the tonic. To remain consistent with Schenker's single-*Kopfton* axiom, the analyst must retain the fifth progression only on the middleground and graph its upper two members as part of a prolongation of $\hat{3}$. Schenker describes the resulting structural relationship as the superimposition of a fifth progression on the final third progression. He goes on to add, however, that "[t]here is no doubt that the primary tone remains the $\hat{3}$; the fifth-progression is merely a final reinforcement."[20] Example 4.5 illustrates. Only the final two members of the descent from $\hat{5}$ make it up to the higher level to complete the larger replica *Urlinie*. Yet this interpretation contradicts the internal melodic indivisibility Schenker normally assigns to linear progressions.[21] Moreover, the status of the dominant shifts from its dependence on the tonic within the transposed second group to a more significant structural role on the scale of the entire recapitulation.[22]

The difficulties in the derivation of the recapitulation from a single replica *Ursatz* are similar to those encountered in reconciliation of the exposition and recapitulation with an undivided background. Theoretical contradictions arise when the analyst must determine which constituents of two replica *Ursatz* structures

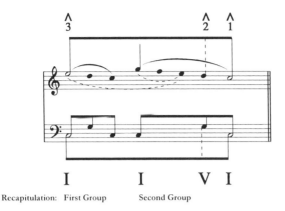

Recapitulation: First Group   Second Group

Example 4.5. Contradictions in Schenker's Interpretation

should join to form a continuous, deeper-level structure. On both the scale of the entire movement and the scale of the recapitulation, the challenge is to find a dominant with sufficient structural weight to connect initial and final tonics. Within the recapitulation of a typical major-mode sonata form that articulates $\hat{3}$ as *Kopfton*, it is often difficult to find such a chord.[23] Ironically, Ernst Oster's comment that the purpose of the fifth progression is "to restate in the main key the diminution which appeared at the first $\hat{2}/V$" cuts to the core of the issue.[24] The new tonal relationships in the recapitulation cannot always be shown to arise out of the diminution of a single replica *Ursatz*. In many cases Rosen's concept of large-scale dissonance resolution provides a more convincing explanation.

These theoretical problems expose some of the limitations of Schenker's approach in dealing with "the confrontation of formal phrase structure relationships and presumably continuous contrapuntal writing."[25] Schenker's theory nevertheless moves well beyond the schemata of *Formenlehre* to reveal aspects of tonal coherence in the sonata forms of the Viennese tradition. In so doing, his theoretical writings provide evidence of both positive and negative effects of anachronistic thinking. By approaching eighteenth-century music from the perspective of a nineteenth-century organicist, Schenker delivers penetrating insight into numerous features of tonal structure, but he simultaneously distorts formal relationships to satisfy his own aesthetic proclivities.

Brahms's engagement with recapitulatory procedures, by contrast, exists in the form of a creative appropriation. He is thus able to realize to its logical extreme the kind of organicist interpretation of sonata form that Schenker later espoused for Haydn, Mozart, and Beethoven. One of the central issues Brahms faced in sonata composition was to reconcile the strong element of repetition inherent in the concept of recapitulation with the late nineteenth-century ideal of continuous motion or growth. The Schenkerian *Ursatz* can also be seen to stem from this predilection, such that Brahms and Schenker embark on intriguingly parallel projects when they

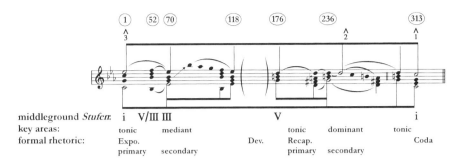

Example 4.6. Background Structure for Piano Quartet

approach sonata form. A comparison of the type 2 derivation with the tonal structure of the first movement of the piano quartet demonstrates the relationship between theorist and composer in their mutual response to sonata form. A parallel structure is merely suggested by the movement's thematic design. Because a divisional element proves illusory from the perspective of middleground counterpoint, the movement fulfills the ideal of continuous tonal evolution that Schenker struggles to reconcile with Classical sonata form.

Across the quartet's exposition and development, large-scale voice-leading coordinates with formal design according to conventions of the Classical period. As we have seen in Chapter 2, the first group prolongs 3̂/i and fuses with a transition that modulates to the relative major for the presentation of secondary material. The first-order linear progression of the second group descends from B♭ back to the E♭ *Kopfton,* which reenters at the structural close of the exposition. The development eventually introduces 2̂/V as part of the retransition, which raises expectations for the recapitulation of the main theme. The anticipated reprise would normally reintroduce 3̂/i and initiate a second replica *Ursatz.* Instead of confirming these expectations, Brahms recomposes the first group to prolong further the retransitional dominant, as described in earlier chapters. Though recapitulatory overlaps of this kind are pervasive in nineteenth-century music and can also be found in the Classical era,[26] in the piano quartet the formal strategy has special significance. It becomes the first stage in a process by which Brahms subsumes the thematic parallelism of sonata form within a unified tonal background. Though limited aspects of the anticipated reprise do materialize, the contrapuntal structure remains continuous; there is no tonal rebeginning and thus no interruption.

Brahms's overlap of development and recapitulation continues across the body of the secondary material with the previously described tonicization of the dominant *Stufe.* The unusual emphasis on the dominant allows Brahms to conflate the return of the tonic and the structural close into a single entity. He thereby merges the divided middleground of sonata form into a continuous background, as shown in Example 4.6. Because the recapitulation avoids a structural rebeginning, the dominant prolongation in the recapitulation resides on the same level as the initial

a) Primary Material

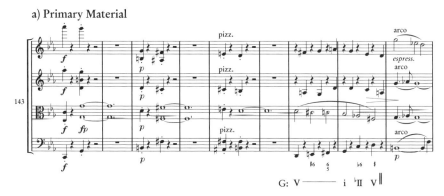

Example 4.7. Tonicization of V in Recapitulation of C-Minor String Quartet
(a) Primary Material

and final tonics. The tonal structure of the exposition and development function unambiguously as the background motion from $\hat{3}$/i to $\hat{2}$/V, as in the type 2 derivation. When the movement is viewed synoptically, it turns out that there is no second $\hat{3}$–$\hat{2}$. The first $\hat{3}$–$\hat{2}$ truly represents a course already run; only the $\hat{1}$ is still lacking. The issue of where to locate the background dominant ceases to be problematic.

It is true that undivided sonata forms like this can be found in earlier repertoires (see note 1). The extended tonicization of the dominant in the recapitulation of the piano quartet, however, takes this compositional strategy to an unprecedented extreme. The apparent recapitulatory element derives not from a parallel voice-leading structure, but from Brahms's evocation of the patterns of themes and keys codified by traditional form theory, which he subsumes within an overarching tonal continuity. Or, as Schenker would ideally have it for all sonata forms, the formal design and the articulations it creates can be understood as part of an indivisible linear projection of the tonic triad.[27]

Though the first movement of the piano quartet represents the most extreme form of dominant emphasis in a Brahms recapitulation, we have seen that there are other sonata forms only one step removed from its progressivism. Through recomposition of his first groups and the original harmonic structure of his second groups, Brahms often grants the dominant a controlling status in a part of the form typically devoted to tonic prolongation on the middleground. As I have highlighted previously, he manages at once to conform to the sonata principle through tonal transposition and to modify its very essence through delay in the reconciliation of the second group with the tonic *Stufe*. Among the movements we have looked at thus far, the Andante of the piano quartet and the first movement of the C-minor string quartet are representative of this type of form.[28]

The string quartet creates an interesting contrast with the piano quartet because Brahms waits until after the recapitulation has begun to introduce a deep-level

b) Secondary Material

Example 4.7. Tonicization of V in Recapitulation of C-Minor String Quartet
(b) Secondary Material

dominant. The tonal structure, in other words, manifests Schenker's type 1 deri-vation of sonata form, in contrast to the type 2 structure of op. 60. It is true that the string quartet focuses more attention on the home key in the recapitulation. The dominant nevertheless does have occasion to function as a local tonic rather than as a harmony clearly under the control of C on the foreground. The string quartet therefore has more in common with the piano quartet than I have even previously emphasized.

   Indeed, tonicization of the dominant in the string quartet occurs in passages within both of the main thematic sections of the recapitulation. Example 4.7 reproduces the relevant material. Brahms recomposes the approach to the [b] section of the main theme (mm. 143–50) so that G moves into the forefront. Similarly the passages in mm. 39–40 and 61–66 of the exposition briefly tonicize the middleground V/III; when the material returns transposed to the tonic key in mm. 180–81 and 202–207, G takes control as local tonic.

The Schenker-Brahms parallelism also provides an illuminating context for my previous analysis of the Andante of the piano quartet. As we have already seen, the Andante also recapitulates secondary material in the tonic key, but nevertheless centers the return around the home dominant. Although Brahms rearticulates a structural tonic prior to the return of the dominant-prolonging B′ section, he does so only toward the end of the A′ section. He thus downplays the sense of division in the form. Once again he displays a proclivity for overarching tonal continuity across a large-scale instance of thematic parallelism. The strategy is less extreme than the approach in the first movement of the string quartet, due to the tonic return late in the A′ section. A compromise between division, as dictated by traditional phrase-formal patterns, and organic unity through continuous contrapuntal writing nevertheless remains a driving force.

In the piano quartet and string quartet movements, as well as in his sonata forms in general, Brahms's adherence to the sonata principle can be viewed as the substantiation of a traditional procedure in the face of late nineteenth-century aesthetics. This practice is undoubtedly an expression of his conservatism, a fidelity to a procedure that he must have considered essential to perpetuate the Viennese sonata tradition. As evidence of his beliefs regarding the underlying principles of sonata form, Brahms's recapitulations express the currently accepted view that tonal transposition of material originally presented outside the tonic was historically a more essential feature than either a full restatement of the primary material or even a coordinated return of main theme and tonic.[29]

But movements like the string quartet and Andante also demonstrate that Brahms's conservatism regarding his second groups may be more apparent than real from the perspective of large-scale tonal structure. When viewed from afar, his adherence to the sonata principle helps maintain a strong element of the form's parallel design. Upon closer scrutiny, however, the transposed restatement may participate in a continuous tonal structure more characteristic of the late nineteenth century. From a Schenkerian perspective, the parallelism in Brahms's formal designs is an aspect of the foreground. The sectionalization it suggests is deceptive in light of a deeper-level tonal continuity.

In movements like these, Brahms reconceives a central component of sonata form: rather than reconcile secondary material with the tonic *Stufe*, the tonal structure of the recapitulation either prolongs or introduces the dominant pole. Through this emphasis on the dominant, Brahms conflates rearticulation of the tonic in the recapitulation and structural closure, in an extreme expression of his compositional economy. The resulting tonal background is truly indivisible, while the articulation at the recapitulation is, in many respects, illusory.

Conversely the Schenkerian analysis of a typical eighteenth-century sonata form can go only as far as a two-part middleground without facing the contradictions that arise when moving to a single *Ursatz*. In more Classically oriented movements, the middleground articulation is real. Derivation from a continuous tonal structure remains problematic. Thus Brahms—perhaps more than any other composer within the long history of sonata form—unequivocally fulfills the ideal of organic unity as conceived by Schenker in his theory of musical form.

5 Brahms's Expository Strategies: Two-Part Second Groups, Three-Key Expositions, and Modal Shifts

The sonata form Brahms inherited from the eighteenth century is a form characterized by articulations and the discontinuities required to create those articulations. As no less an authority on Classical style than Charles Rosen has noted, "discontinuities are, indeed, the principal preoccupation of the late eighteenth-century theorists—Quantz, Vogler, Koch, etc.; what concerns them most is the character and the placing of cadence and half-cadence within any musical form."[1] If one were forced to choose a single primordial discontinuity for sonata form—the most basic level on which the form is divided—a primary candidate undoubtedly would be the articulation that marks the large-scale parallelism of exposition and recapitulation. A close second, however, would have to be the caesura that divides the exposition itself into two distinct key areas. Indeed, motivation for the recapitulation resides in its function as an area of resolution for the tension created by articulation of the exposition into tonally polarized formal areas.

Up to this point I have focused considerable attention on Brahms's treatment of the recapitulatory articulation, and in particular his tendency to evoke this most basic formal discontinuity only to efface it and the larger parallelism it marks. I have also done some preliminary work with issues surrounding articulation of expository key areas in my discussion of dimensional counterpoint in Chapter 2. The current chapter picks up some of the strands that I began to develop there, and now delves further into issues raised by Brahms's approach to strategies of expository articulation.

As with issues of recapitulation, the piano quartet is an appropriate locus for the discussion because it provides a spectrum of key-area types that represent important categories of organization for Brahms's sonata forms in general. Brahms articulates traditional expository key relations throughout the cycle, as noted in Chapter 2. The first and last movements both present their subordinate themes in the mediant (mm. 70 and 55, respectively). The E♭-major slow movement likewise places its secondary material in the dominant (m. 35), as a crucial sonata component of its hybrid form.

The scherzo is the one movement whose form does not follow a sonata trajectory. Nevertheless, even here Brahms includes a sonata-style retransition and double return at the reprise of the opening material (m. 159). The scherzo's A section also articulates two key areas with primary and secondary thematic material (mm. 5 and 23, respectively). As Chapter 3 suggested, however, the material in the dominant functions more like a brief contrasting episode within an essentially one-part form, rather than as a sonata second theme or even a middle section for a ternary form.

One explanation for the choice of the dominant as secondary key in a minor-mode movement is the fact that the scherzo only indirectly engages sonata issues. A brief tonicization of V, within a movement that otherwise clings so closely to the tonic, helps put to rest the extraordinary emphasis on G major in the recapitulation of the first movement, as described in Chapter 3. An exploration of Brahms's expository strategies in this chapter, however, will demonstrate that not only in its modulation to the dominant, but also in its shift in mode, the scherzo's secondary idea reflects larger Brahmsian preoccupations. That is to say, it will become clear that the scherzo manifests proclivities for dominant tonicization and mode shift that Brahms does not hesitate to indulge in forthright minor-mode sonata contexts. Indeed, the idea of a mode shift across a secondary area pervades his major-mode sonata forms as well.

Although the key schemes of the three other movements might appear straightforward, the musical details through which they are articulated is anything but. At first glance, the first movement seems to contain the most conventional key articulation among the cycle's three sonata-form expositions. The arrival of the secondary idea at m. 70 corresponds with the entrance of a middleground E♭ *Stufe,* and the mediant clearly governs the entire secondary area. This island of calm provides a release of tension following the instability of the tonic area. The E♭ tonic is prepared by a dominant-prolonging transition (mm. 42–69) that gradually reduces both energy and thematic content. This de-energizing transition helps to focus a spotlight on the entrance of the E♭ material. In its function as culmination for all that has preceded it as well as in its stability and regal character, the E♭ theme, perhaps more than any other of Brahms's secondary ideas, reflects the central role of the lyrical second theme in nineteenth-century accounts of sonata form. In all of these characteristics—unstable tonic area, de-energizing transition, and resolution into peaceful lyricism—the exposition presents a characteristic Romantic reinterpretation of conventions associated with the medial caesura of Classical sonata form.[2]

Yet it is precisely in the degree of stability that the secondary area reflects an uncommon practice for Brahms. Not only is the E♭ *Stufe* in control from the outset, but the unusual theme and variations form of the secondary area dictates rearticulation of the local tonic every eight or nine measures. Moreover, the harmonic structure of the theme and each variation is constructed around straightforward—one might even say simple—diatonic progressions leading from I to V. (The exceptional passage in this regard involves the half-step shift of material in mm. 98–99. The result is a brief hint of a tonicization of E♮ in variation 3.) This excessively tight-knit manner of organization stands out not only when considered in relation to Brahms's normal approach to secondary material, but also in relation to the approach of his Classical forebears. Eighteenth-century convention favors secondary

Example 5.1. Motivic Connections
(a) Main and Variation Themes
(b) Variation 1

material of looser organization as a contrast to a tight-knit main theme—the reverse of the trajectory Brahms follows in the piano quartet.[3]

Another consequence of the variation process is a secondary area that balances Brahms's characteristic proclivity for developing variation with a focus on relatively stable recurrences of an eight-measure phrase. In other words, thematic orientation around a single self-contained idea complements harmonic orientation around tonic. Signs of developing variation within the variation process are manifest by motivic connections across the two key areas and by more local variation-to-variation continuities. As an instance of the first type of connection, Example 5.1a outlines the second theme's reinterpretation of the main theme's appoggiatura sigh motive. Example 5.1b highlights a more local continuity: development of this half-step idea across the theme and into the first variation.

In addition to continuity of motivic process, Brahms, like any skillful variation composer, endows his variation set with a larger formal shape. He builds momentum toward the climactic variation 4 (m. 102) through increased rhythmic activity in the accompaniment, a registral expansion, and a gradual increase in dynamics. He also develops his material rhythmically by reinterpreting the hypermetrically strong head motive of the theme as an anacrusis gesture in diminution at the beginning of variations 2 and 3 (mm. 86 and 94). In addition to its contribution to the overall rhythmic acceleration, the reinterpretation of the motive results in the irregular hypermetric pattern outlined in Example 5.2. Note that the rhythmic reinterpretation creates continuity across the variations by establishing an anacrusis connection from the dominant into the return of the tonic. The irregular hypermeter thus not only helps to build tension by creating rhythmic dissonance that resolves at the climactic entrance of variation 4: it also contributes to ever increasing continuity within the context of an additive formal process.[4]

Given Brahms's reputation as a composer who was able to overcome challenges of integrating nineteenth-century strategies with traditional approaches to form, an important question arises. How is he able to accommodate a self-contained variation set within a sonata context, while avoiding the kind of episodic writing that often plagues nineteenth-century sonata forms? The motivic connections between the main and variation themes provide one element of integration. Another more overt source of continuity arises from the formal function of the secondary material in relation to the tonic area and transition.

As already mentioned, the E♭ section presents a span of temporary relaxation following the instabilities of what precedes it. Rather than impede the developmental continuity of sonata processes, the island of stability appears motivated as a consequence of these preparatory tensions. It has a reason to exist, in other words, as an area of resolution within the larger sonata trajectory. In this view the C-minor structural downbeat at m. 32 only partially resolves the tension between initiation and preparation in the movement's opening passage. The counterstatement is itself highly agitated despite its tonic pedal, and its energy overflows into the modulatory bridge at m. 42. It is not until the storm gradually subsides across the transition that the form is prepared to relax more fully as it settles into the variation set.

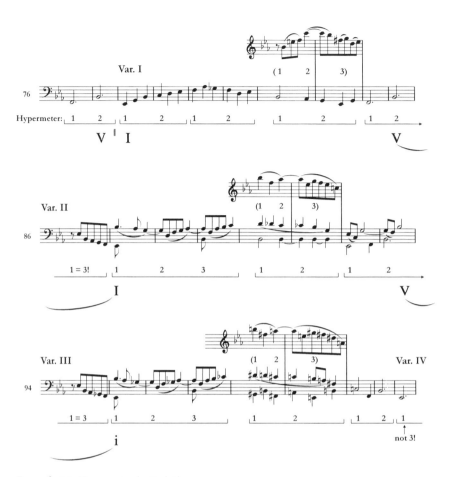

Example 5.2. Hypermeter in Variations

Even more noteworthy with respect to formal integration is the fact that Brahms marshals the stability of the secondary area—at superficial glance, one of the most conventional aspects of form in the cycle—in the service of one of the most unconventional aspects: tonicization of the major dominant in the recapitulation. This factor again demonstrates how a remote consequence of material activated in the recapitulation grows out of properties inherent in its expository presentation. The focus of the secondary area on its local tonic helps the recapitulation overcome the challenge of stabilizing the major dominant in the context of a minor-mode movement.

The relationship between expository presentation and recapitulatory reinterpretation nevertheless represents a special case in at least one crucial respect. Typically Brahms and other nineteenth-century composers build on the kind of anacrusis-to-downbeat trajectory found in the exposition of the quartet. Rather than signaling the beginning of the reprise, unstable opening material can return as part of the retransition. The arrival of the lyrical theme thereby can provide the delayed structural downbeat normally associated with the initiation of the reprise.[5] This is another way in which lyrical stability might appear motivated and thus formally justified in a sonata context.

Brahms does indeed appear to resolve tensions of his recapitulatory formal overlap with the entrance of his secondary idea. Yet the tonal orientation of this "resolution" creates a devastating disjunction between literal and expressed meaning—the crushing irony discussed in Chapter 3. Brahms transforms authentic E♭-major stability into G-major apparent stability—a feature that through its irony creates one of the most extreme forms of tension, rather than resolution, in a Brahms recapitulation.

If the stability of the secondary area in the first movement represents an extreme on one end of a spectrum of Brahmsian possibilities, then the dominant material (mm. 35–67.1) in the slow movement stands at the other. In the one instance, Brahms clings excessively to his local tonic, while in the other, he avoids it entirely, even foregoing a stable articulation at the end of the section. With respect to ternary organization, the dominant material in the Andante functions as a B section. Yet as we have seen, the passage also takes on the role of a sonata-style key area, as evidenced by the fact that part of it returns in the tonic toward the end of the movement (m. 111). The movement also includes a retransition, whose trajectory flows across the return of the A section and in the process develops motivic ideas from the main theme. This sonata-style overlap helps solidify the hybrid character of the form. A process of recapitulatory overlap is a feature the Andante shares with a number of Brahms's other slow middle movements. More often, however, blurred returns in Brahms's slow movements arise through a series of false reprises.[6] The unusual sequential passage based on the augmented triad motive in the Andante must be viewed as a special manifestation of this common Brahmsian strategy.

Equally particular to the Andante is the transposed return of secondary material, a practice common, of course, in Brahms's outer movements but surprisingly rare among his slow middle movements. Of the orchestral slow movements, only the Serenade in D Major, op. 11, and the Fourth Symphony follow this sonata imperative, while the clarinet trio and the F-Major Cello Sonata, op. 99, join the quartet in the practice of large-scale dissonance resolution in a chamber setting. The scarcity of sonata-style reconciliation is a corollary to Brahms's tendency to favor ternary and variation forms for his slow middle movements. If a passage in a secondary key forms the middle section of an ABA form, then there is no reason to expect it to fulfill the sonata principle.

It is true that Brahms often returns to material from his middle sections as part of the codas of his ternary forms. But these references are usually not extensive enough to create the kind of formal parallelism characteristic of a recapitulation of secondary material. Nor do they revolve around the kind of straightforward transposition of large blocks of material that so often characterizes Brahms's recapitulations. The forms still tend to hinge on an ABA alternation with a final reminiscence of the B section contributing to the attainment of closure.

Although Brahms often organizes his ternary forms around third-related keys,

Example 5.3. C♯ Tonicization in F-Major Cello Sonata

he also has recourse to the more unusual strategy of moving to the dominant for his B sections, as noted in Chapter 3. This further highlights the crucial role of the thematic dimension for formal interpretation, notwithstanding the importance of key scheme and large-scale voice leading. In the Andante the presence of a transition joins the multithemed expansiveness of the dominant material to give the section the character of a key area. Other tonic-dominant slow movements have sections governed by V that simply do not fulfill sonata expectations. The just-mentioned slow movement of the F-major cello sonata—a piece that not only moves to the dominant but also goes the extra step of providing a transposed restatement in the tonic—provides an illuminating contrast to the Andante in this regard.

The F♯-major cello movement tonicizes V in a formal context that calls into question a sonata interpretation. Its first main formal section makes only a last-minute move into C♯ for its closing phrase in mm. 16–19. The passage appears in Example 5.3. Brahms neither prepares the C♯ tonicization with a transition, nor does he expand it into a multiphrased thematic outpouring of a key area. Rather, it functions more like a codetta or perhaps the cadential close for the first half of a binary form.

It is true that this C♯ passage returns transposed to the tonic in mm. 60–62. Yet despite the apparent sonata component, the generic dominant for the movement remains ternary form. In part this is because, unlike the B material of the Andante, the middle section of mm. 20–43 does not fulfill a sonata function. If we allow for an interpretation of the C♯ passage as some kind of secondary key area, however imperfectly the term applies, then the big B section should do double duty as a development. Yet this passage fails to produce the motivic working out of themes previously heard, in the manner of a development. Rather, Brahms bases it on new material that revolves around tension between further elaboration of C♯ as a local tonic and as the bass for an augmented-sixth chord in F♮.[7]

If, on the other hand, the B section itself were to function as a secondary area similar to the situation in the piano quartet, then it should presumably follow a transitional passage rather than a phrase that already provides closure in C♯. Moreover, Brahms would need to return to the B material later in the movement to reconcile it with the tonic according to his standard sonata practice. It is true that he mingles thematic fragments from the A and B sections in the coda of mm. 63–71. Yet this again would appear to be an echo of sonata practice sounding within an overall ternary context. Sonata characteristics are less active than is the case in the Andante, where there is a brief yet independent transition, an extensive elaboration of the dominant key as a quasi-independent section, and a recapitulation of a substantial portion of this secondary material in the standard tonic transposition.

The example of the cello sonata notwithstanding, a number of Brahms's middle movements tonicize the dominant in what appears to be a sonata context, yet nevertheless fail to produce a tonally transposed return. The Andante is unusual, in other words, not only for the expository character of its A and B sections, but also for fulfilling the expected recapitulatory response. All the symphonies, with the exception of the first, include slow movements in major keys that place their secondary material in the dominant. Moreover, these movements contain distinctly developmental-like middle sections. The Fourth Symphony recapitulates its secondary material in the tonic, providing strong grounds for a sonata interpretation.[8]

In the Second and Third Symphonies, Brahms eschews restatement of secondary material in the tonic key or otherwise. (In the Third Symphony, the secondary material does return, but in the finale.) In the back-and-forth between sonata and ternary interpretation that characterizes the listening experience of these and other Brahms slow movements, a final synoptic perspective favors the idea of ABA′ form, similar to the situation in the cello sonata.[9] To summarize, within a general tendency toward formal hybridization in slow movements, the Andante of the piano quartet stands out not only as a piece that tonicizes the dominant as a secondary key. It is also noteworthy for the fact that it responds to this and other sonata characteristics of its "exposition," with a reprise section that follows through with transposition of subsidiary material to the tonic.

In addition to these distinguishing characteristics, internal details of the Andante's secondary material mark it as atypical. The Andante, like the opening Allegro, articulates the beginning of its secondary area with a textural break (m. 34). Yet as noted in Chapter 3, the secondary material continues to prolong the F♯ dominant introduced in the transition. The material is marked by a duality, in other words: the two main thematic ideas of the section—one characterized by a syncopation (mm. 35–36.1), the other by a dotted rhythm (mm. 39–45)—are stable enough to give the section the character of a theme group. Yet Brahms refuses to provide a resolution to the local tonic and therefore sustains a transitional trajectory. Multiple statements of a characteristic form of the prolonged F♯ dominant heighten this element of continuity with the transition. The dominant returns with a G♮ ninth at the articulation points of mm. 36–37, 45, and 52, just as it originally appeared at the crossover from the transition into the secondary area.

The tendency to keep returning to the dominant ninth chord points to two other unusual aspects of the secondary material: its circularity and its character of tense stasis. Circularity and stasis are manifest in both the harmonic and thematic dimensions and with respect to large-scale organization and the more moment-to-moment evolution of the material. In addition to the overarching V/V prolongation and tendency to return to the characteristic ninth chord, the tonal structure exhibits a remarkable fixation on F♯. The syncopated theme unfolds almost entirely over an F♯ pedal, first in the piano of mm. 35–37 and then in the viola when the material returns in mm. 46–50. When the bass does finally move toward the end of these passages, it is only to create yet further emphasis on F♯, which reenters to initiate the dotted-rhythm material at mm. 39 and 52.

Rather than provide some contrast to this F♯ fixation, the dotted-rhythm theme merely shifts the means of emphasis. The material consists of an incessant alternation of V^7 and I in which the local tonic embellishes the controlling F♯ dominant. Brahms heightens the feeling of circularity by means of an accompaniment that not only repeats the same pattern over and over but also moves around and around in contrary motion. The activity is continuous, but it never leads anywhere. As is the case for the syncopated theme, both statements of the dotted-rhythm material maintain harmonic stasis until the second of the passages finally leads via a climactic crescendo to the arrival on B as home dominant at m. 62.

A conspicuous absence of Brahmsian thematic evolution on both global and local levels complements the harmonic circularity. With respect to large-scale organization, the B section consists of a simple alternation of the syncopated idea and the dotted-rhythm material. The dual statements of each passage are marked by very little in the way of development, with each repetition closely following the template of the original. Example 5.4 summarizes the clear parallelisms. All four passages are also noteworthy for their high degree of internal repetition, also outlined in Example 5.4. Admittedly the first statement of the syncopated idea merges into a two-measure unit (mm. 37–38.2) that anticipates the contrasting dotted-rhythm phrase; the dotted material proper begins only in m. 39. Yet the second statement of the syncopated material replaces this element of continuity with an internal repetition based on a shift of the melody from violin to cello (mm. 50–51.2).

The dotted material contains an even higher degree of internal redundancy. The dialogue between cello and viola in mm. 39–40.1 is repeated immediately by the violin/cello and viola. There is even the beginning of a third repetition before a process of liquidation leads into the cadence on F♯ at m. 45. The two-measure units themselves also consist of internal repetitions of the dotted-rhythm figure. The large-scale repetition of the whole unit follows the same pattern before the aforementioned climactic crescendo begins in m. 55.

It is true that the pattern of repetition and liquidation within each of these phrases can be explained as an instance of a Schoenbergian sentence, that is, as a conventional rather than exceptional means of organization.[10] Two points counter this argument, however. First, the kind of clear-cut statement and repetition in the dotted-rhythm theme is far more characteristic of Beethoven than of Brahms. More often in Brahms's sentences, the development of material begins immediately following a single statement of a basic idea rather than after a statement and repetition. (Among pieces discussed in earlier chapters, the opening phrase of the C-minor string quartet [mm. 1–8] provides a representative example.) Second, the repetition of the basic idea in the dotted-rhythm theme does not shift to a different transposition level and harmonic orientation. Although some sentences consist

Example 5.4. Thematic Relations in B Section

Statement	Repetition
Syncopated Theme	*Syncopated Theme*
mm. 35–36.1: Syncopated idea in vl.	mm. 46–49: Syncopated idea (expanded) in vl.
mm. 37–38.2: Anticipation of dotted-rhythm idea	—
	mm. 50–51.2: Repetition of syncopated idea in cello
Dotted-Rhythm Theme	*Dotted-Rhythm Theme*
mm. 39–40.1: Basic idea in cello and vla. with internal repetitions of rhythmic motive	mm. 52–53.1: Basic idea in vla. and vl. with internal repetitions of rhythmic motive
mm. 41–42.1: Repetition of basic idea in vl./cello and vla. with internal repetitions of rhythmic motive	mm. 54–55.1: Repetition of basic idea in vla./cello and varied continuation in vl./cello, all with intensification of internal repetition pattern on the rhythmic motive
mm. 43–45: Continuation with liquidation of rhythmic motive leading to cadence on F♯ as V/B	mm. 56–61.1: Liquidation of dotted-rhythm idea and transition to arrival on B as V/E

of this type of literal repetition—the opening phrase of the piano quartet's first movement, for example—the restatement of a basic idea more conventionally involves transposition up a step so that the harmonic orientation shifts from tonic to dominant.

The idea that the Andante's emphasis on V/V represents an extreme among Brahms's expository strategies rests not merely with the fact that a structural B harmony arrives only toward the end of the section (m. 62). It is also manifest in the identity of this delayed B chord itself as a dominant seventh directed toward resolution to E. More often in Brahms, a key area focused on its local dominant will resolve to a stable tonic, even if the harmonic delay extends to the end of a section. In a sonata context, for instance, Brahms almost always chooses to mark the end of his expositions with structural closure before he begins the development.[11] This is the case in the first movement of the C-minor string quartet, a sonata form that like the Andante has secondary material focused entirely around the dominant of the secondary key, as discussed in previous chapters.

By contrast, the secondary material in the Andante merges seamlessly into a retransition. The harmonic tension of the passage never resolves to a stable B harmony. A last chance for a delayed articulation of the tonicized dominant is instead replaced by a new form of anacrusis trajectory at m. 62. The conflation of harmonic functions reflects the pervasive tendency for formal bivalence throughout

Example 5.5. B–C♮ Neighbor Motive in Retransition

the cycle. In addition to the just-mentioned duality of transitional-like harmonic tension and thematic stability of the B section, other instances in the Andante include the overlap of closing and transitional functions for the material in mm. 27–34, the overlap of retransitional and recapitulatory formal functions at the reprise described in Chapter 3, and finally the overall hybrid character of the movement's form.

A final brilliant stroke with respect to unresolved dominants emerges in the path the Andante's retransition takes as it leads back to the tonic key. Brahms first expands the B dominant through neighboring progressions to iv⁶ and ♮VI at mm. 63 and 65, respectively. These progressions provide bass articulations of the B–C♮ neighbor motive originally embedded within the voice leading of the opening of the movement's main theme. Example 5.5 clarifies the relationship. The neighbor motive also has returned earlier in the B section, both in the form of ♮9 in the aforementioned dominant ninth chords and at the points highlighted in Example 5.6. The emphasis on ♮6̂ in the major-mode context of the Andante provides another example of how elements of tragic foreboding can seep into a part of the quartet that otherwise appears to provide a reprieve from suffering. In Chapter 6 we will explore how this motivic component joins the above-described idiosyncrasies of the B section to undercut the apparent expressive contrast provided by the Andante.

A connection between the retransitional neighbor progressions and the main theme becomes explicit at m. 70, where the 5̂–♮6̂ motive continues to function as a means of avoiding tonic resolution. The return of the opening idea here, as part of the V–♮VI progression, initiates the sequential passage that develops the material's augmented triad motive, as described in Chapter 3. This motivic expansion leaves the retransitional dominant hanging without tonic resolution at the beginning of the reprise (m. 78). The graph of the passage in Example 3.17 of Chapter 3 (p. 102) depicts this harmonic reinterpretation of the opening phrase. Recall that Brahms picks up the dominant again only when the middle section of the A material re-

Example 5.6. $\hat{5}$–$\natural\hat{6}$ Neighbor Motive in B Section

turns in its original form at m. 86. Now, however, the dominant is tonicized. It thus calls to mind the tonicized dominant that failed to materialize in the B section. This tonicized dominant, though displaced to the "wrong" part of the form, finally behaves as it should: it functions as a local tonic for the beginning of a section (m. 86) and returns as home dominant at the end (m. 93). The displaced status of the dominant is confirmed by the fact that it resolves to the type of tonic that Brahms withholds from the beginning of the A′ section: a middleground structural harmony articulated by a restatement of the opening theme (mm. 93–94).

Despite all of the noteworthy characteristics of second-key articulation in the quartet's first three movements, it is important to reemphasize a point made at the outset: the point of initiation for each secondary area remains essentially unambiguous. Formal clarity in the first movement and scherzo results from Brahms's coordination of a middleground harmonic arrival with the entrance of a new theme at this crucial hinge in the form. Although the Andante fails to provide similar coordination—there is no new harmony introduced at the beginning of the B section—it nevertheless marks a formal division via elements of articulation in the thematic dimension.

The exposition of the finale is an entirely different matter. Here Brahms projects the type of extreme formal multivalence familiar to us from the crossover into the recapitulation of the first movement. The formal complexity in part arises from the organization of the secondary material into two main parts (mm. 55–74 and 75–95). This type of two-part division has long been recognized as an important component of Brahms's approach to sonata form. It was James Webster who argued, in a seminal study now more than twenty years old, that certain innovations of Schubert's had a decisive influence on Brahms's approach to sonata form.[12] Central to Webster's argument is the idea that Brahms adopted from Schubert the practice of sometimes organizing his secondary material "into two separate sections in different keys. . . . The result is a 'three-key exposition,' comprising a first group and a 'double second group.' "[13] The insight has proven valuable for both analytical and historical understanding of sonata form. For if Charles Rosen is correct and eighteenth-century sonata form hinges on the creation and resolution of a polarity between two keys, then a three-key pattern would indicate a significant adjustment, if not a transformation, of the Classical model.[14]

Although Webster emphasizes the influence of Schubert on the works of Brahms's first maturity, many of the characteristics he traces to Schubert can be heard in Brahms's later sonata forms. The exposition of the finale is a case in point. Brahms hesitates to leave the tonic, and when he does in mm. 51–55, he modulates abruptly and without recourse to a key-defining transitional dominant. Once the exposition reaches its secondary key at m. 55, it almost immediately destabilizes the new tonal center and merges into a transitional-like passage. Finally, before making a more conventional move into the arrival of the exposition's third part, the middle section refers back to the tonic key through several ii^{ø7}–V–(i) progressions in mm. 67–70. Indeed, there is some ambiguity, given the previous abrupt and weakly articulated modulation, as to whether the exposition has truly left the tonic, until the third part of the exposition at m. 75. In all of these features, the exposition behaves in ways that Webster associates with Schubert.

Yet it is also the case that aspects of the movement call into question the notion that Brahms's double second group reflects a singularly Schubertian influence. First, the choice of second key is the conventional mediant rather than the type of remote tonal center characteristic of Schubert's middle areas. Moreover, the second and third parts center on a single key; an overall three-part layout arises out of a shift, from an E♭ major inflected with elements borrowed from the parallel minor, to a more diatonic E♭. Equally decisive for the articulation is the thematic contrast between the appassionata "hailstorm" material of m. 55 and the chorale of m. 75.[15] In other words, it appears that Brahms blends some Schubertian strategies with an approach that perhaps derives from other sources.

The duality of the situation raises broad questions about Brahms and the topic of two-part second groups. Since Webster's study, the concept of a three-key exposition has become part of standard sonata nomenclature. Absorption of the idea into analytical discourse has led to a situation in which the meaning of the term often seems to be taken for granted. This is dangerous because there is still much to be clarified about the concept of a three-key exposition. First of all, while the three-key terminology has passed into the literature, Webster's more all-embracing idea of a double second group seems to have been left behind, without sufficient attention to the slippage. Emphasis on three keys rather than Webster's concept of a double articulation within the nontonic area can conceal a number of qualitatively different formal strategies.

Within Brahms's oeuvre alone, there are significant distinctions among expositions that scholars have grouped under the three-key rubric. The finale of the quartet reflects only one of a number of diverse strategies of organization for a double second group. Yet despite the variety of Brahms's practice, Webster's article and Roger Graybill's 1983 dissertation remain the only attempts to codify different ways in which he organizes his two-part second groups.[16] One purpose of the present chapter will be to continue the work initiated by Webster and Graybill. The immediate goal will be to provide an appropriate context in which to interpret the particulars of second-key organization in the finale. The discussion, however, will also provide a framework for future exploration of Brahms's expository strategies.

Before looking more closely at the exposition of the finale, it will be helpful to have an overview of Brahms's double second groups in order to suggest the possibility for refinements in the interpretation of his diverse strategies. A survey will afford the opportunity to explore some of the ways in which different subtypes of Brahms's two-part second groups relate to the practice not only of Schubert, but also the practices of Haydn, Mozart, and Beethoven. An overview will also establish a context for the final section of this chapter. There an in-depth look at the finale will be further contextualized through comparison with Brahms's approach in the finale of the E♭-Major Horn Trio, op. 40, and the first movement of the First Symphony.

These analyses will allow for more detailed observations on the complex interaction of thematic design, key scheme, and voice leading in Brahms's double second groups. They will also demonstrate that aspects of Brahms's approach are rooted solidly in the Classical tradition, rather than in Schubertian innovations. The topic is crucial for the current project because the idea of a double second group provides not just an important structural resource but also a powerful medium for musical expression. An exploration of the relationship between Brahms's approach and the strategies of his Viennese precursors will allow for further insight into both his special brand of dimensional counterpoint and issues of meaning in the finale of the quartet.

First, it is necessary to clarify the meaning of the terms *double second group* and *three-key exposition*. In addition to expositions that articulate three distinct keys, Webster and Graybill address two other alternatives to Classical two-part organization: secondary areas that present a tonally unstable or even ambiguous area between tonic and dominant, and expositions that create an overall three-part division through a mode shift within a single secondary key.[17] Their inclusion of these two categories indicates that the term *three-key exposition* is somewhat of a misnomer, unless its application is limited to movements in which a relatively stable tonal area sits between tonic and dominant.

The potential for confusion is especially strong in the case of the mode-shift category, considering the emphasis on modal mixture in the nineteenth century and the apparent shift from the twenty-four-key system of earlier music into a twelve-key approach. On the other hand, Brahms often presents a sharp contrast between major and minor forms of a key in his secondary areas and thus takes advantage of a resource of the older approach to tonality. It is also true that, in Schubert and Brahms, arresting melodic invention often occurs in tonally ambiguous middle sections. The idea of a quasi-independent expository area thus seems appropriate in these cases despite the absence of tonal stability. This is all to say that expositions that fall into either of Webster's and Graybill's alternative categories often do break down into three distinct formal sections. They therefore present alternatives to bipartite organization that are related to, if not coextensive with, a design based on three distinct keys.

The finale provides a prototypical example of a secondary area that divides into two parts despite the absence of a third expository key. The manner of organization is most like expositions that fall into the mode-shift category. Although Brahms holds to a major E♭ tonic throughout the two parts of the secondary area, his emphasis on iv (minor) and ii°6 (diminished) harmonies gives the intermediate passage at m. 55 an E♭-minor cast. (The remaining chords in the beginning of the passage, V6/5/V and V harmonies, are modally "neutral" and can be tipped either way based on context.) The melodic emphasis on ♭6 underscores the minor coloration. Contrast this with the third part at m. 75, where Brahms emphasizes the diatonic 6̂, and even highlights C♮ via D♭ upper neighbors. He likewise articulates a ii chord as the goal of the third part's second phrase at mm. 83–84, in contrast to the previous emphasis on the diminished version of the supertonic.

A three-part division is also suggested by the sharp contrast between appassionata and chorale material, as previously noted. The two ideas articulate a shift in character from the tension and struggle of the minor-colored appassionata theme to the relative calm of the more purely major chorale. This type of thematic contrast is not unusual for double second groups in general. It takes on a crucial function, however, in the context of the mode-shift type where melodic duality becomes a powerful articulative resource. The thematic contrast in the finale thus contributes to an association with movements in the mode-shift category even though a major E♭ tonic is present throughout both parts.

Although the three types of double second group represent modes of organization distinct from more straightforward two-part expositions, it is not the case that they all derive from Schubert as innovations apart from eighteenth-century conventions. Webster's argument that either an intermediate key area or a tonally ambiguous middle section represent quintessentially Schubertian contributions to the evolution of sonata form rings true.[18] The mode-shift type, however, was not an important Schubertian resource. This is not to say that Schubert avoided modal mixture or sharp juxtapositions of major and minor; his incomparable skill with both compositional resources has long been recognized. Rather, the point is that Schubert did not consistently create two-part secondary areas through a division into minor and major sections, both under the control of a single tonic.

The first movement of the A-Minor Piano Sonata, D. 845, for example, includes an important shift to minor within its secondary area. The C-minor passage of mm. 64–76, however, is an expressive detour within a section that begins and ends in C major. Similarly, the secondary area in the finale of the B♭-Major Piano Sonata, D. 960, presents a dramatic shift in character for a stormy episode in the minor dominant (mm. 156–84). The passage, however, is framed by material in F major. Closer to the mode-shift type is the first movement of the *Death and the Maiden* String Quartet, which includes a motion from A major (mm. 102–14) to A minor, the key in which the exposition closes (mm. 115–40). If the section in A is regarded as two-part, then the exposition is an example of a four-part layout since an F-major theme group (mm. 61–82.1) sits between tonic and dominant areas.[19]

The *Death and the Maiden* example notwithstanding, the mode-shift alternative remains far more characteristic of Brahms than of Schubert. Brahms's affinity for the mode-shift type becomes clear from a glance at Example 5.7, which presents summary information about all of his double second groups. (The work designations in the leftmost column refer to first movements, unless otherwise noted; the same holds true for subsequent references to works in the text.) The first set of pieces in the table, beginning with the B♭ sextet and ending with the E♭ horn trio, fall within the period that Brahms scholars, expanding somewhat on Tovey, have identified as the composer's first maturity. The characteristics of these pieces are important because it is here that Webster, again following Tovey, argues that Schubert's influence is most strongly felt.[20]

Although Webster bases his thesis on a number of interrelated Schubertian innovations, the three-key idea stands at the center of his argument. Yet as the summary of expository key schemes in the second column indicates, there are actually very few expositions from Brahms's first maturity that follow patterns of three-key organization traceable to Schubert. The B♭ sextet is one example. In a process similar to Schubert's approach in the C-Major Cello Quintet, D. 956, the secondary thematic idea of mm. 61–84.1 hovers between two third-related keys before it pushes on to the stable arrival of the dominant at the beginning of the third part. Example 5.8 (pp. 141–45) highlights this and other similarities between the two passages. The finale of the A-Major Piano Quartet, op. 26, also articulates a tonally unstable middle area in mm. 85–113.1. In this case the emphasis is on the dominant of a third-related key. In a familiar enharmonic procedure, Brahms reinterprets the emphasized V^7/F as a German augmented-sixth chord (mm. 105–106) to form a transition from the unstable middle area into the section in the dominant.[21]

These two movements, however, are exceptional cases. Brahms otherwise uses mode shifts to create subdivisions within the four other two-part second groups of the first maturity. There are no examples of the other Schubertian strategy in which the middle section stabilizes a key between tonic and dominant poles. Brahms's use of both types of Schubertian double second group becomes more prevalent in his later works. The Second Symphony, for instance, includes another example of an unstable intermediate area like the B♭ sextet; the finale of the C-Major Piano Trio, op. 87, and the first movement of the A-minor clarinet trio are cases in which the exposition tonicizes a relatively stable mediant before the tonal process continues on to the dominant. But even in later sonata forms, expositions of the mode-shift type still outnumber Schubertian three-key patterns by a margin of 9 to 8. This is surprising in light of the presumed influence of Schubert, especially with respect to the first maturity.[22]

Although it is clear that Schubertian innovations had a decisive influence on Brahms's overall approach to sonata form, the younger composer's attention to alternative patterns of three-part organization suggests other sources of inspiration. The recent revival of a *Formenlehre* approach to late eighteenth-century music in the writings of the musicological team of James Hepokoski and Warren Darcy provides the background to explore these other possible sources. Their recent study of

Example 5.7. Brahms's Double Second Groups

Work	Key Plan: Exposition and Recap.	Harmonic Character of 1st Part of 2nd Group	Arrival of Middleground Harmonic Goal (Expo.)	Webster and Graybill Classification
First Maturity				
B♭-major sextet	B♭—A—F B♭—D—B♭	Unstable: hovers between A and F (but does have 2nd theme)	Beg. part 2 of 2nd group	Both
G-minor piano quartet	g—d—D G/g—E♭—g	Stable	Beg. part 1 of 2nd group	Both
A-major piano quartet (IV)	A—V^7/F—E A—V^7/B♭—A	Unstable: emphasis on V^7-Ger. duality (cf. mvt. II)	Beg. part 2 of 2nd group	Webster–yes Graybill–no
F-minor piano quintet	f—d♭——D♭ f—f♯—f—F—f	Stable	Beg. part 1 of 2nd group	Both
E-minor cello sonata	e—(C)—b—B e—(F)—e—E	Stable	Beg. part 1 of 2nd group	Both
E♭-major horn trio (IV)	E♭—b♭—B♭ E♭—e♭—E♭	Unstable: prolongs back-relating V/E♭ with no 2nd theme	Beg. part 2/closing theme	Both
Later Works				*Graybill Classification*
C-minor string quartet	c—e♭—E♭ c—c—C—c	Unstable: prolongs V/e♭	End part 2 of 2nd group	Yes
C-minor piano quartet (IV)	c—"e♭"—E♭ c—"c"—C—c (with Picardy 3rd)	Unstable: E♭ trapped within prolongation of opening tonic	End part 2 of 2nd group (anticipated by beg. part 2)	No

Continued on the next page

Example 5.7. *Continued*

Work	Key Plan: Exposition and Recap.	Harmonic Character of 1st Part of 2nd Group	Arrival of Middleground Harmonic Goal (Expo.)	Graybill Classification
C-minor symphony I	c—E♭—e♭ c—C—c (with Picardy 3rd)	Unstable: Multiple medial caesuras but no E♭ or 2nd theme	End part 2 of 2nd group (anticipated by beg. part 2)	Yes
IV	C—G—e —C—c—C	Stable	G: Beg. part 1 e: End part 2	Yes
D-major symphony	D—f♯—A D—b—D	Unstable: Some emphasis also on D and A (but does have 2nd theme)	End part 2 of 2nd group (anticipated by beg. part 2)	Yes
D-major violin concerto	D-—A———a D—(F♯)—D—d	Unstable (but does have 2nd theme)	End part 2 of 2nd group	Yes
C-major *Academic Festival Overture*	c/C—E——G C—C—(E♭)—C	Stable, but very brief	E: Beg. part 1 G: Counterstate-ment of part 1 theme	Yes
D-minor *Tragic Overture*	d—F—f —D—d	Stable	Beg. part 1 of 2nd group	No
B♭-major piano concerto	B♭—F——f B♭—B♭—b♭—B♭	Unstable	Part 2 of 2nd group, 3rd phrase	Yes
C-major piano trio (IV)	C—e—G C—a—C	Stable, but brief	e: Beg. part 1 G: Beg. part 2	Yes

Continued on the next page

Example 5.7. *Continued*

Work	Key Plan: Exposition and Recap.	Harmonic Character of 1st Part of 2nd Group	Arrival of Middleground Harmonic Goal (Expo.)	Graybill Classification
F-major symphony				
I	F—A—a F—D—d—F	Stable	Beg. part 1 of 2nd group	Yes
IV	f—C—c f—F—f	Unstable: Prolongs V/C (but does have 2nd theme)	Beg. part 2 of 2nd group	Yes
E-minor symphony	e—b—B e—e—E—e	Unstable: Prolongs V/b (but does have 2nd theme)	Beg. part 2 of 2nd group	Yes
F-major cello sonata	F—C—a F—F—d—F	Stable	C: Beg. part 1 a: End part 2	Yes
D-minor violin sonata (IV)	d—C—a d—F—d	Unstable: Immediately sequential (but does have 2nd theme)	End part 2 of 2nd group	No
A-minor clarinet trio	a—C—e a—F—a—A—a	Stable, but brief	C: Beg. part 1 e: Beg. part 2	Yes
F-minor clarinet sonata	f—D♭—c f—F—f (with Picardy 3rd)	Unstable: Prolongs D♭ as offshoot of opening F tonic *Stufe* (but does have 2nd theme)	End part 2 (anticipated by beg. part 2)	Yes

the medial caesura establishes a nuanced scheme of categorization for expository strategies in Classical sonata form and thus lays the groundwork for a more refined understanding of Brahms's practice.[23]

An exhaustive treatment of Brahms's exposition types would carry us beyond the scope of the present chapter. Indeed, the topic could easily blossom into a book-length study of its own. The focus here will be on organizational schemes within

a)

Common-Tone Modulation

F: $\hat{3}$ = A: $\hat{1}$

poco rit. - - - - - - - - - in tempo

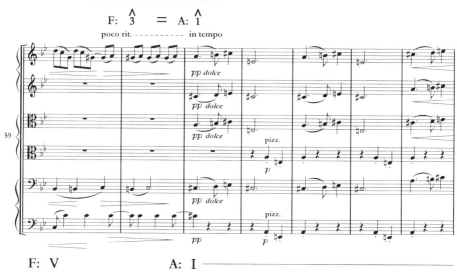

F: V   A: I

Example 5.8. Double Second Group in
(a) Brahms's B♭-Major Sextet
Continues on the next page

Example 5.8. Double Second Group in
(a) Brahms's B♭-Major Sextet

A: I   F:V⁷/IV   IV⁵ ⁻ ⁶   V   I

Example 5.8. Double Second Group in
(a) Brahms's B♭-Major Sextet

the mode-shift category. Attention to the mode-shift type is logical not simply because Brahms adopts a similar strategy in the exposition of the finale. It is also
appropriate because, in mode-shift expositions, Brahms is less directly in debt to
Schubert than in the case of other expository strategies. Indeed, it is not at all unusual for Classical-period composers to articulate a two-part second group through
a shift in mode. Comparison of Brahms's approach to eighteenth-century precedents will yield insights into formal expression unavailable if Schubert is taken to
be the sole model for his double second groups.

Instances of mode-shift division occur in such well-known works as the finale
of Mozart's F-Major Piano Sonata, K. 332, and Beethoven's *Pathétique* Sonata.
Example 5.9 (pp. 146–49) presents the beginning of the minor- and major-mode
sections from these two movements. Although Beethoven had a proclivity for this
technique in his early period, he also took advantage of it in some of his most
important later works, for instance, the *Appassionata* Sonata, also excerpted in Example 5.9 (p. 150). These three expositions demonstrate that mode shifts occur in
both major- and minor-mode works and that the shift may proceed from either
form of the secondary tonic.

The final segment of Example 5.9 (p. 152) outlines Brahms's adaptation of the
mode-shift strategy for the second key area of the piano quintet. It is not much of
a stretch to hear the quintet's secondary area within the same tradition as the mode
shift in the *Appassionata*. Similarities between the two works also include motivic
treatment of D♭–C neighbor figures within a common F-minor tonality, and a
number of striking similarities of formal organization in the exposition and recapitulation of main-theme material.[24] It is true that Brahms places his secondary
material in D♭, not the mediant like Beethoven, but Beethoven was also fond of the

Example 5.8. Double Second Group in
(b) Schubert's Cello Quintet

Example 5.8. Double Second Group in
(b) Schubert's Cello Quintet

Example 5.9. Secondary Areas Subdivided by Mode Shift in
(a) Mozart's Piano Sonata, K. 332

Example 5.9. Secondary Areas Subdivided by Mode Shift in
(a) Mozart's Piano Sonata, K. 332

submediant as a secondary key. He was also not shy about tonicizing chromatically altered *Stufen,* like the vi♭⁻♯ in the Brahms quintet. He articulates III♯ as a key area in the *Waldstein* Sonata, tonicizes VI♮ in both the *Hammerklavier* Sonata and the *Archduke* Trio, and moves to ♭VI for the secondary area in the exposition of his B♭-Major String Quartet, op. 130.

The two other minor-mode works from Brahms's first maturity that articulate three-part expositions—the G-minor piano quartet and the E-minor cello sonata—adapt the mode-shift strategy to tonicizations of the dominant. Classical-period composers make use of mode shifts within the dominant in major-mode works. The Mozart movement just mentioned is one example. Other examples from Beethoven include the C-Major Piano Sonata, op. 2, no. 3, the G-Major String Trio, op. 9, no. 1, and the A-Major String Quartet, op. 18, no. 5. The practice of consistently doing so in minor, however, would seem to be a peculiarly Brahmsian idiosyncrasy. The mode shift in the dominant of the C-minor piano quartet's scherzo, mentioned at the outset of this chapter, therefore reflects a personal stylistic tendency. Even though the shift in the scherzo does not occur in a sonata context, it follows an approach to key relations that Brahms engages in many of his minor-mode sonata forms.

For Haydn, Mozart, and Beethoven, a dominant key area in minor remains exceptional, regardless of the separate issue of a mode shift.[25] And although Schubert often closes minor-mode expositions in the dominant—for example, in the *Death and the Maiden* quartet and the *Quartettsatz*—the V *Stufe* typically follows an intermediate key. A basic three-part layout normally does not arise through a mode shift. The motion from major to minor within the third part of the *Death and the Maiden* exposition is a special case for Schubert. For Brahms, motion to the dominant without an intervening third relation as well as the division of V via a mode shift are common options in the minor mode.

Be this as it may, similarities between Brahms's mode-shift strategies and the approach of his eighteenth-century forebears extend beyond generalities of key scheme and modal inflection. Brahms, like the Viennese classicists, often plays with conventions governing medial caesuras in these mode-shift expositions to create formal ambiguities and tonal delays. With this mutual play with convention in mind, we can refine our understanding of Schubert's influence on Brahms. There is little doubt that Schubert developed expository strategies that represent innovations apart from the traditions of formal multivalence that are the topic of the presb)

Example 5.9. Secondary Areas Subdivided by Mode Shift in
(b) Beethoven's *Pathétique* Sonata

ent discussion. It also seems clear that Brahms absorbed some of these innovations into his own sonata practice.

Yet it is also the case that Brahms—and perhaps Schubert as well—participated in a more all-embracing tradition of play with conventions of medial articulation that dates back to the eighteenth century. The distinction is important because interpretation of an exposition that revolves around traditional ambiguities of medial articulation will differ from analysis of an exposition that carves out new approaches to expository relationships. Movements like the opening Allegro of Brahms's First Symphony or the finales of his C-minor piano quartet and horn trio create formal expressivity through engagement with a different set of conventions than pieces like his B♭ sextet and Schubert's cello quintet.

Example 5.9. Secondary Areas Subdivided by Mode Shift in
(b) Beethoven's *Pathétique* Sonata

Generally speaking, there are two ways in which thematic design and structure interact in the context of a mode-shift exposition. In the first case, a single middleground *Stufe*—the local tonic for the exposition's second key—controls the area in which the mode shift occurs. In the second case, the first part of the mode shift participates in a delay of the goal *Stufe* until the arrival of the second part. The Mozart movement in Example 5.9 (p. 146) provides an instance of the first type. As the graph in Example 5.10 indicates (p. 154), the exposition's middleground C *Stufe* enters along with the minor-mode material at m. 50 and remains in control across the shift to major at m. 65.

Beethoven's *Pathétique* falls into the second subcategory. Although the thematic entrance at m. 51 follows a B♭ medial caesura, its E♭ chord of departure is in $^6_4$ position. Indeed, B♭ persists in the bass across the entire opening phrase. In addition,

c)

Example 5.9. Secondary Areas Subdivided by Mode Shift in
(c) Beethoven's *Appassionata* Sonata

the passage very quickly becomes sequential and modulatory. The result is that an E♭ *Stufe* enters only at the shift to E♭ major at m. 89. Example 5.11 (p. 154) reproduces Ernst Oster's graph of this process of delay.[26]

The Mozart and Beethoven movements also provide prototypical examples of a type of thematic treatment characteristic of mode-shift contexts. In both expositions the more arresting melodic idea enters at the first part of the secondary area. The second part is marked by more generic material that initiates a drive toward closure. The contrast of thematic material helps to articulate a sharp division between the two sections. Reciprocally, the minor-mode inflection provides an intensity of expression that helps make the first of the themes more characteristic.

The Beethoven movement also demonstrates a typical way in which thematic contrast can contribute to the potential for formal multivalence. From the perspective of thematic rhetoric, the *Pathétique*'s characteristic passage at m. 51 signals the beginning of the secondary area. This intuition is contradicted, however, by the B♭ pedal and the subsequent sequential treatment of the material. The more generic idea of m. 89, on the other hand, finally provides the arrival of the middleground harmony normally in control from the outset of a secondary group. But its thematic character signals the final push toward closure—the beginning of the end of the exposition as it were.

Example 5.9. Secondary Areas Subdivided by Mode Shift in
(c) Beethoven's *Appassionata* Sonata

The shift to major thus has a dual meaning. It partly confirms the notion that the earlier thematic entrance was too unstable to initiate the secondary area, but it also partly supports the perception that the earlier point was in fact the beginning of the subordinate section. At no point does Beethoven allow us to settle comfortably into a univalent interpretation, a significant source of dynamism for this music.[27] Thus although I agree with Oster's structural analysis in Example 5.11, I take exception to his statement that "the initial 'Eb minor' $^6_4$ chord [at the beginning of the characteristic passage] has nothing to do with Eb minor."[28] Rather, I prefer to use principles of analysis based on dimensional counterpoint to assert a key-scheme relationship between the Eb-minor phrase at m. 51 and the later arrival of Eb major, despite the absence of a voice-leading connection.

The exposition of the finale of Brahms's horn trio—the only work that we have

d)

Example 5.9. Secondary Areas Subdivided by Mode Shift in
(d) Brahms's Piano Quintet

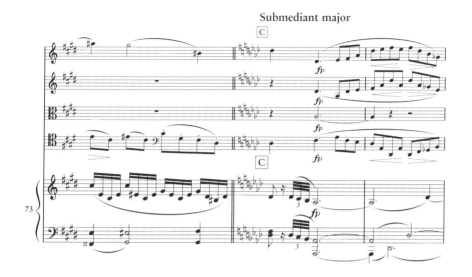

Example 5.9. Secondary Areas Subdivided by Mode Shift in
(d) Brahms's Piano Quintet

yet to mention from the first-maturity section of Example 5.7 (p. 138)—creates a
tonal delay similar to the situation in the *Pathétique*. The trio also provides an example of a type of thematic treatment distinct from the Mozart and Beethoven
examples, but nevertheless also characteristic of the Classical era. Example 5.12
(p. 155–58) provides a score excerpt of the relevant passage. Webster and Graybill
both include the trio in their discussions of three-key movements, and its exposition does indeed fall into three parts: a tonic area (mm. 1–44); a contrasting middle
section in the dominant minor (mm. 45–82); and a third part in the dominant

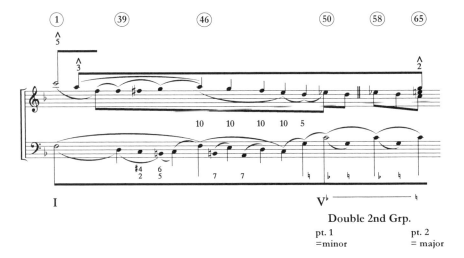

Example 5.10. Middleground Graph for Exposition of Mozart, K. 332

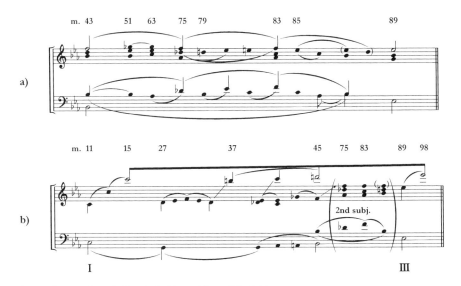

Example 5.11. Oster's Graph for Exposition of *Pathétique*

major (mm. 83–90.1). The voice-leading graph in Example 5.13 (p. 159) outlines the relationship between these formal parts and the exposition's middleground structure.

As with all mode-shift expositions, Webster and Graybill are careful to point out that the three-part division does not articulate three distinct keys. It should also be noted, in fairness to Webster, that he does not subject the trio to close analysis, but rather mentions it only in passing as part of the peroration of his Schubert/Brahms

Example 5.12. Secondary Area of Horn Trio Finale
Continues on the next page

Example 5.12. Secondary Area of Horn Trio Finale

Example 5.12. Secondary Area of Horn Trio Finale
Continues on the next page

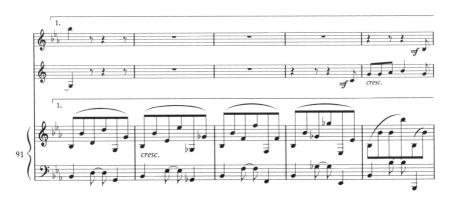

Example 5.12. Secondary Area of Horn Trio Finale

study. He nevertheless refers to the trio in a context in which he argues for the persistence of Schubert's influence on works of the later first maturity.[29] Moreover, two of the three examples from the first maturity that Webster does explore in detail—the piano quintet and the G-minor piano quartet—are of the mode-shift variety.[30]

Yet in neither of these movements does Brahms follow any of the other strategies that Webster identifies as Schubertian innovations. The movements do not hesitate to leave the tonic, modulate abruptly or by common tone, prepare a key different than the one they arrive at, avoid V of the secondary key as transitional goal, or refer back to the tonic before pushing on to the third part. Furthermore, Brahms's choice of $vi^{\flat-\natural}$ as a key area in the quintet can be traced as easily to Beethoven as to Schubert, while the quartet's mode shift in the dominant reflects Brahms's own standard practice, as already discussed. These factors indicate that the two-part division of the secondary area must stand at the center of Webster's argument (along with perhaps the ABA′ design of the main theme in the quartet), despite the fact that there is clear Classical precedent for the mode-shift option.

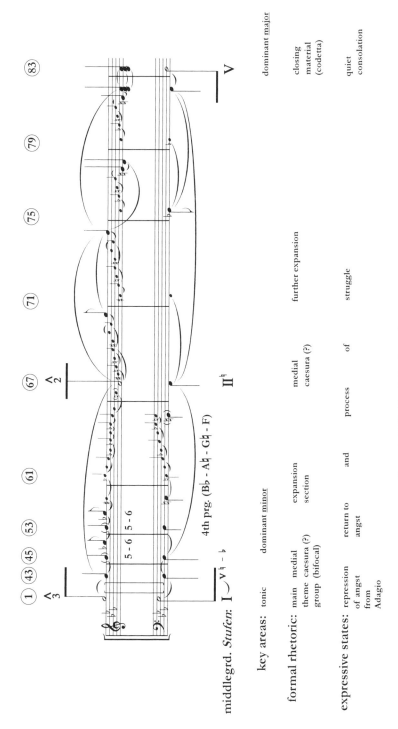

Example 5.13. Graph for Secondary Area in Horn Trio

But to return to the horn trio, Graybill is closer to the mark when he suggests that the movement's formal characteristics are in many respects closely modeled after strategies of the late eighteenth century.[31] The movement has an overall neo-Classical character, in no small degree a consequence of the hunt and pastoral topics that inform its musical materials. The Classicizing tone also extends to aspects of the tonal structure. As Example 5.12 highlights, the first part of the exposition ends at m. 43 with a bifocal close—that old eighteenth-century alternative to a modulatory transition in which an arrival on the home dominant functions as medial caesura.[32] Most commonly this type of medial articulation is followed by the entrance of a second theme immediately in the dominant key, so that the new tonal center, although not prepared by a modulation, asserts itself at the outset of the exposition's second part. Brahms, however, chooses to exploit an alternative approach, which nevertheless also has its roots in the eighteenth century.

Although Webster interprets the B♭-minor passage at m. 45 as a Schubertian middle section, the passage's formal rhetoric centers around the late eighteenth-century strategy that Hepokoski and Darcy call bait-and-switch.[33] In order to understand bait-and-switch principles, it is first necessary to have in mind two general types of exposition in the Classical tradition: the standard two-part design and the Haydnesque alternative of a continuous exposition. In the familiar two-part type, a clearly defined medial caesura is followed by a thematically and tonally stable secondary area. A continuous exposition, by contrast, is noteworthy for the absence of either of these features. The tonic area merges into an unstable *Fortspinnung* section, which comes to rest only with the arrival of closing material toward the end of the exposition.[34] The bait-and-switch strategy plays off a listener's response to musical cues that normally signal which of these two types of exposition is underway. What at first appears to be a medial cadence—a surefire indicator that a two-part exposition has been launched—is denied that status when an expansion section, rather than second-theme rhetoric, ensues.

This is precisely what happens in the horn trio, as annotations in Example 5.12 highlight. Brahms leads us to believe that we have arrived at the dividing point for a two-part exposition, only to shift to a continuous pattern with the entrance of unstable material in B♭ minor. Note the contrast with the *Pathétique*. In Beethoven's movement, second-theme rhetoric emerges following the medial caesura, regardless of the tonal instability. In Brahms's movement, the instability is thematic as well as tonal.

The sense of reversal at this point in a bait-and-switch exposition is perhaps even more salient for Brahms than for his Classical forebears, given the role of the lyrical second theme in nineteenth-century descriptions of sonata form. Although recent thinking about sonata form tends to downplay this concept as it relates to eighteenth-century repertoire, the notion remains historically valid for the Romantic era. Nineteenth-century *Formenlehre* provides evidence of the powerful expectations for an arresting idea at the arrival of the second key. It must have been all the more striking for Brahms's audience when he circumvents this convention.

Brahms continues to encourage retrospective formal reevaluation when he uses the B♭-minor passage to lead to a big arrival on the dominant of B♭ major, in the manner of a modulating transition. As Example 5.13 outlines, it is not until this second medial articulation, at m. 67, that the tonal structure makes a middleground move away from the opening E♭ *Stufe*. The voice leading thus suggests that the thematic entrance at m. 83 constitutes the true onset of the second key, and therefore that the earlier bifocal articulation represents a false medial caesura.

Yet, on the other hand, when he does resolve the F dominant at m. 83, it is just seventeen measures before the end of the exposition and with material of closing character. Thus there is yet a further element of retrospective reevaluation: perhaps that bifocal close at about the halfway point of the exposition (47 percent) really did signal the onset of the secondary area. In the final analysis, the formal rhetoric shuns the idea of an unambiguous decision regarding *the* medial cadence or *the* entrance of the second key. Brahms's compositional strategy, like Beethoven's, centers on a dynamic process in which the meaning of formal signals fluctuates.

Although skeptics might concede that the dynamic process Brahms creates in the horn trio owes more to eighteenth-century traditions than to Schubertian innovations, they might also argue that the trio represents a special case. Given the overall Classicizing tone of the movement, it is not surprising that the exposition adopts strategies of three-part organization traceable to Haydn, Mozart, and Beethoven. Similar ambiguities of key articulation, however, inform other, less overtly Classicizing, double second groups, including the secondary material from the finale of the C-minor piano quartet. Similar to the trio, the quartet delays the arrival of the exposition's goal *Stufe* until the third part. Yet by contrast, Brahms presents at least the beginnings of second-theme rhetoric earlier at m. 55 with the entrance of what I have previously referred to as appassionata material. In this sense, the finale is more like the *Pathétique* movement. The situation is complicated by the unusual means through which Brahms blurs the crossover into the secondary material. As already noted, he modulates abruptly through reinterpretation of vi/C as iv/E♭, but he does so without recourse to a modulating dominant. He simply allows the bass to slip down a half step and sneaks in an E♭$^6_3$ chord as point of departure.

One source of coherence for this bass motion derives from its connection to A♭ neighbor gestures in the main theme and transition. Example 5.14 illustrates. The A♭–G progression also reflects the trend in the quartet to engage $\hat{5}$–$\hat{6}$ neighbor motives at important points of formal articulation or overlap. Chapter 3 demonstrated that $\hat{5}$–$\hat{6}$ motions are crucial components of the blurred reprises in the first and third movements. The scherzo, by contrast, clearly articulates its main-theme return in part through a resolution of A♭ to G. We will see that, in the finale, idiosyncratic treatment of the motive occurs not only at the beginning of the appassionata theme but also at the arrival of the exposition's third part. At both locations the dyad participates in a process of delay that pushes the arrival of the E♭ *Stufe* ahead to the close of the exposition.

The connection between the bass motion and the neighbor figure represents just one type of motivic relationship that Brahms exploits at the arrival of the appassionata theme. In this first type of relationship, an untransposed repetition undergoes functional reinterpretation due to changed tonal circumstances. The A♭–G

Example 5.14. A♭–G Motive in Exposition

pitch-class pairing remains invariant as does the neighbor relationship between the pitches. What changes is the scale degree identity of the motive: $\hat{6}$–$\hat{5}$ is reinterpreted as $\hat{4}$–$\hat{3}$.

In the second type of motivic relationship, a figure returns in transposed form in a new key, such that degree identity becomes the basis for a connection. This occurs when the $\hat{6}$–$\hat{5}$ motive returns in the E♭ section as a C–B♭ figure. The transposed version begins to emerge in the accompanimental pattern of mm. 51–55, as highlighted in Example 5.15 (p. 165). The example traces how the motive then becomes increasingly more prominent as the appassionata theme unfolds, culmi-

Example 5.14. A♭–G Motive in Exposition
Continues on the next page

nating in the C–C♭–B♭ motion in the top voice just prior to the entrance of the chorale. The chorale itself also contains multiple repetitions of the figure, as shown in the example.

All of these transposed repetitions take on heightened significance in the recapitulation. There the return of the secondary material in the tonic transforms the functionally based connections of the exposition into connections of the pitch-specific kind. Example 5.16 demonstrates (p. 165). Conversely, what had been untransposed A♭–G repetitions lose some of their motivic salience. Because they return as F–E♮ dyads in the recapitulation, they share neither pitch identity nor $\hat{6}$–$\hat{5}$ status with the original form of the neighbor motive.

Before we return to issues of form and key articulation, one final point should

c)

Example 5.14. A♭–G Motive in Exposition

be made about motivic processes. It relates to the fact that the E♭ passages of the exposition include both diatonic and chromatic forms of the 6̂–5̂ motive. The inclusion of ♭6̂ in these passages enriches the web of motivic connections. Example 5.17 (p. 166) outlines an additional relationship with the head motive of the finale's main theme and even with the final melodic gestures of the Andante. A salient factor in this strand of motivic continuity is the concomitant change in the status of B♮/C♭ from chordal fifth, to leading tone, to chromatic neighbor or passing tone. Connections that arise via the B♮/C♭ enharmonic relationship as well as the 6̂–5̂ figure have important consequences for expressive interpretation. The discussion here merely lays the groundwork for the exploration of these expressive implications in Chapter 6.

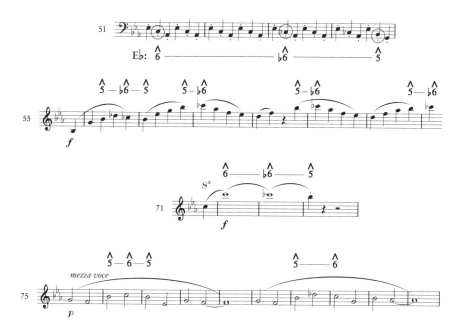

Example 5.15. C–B♭ Motive

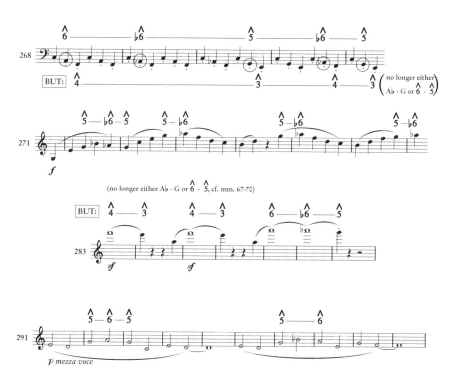

Example 5.16. Recapitulation of Motivic Relationships

Example 5.17. Motivic Connections Involving B♮/C♭ Enharmonic Relationship

For now, let us return to the unusual formal articulation at the entrance of the appassionata theme and interpretation of the exposition's double second group. The idea of beginning a key area with a first-inversion triad, although certainly not the most common option in the Viennese tradition, does have significant precedent.[35] What is more strikingly unconventional about the passage in Brahms's finale is the absence of a dominant as preparation for the entrance of the new formal section. As Chapter 2 suggested, the crossover into E♭ nevertheless mimics the kind of textural articulation associated with a medial caesura. Following a dramatic buildup of energy and liquidation of motivic content, A♭ arrives as a kind of impostor medial harmony. The articulation of a new tonic with a thematic entrance then marks the beginning of the subsequent section. Even the repetitions of the A♭ chord can be heard in relation to eighteenth-century precedent: they fill the gap of silence that more conventionally divides the arrival of a medial dominant and the entrance of a new key area—the technique that Hepokoski and Darcy call caesura-fill.[36] Precisely this type of caesura-fill occurs at the authentic medial caesura at mm. 73–74.

Although we have seen that the thematic layout of the finale is similar to the pattern in the *Pathétique,* the tonal situation is more like the middleground structure in the horn trio. Brahms first hints at the second key at the beginning of the appassionata theme, but the tonic *Stufe* remains in control. This was a central point of the discussion of dimensional counterpoint in the finale in Chapter 2. As the graph in Example 5.18 outlines, it is not until the B♭ dominant enters in m. 73 that there is a middleground motion toward E♭ as a structural harmony. In the *Pathétique,* the middleground V/III enters much earlier, at the end of the transition.

The delayed arrival of E♭ is only one aspect of a complex process of multivalence in which multiple formal functions arise through conflicting signals in the musical narrative. The process begins as far back as the passage that leads into the impostor A♭ medial harmony. This section (mm. 35–51) is characterized by transitional thematic character, but it remains in the tonic key. The conflict is intensified by the fact that the continued presence of the overriding middleground C *Stufe* is felt directly on the foreground. Note in this regard the C-minor arrivals in mm. 43 and 45. These C-minor tonics prepare the articulations of the A♭ pivot in mm. 47 and 49 so that they clearly sound as deceptive progressions in the home key.

As has already been noted, the entrance of the appassionata theme has some of the character of the beginning of a key area. Yet it is only after this thematic beginning that the harmonic structure makes its way to a key-defining dominant at mm. 58 and 60. In other words, Brahms presents a theme that articulates a transitional harmonic motion and thus functions in part as a bridge theme. But even this tonal signal and the resulting formal message prove illusory, since the progressions to the B♭ dominant reside on the foreground. Moreover, the theme enters too late to function as an unequivocal transition theme. It not only follows a mock medial caesura, but also arrives just beyond the midpoint of the exposition (56 percent), two signals for second-theme status.

Yet no matter how the theme is interpreted—either as second theme proper or as transitional theme—the C *Stufe* remains in effect on the middleground. This

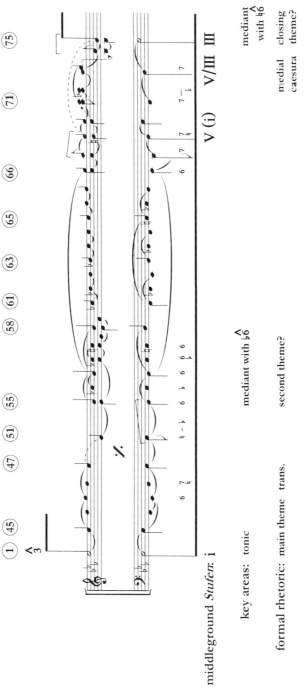

Example 5.18. Middleground Graph of Secondary Area

would indicate that, at least from one crucial perspective, the material is neither bridge nor second theme. It is important to observe, however, that the C tonicity fades from the foreground during the E♭ appassionata passage, in contrast to the situation in the earlier nonmodulating transition. The E♭ progressions therefore have more form-defining potential, at least in a local context. Not until the turn back to the home key at mm. 67–70 does it become clear that the E♭ motion merely feints at a more decisive move yet to come. Put otherwise, analysis by theme and key supports two possible formal interpretations, while middleground tonal structure dictates yet a third.[37]

A final formal duality is manifest in the chorale, which presents a conflict between functions as second theme and closing theme. The material finally articulates a root-position E♭ harmony as point of departure for the first two of its phrases. One way to interpret this E♭ expansion is as initiation of the middleground mediant *Stufe* that has thus far failed to emerge. A reading along these lines appears in Example 5.18. Although I believe that the idea of middleground E♭ control ultimately proves unsatisfactory, it is certainly a reasonable interpretation that some aspects of the music appear to justify.

First and foremost, the chorale entrance follows directly from the B♭ structural dominant that stands as the culmination of the previous passage. In addition, details of voice leading can be marshaled in support of the idea that the chorale resolves instabilities of the appassionata section. From this perspective, the chorale corrects some of the problems of the earlier ambivalent passage and thus functions as a stable formal area, perhaps even a second theme. One way in which this occurs is through a shift from the urgency and pain of free dissonance treatment in the sequential passages of mm. 61–66 to the more conventional voice leading of the chorale.

Somewhat more complex is the manner in which the tonal structure reengages the A♭–G motive. Brahms transfers the figure into the top voice in mm. 67–70 as part of the climactic buildup to the authentic medial caesura. Crucially, this occurs at the point that the tonal structure touches back on C minor via rearticulation of its G dominant harmony. It is as if to say: all that previous E♭ activity was illusory; now we must return to our original C-minor key, pick up our 6̂–5̂ motive, and proceed properly to the mediant. As the graph in Example 5.18 shows, A♭ moves into an inner voice when the progression shifts to E♭ major. (At this point a C–[C♭]–B♭ version of the 6̂–5̂ motive reaches over into the top registral position.) A♭ reemerges in the top voice again at the end of m. 74. In the reading of Example 5.18, this A♭ resolves to G at the entrance of the chorale. The idea here is that more generic treatment of the A♭–G motive corrects the earlier anomalies of its bass-line appearance at m. 54. This correction contributes to the sense in which the chorale provides a delayed resolution of ambiguities in the earlier medial articulation.

Articulation of G as melodic point of departure has additional significance with respect to the question of whether the chorale functions as secondary or closing theme. A local 3̂ in the top voice makes the E♭ tonic sound more like a point of departure for a key area than for a closing theme. A closing theme typically enters with the arrival of 1̂/I, at a point of formal overlap with the end of the main body of the secondary area. In the finale there is a caesura-fill between the dominant arrival and the entrance of the tonic, not an overlap of sections. Recall that caesura-fill is one of the typical means of articulation at the beginning of a secondary area.

Moreover, a structural descent from $\hat{3}$ occurs across the chorale with $\hat{1}/I$ arriving in mm. 93–94. This melodic motion creates a crucial distinction between the chorale and the similarly ambiguous theme at the end of the exposition in the horn trio. In the trio the third part presents no descending motion from F, as indicated in Example 5.13. The middleground melodic stasis contributes to a closing character, even though the section provides the first articulation of the B♭ *Stufe*. The scales are therefore tipped more clearly toward a codetta function than is the case in the quartet.

The quartet's chorale theme nevertheless has the compactness and simplicity of closing material. It also enters too late—after approximately three-fourths of the exposition have passed (76.5 percent)—and after too much second-theme rhetoric in the appassionata material, to function as a straightforward second theme. Moreover, unlike mm. 113–21 of the *Pathétique*, the finale includes no codetta material following the third part of the exposition. Rather, Brahms sustains formal multivalence all the way to the end of the exposition.[38]

Additional aspects of this sustained multivalence give rise to my aforementioned doubts about the reading shown in Example 5.18. Despite its importance to interpretation of the chorale, the graph reflects only a partial view of the passage's complexity. For although it traces voice-leading continuities across the formal hinge, it fails to respond to some powerful idiosyncrasies of the material. Indeed, Brahms extends the idea of tonal delay across the chorale, as part of the multivalence of the passage. The arrival of the chorale may not be quite as strange as the crossover into the appassionata theme, but it falls well short of the standard formal articulation implied by the graph.

The peculiarity flows from the way in which foreground details work against the factors cited in support of the normative resolution outlined in Example 5.18. Note in particular the abrupt shifts across mm. 74 and 75 in the dimensions of dynamics, rhythmic patterning, articulation, and instrumentation. These elements of discontinuity prevent the E♭ chord from providing the sense of arrival that should accompany a middleground resolution. Instead there is a feeling that the bottom has dropped out precisely at the point that the music has led us to expect a moment of fulfillment.

A more sensitive interpretation does not discount the view presented by the graph in Example 5.18. Rather, it absorbs the idea of resolution as a potential that Brahms evokes but ultimately denies in favor of a further delay until the chorale's closing cadence (m. 93). This alternative interpretation appears in Example 5.19. It is important to note that even at the close of the chorale, Brahms sustains tension until the bitter end by staggering points of resolution in the different voices. The violin and viola present 7–8 and 4–3 suspensions above the cello's V–I bass motion, and the piano maintains the rhythmic activity even further until the arrival of its low E♭ at m. 95. Moreover, even the low E♭ is less than fully satisfactory. By the time it enters the strings have dropped out so that hollow octaves mark the moment of

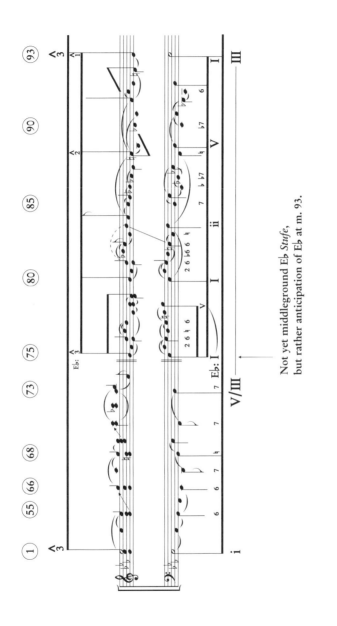

Example 5.19. Alternative Interpretation of Secondary Area

arrival. These octaves are themselves disturbed by the intrusion of a grating D♮ and the adumbration of the main theme in the strings.

The passage thus constitutes yet another example of Brahms's by now familiar practice of conflating three formal functions: the delayed arrival of a middle-ground harmony normally expected at the beginning of a section, structural closure for that section, and the initiation of a transition to a subsequent formal unit. The sense of denial throughout the chorale also reflects the tendency in the quartet for Brahms to carry his compositional strategies to extremes that push beyond even his own proclivity for tension and multivalence. This strategic excess suggests expressive rather than purely structural motivations, as has already been noted. On the face of it, the finale's secondary material may not appear as exceptional in its tonal characteristics as the dominant focus for the recapitulation in the first movement. But it does indeed present the same type of conflict among dimensions that characterizes much of the quartet.

A central point of this chapter has been that consideration of the diversity of eighteenth-century sonata conventions can lead to greater insight into Brahms's double second groups. It hardly counts as an original insight to argue that Brahms absorbed Schubertian innovations into a practice based solidly on the Viennese Classical tradition. What is remarkable is that Brahms still manages to draw on eighteenth-century precedents even within one of the areas in which Schubert's influence is presumably strongest. His responsiveness to the range of expository strategies established by Haydn, Mozart, and Beethoven—in addition to more distinctly Schubertian alternatives—demonstrates his famously deep insight into the music of his precursors. Rather than limit himself to an outlook that hears only Classical two-part expositions on the one hand or Schubertian three-key expositions on the other, Brahms absorbs all of the subtlety and variety of his predecessors into his own compositional voice. Our challenge remains to respond to his music—as well as to the music of the tradition that he loved—with a comparable degree of sensitivity.

Up to this point, issues surrounding double second groups have been dealt with in terms of abstract formal relationships. The impact of this type of exposition can also reverberate beyond issues of form to engage the emotional content of a movement or even an entire multimovement cycle. Dramatic contrasts between sections of a bipartite secondary area are an important resource for expression in a piece like the piano quartet. Although the topic of expression will be taken up in earnest only in Chapter 6, it will be helpful to lay some groundwork here with respect to the expressive potential of double second groups. The finale of the horn trio provides a useful starting point for the discussion. The final section of this chapter will then move on to compare the expressive meaning of bipartite secondary areas in the First Symphony with Brahms's approach in the piano quartet.

As we have seen, Brahms composes the trio's secondary material to delay the arrival of the exposition's goal B♭ *Stufe* until the final codetta-like section. The delay, however, is not only significant with respect to the counterpoint between formal design and middleground structure. The contrast of material in the secondary

Example 5.20. Elaboration of vii°⁷ Chord in Secondary Material

area helps to mark the articulation at m. 83 not merely as a delayed point of harmonic resolution but as an expression of emotional consolation. The idea is that the emotional difficulties of the main body of the secondary area give way after some struggle to the inner peace of the closing section.

This interpretation is not merely fanciful, I believe, but rather can be grounded by reference to specific technical aspects of Brahms's material. Attention to these technical aspects will bring us closer to the structural individuality of the movement, while simultaneously opening up interpretation of expressive content. From a generic perspective, the shift from minor to major constitutes an obvious source for the emotional transformation, as does the progression from the tension of a tonal delay to the release provided by resolution. Yet the expressive shift also results from more idiosyncratic characteristics particular to the trio.

The first hint of emotional disquiet, following the carefree romp of the tonic area's hunt material, emerges just after the onset of the B♭-minor section at m. 45. Although the passage begins with a major ⁶₃ chord instead of a darker-sounding minor tonic, it quickly becomes mired in the expanded vii°⁷ harmony of mm. 49–52. (The major ⁶₃ chord is an apparent G♭ triad. It does not function as an inversion of a G♭⁵₃, but arises instead out of an implied 5–6 contrapuntal motion over B♭, as shown in Example 5.13 (p. 159).) Brahms heightens the expressive tension of the fully diminished sonority—its tendency to be associated with emotional angst due to its high degree of dissonance—through emphasis on the neighbor motions highlighted in Example 5.20. Of special significance are the neighbor figures in the piano: minor 5̂–6̂ motions traditionally have stood as symbols for suffering or lamentation. Observe also the major-second clash of the chordal C against the B♭ pedal in the left-hand part of the piano.

The repetitive structure of this first phrase of the secondary area contributes to a feeling that the anguish that begins to emerge here will not be dispensed with easily. The second phrase at m. 53 only heightens the effect. It begins just as the first phrase had, but the major ⁶₃ chord almost immediately collapses into a darker minor sonority. A shift to angry *forte* and *marcato* following the *piano* and *legato* of the previous material complements this sudden change in color. The continuation tonicizes G♭ minor, now enharmonically respelled as F♯ and in root position. The effect is to make the painful yet more palpable. In addition to emphasis through tonicization, the repetitions of the $\hat{5}$–$\hat{6}$ neighbor (F–G♭), briefly reinterpreted as a $\hat{7}$–$\hat{8}$ alternation (E♯–F♯), become even more incessant. Note also the rhythmic dissonance created by the syncopated pattern and the shift of the neighbor motive into the more extreme upper register. The result is a progression from mere hints of disquiet in the opening phrase to more urgent cries of anguish in the second.

The local $\hat{7}$–$\hat{8}$ alternations return to their original $\hat{5}$–$\hat{6}$ function and spelling as the passage shifts back to B♭ minor for its climax and dramatic descent in mm. 61–66.1. It is perhaps no coincidence that this high point of expressive tension corresponds with repetitions of the $\hat{5}$–$\hat{6}$ alternation now in the registrally highest voice, given the aforementioned association of this figure with pain or angst.

The passage is able to pull itself together only abruptly at the arrival of the middleground V/V chord at m. 67. Yet this moment of harmonic clarity cannot by itself put to rest the anguish of the preceding passage. The exposition needs more time to recover, and Brahms therefore expands V/V via further development of the $\hat{5}$–$\hat{6}$ motive in both the top voice and bass, as shown in Example 5.13. It is interesting to note that the shift to G♮ at the beginning of the passage helps to alleviate some of the suffering that arose via emphasis on G♭ in the previous section. Measures 67–74 certainly are more settled than what has preceded them, despite Brahms's further deferral of B♭ resolution.

G♭'s threat nevertheless remains real: ♭$\hat{6}$ returns in the bass of mm. 75–80. It is only at the last minute, with the long-delayed resolution to B♭, that the exposition is able to put to rest this source of anxiety. Moreover, G♭ is not all that the closing material puts to rest. The codetta replaces the aggressive rhythmic dissonance and *forte marcato* of the crisis point with a gentle three-against-two pattern sung out *piano dolce*. It also transforms the earlier passage's clashing B♭ pedal into an anchor of emotional calm. It is in this sense that the arrival of the closing material does not merely articulate a moment of harmonic resolution: it expresses emotional consolation following the torment of the previous harmonic delay.

This much seems clear, perhaps, but several questions remain unanswered. What is a possible motivation for the angst in the B♭-minor passage? And does the treatment of this angst in the finale have any larger significance for the work as a whole? The answers to these questions are interrelated. Although no explicit statement from Brahms survives in his correspondence or elsewhere, the Adagio mesto movement of the trio has been interpreted, along with the *German Requiem,* as Brahms's artistic response to the death of his beloved mother. Given the time of the work's completion—1865, the year of Brahms's mother's death—the *mesto* designation, and not least the elegiac tone of the movement, this seems to be a reasonable conjecture.

If we can accept an interpretation of the slow movement as a lament on the death of a loved one, then the sunny jocularity of the finale might indicate the potential solace that a retreat into the natural world can offer. A relationship along these lines is anticipated within the Adagio itself. Within the movement's A′ section, Brahms briefly allows a ray of light to shine through via anticipation of the finale's hunt theme in mm. 59–60.1 and 63–64.1.[39] Yet that is all these measures represent—rays of hope that cannot be sustained within the Adagio's overall expressive trajectory.

Following a final *passionata* climax on the movement's main theme at m. 69, the Adagio concludes in a state of deep despair. The hunt and pastoral music that dominates the finale provides a jarring contrast to this despondency. Indeed, the abrupt expressive shift might strike some listeners as unconvincing. How is it possible after the emotional intensity of the Adagio to achieve such a positive outlook without a more gradual transition from mourning to recovery?

In this context, the outburst of angst in the Bb-minor passage functions as a signal that the high spirits of the movement may not be as secure as they first appear. The hunt material of the tonic area could even perhaps represent a kind of overcompensation in a struggle with painful emotions. The feeling of consolation in the exposition's closing material would then constitute a more emotionally convincing response. The closing material follows a return, in the Bb-minor section, to the angst that had been repressed in the tonic area, and it achieves its inner peace as the culmination of a gradual process. The closing material also soothes through understatement and thus seems more emotionally secure than the romp in the countryside that enters without preparation at the outset of the movement.

The recapitulation brings the process of healing even closer to home, as it were, through the standard transposition of secondary material into the tonic key. The transposition works its effect in two ways. First, it reorients the first part of the double second group around Eb minor at m. 213, specifically recalling the key of the Adagio mesto. Second, it puts the resolution of the passage's tension at m. 251 into the home key and thus binds it more intimately with the hunt material of the tonic area. A connection with the tonic area becomes more explicit when the brief transition of mm. 259–62 leads from the closing material into the hunt material of the coda. In the coda the hunt material reaches an even higher degree of jubilation. Its emotional exuberance nevertheless finally comes across as convincing because the coda helps to sustain a restoration of positive feeling that has been earned rather than willed.

The example of the horn trio demonstrates the importance a mode shift across secondary material can have for expressive interpretation. The connection between the Adagio mesto and the death of Brahms's mother also highlights the significance of Eb minor as a key to which Brahms would turn to express difficult emotions of possible personal significance. We will see in Chapter 6 that Eb plays a similar role in the piano quartet. The key is also significant for the First Symphony, a work whose relationship with the quartet has already been noted. Yet although the quartet and the symphony share some compositional and biographical attributes, the differences in the way they treat the expressive potential of a double second group are as striking as the similarities. A comparison of these differences will help to illuminate critical aspects of the two works.

A good place to begin is with the first movement of the symphony. It will be necessary to continue briefly with discussion of abstract formal relationships before it will be possible to address issues of expression. Although I did not draw attention to the point in Chapter 2, the movement's exposition provides another example of Brahms's affinity for mode-shift conventions of the Classical era. The symphony's secondary area, like the trio's and quartet's, falls into two parts (mm. 121 and 157), both oriented around the mediant key. The trajectory here, however, is from major to minor.

It will be helpful to reconsider the analysis of Chapter 2 in light of the mode shift idea. A glance back at Example 2.4d (p. 39) will bring back to mind salient aspects of counterpoint between thematic design, key scheme, and structural bass discussed in Chapter 2. In general terms, the symphony's secondary area unfolds somewhat more along the lines of the mode shift in the horn trio, rather than in either the quartet or the *Pathétique* sonata. Like all three of these movements, it delays the arrival of its expository tonal goal, in this case via the large-scale B♭–G–E♭ bass arpeggiation outlined in Example 2.4d. What it shares with the horn trio, in particular, is the absence of a melodically distinct second theme and the resulting suggestion of a continuous exposition. (In both the *Pathétique* sonata and quartet, recall that second-theme rhetoric emerges at the midpoint of the exposition despite middleground tonal delay.) Yet, as is often the case in eighteenth-century examples and in the trio, this continuous character in the symphony involves periodic suggestions of two-part rhetoric in the manner of a bait-and-switch approach.

A bait-and-switch strategy is initiated by the brief modulatory passage and dramatically articulated arrival of the middleground B♭ dominant harmony in mm. 89–96.1—both straightforward signs of a medial caesura. Brahms luxuriously expands this dominant in a manner that heightens expectation for resolution to an E♭ tonic. What happens instead reflects a typical Brahmsian equivocation. As described in Chapter 2, the dominant does resolve, at least on the surface, but to an E♭$^6_3$ chord at m. 121—the same type of unstable tonic that Brahms presents at the beginning of the secondary area in the quartet.

Examples 2.5a and b (p. 43) in Chapter 2 suggested two possible structural interpretations. In the first, B♭ remains in control across the first articulation of the E♭$^6_3$ chord. Yet even if the $^6_3$ chord at m. 121 is heard as a more fundamental resolution of the dominant, as graphed in Example 2.5b, it nevertheless remains part of an arpeggiation from dominant $\hat{3}$ to tonic $\hat{3}$. The bass G is a stepping stone that connects a deeper-level motion between root-position *Stufen*.

Moreover, although the material throughout the E♭-major area provides a respite from the relentless *scherzando* of the surrounding sections, Brahms continues to work with fragments from the tonic area. In other words, the listener is presented with the first signs that this is perhaps not a two-part but a continuous exposition. An observation from earlier in this chapter bears repeating here. A sense of thwarted expectations following the medial caesura must have been strong for Brahms's audience given the reification of the lyrical second theme in nineteenth-century accounts of sonata form. This is perhaps especially the case for Brahms's long-awaited debut in the public genre of the symphony, where not just the absence of lyricism but monothematicism in particular would have appeared out of place.

A bait-and-switch process of equivocation continues with each new formal cue. Consider the big dominant arrival at m. 130. From the perspective of an analysis that places the beginning of an E♭ prolongation at m. 121, this articulation functions as an internal half cadence. But the absence of thematic and tonal stability in the passage initiated by the E♭$^6_3$ chord makes this new dominant arrival sound like another attempt at a medial caesura. Moreover, as Example 2.5a outlines, the return to the dominant forms a strong connection with the previous B♭ articulation: the formal process is once again poised for both a thematic entrance and a middleground resolution to E♭.

The subsequent passage, however, yet again presents conflicting signals. Although new thematic material enters, it is hardly a full-blown melodic idea. Moreover, the dominant fails to resolve to tonic. What little thematic stability is manifest dissipates until we are left with a fragmentary dialogue between horn and woodwinds that alternates dominant $^4_2$ and tonic $^6_3$ chords in mm. 148–56. Regardless of whether one hears this alternation in relation to a previous dominant prolongation, as in Example 2.5a, or tonic prolongation, as in Example 2.5b, the main point is that Brahms withholds root-position E♭ stability across the first part of the mode shift. As in previous examples, the compositional strategy centers not on a single unambiguous interpretation, but on a formal process in which the meaning of events fluctuates.

Brahms finally articulates a root-position tonic at the thematic entrance of m. 161—four measures after the beginning of the E♭-minor section. In light of both normal expository proportions and the previous suggestions of medial caesuras, a formal articulation after 82 percent of the exposition has passed is too late to constitute the beginning of a secondary area in a two-part exposition. Rather, the character and timing of the E♭-minor section follow Haydn's tendency to terminate his expansion passages with the arrival of closing material. This is the same strategy Brahms adopts in the horn trio.

Yet even here Brahms does not allow the symphony's middleground V/E♭ to resolve directly to the tonicized mediant, as can be seen in Example 5.21. Instead he introduces E♭ via a common-tone dominant ninth chord on F in mm. 157–59. This unusual articulation—certainly one of the most disturbing moments in Brahms's oeuvre—distinguishes the symphony from the horn trio and *Pathétique* sonata. Recall that in each of those expositions there is a direct V–I motion at the beginning of the third part.[40] In the symphony the E♭-minor tonic at m. 161—although it connects to the middleground E♭ *Stufe*—functions as an anticipation of the structural E♭$^5_3$ that arrives only at the end of the exposition (m. 185). The unusual preparation for the E♭ tonic forms a corollary to the absence of normal second-theme rhetoric following the arrival of the middleground dominant: foreground patterns of prolongation create a gulf between B♭ and E♭ middleground harmonies. In this sense the symphony is more like the finale of the piano quartet. There too the E♭ harmony at the beginning of the exposition's third part functions as an anticipation of the structural mediant that arrives only later at the point of closure.

The gulf between the B♭ and E♭ *Stufen* has a profound impact on Brahms's approach to tragic expression in the symphony. The schism is part of the separa-

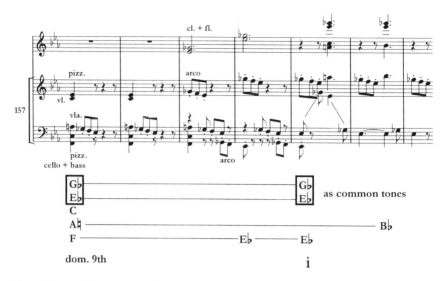

Example 5.21. E♭-Minor Articulation in First Symphony

tion Brahms creates between the intimacy of the major-mode section and the tragic intensity of the *scherzando* material that surrounds it. It is noteworthy that the attempts to achieve lyrical stability are thwarted in both the thematic and tonal dimensions. As we have seen, a full-blown theme and E♭ tonic $\frac{5}{3}$ articulation emerge only at the shift to minor. In other words, the desire for personal intimacy —perhaps even a love relationship—reflected in the fragmentary clarinet and horn duet, is thwarted by the pressing demands of fate.[41]

Yet although the *scherzando* material dispenses with any feelings of hope in the exposition, the motion to minor returns in the recapitulation, where it prepares for a final shift to major in the coda. On the one hand, the turn to major is far too tentative to put to rest the dark intensity that characterizes so much of the movement. Moreover, the coda itself maintains both the ominous pulsing of the timpani and what Kalbeck calls the fate motive (*Schicksalsmotiv*), the rising chromatic figure (C–D♭–D♮) of mm. 495–503. Both ideas originate in the slow introduction and are pervasive throughout the movement. There is a real sense, therefore, in which the coda falls under the shadow of the tragic intensity that has come before it. Yet at the same time, the arrival of the major tonic foreshadows the shift in mode that is to occur across the entire symphony. The coda thus begins to signal the work's connection to the *per aspera ad astra* plot archetype that became a hallmark for symphonic music after Beethoven.

The symphony's finale takes on heightened importance within this archetypal pattern, as culmination for a process leading from difficulties to the stars. What is of particular relevance to the current discussion is the role that double second groups and expository mode shifts play in Brahms's finale. The connection of these mode shifts with tragic expression is even more direct in the finale than in the first movement.

The key scheme of the finale's exposition unfolds according to a variation of a Schubertian approach in which Brahms tonicizes the major dominant before a section in a third-related key.[42] The G-major section begins in m. 118 as if it were the normal secondary area for a two-part exposition. By m. 142, however, the tonal orientation begins to shift to the mediant, and the exposition closes with an emphatic cadence in E at m. 183. Note that the overall C–G–E pattern articulates a shift in mode as well as key since Brahms chooses to orient the third part around the diatonic mediant, E minor.

This type of expository turn to minor is common in Brahms's symphonic music, where it can join aspects of orchestration, dynamics, and thematic character to create a sense of catastrophe, perhaps not suited or even possible in a chamber context. The potential for contrast between light orchestration and solo writing in a major-mode passage and an enormous *forte* tutti in minor at the end of an exposition is greatest with symphonic forces. Although the finale of the first symphony combines this approach with a change in tonal center, Brahms often achieves a similar effect through a mode shift within a single key. This is the case not only in the first movement of the symphony, as we have just seen, but also in both outer movements of the Third Symphony and in the *Tragic Overture*.

It is also the case for the recapitulation in the First Symphony's finale, where both key areas return in the tonic (mm. 302 and 326, respectively) so that the explicit three-key plan of the exposition is transformed into a mode-shift pattern. The recapitulation of the finale thus follows the same C-major-to-minor pattern as the recapitulation of the first movement. In the finale, however, the turn to minor prepares the famously emphatic shift to major in the work's coda, which fulfills the promise for transcendence made only tentatively at the end of the first movement.

This is where we see a decisive difference between the symphony and the quartet. In the quartet there is also a turn to major in the recapitulation of the finale. The material of the tonic area (m. 217) rearticulates C minor before the first part of the secondary area shifts to the tonic major (m. 271). Brahms's practice of closely following the original template of his secondary material, however, ensures that the major tonic enters only in $^6_3$ position. In addition, he maintains all other elements of tonal instability, the same minor-mode colorations, and the appassionata character the passage had in the exposition. It is only with the chorale that the recapitulation introduces a purer major at m. 291.

Yet as was the case in the exposition, the entrance of the chorale fails to articulate a structural tonic $^5_3$ following the tonal delay of the appassionata theme. The further delay prepares for a final shift, in the coda (m. 328), back to the modally mixed coloration of the first part of the secondary area. The apparently peaceful major of the chorale proves ephemeral when the coda repositions the major tonic within an otherwise minor context. The result is not a standard Picardy third ending but a close on a tragic major tonic, as suggested in Chapter 3.

In the symphony the minor-to-major trajectory expresses authentic transcendence. The mode shift in the quartet instead functions as a form of tragic irony. The idiosyncrasy of a major tonic throughout the quartet's otherwise minor-mode coda creates a strong associative connection between the hailstorm music and the close of the movement. There is thus an additional sense in which the chorale assumes an ironic function. Not only does it fail to provide a satisfactory major tonic, but it also collapses back into the tragic major first hinted at in the appassionata section.

A final point of comparison between the symphony and quartet—Brahms's incorporation of chorale writing in the two works—underscores their expressive differences. The chorale topic of the symphony's tonic area functions as an important component of the work's trajectory of transcendence, as has often been remarked. Nature, as represented by the alphorn theme of m. 30, also plays a role as it did via hunt material in the horn trio. The alphorn material enters as part of the finale's slow introduction, as the introduction turns from minor/darkness to major/light. The process culminates with the entrance of the exposition's chorale theme.

The slow introduction also includes an additional chorale phrase that alternates with statements of the alphorn theme at mm. 47–51. Brahms's incorporation of these musical topics as the symphony turns decisively to C major expresses a belief in the potential transcendental powers of nature and religion.[43] Yet when the chorale material of m. 47 famously returns in m. 407 of the coda, it does so with a sense of strain that betrays a discomfort Brahms may have felt with a transcendent outcome for the cycle—an outcome perhaps forced on him by symphonic traditions.[44] Indeed, the bombast of the entire coda may strike many listeners as excessive.

By contrast, in the quartet's recapitulation, a similar failed attempt at apotheosis for chorale material (m. 311) is effective due to its irony. Brahms uses it to prepare for a tragic close that fulfills the necessities of this highly idiosyncratic work. Rather than end the secondary area quietly, as he had in the exposition, Brahms allows the piano to take over the chorale material in a final desperate attempt to avoid tragic fate, as described in previous chapters. The percussive sound of the keyboard, following the warmth of the strings, highlights the desperation of the piano's endeavor. Here, rather than participate in the kind of no-holds-barred victory of the symphony, bombast crumbles into the pathetic resignation of the coda. It will be the task of Chapter 6 to explore the remarkable expressive path that culminates in this desolate close.

Part Two

6 Toward an Expressive Interpretation: Correlations for Suicidal Despair

How is it possible to discuss musical expression? The question has vexed musicians for centuries. Although there is no end in sight to the debate—nor should there be—scholars have made significant progress in recent years to address the topic. My purpose here is not to survey and critique, in any comprehensive way, the large body of literature that has grown up around issues of musical meaning. Such an endeavor, although fascinating on its own terms, would carry us too far afield from our goal, which is to come to grips with expression in the piano quartet. Establishing a broader context for my interpretation nevertheless will be helpful as a backdrop for the main work of this chapter. The idea will be to tease out salient methodological points from the most relevant style of analysis that has emerged over the past decades within the large body of research dedicated to questions of expression. These methodological points will then serve as a basis for engagement with issues of extra-musical significance in the quartet.

In a recent essay on musical meaning, Nicholas Cook identifies two main schools of thought among scholars concerned with expressive interpretation.[1] Although Cook's categories tend toward an extreme of schematic reduction, they nevertheless provide a framework in which to highlight fundamental distinctions among approaches to extra-musical significance. One of Cook's categories—what he calls a formalist approach to expression—centers on the belief that meaning adheres in the structure of music—that meaning is inherently musical, in other words. Cook traces this line of thought all the way back to Hanslick and juxtaposes it with a second and contrasting interpretive tradition. Cook sees the work of Adorno as the inspiration for this alternative school in which the social construction of meaning is paramount. With its emphasis on cultural forces as opposed to reputedly objective musical structure, this second style of analysis overlaps to a significant degree with the work of New Musicology. Indeed, Cook focuses much of his critical discussion of constructivist approaches around a famously provocative Beethoven analysis by Susan McClary, one of the leading figures in the New Musicological movement.[2]

The contrasting priority given to structure versus social context in Cook's categories might, on the face of it, appear to map onto the traditional disciplinary rivalry of historical musicology and analytical music theory. The picture, however, is more complex. Some of the writers Cook references in his exploration of expressive formalism are historians, not theorists. Anthony Newcomb and Leo Treitler, for example, hardly stand as advocates for music theory, much less as leaders of any kind of rear-guard, old musicology movement. Indeed, Treitler has been forthright in his criticism of theoretical approaches in general and Schenkerian analysis in particular.[3] Yet given the crucial role of structure and thus of technical analysis in the so-called formalist approach, it is not surprising that some of the leading exponents of Cook's Hanslickian tradition also turn out to be music theorists. Two of the most prominent cited by Cook are Edward Cone and Robert Hatten.[4] To his list of formalists, Cook could add me, for with a few adjustments or clarifications, my ideas about expression in the quartet follow this school of thought.

I am not embarrassed to join this list, even though Cook uses the term "formalist" with the pejorative connotation it has acquired in the current musicological scene. (Sticks and stones may break my bones, but names will never hurt me.) Formalists are supposedly those obdurate or naive types who still believe in "traditional theoretical assumptions regarding the autonomy of music."[5] They stubbornly hold fast to this myth of autonomy even in the face of the presumably persuasive arguments of New Musicologists regarding the truism that all musical meaning, structural or expressive, is socially constructed. Although such a characterization of writers like Cone and Hatten dangerously oversimplifies their interpretive perspectives, Cook nevertheless correctly sees their emphasis on structural analysis as a defining characteristic of their approaches to expression. For lack of a better term, I will adopt his formalist label to describe analysts working in this tradition.

Because my approach to meaning in Brahms has been inspired by writers such as Cone and Hatten, among others, I would like to begin by surveying some formalist constructs in order to establish a theoretical framework for my expressive interpretation. I also would like to discuss formalist methodology in light of some of Cook's critical points, not so much because I agree with his conclusions, but because reference to his concerns will help to situate my own methodology in relation to contemporary debates about musical expression. A fruitful place to begin is with an essay that stands as one of the most eloquent statements of expressive formalism: Cone's classic article "Schubert's Promissory Note: An Exercise in Musical Hermeneutics."[6]

Cone sets his "exercise" in motion by raising an age-old problem for expressive interpretation. How might it be possible for discussions of extra-musical significance to move from generic categories of meaning to "true content—the specific expression uniquely embodied in a work"?[7] To illustrate the dilemma, Cone cites Beethoven and Chopin, who along with countless other composers both wrote funeral marches. These marches share many aspects of surface generality: slow tempo, minor mode, march rhythms, low registration, soft dynamics, and so forth. But as Cone argues, we are not interested in engaging a funeral march by Beethoven or Chopin primarily on this generalized level of expression. Rather, our fascination with a composition emanates from its uniqueness, in both structure and expression. Although two funeral marches—specific *tokens* of the same *type* of piece, to use the terminology of C. S. Peirce—by definition will share expressive points of contact, they will not have one and the same meaning.[8] The challenge then is to move from observations about generic stylistic features—what music semiologists call topics, in this case the topic of funeral march—to the specific expressive content of an individual work.

Cone suggests that the solution to this challenge lies in a process by which expressive interpretation is refined through detailed structural analysis. Structural analysis should not ignore generic topical characteristics, to be sure. It must nevertheless subsume topical features within a more comprehensive interpretation that addresses "*all* [of a work's] sonic elements and relates them to one another in a significant temporal structure."[9] The task then is to "derive from the structural analysis of a composition an account of its expressive content."[10] It is here, with Cone's idea of derivation of expression from structure, that we see the prioritization of inherently musical relationships that Cook identifies as emblematic of a formalist approach. Music theory's characteristic attention to detail and idiosyncrasy thus serves as a bridge to a more-particularized response to a work's individual expressive profile. For it is only through the combination of generic stylistic attributes and more characteristic features that a type becomes a token and thus acquires its own specific expressive content.

Cone demonstrates his analytical agenda through a three-stage analysis of Schubert's Ab-major *Moment Musical,* op. 94, no. 6. Following discussion of the piece's most important structural idiosyncrasies, he deduces what he calls the work's expressive potential, a "wide but not unrestricted range of possible expression."[11] Although he deals on a fairly generic level of meaning here, Cone already begins to constrain and particularize his expressive interpretation. He does so by emphasizing the notion that any deduced content must be congruous with details of musical organization uncovered through his structural analysis. It is through this relationship of structure and meaning—the hallmark of Cook's formalist category—that expressive potential, although largely open-ended and thus subjective, begins to emerge as delimited and intersubjective.

Once he establishes an expressive potential for the *Moment Musical,* Cone moves on to evolve a series of more narrowly circumscribed human experiences (along with their emotional corollaries) that nevertheless remain isomorphic with structural relationships. The process culminates in the most detailed level of structural-expressive isography: speculation on the expressive significance the *Moment Musical* may have had for Schubert himself. In the case of some compositions, this kind of biographical significance may relate to human situations a composer could only have imagined, as opposed to actual experiences or thoughts for which there is documentary evidence. A composer's mental world—a world available to us for the most part only through speculation—might just as easily be the wellspring for content expressed in tones. Moreover, in some cases it is possible that a composer might not even have been aware of the precise expressive motivations for a particular composition. Musical meaning can just as easily emanate from a subconscious psychological level.

In the absence of any extant evidence of intentionality, tying an expressive interpretation to a composer's life therefore can be a dangerous game, as Cone admits. He nevertheless suggests that his interpretation of the *Moment Musical* "as a model of the effect of vice on a sensitive personality" can be mapped even more specifically onto Schubert's own struggles with a syphilitic infection.[12] This may very well be true. Yet it is entirely possible that Schubert struggled with other vices—or at least what in his time would have been considered vices—that could have served as biographical corollaries for the musical vice, the disquieting E♮ promissory note, that has such a devastating impact on the movement. More recent Schubert scholarship, for instance, has drawn attention to the composer's reputed homosexuality and in particular his possible attraction to young men.[13] Be this as it may, Cone's willingness to speculate on the relationship between biography and expression lends a certain interpretive force to his reading of the *Moment Musical*. The last stage of his "hermeneutic exercise" provides a poetic apotheosis for an incisive piece of criticism, regardless of more nitty-gritty concerns regarding issues of historical verification.

Beyond concerns of historical veracity, another more substantive criticism of Cone's methodology—and thus of my own approach to meaning—relates to the aforementioned defining characteristic of expressive formalism. The sticking point is the priority Cone grants to the results of technical analysis as an autonomous structure from which extra-musical meaning is generated. Cone treats his structural interpretation as more or less objective information that appears to emerge prior to any exploration of extra-musical significance. Put otherwise, he grants priority to structural analysis above all other routes to expressive interpretation, much the way a strict Schenkerian claims, within the more narrow realm of technical analysis, to derive all the diversity of a composition's foreground from its *Ursatz*. By this late date, it is not hard to reconstruct the postmodern objection to this formalist mode of thought. In stark contrast to the tenets of New Musicology, music is held to have its own, inherently musical principles of organization and coherence. Formalism purports that there is an objective and self-contained musical structure that exists apart from our construction of it. Structure exists in the piece. Analysis does not create it but, rather, uncovers it.

Rather than portray the notion of structural priority in negative terms, Cone sees a distinct advantage to ideas of musical autonomy. As I have already mentioned, he defends technical analysis as a means to circumscribe the more subjective realm of expressive interpretation. In addition to providing a path from type to token, attention to structural process provides, if not absolute truth, at least grounds for *intersubjective corroboration* for an expressive account of a work. Indeed, the idea of intersubjective corroboration is perhaps the most frequently cited benefit in defense of formalist approaches to expression. A focus on musical relationships provides one avenue by which an analyst can argue for the validity of an expressive interpretation. Otherwise there is a danger that attribution of extra-musical significance might appear arbitrary. Cook himself acknowledges the positive function of structural analysis in this regard. This does not mean that there need be one and only one correct expressive interpretation or structural analysis. Rather, it means that there will at least be some basis for debate. Two interpreters might argue back and forth about the validity of a structural analysis and of the expressive interpretation that flows from it, not in any absolute sense, but at least within the framework of a theory.

For example, it is not hard to imagine a case in which the expressive significance of, say, a recomposed recapitulation might hinge on interpretation of a tonic chord at the entrance of the reprise. One analyst might cite the middleground status of this tonic in support of one line of expressive interpretation. Another might argue that the chord functions as an apparent tonic and thus has quite a different extra-musical significance. The expressive distinction, for instance, might center around the idea of straightforward versus ironic expression, as these oppositions of meaning map onto the structural opposition of middleground versus apparent function. Debate about structure, and by extension about meaning, could then unfold rationally based on the criteria by which Schenkerian theory draws distinctions between different types of tonics, as supported by reference to actual musical details.

More often than not, one interpretation will prove to be more persuasive, at least within the heuristic framework of a particular theory. In other situations, in which there may be a strong case for structural bivalence, the potential for competing interpretations itself may be a source of expressivity.[14] In all of these scenarios, however, the point would *not* be that we are dealing with the pursuit of some absolute truth, but rather with matters of interpretation. Anyone with just a little experience with Schenkerian analysis realizes that expert practitioners can produce different, yet essentially well-formed, analyses of the same composition. To repeat a point made earlier, the idea behind formalism, as I understand it, is not that there is one and only one correct interpretation, but that interpretation should be grounded in the materials of the music.

This interpretive, as opposed to scientific, conception of formalism allows for the very real possibility that the same structural data might be marshaled in the service of alternative expressive interpretations. Two writers might agree about structure and process, in other words, but differ in regard to their precise expressive significance. This is why Cone begins his interpretation of meaning with the idea of expressive potential and only then moves gradually to more narrowly circumscribed interpretations. The idea of a formalist approach, as I see it, is not to force interpretation to become a mechanism through which structure somehow automatically dictates meaning. Rather, the intention is simply to have some common ground for discussion, before a move is made toward increasingly more specific attributions of extra-musical significance. Thus readers can at least understand the rationale for Cone's idea that the *Moment Musical* expresses "the effect of vice on a sensitive personality," even if they interpret it otherwise. Moreover, beyond seeing Cone's interpretation as minimally defensible, they might even find it convincing, notwithstanding possible reservations about its reputed biographical significance.

In any case, it is important to note that even the most informal analytical discussions depend on theory, whether the interpreter cares to acknowledge this fact or not.[15] Even some of the harshest critics of theoretical approaches nevertheless often go on to engage music with such concepts as Roman-numeral chord function, modulation, chromatic harmony, key relations, sonata form, and so forth—concepts that exist only as a consequence of theory. Or they may work with yet more abstract but nevertheless implicitly theoretical notions such as relative degrees of continuity and discontinuity or tension and relaxation. And this is where a glaring inconsistency often arises in the work of New Musicology. Practitioners of New Musicology bring to bear the most careful scrutiny on just about every aspect of musical study but characteristically fail to interrogate their own analytical methods. The polemical edge of their work emerges from their considerable skill in teasing out contradictions and problematic assumptions in traditional approaches to musical scholarship. Yet all of a sudden when it comes to their own analytic tools they fall into the very habits of unreflective acceptance of received notions that they excoriate in others.[16]

The advantage of a highly developed system like Schenker's is that much of the work of critical self-evaluation regarding concepts of tonal analysis has already been done. Schenkerian theory allows us to approach tonal structure with precisely defined concepts, concepts that have been put to the test both in Schenker's own writings and through the significant body of scholarship that has followed in his wake. The terms of the debate themselves have been thoroughly scrutinized so that interpretation emerges from a solid foundation rather than on an ad hoc basis. Although contemporary theory has scarcely yet to answer all questions about tonal structure—or rhythmic-metric processes or formal design, for that matter—the scholarly community has nevertheless made considerable progress in gaining insight into all of these dimensions of musical organization. It represents nothing less than a missed opportunity for interpreters of extra-musical significance to turn their backs on these advances.[17]

In fairness to Cook, it is important to note that, while he is critical of formalist approaches, he nevertheless acknowledges the contribution structural analysis can make to expressive interpretation. His point is not to throw out the analytical baby with the ideological bath water, but to promote a methodology in which we confront extra-musical significance in the space between "an approach that sees meaning as inherent in the music . . . and one that claims it to be a purely social construction."[18] An advantage of this methodological compromise—what Bill Clinton or Tony Blair would call a third way—is that it allows for the possibility for circularity of interaction as opposed to a unidirectional flow from structure to expression. Cook promotes circularity as an improvement over the prioritization of structure that we have observed in Cone's essay and that Cook sees as equally omnipresent in the work of Hatten and other formalists. For Cook, the main problem with formalist expressive interpretation is that it might disguise the fact that what is really being offered is either a structural interpretation merely translated into emotional vocabulary or a standard analysis with "expressive meaning grafted onto it at the last moment."[19] Theory appears to reach out and embrace the idea of expressive interpretation and thus to respond to the criticism that it is too narrowly focused on reputedly autonomous structure without regard for extra-musical significance. Formalists nevertheless remain stuck in old habits, according to Cook.

As a route to what he sees as more authentic progress, Cook proposes that we level the playing field of expressive interpretation, so that one perspective—structural or cultural—does not dominate the other. In Cook's view, writers like Hatten and Cone fail to reap the benefits that can accrue from allowing structural analysis itself to be shaped by ideas about expressive potential. In the case of Hatten, he finds that "it is telling that [he] often begins with a stylistically informed expressive characterization and then refines it through structural analysis, but he never reassesses a formal analysis on the basis of his expressive interpretation; only sporadically . . . do we get a sense of the expressive analysis genuinely counterpointing the structural one—for example, by demonstrating expressive coherence just where the music is structurally incoherent."[20] Put otherwise, despite all the ink spilled by New Musicologists, formalist modes of interpretation still hold fast to traditional notions of structural priority—the authority of the text as an autonomous object—and thus to the disciplinary authority of theory.

My understanding of the situation is a bit different. First of all, Cook, like many academics seduced by postmodernism, writes as if the debate about musical autonomy has been settled. For instance, he merely dismisses as an ineffective, "scattergun approach" Pieter van den Toorn's extended polemic in defense of traditional notions of theory and analysis, without actually engaging any of the specific arguments van den Toorn offers.[21] Although Cook may believe that New Musicology has dealt the knockout punch to theory, his long and diverse list of writers who approach expression from a formalist perspective would seem to indicate that the referee's count is not yet over. In addition, although Cook undoubtedly makes a good point about the potential benefits of circularity, I also think that he overstates his case. What he finds lacking in formalist approaches is, at least in part, I believe, a matter of his own misreading of these approaches.

In the case of Hatten, for example, Cook fails to acknowledge that even in his preliminary analysis of the Adagio sostenuto from the *Hammerklavier* Sonata, Hatten bases his hermeneutic interpretation on several anomalies—in effect demonstrating expressive motivations for characteristics not easily explained on structural grounds alone.[22] Moreover, although Cook faults writers like Hatten and Cone for the priority they grant to structural analysis in their interpretive process, neither of them ever claims that musically insightful analysis can emerge without sensitivity to the expressive dimension. This would be a bit like saying that, since Schenker narrates his finished graphs as background-to-foreground derivations, then he must advocate a process of analysis in which the background of a piece could somehow be assigned without knowledge of the piece's foreground details. Clearly the process of Schenkerian analysis, like expressive interpretation, involves circularity. To have any musical validity, a proposed background needs to be confirmed by foreground details just as foreground details need to be interpreted in light of the background they embellish. The same can be said for the relationship between structural and expressive interpretation, analytical perspectives that also need to travel around the hermeneutic circle, as Hatten argues in developing his own methodological dialectic.

Presentational style is nevertheless a component of analysis that should hardly be dismissed as irrelevant. The serial priority Schenker grants to the *Ursatz*—in the narrative unfolding of both his theory and his analysis of specific pieces—clearly reflects the conceptual priority he assigns to the background as the source for the musical unity he perceives in the works of the masters. There can be no doubt as well that Cone and Hatten grant interpretive authority to structural analysis. But it is also important to acknowledge—in a way that Cook never does—the influence expressive interpretation has on the *kinds* of analysis they each engage. Hatten, for example, develops an entirely new framework for analysis—a fresh set of categories in which to engage analytical observations—whose very basis grows out of a desire to interpret meaning.

Moreover, Hatten's and Cone's work hardly follows the model of a totalizing theory like Schenker's—the perspective that New Musicologists wrongly take as not merely representative but somehow essential to the discipline of theory.[23] First of all, their analytic methods are flexible and eclectic. Second, they lavish considerable attention on how musical processes interact dynamically with ideas of expression. Cook may feel otherwise, but after reading an essay such as Cone's, I am hardly left with the impression that all Cone has done is graft an expressive interpretation onto a standard structural analysis or engage in a mechanical act of translation. Rather, his ideas about expression in the *Moment Musical* emerge organically out of the careful way in which he presents his structural interpretation, both in its analytical focus and in the language he uses to communicate his insights.[24] Indeed, when Cone arrives at his most specific level of expressive interpretation, the connection of structurally derived meaning with Schubert's own life enters not as an afterthought, but rather as a highly poetic culmination.[25]

Cook himself anticipates these types of objections to his formalist critique, also via an analogy with Schenkerian analysis. The idea that all Hatten—or Cone, or me, or any other formalist—is doing is translating meaning deduced from structure into words is, as Cook puts it, "a bit like complaining that Schenker reduced everything to 'Three Blind Mice.'" In somewhat of an eleventh-hour backpedal, Cook belatedly admits that "the focus of Hatten's analyses is not on the emotional identification as such, but on the manner in which expressive qualities are constructed, supported, undercut, or negated by the music."[26] From this perspective, the interest of my analysis of the piano quartet resides not in the simple notion that the composition is about suicidal despair, any more than the interest of Schenker's analysis of the first movement of the *Eroica* centers on the idea of an *Ursatz* with $\hat{3}$ as *Kopfton*.[27] Brahms's letters and Schenker's graphs tell us as much from the outset. The interest rather lies in *how* a piece in all its details can embody suicidal despair or derive from an *Ursatz* and *what* we can learn about that piece from viewing it in these ways.

What, then, are some of the means that Hatten develops to explore music's ability to construct, support, undercut, or negate expressive qualities? It is in these areas of theory development, in addition to his insights into actual compositions by Beethoven, that Hatten makes his most important contribution. The core of his theory centers around the concepts of *stylistic correlation, strategic interpretation,* and *markedness.*[28] What these concepts provide is a theoretical complement to both the somewhat more informal approach to expression outlined by Cone in his essay on

Schubert and his more extended discussion of the topic in *The Composer's Voice*. Hatten develops a useful framework in which to fulfill Cone's desiderata to "derive from the structural analysis of a composition an account of its expressive content." It is this theoretical framework that I will adopt as a starting point for my own interpretation of Brahms's piano quartet. Thus, notwithstanding the quartet's biographical significance, my approach steers clear of the trend in recent Brahms scholarship of viewing expression largely as a consequence of putative musical ciphers and allusions, in favor of Hatten's categories of analysis.[29]

Central to Hatten's work is his insight that various types of musical opposition can function as a basis for expressive interpretation.[30] It is often difficult if not impossible to pin down the extra-musical significance of a passage in any absolute terms. Musical materials acquire meaning not in isolation, but rather as they interact with generalized stylistic and topical concepts, on the one hand, and particularized structural processes actually manifest in a composition, on the other. Returning to Cone's example of a Beethoven or Chopin funeral march, Hatten's theory asserts that expression derives from both generic characteristics of the funeral topic and the more individualized processes specific to the particular funeral march at hand. In the case of generic features, Hatten accesses meaning through his notion of *stylistic correlation*. His concept of *strategic interpretation*, on the other hand, provides a route toward expressive interpretation of idiosyncratic characteristics.

It is in the process of accessing meaning in these two modes of analysis that the notion of opposition comes into play. In the case of both stylistic correlation and strategic interpretation, Hatten conceives the analytic process as a series of "mappings of expressive oppositions onto oppositions in musical structures."[31] As Hatten describes them, correlations "typically involve general *cultural units* or expressive states defined by basic semantic oppositions in a culture (sad vs. happy; tragic vs. nontragic). These cultural units are mapped onto general stylistic types, as oppositionally defined by traditional or other theories (minor vs. major). Interpretations, on the other hand, further specify or contextualize expressive states as they relate to *entities*—structures or processes—actually manifested in musical works (i.e., *tokens* of their stylistic types)."[32] Crucial to this conceptual framework is the notion of markedness, the idea that "the two terms of an opposition will have an unequal value or asymmetry, of marked versus unmarked, that has consequences for the meaning of each term."[33]

A brief review of my partial expressive interpretation of Brahms's horn trio from the end of Chapter 5 will provide a means to illustrate Hatten's concepts of correlation, interpretation, and markedness. Recall that my analysis first of all focused attention on the generic opposition of major and minor modes, expressed both between the two movements and within the finale itself. In addition, the discussion highlighted the Adagio's lament topic and the finale's hunt characteristics. All of these features function on the level of stylistic correlation. Although I did not couch my analysis in terms of Hatten's theory, essentially what I was engaged in was a mapping of oppositionally defined stylistic characteristics onto oppositions of expressive state. To reframe the analysis in Hatten's terms, we could say that the Adagio's minor mode correlates with the idea of a tragic expressive state in opposition to the nontragic major of the finale.

The minor mode, moreover, is marked in relation to what we could think of as the default-option status of major in the tonal system. Minor-key tonality represents not just one of two, equally weighted options, but a special case. This special case or marked status tends to endow minor-mode pieces with a heightened expressive significance. In the case of the Adagio, I presented the idea that the minor mode interacts with the movement's more specific lament characteristics to create a correlation not just for sorrow, but in particular the sorrow one feels at the loss of a loved one. From the context of this expressive potential—Cone's wide but not unrestricted range of expression—I narrowed the interpretation further to embrace the widely held notion that the Adagio represents Brahms's artistic response to the death of his mother.

The focus of my analysis nevertheless was not the Adagio, but the finale. It is in the finale, therefore, that I was able to combine attention to stylistic correlations with actual strategic interpretation to deduce a somewhat more nuanced view of meaning. Recall that, on a stylistic level, the shift from the Adagio's minor mode to the finale's major tonality correlates with an expressive shift from tragic to nontragic states. Yet given the more specific lament characteristics of the Adagio, the analysis was able to move from a generic interpretation of the finale as nontragic to the more specific notion of the movement as a vehicle for emotional recovery. Still more specifically, the finale's hunt characteristics suggested the idea of both natural beauty and outdoor activity as sources of solace in the mourning process.

What my analysis tried to show, however, was that the return to minor at the beginning of the double second group, along with the abruptness of character change at the beginning of the finale, together raise doubts about the security of the emotional recovery. It was in this stage of the discussion that I combined observations about the finale's generic stylistic characteristics with attention to its idiosyncratic processes of motivic development and tonal delay. Strategic interpretation supported a view of expression in which a willed euphoria at the beginning of the movement becomes an earned recovery by the end of the secondary area. The middleground structure of the exposition; the counterpoint of this structure with segmentations in the key scheme and thematic dimensions; the rhythmic, registral, and dynamic characteristics of the thematic materials; the function of $\flat\hat{6}$ and $\natural\hat{6}$ neighbor motives on multiple structural levels: all of these piece-specific elements join to create musical processes that correlate with this extramusical idea.

Although my horn trio analysis illustrates some of the basic components of Hatten's theory, it is important to note that it does not by any means constitute a thoroughgoing expressive interpretation. First and foremost, it falls far short of Cone's requirement for engagement with *all* of a work's sonic elements. Even within an analysis focused narrowly on the change of character between the movements, a proper expressive interpretation would require structural analysis—Hatten's strategic interpretation—of salient passages in the Adagio. Chapter 5, in any case, was not focused primarily on issues of expression, but rather on technical and stylistic aspects of three-key expositions and double second groups. My intention at the end of the chapter merely was to highlight some potential expressive ramifications for Brahms's expository strategies. My review of the analysis here likewise has been limited to illustration of Hatten's core analytical categories, not a full-fledged expressive interpretation.

In the case of the piano quartet, the extensive discussion of structure in previous chapters provides a foundation for expressive interpretation that at least approaches Cone's ideal of thoroughness. Moreover, we already have some fairly concrete ideas about expressive potential as well as more specific notions of extra-musical significance. Brahms himself articulated an interpretation halfway between the wide range of possibility manifested in Cone's notion of expressive potential, on the one hand, and the specific experiences in Brahms's life that may have been relevant to the composition, on the other. In the letter I quoted at the very outset of this study, the composer advises that in confronting the quartet a listener should "imagine a man"—not Brahms, but a man—"who is about to shoot himself, and for whom there is no other way out."[34]

On the one hand, this image already significantly delimits the range of possible expressive interpretations the quartet could support. It is hard not to hear the piece as an expression of some kind of extreme and unrelenting despair. Brahms, however, ups the ante by referring not merely to suicide—that alone would have signaled an uncommon expressive extreme—but specifically to the uniquely agonizing moment just before an act of self-murder. Note nevertheless that Brahms's image does not specify the source of the protagonist's overwhelming despondency. Nor does Brahms identify himself as the suicidal individual. It is in this sense that he articulates an interpretive context halfway between Cone's expressive potential and any possible connection of the work to specific events in his life. His references elsewhere to Goethe's *Werther* nevertheless have tempted many interpreters to make this final biographical leap of faith. Indeed, it requires great willfulness not to associate Brahms with "the man" and the situation for which there is no other way out, his relationship with the Schumanns.

My own view of the connection between Brahms's life experiences and the work is a bit more complex, and I will therefore reengage the question later. For now I return to Cook's eleventh-hour acknowledgment of Hatten, and emphasize that our task is not to focus on "the emotional identification as such, but on the manner in which expressive qualities are constructed, supported, undercut, or negated by the music."[35] The interesting question, in other words, is not *what* the quartet is (or can be) about. We already have a pretty clear idea of that. Rather, the source of fascination is *how* a composer like Brahms might create musical correlations for the extreme despair associated with his image of suicide. By what means does Brahms marshal techniques of common-practice tonality and form in the service of an emotion as extreme and rare—not only in life but also in the long history of musical expression—as suicidal despair?[36]

Oxymoronic as it might sound, a fruitful place to begin exploration of musical expressions of suicidal despondency is with one of the quartet's most stylistically unremarkable characteristics: the first movement's expository modulation from C minor to E♭ major. Brahms's treatment of this standard key scheme creates an expressive opposition that, as we will see, emerges as a central topic of discourse not just within the movement, but indeed across the entire cycle. The opposition between the active character of Brahms's primary material and the tranquility of his lyrical second theme joins the C–E♭ mode shift to create an expressive progression from angst to serenity. In Hatten's terms the generic opposition of tragic and nontragic expressive states maps onto, or correlates with, the generic stylistic opposition of minor and major modes. This dichotomy, however, doesn't just emerge from the conventional key scheme and pattern of thematic contrast—that is, from matters of stylistic correlation. Otherwise the expressive progression would be indistinguishable from the change of character engendered by the mode shift across the final two movements of the horn trio or from countless other sonata expositions that modulate from minor tonic to major mediant. As Hatten would have it, the expressive progression takes on a more particular profile as a consequence of idiosyncrasies specific to the quartet. These idiosyncrasies need to be addressed through strategic interpretation, which in counterpoint with stylistic correlations will form the beginnings of a more particularized expressive interpretation.

Idiosyncrasies of the tonic and mediant material help to establish an individualized expressive arc that is crucial to the despondency of the quartet. The exposition offers glimmers of hope only to undercut these suggestions of the possibility for emotional healing. We will see that the same pattern occurs in other guises throughout the four movements. Brahms conspicuously avoids breaks from intensity in favor of an extreme relentlessness that relates to the work's unusual affective motivations. Idiosyncratic and even at times bizarre characteristics help to stir fateful energies that are excessive compared to other Brahms works and that are traceable to the quartet's association with the idea of suicidal despair. Even in the rare passage like the secondary area, in which Brahms seems to suggest the possibility for an escape from anguish, he nevertheless hints at the impossibility of transcendence—the notion that there is no way out other than suicide. This pessimism is a consequence of the aforementioned piece-specific structural processes through which Brahms contextualizes stylistic correlations. Strategic interpretation of these processes will allow us to move from generalized concepts of the tragic to the more particular extremes of suicidal despair that Brahms expresses in the quartet.

Before we explore more particularized expressive correlations for the C-minor/E♭-major opposition, however, we first need to interpret aspects of meaning within the tonic area itself. The two paragraphs of the tonic area provide a further demonstration of how generic stylistic and topical characteristics interact with structural idiosyncrasies to create a progression of expressive states. That the opening paragraphs, like the C and E♭ key areas, articulate a structural/expressive dichotomy allows for a parallel strategy of interpretation on the more local formal level. Hatten's notion of opposition as a route to expressive interpretation proves useful once again. The smaller-scale dichotomy, however, involves two types of negative emotion, as opposed to the more extreme opposition of despondency and hope that maps onto the exposition as a whole. The first paragraph establishes a tone of gloom and foreboding. The second responds with a sudden outburst of anger that extends throughout the ensuing expansion of an unyielding C-minor tonic—a symbol for the despair from which Brahms's man can find no escape.

As annotations in Example 6.1 highlight, the opening paragraph (mm. 1–31.1) includes a descending tetrachord from C to G, as well as a prevalence of falling half-step motion. These falling half-step figures occur in the form of both an appoggiatura sigh motive and in longer chromatic successions leading downward to the dominant. All of these thematic configurations represent traditional topical signs for death or lamentation. Also crucial to the foreboding of the opening paragraph are the piano octaves, the rhythmic stops and starts, the arrival on the empty dominants at mm. 9 and 27, and the slower surface rhythms relative to the second paragraph (mm. 32–41.1). These features invoke a slow-introduction topic with its associated expressive character of tense anticipation. In terms of yet more idiosyncratic features, a feeling of disquiet grows out of the *unheimlich pizzicato* E♮'s, which enter inexplicably within an inactive yet tense dominant. Moreover, Brahms answers both the opening phrase and the *pizzicato* E♮'s with abrupt shifts, in the first case to the sequential thematic statement in B♭ minor and in the second case to the angry tone of the second paragraph.

Rather than lead to some form of relief, the tense anticipation of the opening is swallowed up by a C minor that is demonic in its relentlessness. The second paragraph or counterstatement expresses this crushing resolution of anxiety into overwhelming despair through both rhythmic and tonal means. Not only does it unfold entirely over a tonic pedal, but the pedal itself consists of incessant eighth-note repetition. The unyielding character of these eighth notes is one manifestation of a more general tendency toward emphatic metric articulation—a kind of rhythmic weightiness—that colors many passages throughout the work. As we shall see, this weightiness is one resource through which Brahms suggests the oppressiveness of an emotional crisis that affords no escape.

Another manifestation of excessive metric emphasis results from transformation of the tremulous rhythmic character of the strong-weak appoggiatura sigh motive, as outlined in Example 6.2. Brahms exploits the potential for $\frac{3}{4}$ meter to express either strong-weak-weak waltz rhythm or strong-strong-weak sarabande rhythm in order to reinterpret the sigh figure as a repeated hammer blow. The new strong-strong emphasis has an incessant character not unlike the C pedal, and Brahms similarly repeats the hammer blows throughout mm. 32–37. The newly unleashed anger of the counterstatement culminates in the climactic arrival on the C-minor tonic that initiates the transition at m. 42.

The stability of the E♭ material of m. 70 appears to hold out hope for escape from the tonic area's progression from foreboding to anger. Crucial to this expression of hope is the complex relationship manifest between the key areas and the concept of large-scale dissonance often associated with Classical and Classically oriented sonata forms.[37] In eighteenth-century movements primary material typically establishes a stable tonic pole before a transition leads to a secondary key. Brahms partly follows this pattern when he transforms the tonal instability of the

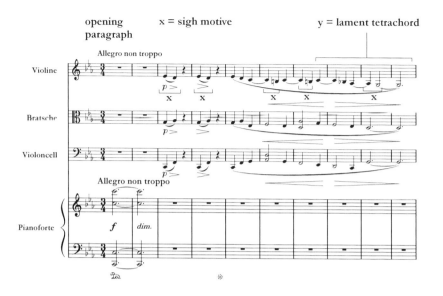

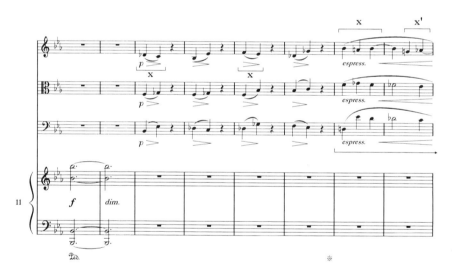

Example 6.1. Topical Signs for Lamentation in the Tonic Area

opening paragraph into the relentless tonic focus of the counterstatement. Yet as we have seen, the agitation and increased rhythmic activity of the counterstatement push onward into the transition. The result is that the entire opening of the movement functions as anacrusis to the arrival of E♭ major at m. 70. The progression from angst-ridden instability to a more stable and affirmative E♭-major suggests that the quartet may eventually overcome C-minor difficulties. C-minor

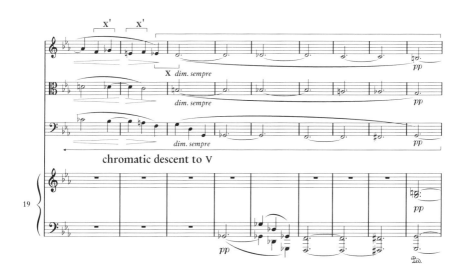

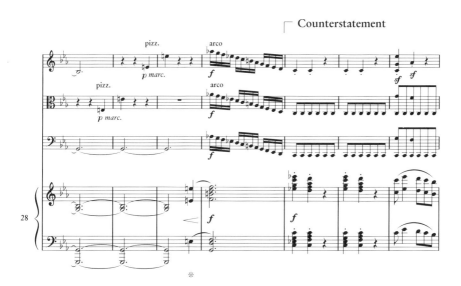

Example 6.1. Topical Signs for Lamentation in the Tonic Area

anxiety appears to fade away, by means of both the long deenergizing transition and the arrival of a more securely articulated area of major-mode solace.

Two aspects of this resolution heighten the potential for solace offered by the secondary material. First, although the turn from darkness to light occurs only with a shift away from the tonic, the area of repose nevertheless articulates a conventional secondary key. Conformity with convention suggests that the positive feeling may represent sustainable emotion, rather than ephemeral expression, as

① strong-weak tremulous sigh motive   becomes ② strong-strong hammer blows

Example 6.2. Rhythmic Transformation of Sigh Motive

might be the case with a remote key. Generalizing from this interpretation leads to an important principle applicable to both the quartet and analysis of meaning in general: conventional formal relationships tend to correlate with literal as opposed to ironic (or other) expression. In the case of the E♭ material, this means representation of positive emotions with real force, as opposed to expression that must, in the end, give way to the negative world of the C-minor home tonic.

Second, and also related to formal convention, is the idea that the conventional tonal course of the exposition creates an expectation that the recapitulation will answer with transposition of secondary material into the tonic major. If this possibility were indeed to materialize, it would leave the expressive outcome of the movement up in the air until the coda. Closing material that would maintain the tonic major might validate a sense of consolation if not in fact outright triumph over despair. A turn back to minor, on the other hand, could expose the affirmative character of secondary material as a form of tragic irony. As we have seen in previous chapters, Brahms opts for something along the lines of the second option. Indeed, he heightens an ironic effect through the dominant recapitulation of the secondary material, about which I will have more to say later.

A closer look at details of the secondary material—its strategic interpretation—would appear to confirm the idea that the E♭ area poses a legitimate emotional challenge to the turbulence of C minor. The unusual theme and variations form of the material ensures that the local E♭ tonic will be rearticulated every eight or nine measures. The material, furthermore, neither wanders like the opening paragraph of the tonic area, nor is mired in its tonic along the lines of the counterstatement of the main theme. The form thus has made a fundamental shift. In addition to the progression from minor to major, the exposition has moved from quasi-introductory character to an extended sense of arrival, and from material characterized by abrupt tonal shifts and seemingly inexplicable details to a section of straightforward tonal continuity. It would seem, therefore, that the tonic area is marked in opposition to the E♭ material.

Yet although the theme and variations section is perhaps not as odd as the C-minor material, it does cling more closely to its tonic than is usually the case in Brahms's secondary areas. In other words, it is itself marked by virtue of excessive tonal stability as well as by fixation on a single thematic unit. The variation form and the resulting tonal stability can be seen as symptoms of overearnestness—an attempt to sustain a formal process/emotional state that ultimately must give way to sonata exigencies/tragic fate. The markedness correlates with the overcompensation characteristic of an attempt to deny or escape reality. Even within the exposition, a hint of irony begins to emerge within the secondary material.

Thematic and tonal details enforce this intimation of a divergence between literal and expressed meaning. Even the relatively calm secondary area is haunted by ominous resonances from the main theme. As Example 6.3a shows, developing variation of the main theme's sigh motive first described in Chapter 5, interacts with modal mixture to allow an undercurrent of C-minor angst to flow into the secondary material. Similarly, Example 6.3b traces the origin of the second theme's head motive in the quarter-note idea originally associated with the descending chromatic motion in mm. 21 and 23. In the third variation (m. 94), tragic undercurrents push through to the surface with an outright shift to the E♭ minor hinted at in variation 1. From one perspective, this modal shift functions as preparation for a triumphant arrival back on E♭ major at the climax of the secondary area at m. 102. Locally it might introduce an element of foreboding, but from a slightly larger perspective, it perhaps participates in an affirmation of the variation form's expression of major-mode solace.

Yet although the climax enters approximately two-thirds of the way into the secondary area and is followed by a dénouement—both stylistic characteristics of a conventional dramatic trajectory—strategic interpretation reveals it to be somewhat brittle and forced. The unsatisfactory character of the climax further hints at the inability of the E♭ material to overcome fate, despite surface appearances to the contrary. The brittleness is a consequence of the registral shifts across the formal hinge at m. 102, which prevent the climax from entering as a straightforward structural downbeat. Instead there is a slight break—or perhaps even a grouping subdivision—between the dominant and climactic tonic. The eighth-note activity of the last variation also contributes to a feeling of agitation for the climactic moment.

Finally, when the material settles down for closure, it merges into a return of the main theme at m. 110. Here is another instance in which Brahms exploits formal convention in the service of his unique expressive aims. Main-theme material often returns as part of a codetta at the end of an exposition. In the case of the quartet, this practice becomes a strategic means to undercut further the affirmative character of the secondary area. The final variation fails to achieve 1̂/I closure, but instead leads to an articulation of 3̂/I at the return of the main theme at m. 110. A sense of failure, moreover, arises not simply from this delayed closure. It also emerges from the fact that the bottom drops out of the last variation with the sudden cutoff of the strings at m. 108. Despite the buildup to an affirmative climax at the beginning of variation 4, the form finds itself suddenly vulnerable again to the despair with which the movement began. The tenuous character of the closing E♭ tonic—multiple E♭'s with only a G in the viola (mm. 118–19) followed by octave E♭'s in the piano (mm. 120–21)—embodies the anxiety engendered by a sudden realization of this vulnerability.

The presence of C♭ throughout the codetta joins the reemergence of the main theme to cast a shadow over the mediant. This element of disquiet hints at the reemergence of the minor mode and, in the process, creates a link with the begin-

Example 6.3. Motivic Connections between Primary and Secondary Material
(a) Development of Sigh Motive and Modal Mixture in Variations
(b) Motivic Origin of Head Motive

Example 6.4. Formal Outline of the Development

Pre-Core	Core: Part 1	Core: Part 2	Retransition
mm. 122–33 and 134–41	mm. 142–53.1 and 154–63	mm. 164–75.1	mm. 176–98
E♭ minor to B♮ as V/E	B♮ major as tentative local tonic and then as dominant	G major as tentative local tonic and then as dominant	G major as dominant
Main theme	Grandiose transformation of main theme	Grandiose transformation of main theme	Ideas derived from variations 2 and 3 of secondary area

ning of the development. There the main theme continues to dominate, but now it articulates an outright shift to E♭ minor. This shift back to minor completes a process whereby E♭-major hope is framed within C-minor and E♭-minor despair.[38] The second statement of the main theme in the development (m. 134) even adds a restless undercurrent of tense sixteenth-note motion to heighten the change in character. With respect to tragic expression, the E♭ major of the affirmative secondary area falls into the grip of both E♭ minor and the foreboding main theme, a shift already anticipated by modal mixture and motivic details within the variations themselves.

In the context of a strictly formal analysis, it is standard practice to interpret the progress of a sonata's development and recapitulation as a response to expository relationships. The choices composers make in the latter two-thirds of a sonata movement often derive from characteristic features stated either explicitly or implicitly at the outset. Chapter 3 demonstrated the special resonance of this strategy for analysis of Brahms, given the composer's tendency to avoid needless repetition in favor of developmental possibilities. Might such an approach work with a focus on expressive meaning? Indeed, it is my contention that issues of meaning in the first movement continue to swirl around the expressive dichotomy Brahms establishes between his primary and secondary material.

The central area of emotional crisis for the movement, and indeed for the entire quartet, falls at the crossover from the retransition into the recapitulation. Before we can zero in on the expressive significance of this recapitulatory overlap, it is first necessary to explore how the development sets the stage for the reprise. As outlined in Example 6.4, the development unfolds in four stages. In the process of articulating this four-part structure, note that Brahms retraverses the thematic path of the exposition: the first three sections focus on main theme material, while the retransition shifts to ideas derived from the second and third variations of the secondary area.[39]

The process of retraversal, however, finds the expressive correlations of the expository ideas reversed. This expressive reversal begins with the grandiose trans-

Example 6.5. Harmonic Preparation for B♮-Major and G-Major Tonicizations

formation of the foreboding main theme, in the second and third sections of the development. The grandiose passages follow the pattern mentioned earlier of sections that suggest positive emotions—in this case victory over despair—but that are nevertheless undercut by an overriding tragic arc. In a different formal context, the character transformation of the main theme might have signaled the authentic possibility to overcome the despondency expressed by this material at the outset of the movement. Yet even as the passages of triumph unfold, a number of tonal factors immediately contradict the idea of transcendence.

The first point to consider is the fact that the putative victory occurs in the development, a part of the form far from home, as it were. The transformed theme also arrives initially in the remote key of B♮ major—a further suggestion of distance—and then in G major, a key that points toward resolution to the fateful minor tonic. The fact that neither local tonic enters via its dominant further undermines the staying power of the character transformation. The first arrival emerges out of itself, with an articulation of B♮ preceding the thematic entrance at m. 142. The second, G-major articulation follows a local C-minor expansion in mm. 162–63. As Example 6.5 highlights, both preparatory contexts hint at the long-range function of the tonicized chords as dominants. Indeed, toward the ends of the two phrases (mm. 152 and 174, respectively), Brahms transforms B♮ and G into V⁷ chords on the musical surface.

In expressive terms the chords each lose what little hold they have on reality and

a)

Heard as notated or with metric shift?

b)

Notated hemiola or shifted hemiola?

Example 6.6. Metric Ambiguity Following B♮-Major Section

lead into passages of great turbulence. The process correlates with the idea of a despondent individual who can briefly fantasize a triumphal escape from despair, but who ultimately finds himself nevertheless overcome by inescapable anguish. In the case of B♮, the progression to instability involves a formal unit in mm. 154–63 that exploits the rhythmic ambiguity of the main theme's head motive to undermine the vision of victory in the preceding passage. Example 6.6 outlines elements of this rhythmic process as it contributes to the metric/expressive tension of the

Ins Gebüsch verliert sich sein Pfad,	But there, apart, who is it?
Hinter ihm schlagen	He has lost his way in the thicket.
Die Sträuche zusammen,	The undergrowth closes upon him.
Das Gras steht wieder auf,	The grass springs up again.
Die Öde verschlingt ihn.	The wilderness entangles him.

Example 6.7. Augmented Triad in the *Alto Rhapsody*

passage. In the case of G, the shift comes about through the onset of the retransition, one of the most tension-filled passages in the entire quartet.

It is also noteworthy that the large-scale tonal structure of the development—its E♭–B♮–G *Stufengang*—articulates a version of the quartet's augmented-triad motive discussed in previous chapters. The expressive significance of the progression derives from the fact that augmented triads often function as symbols of emotional anguish in Brahms. The apparent transcendent passages are thus embedded within a larger tonal trajectory of negative connotation. Perhaps the most famous example of a more direct use of an augmented triad for negative expression occurs in the opening passage of the *Alto Rhapsody.* There the triad appears on the musical surface, as can be seen in Example 6.7. The example also quotes the text that the material sets when it reenters later as accompaniment to the entrance of the vocal soloist at m. 20. The text excerpt illustrates that although expressive meaning is certainly not identical in the *Rhapsody* and quartet, the two works wrestle with similar forms of intense despair.

A relationship between the *Rhapsody* and quartet also emerges through a common strategy of enlargement for the triad. Similar to his approach in the development of the quartet, Brahms expands the motive as the basis for the middle section of the *Rhapsody's* closing chorale (mm. 128–45; see Example 6.8).[40] Likewise, we will see shortly that the augmented triad at the head of the main theme in the quartet's finale serves as a means to shift from the positive emotions of the otherworldly Andante back to the grim realities of tragic fate. Example 6.11 (p. 216) highlights this motivic repetition at yet another crucial turning point in the expressive trajectory of the quartet.

A relationship between the *Alto Rhapsody* and the quartet is solidified by the fact that in each of these passages the motivic triad is built from the same pitch classes. The two works are further linked by their shared tonalities and the fact that they

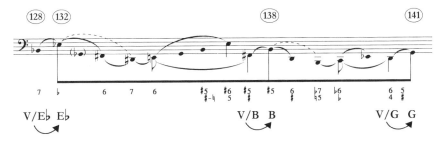

Example 6.8. Enlargement of Augmented Triad in the *Alto Rhapsody*

fall in relatively close proximity in the chronology of Brahms's works. Themes of solipsism and despair, as well as authorship by Goethe, are also common to both the *Alto Rhapsody*'s text and *The Sorrows of Young Werther,* which Brahms himself associated with the quartet. The pieces nevertheless articulate very different outcomes as they wrestle with the topic of emotional anguish. We will return to the comparison later, for the differences are as instructive as the similarities.

For now let us return to the quartet's development and the more pressing issue of the character shift that occurs as the grandiose passages give way to the retransition. We have seen that the grandiose passages attempt to transform the main theme into a vehicle for triumph. The retransition does just the opposite with the secondary material. It picks up what once created a section of authentic reprieve and absorbs it into part of the preparation for the central area of crisis in the entire quartet. The difference is that the two attempts at victorious transformation prove ephemeral, whereas the retransition drags the second theme into emotional suffering that will prove inescapable.

The retransition builds enormous tension through three sets of imitative entrances based on the head motive from the second and third variations, at mm. 177, 185, and 191. The points of imitation initiate successively shorter phrases and enter in increasingly tighter stretto. The pulsing triplets and rising chromatic bass in the piano, the angry *marcato pizzicato* figures in the cello, the crescendo from *piano/ pianissimo* to *fortissimo,* and the *agitato* of the last phrase join the stretto imitation to embody musically a buildup of unbearable emotional agony.

The retransition's multiplicity of materials and voices correlates with the tangle of conflicted emotions that can overwhelm a mind in turmoil. The abrupt shift to octave G's at m. 196 constitutes a push past the breaking point. The retransition loses its ability to keep up with its own anguish and can no longer continue the struggle to regain a coherent line of thought. To break out of this crisis, the enraged G's push up to A♭'s in a last burst of anger. Following this scream of anguish, the music collapses, as if a suffering individual has thrown himself or herself onto the floor.

What emerges in the midst of the climax's abrupt dissolution is the main theme, at m. 199, in a form similar to the opening of the movement. Despite the experience of positive emotions in the secondary area and attempts at victorious transforma-

Toward an Expressive Interpretation 205

tion in the development, the movement finds itself mired again in the misery of the opening phrase. Yet now the main theme enters not from silence as part of a quasi-introductory opening paragraph: it follows the enormous buildup of the retransition. The expressive intensity that has accumulated in the retransition cannot simply disappear following the sudden collapse after the climax. Yet the elements of overlap across the entrance of the recapitulation described in Chapter 3 prevent the thematic entrance from restoring either musical or emotional stability. Indeed, as Chapter 3 emphasized, the main theme culminates in the thematically empty chords in the piano of mm. 205–208, followed by fragmentary statements of the head motive in which the idea loses its metric/emotional grip.

How can the recapitulation pull itself together following this catastrophic collapse? In the exposition, the transition—and indeed the entire tonic area—functions as preparation for the section of authentic reprieve provided by the secondary area. In the recapitulation, the transitional material reenters in m. 213 and, as noted in Chapter 3, momentarily points toward a recapitulation of the theme and variations in the major tonic. In expressive terms, such a recapitulation would fulfill the promise of emotional recovery indicated by the conventional tonal plan of the exposition. This first attempt to regain composure, however, is not nearly strong enough in the face of the emotional breakdown. After several measures the putative transition to C major collapses back into material analogous to the dominant arrival at the end of the quasi-introductory first paragraph of the main theme (mm. 217–26).

It is only through the alien *pizzicato* E♮'s that the recapitulation is able to muster enough composure to make a successful move toward the secondary material of m. 236. But this apparent recovery comes about only with a break from reality, as represented by the shocking divergence from formal convention discussed in Chapter 3. Development of E♮—an element foreign to the real world of C minor— carries the recapitulation away from despair to a G-major area that provides relief on the surface, but that nevertheless remains highly dependent on tonic resolution. Brahms never stabilizes E♮, despite the hint of tonicization in mm. 227–30. Similarly, the major dominant, although it functions as an extended key center, must give way to C. Indeed as Chapter 3 argued, G major has already been exposed as a harmony destined to collapse into tragic C minor via its prolongational connection with the home dominant of the retransition.

In place of the conventional route of the exposition, Brahms follows a tonal path in extreme conflict with formal norms. Tonicization of the major dominant for the recapitulation of secondary material is not merely a marked procedure. It is, as has already been noted, without precedent in the Viennese sonata tradition. Moreover, the emphasis on G occurs precisely at the point that a less idiosyncratic sonata could have expressed transcendence via recapitulation of the peaceful secondary material in C major. This is the essence of the expressive irony: the recapitulation regains composure only via tonal materials that remain hopelessly unsustainable within the overriding C-minor arc of the movement. The resulting undivided *Ursatz* overwhelms the stability normally afforded by sonata recapitulation and obliterates the potential for resolution into C major. Part of the pathos grows from the fact that, despite the foreground stability of the secondary material, this last attempt is doomed from the outset. The hope provided by E♭'s authentic challenge to the tonic in the exposition is thus crushed by the remainder of the sonata form.

If, as Edward Cone suggests, formal repetitions are best understood as events rehearsed in memory, then the consoling power of the secondary material remains something of the past.[41] Its inability to return in the tonic major symbolizes the psychological distance of positive memories from the reality of the recapitulation. The recapitulation can recall the contentment of the theme and variations, but memory cannot lead to emotional recovery, as it might if the material had returned in C major. New extremes of dynamic and expressive markings join the G-major tonicization further to suggest the poignancy of a memory whose experience can never be relived. Note both the *molto dolce* indication at mm. 244–51 and the *piano con molto espressivo* directive at m. 271. The instrumental interplay between viola and piano in the theme and in the second and third variations (mm. 236, 252, and 260, respectively) likewise contributes to a heightened intensity of expression.

The dreamlike character of the new variations breaks when the material of the second and third variations of the exposition return, at mm. 270 and 278, as the basis for the fourth and fifth variations in the recapitulation. The shift to G as dominant-seventh chord at m. 279, in particular, begins to drag the otherworldly secondary material back into the grip of grim reality. It is at this point that the dream of G as stable tonic wakens to the reality of a chord destined to collapse into C minor.

In the exposition we have seen that the second and third variations build to a brittle yet nevertheless climactic arrival on E♭ at m. 102. Where does the recomposed version of these variations lead in the recapitulation? Instead of a climax, the gradual return to reality in the recapitulation prepares a still more unstable articulation of C major at m. 288, as discussed in Chapter 3. Once again we see that Brahms recomposes his material in order to allow the tragic sweep of the recapitulation to overwhelm a passage that otherwise could have provided transcendence via a climactic arrival on C major.

The cancellation of the possibility for transcendence at m. 288 emerges from thematic as well as harmonic considerations. Brahms replaces what had been further variation of the affirmative second theme at this point in the exposition with the negative connotations of a return to main-theme material. This thematic substitution participates in yet another reversal of the expressive correlations for the movement's expository ideas. Brahms's exposition consists of a foreboding C-minor main theme that functions as anacrusis to a secondary area of authentic reprieve. In the recapitulation he reinterprets his material to create a deceptively stable G-major area of solace that must give way to the C-minor primary material, with its tragic corollaries.

Recall from Chapter 3 that the arrival at m. 288 functions as the first of a number of failed attempts at tonic resolution throughout the coda. Even the return to dark C minor thus is characterized by struggle and frustration. Or perhaps the inability of the music to settle on a C tonic represents ever more desperate attempts to avoid a fate that proves inevitable. The coda's thematic character heightens the frustration created by this overexcessive tonal delay. Throughout, the appoggiatura lament motive from the head of the main theme dominates. It appears in its original quartet-note form (mm. 288–91), but now also in rhythmic diminution (strings, mm. 292–303), to create an overall mood of anger and frustration. This is especially the case for passages in which the motive repeats at a single pitch level, for example, the *marcato* reiterations in mm. 292–93. At other times, mm. 296–98 for instance, there is almost a feeling of nausea—perhaps an embodiment of a kind of existential queasiness—as the positive memories of the second theme have given way to material of the tonic area.

The coda's tonal delay makes the tonic all the more devastating when it finally arrives at m. 313 in the form of the C octaves from which the struggles of the movement began. The activity comes to a sudden standstill on these C's, similar to the manner in which the crisis of the retransition hits a wall of unison G's. A parallelism between the passages further emerges through the triplet pedal on G common to both. (Cf. the piano of mm. 176–95 with the cello and viola of mm. 308–12.) The piano in the coda also focuses on triplets, but now in an even more intense sextuplet alternation between left and right hands in mm. 308–12. All of these triplet passages provide further examples of the quartet's tendency toward overemphatic rhythmic articulation, first mentioned in discussion of the counterstatement of the main theme in the exposition. The triplets also form important links with passages in subsequent movements that likewise express the oppressiveness of an inescapable emotional crisis through unyielding rhythmic intensity. This is the case, for example, with the triplet motor rhythms that dominate the entire scherzo and with the alternating sextuplet version that reemerges in the hailstorm music of the finale's secondary area (mm. 51–74).

The connections between the coda and the retransition in the first movement allow the final measures to recall the extreme emotional anguish at the reprise, at the same time that they tragically fulfill the dark foreboding of the octave C's of mm. 1–2. The coda also swallows up the E♮ *pizzicato* motive—the figure that provided a means of apparent escape from the emotional collapse at the beginning of the recapitulation—into tragic C-minor destiny. As was noted in Chapter 3, the motive appears transposed to the C pitch level, timbrally normalized, and without metric ambiguity, in mm. 314–17.

To summarize the process whereby Brahms leads to this bitter conclusion, Example 6.9 depicts the expressive arc of the first movement in capsule form. The summary traces a series of emotional states in counterpoint with aspects of large-scale structure and form, similar to the more strictly technical depictions of dimensional counterpoint in earlier chapters. Perhaps the most important point to observe is how the development and recapitulation join together in response to the dichotomy between foreboding and hope articulated by the exposition. The development begins by dragging the E♭-major secondary area into the darkness of E♭ minor, suggesting the ephemeral nature of expressions of solace in the movement. The core of the development and the recapitulation then make three attempts to overcome emotional anguish. The first two of these attempts, the passages of grandiose triumph in the development, are most obviously doomed to failure. They are

Example 6.9. Summary of Expressive Trajectory

Exposition				Development				Recapitulation			Coda
Primary Material		Transition	Secondary Material	Pre-core: Primary Material	Core: Primary Material		Retransition: Secondary Material	Primary Material	Transition	Secondary Material	Primary Material
Part 1	Part 2				Part 1	Part 2					
			Variations and codetta					Part 1 only		Theme and new variations	
C minor		To E♭ major	E♭ major (with hints of minor)	E♭ minor	B major	G major	C minor but on G	C minor but on G	To G major via E♮	G major as tonic, then as dominant	C minor
Foreboding and anxiety (Part 1) lead to angry outburst (Part 2).		*Long and gradual recovery of emotional control prepares*	*reprieve from suffering although solace is colored by underlying hints of anxiety.*	*Return to minor completes framing of E♭ solace by overwhelming despair.*	*Fantasy of triumphal escape from despair.*		*Rude awakening from fantasy to the reality of unbearable emotional agony that builds to*	*scream of anguish and catastrophic emotional collapse.*	*Process of apparent recovery of composure allows for*	*hopelessly unsustainable memory of earlier time of solace.*	*Reverie of past solace awakens to grim reality, followed by ever more desperate attempts to avoid a fate that proves inescapable.*

in remote keys, in a distant part of the form, and immediately collapse into tension and instability.

At first glance, the second theme's response to the catastrophe of the recapitulatory overlap is more promising. The turn to major and tranquility falls in the right part of the form and is expressed by the very thematic material that offered hope in the exposition. Yet G major has already been unmasked as an impostor tonic through its prolongational connection to the dominant of the retransition. Despite extended tonal stability, this last attempt is fated from the start—a significant source for the poignancy of the G-major tonicization, on the one hand, and the bitterness of the C-minor coda, on the other. The events that ensue in the development and recapitulation conspire to crush the optimism provided by E♭'s authentic challenge to the tonic in the exposition.

The extreme devastation of the first movement's coda would be hard to overcome in later movements without a deep aesthetic disjunction that might be disastrous for the continuity of the cycle. Although a tragic close therefore seems preordained, the quartet's expressive outcome nevertheless falls into the hands of the remaining movements. Brahms has set himself up for a major challenge: how does a composer continue after pushing the expressive envelope to such a degree in an opening movement? His solution is to follow with middle movements and a finale that, as we have already seen, match the extreme degrees of structural idiosyncrasy of the opening Allegro. As in the Allegro, these idiosyncrasies create musical correlations for the unrelenting despair of Brahms's unnamed man who can find no escape from anguish other than suicide.

Expressive interpretation thus far has demonstrated the crucial role of the C-minor/E♭-major key dichotomy, as that dichotomy plays itself out in the sonata drama of the first movement. What possible part might this dichotomy play in the emotional world of the scherzo? The duality does indeed resonate in the scherzo but through E♭'s conspicuous absence. Indeed, with the exception of the brief move to G in the A section and the even weaker hint of F minor in the middle section, the movement maintains a relentless focus on C minor, as previously described. In expressive terms Brahms further emphasizes the irony of the Allegro's G-major tonicization through an unyielding obsession with C minor throughout the scherzo. He thereby tightens the grip of despair applied by the arrival of C minor in the Allegro's coda.

The flip side of the argument is that, by avoiding E♭ major, the scherzo eliminates the potential for consolation offered by the mediant in the first movement. The first movement's recapitulation was at least able to return to the theme and variations, albeit only as an unsustainable memory in the major dominant. The scherzo carries despair a step further by removing the mediant from consciousness and with it the hope for an eventual turn to the tonic major. It is not simply a matter of an inability to reexperience feelings of hope or consolation; from the vantage point of the scherzo, such feelings can no longer even be recalled. Indeed, the only stable key the two middle movements offer as a reprieve from C minor is the otherworldly E♮ major of the Andante's A section. (The Andante's B-major secondary area centers on its local dominant and thus is tension-filled, as noted in earlier chapters.) The cycle returns to E♭ only in the finale's secondary area, and there, as we have already seen, the mediant is barely able to assert itself in the face of the tonic's power.

It is true that the scherzo's A section modulates to the dominant for its brief contrasting idea in mm. 23–33. The material nevertheless begins in sorrowful minor, and, as Chapter 3 argued, it hardly constitutes a full-fledged key area. In an echo of the Allegro's recapitulation, the very factor that manifests some optimism—the turn to the major dominant in m. 27—is the very attribute that simultaneously signals the inevitable return of the minor tonic. The difference is that, in the scherzo, C minor reenters immediately without the kind of extended delay of the first movement. G major has lost its ability to suggest even an ironic expression of hope. It is directly at the mercy of the demonic minor tonic.

The scherzo's C-minor focus is complemented by the lack of thematic contrast noted in previous chapters. It is not unusual, of course, for a scherzo to have a narrower expressive range than a first-movement sonata form. Brahms nevertheless reduces the emotional compass even more than is customary. The G-minor/major episode provides one of the only areas of contrast. Yet this material hardly poses a challenge to the affective dominance of what surrounds it. The secondary idea fails to interact with the C-minor material and therefore to suggest the possibility for the negative expressive thrust of the movement somehow to transform into a more positive disposition. Rather, the G-major theme stands in isolation, like a tiny island within the middle of a vast and stormy sea. Its *piano* and *più piano* dynamics follow *subito* from the *forte* of the preceding cadence and create a feeling of distance, not unlike the effect of the freshly intense expressive markings in the G-major recapitulation of the Allegro's theme and variations discussed above.

In addition, it is important to observe that, notwithstanding the contrast provided by the secondary idea, the material is hardly relaxed. It maintains the scherzo's *Allegro* tempo and rhythmic energy via accent marks, thus standing on its toes, as it were, until a last-minute *poco ritard*. It also never achieves a tutti texture, but instead presents strings and piano in alternation. In its isolation the secondary idea mirrors the sharp contrasts created both by the theme and variations in the context of the first movement and by the Andante in relation to the entire cycle. Yet, unlike either of these sections, the secondary idea barely has a chance to come into existence before it is over. It is dwarfed by the wrathful energies of the scherzo. The sudden return to C minor via two abrupt tonic chords in m. 34 has the character of a muddy boot crushing a delicate flower. The G-minor/major episode thus functions like a brief reverie cut off by the sudden realization that any positive feeling it might have engendered was nothing more than a momentary escape from reality.

Another point worth recalling from Chapter 3 is the idea that a sweep of intensity similar to the continuity within the scherzo's A section likewise flows across the movement's large-scale ABA form. In expressive terms this intensity provides yet another way in which the scherzo ceaselessly extends the bitter despondency of the first movement's coda. Although the B section of mm. 72–158 centers on a new idea, it does not provide the type of lowering of tensions that we normally expect from a trio, but rather sustains the relentless eighth-note motion from the surrounding A sections. Moreover, the B section is further integrated through the enormous development and retransition formed by its second part (mm. 115–58). The motivic development centers entirely on A-section material, and the retransition prepares the return of the tragic C-minor tonic with the dynamically charged character of a structural anacrusis. Thus, the B material both grows out of and leads inexorably back into the C minor from which, as Brahms so aptly put it, there is no escape.

A yet further aspect of continuity between the A and B sections that similarly undercuts any hope for emotional relief emerges in the harmonic dimension. The A material includes a Picardy third in its closing tonic of mm. 62–71, a stylistic gesture that typically correlates with some form of expressive affirmation. Yet, as we might by now expect, Brahms articulates this C major only tentatively, denying it any lasting stability. He immediately picks up the major tonic in the middle section and reinterprets it as V of F minor. A characteristic of the scherzo that might otherwise provide a ray of hope is promptly undercut through dominant reinterpretation. The new function of C as V/F echoes the abrupt shift from G major to C minor at mm. 33–34. In both cases a tenuous shift to the affirmative major mode proves unsustainable in the face of the negative minor. At the end of the scherzo (m. 228), in the parallel passage of the A′ section, the more solid attainment of C major is nevertheless similarly undercut by what follows in the Andante. We will see shortly that this is the case even though, on the one hand, the scherzo's conclusive C major seems more authentically triumphal, and on the other, the Andante undercuts it in a manner more subtle than the turn to the subdominant of the middle section.

A simple lack of thematic contrast alone, of course, will not necessarily result in an extension across the scherzo of tragic energies unleashed by the first movement. The specific character of the scherzo's materials complements the movement's focus on C minor to sustain the anguish of the Allegro's close. Chapter 3 has already summarized a number of ways in which the scherzo liquidates characteristic features of the first movement in a kind of dissolution into unremitting despair. One important link, for example, is the scherzo's repetition of the G–A♭ cry of anguish first heard at the end of the first movement's retransition. We have also seen a more general element of continuity in the connection between the scherzo's eighth-note motor rhythms and the pulsing triplets that characterize both the retransition and coda of the Allegro. The concentrated anguish of these passages from the first movement thus reverberates across the entire scherzo, where the emotional pressure of triplet repetition becomes omnipresent.

Recall that the Allegro was eventually able to pull itself together, following the G–A♭ cry of anguish, enough at least to lead to the G-major reverie of the theme and variations. The scherzo, by contrast, immediately follows its G–A♭ outburst with a plunge into the depths of unrelenting C minor at m. 5. Individual listeners undoubtedly will respond to the thematic material that ensues with different shadings of verbal characterization. The range of adjectives that might be used to describe the nearly ceaseless rhythmic energy of the material nevertheless will likely include: relentless, tense, agitated, driving, obsessive, angry, aggressive, anguished, and demonic.

In addition to these characterizations, the *sforzandi* or *fortepiano* markings that Brahms places on anacrusis eighth notes in the main theme create a tone of disquiet. The same can be said for the rhythms in the development and retransition, where the anacrusis motive appears as a fragment in obsessive repetition. No matter how virtuosic the performance, the timbre in these passages will tend to be rough with octave leaps, *staccato* markings, accents, and *forte* dynamics in the strings, all at an *Allegro* pace. The wrathful character of the anacrusis motive increases as the leaps are batted back and forth between the instruments in imitation as part of an enormous buildup to the return of the A section.

Also noteworthy is the fact that the scherzo's motor rhythms often unfold across extended passages of *forte* or *fortissimo,* for example, in the bulk of both the [a′] section and the retransition (mm. 52–68 and 131–58, respectively). The sustained loud dynamics join both the rhythmic *moto perpetuo* and the absence of either tonal or thematic contrast to embody the force of overwhelming anguish. This anguish comes to a head as the ever-increasing tension of the retransition culminates in a yet-more-climactic statement of the cry-of-anguish motive at m. 155.

The retransition's emotional trajectory resembles the buildup of anxiety in the retransition in the first movement: a contrapuntal fight among voices depicts the inner strife of a mind in the midst of ever-increasing emotional torment. Once again, the only way out of the crisis is through an abrupt shift to unity among the voices in which the G–A♭ motive represents the individual pushed past the breaking point. At this point, however, the cry of anguish leads to the tonic bass of the main theme *senza decrescendo* and via both full dominant harmony and a complete stepwise descent from $\hat{5}$ to $\hat{1}$.

All these characteristics contrast sharply with the deferral of tonic resolution at the beginning of the first movement's recapitulation and even with the motion to the tonic at the beginning of the scherzo. Recall from the discussion in Chapter 1 the odd sense of frustration at the beginning of the scherzo, due to both a *decrescendo* and missing $\hat{2}$ in the $\hat{5}$–$\hat{4}$–$\hat{3}$–$(\hat{2})$–$\hat{1}$ bass descent. The C minor at the scherzo's reprise instead recalls the emphatic tonic arrival in the coda of the first movement. These two formal moments—more than any other of the quartet's passages —crystallize the work's position at the opposite end of the expressive spectrum from the kind of C-major triumphalism often found in nineteenth-century compositions that engage the C minor/major topos. If the first movement's recapitulatory overlap represents the central emotional crisis of the entire cycle, then the C-minor articulations in both the Allegro's coda and the scherzo's reprise constitute the most visceral expressions of the quartet's darkest impulses.

What can be said, however, of the closing tonic of the scherzo? Following a note-for-note repetition of the A section, Brahms expands the final cadence in mm. 216–34 in order to build to an extended and stable tonic with Picardy third. Recall that the major tonic at the parallel point at the end of the A section was destabilized by transformation into V/iv. At the end of the movement, the Picardy third would appear to be conclusive. But is it?

An obvious way for Brahms to confirm the arrival of an affirmative tonic would be to set the Andante in C major. He follows that very strategy in the third movement of his C-minor piano trio following a similar focus on C minor in the first two movements. The finale of the trio then begins back in C minor but eventually turns to major for its conclusion, in the familiar darkness-to-stars trajectory. It is certainly the case that, at least in its opening section, the Andante of the quartet presents a reprieve from the struggles of the first two movements. In a very general sense this is not unlike the affective shift that occurs at the beginning of the third movement in the op. 101 trio. Yet, in the quartet, a change in mood can be achieved only via a leap into the distant world of E♮ major. The E♮ Picardy third—the pitch class that might have represented a momentary victory over darkness in the context of a C tonic—immediately transforms into the tonal nexus for an exotic other-worldly place. The scherzo's C-major closing tonic thus functions as part of a transition away from reality—not part of a sustainable reality of its own.

Indeed, the Andante's otherworldly character stems in part from the prominence of C♮ in its main theme. As part of both an augmented triad in the melodic dimension and a plagal iv$_5^{(6)}$ chord in m. 1, Brahms transforms C♮ from a symbol of tragic destiny to an element of sensual coloration. In voice-leading terms, the arrival of positive affect reduces C♮ to the status of chromatic neighbor. The new relationship between C♮ and E♮ presents an expressive inversion of the situation in the first movement. There, in the midst of the ominous quasi-introductory opening material, E♮ intrudes as a foreign element. Now, in a context of emotional calm, C♮ stands out as exotic and ephemeral. What remains impossible is for the quartet to present these two pitches—the very tones that would have to come together to effect a C-minor/major transformation—as part of a sustained affirmation of positive emotion. Although the local character of the Andante is one of comfort, the message in the larger context is a negative one. The movement represents that which cannot be maintained in the real world where C♮ functions as tonic.

Earlier I noted a tendency for augmented triads to function as tragic symbols in Brahms, via a comparison between the quartet and the *Alto Rhapsody*. A tragic connotation for the triad is clearly not manifest at the beginning of the Andante. The emotional context instead resembles Brahms's incorporation of a similar sensual harmony involving ♭$\hat{6}$ in the opening section of another vocal-orchestral work, the *Song of Destiny*. Example 6.10 presents the relevant passage and text excerpt from the *Song*'s opening section, set above the incipient from the Andante. Admittedly the parallelism is inexact. Beyond the obvious difference of key context, the sensual harmony in the Andante is iv$_5^{(6)}$ while in the *Song* it is vii°7 above a tonic pedal. The distinction, however, is actually slighter than Roman-numeral labels alone might indicate. Both harmonies contain $\hat{2}$, $\hat{4}$, and ♭$\hat{6}$, the difference being that the Andante holds fast to $\hat{1}$ in its inner voices while the *Song* introduces $\hat{7}$ above its tonic pedal. Moreover, as Example 6.10 illustrates, both passages highlight neighboring $\hat{3}$–$\hat{4}$–$\hat{3}$ and $\hat{5}$–♭$\hat{6}$–$\hat{5}$ motions as they coloristically embellish the tonic to initiate a section devoted to portrayal of an otherworldly realm.

With respect to key relations, a more specific parallelism between the works re-

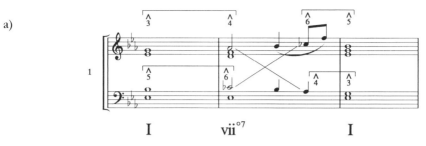

a)

I   vii°⁷   I

Ihr wandelt droben im Licht	You make way there above in the light
Auf weichem Boden, selige Genien!	On smooth ground, blessed spirits!
Glänzende Götterlüfte	Lustrous divine breezes
Rühren euch leicht,	Touch you gently,
Wie die Finger der Künstlerin	Like the fingers of the Muse
Heilige Saiten.	The holy strings.
Schicksallos, wie der schlafende	Fateless, like the sleeping
Säugling, athmen die Himmlischen;	Infant, the heavenly ones breathe;
Keusch bewahrt	Chastely kept
In bescheidener Knospe,	In modest bud,
Blühet ewig	Eternally blossoms
Ihnen der Geist,	Their spirit,
Und die seligen Augen	And their blessed eyes
Blicken in stiller	Gaze in silent
Ewiger Klarheit.	Eternal clarity.

b)

I   iv⁵₄ (6)   I

Example 6.10. Motivic Usages of ♭6̂
(a) Opening of the *Song of Destiny*
(b) Main Theme of the Andante

lates to the potential for E♭ to point toward a positive outcome in a C-minor/major context. As the *Song of Destiny* shifts from the E♭ spiritual world of angels to the misery of the physical world of humankind, the form modulates to C minor. As in the *Alto Rhapsody,* C minor represents the darkest realms of human experience. Although Brahms chose to set the one instrumental work he explicitly labeled as tragic—the op. 81 overture—in D minor, the traditional association of C minor with tragic expression clearly must have resonated with him.[42] In both the *Song of Destiny* and *Rhapsody,* hope for salvation comes in the form of a concluding section in C major, the fundamental turn from darkness to light that is conspicuously ab-

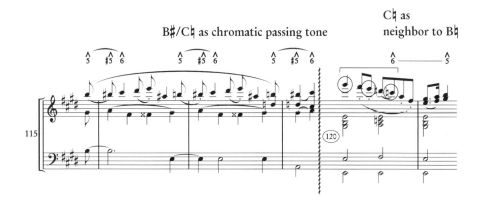

Example 6.11. Augmented Triad and Reinterpretation of C♮–B Dyad

sent in the piano quartet. Moreover, the *Song of Destiny* achieves this transcendence specifically through transposition of the opening E♭ material into C major—the very formal procedure Brahms takes pains to avoid in the first movement of the piano quartet.[43]

What happens instead in the quartet is a vaporization of the heavenly calm of the Andante, as the cycle shifts back to C minor for the finale. Beyond the obvious shift in key and mode—elements of stylistic correlation—motivic connections between the Andante and finale contribute to the character of a rude awakening from a dream world. Repetitions of the G♯–E♮–C♯–(A) head motive in the cello and piano in the final measures of the Andante (mm. 119–20) sink down to the G♮–E♭–B♮–(C) of the violin at the start of the finale. Example 6.11 illustrates this motivic connection first highlighted in Chapter 5. The sensual version of the augmented triad, in other words, slips down a notch to a level that symbolizes tragic fate, just as E♮ is abandoned and C♯ reemerges as tonal center.

Note, as part of this slippage, the telling reversal in the function of the C–B♮ dyad. In both the closing tonic expansion of the Andante and the recapitulation of the Andante's secondary material (mm. 111–18.1), C functions as embellishment to a structural B♮. Example 6.11 illustrates the neighboring and passing functions for B♯/C♮ in these passages. At the beginning of the finale, B♮ suddenly reemerges as leading tone. The reinterpretation of the dyad correlates with the shift from a dream world of solace, where B♮ can function temporarily as stable fifth of an E♭ tonic, back to grim reality where it must resolve as leading tone to C. The violin's repetitions of the painful E♭–B♮ diminished fourth, in mm. 1, 3, 9, and 11 of the finale, emphasize the despair engendered by this abrupt awakening to reality.[44]

An additional reversal arises through the extended solo-sonata instrumentation, which joins the augmented triad motive in creating a parallelism between the openings of the two movements. The warm, comforting, perhaps even paternal cello of the Andante is replaced by the more vulnerable and anxious violin of the finale. A sharp contrast in the character of the respective accompanimental patterns contributes to this affective transformation. The restless eighth-note activity of the finale replaces the solidity of sustained half notes and gently rocking syncopation of the Andante.

The transformation even engages issues of hypermeter. Both themes unfold according to two- and even four-measure periodicity, as outlined in Example 6.12a and c. The cello line in the Andante, however, is less methodical in its hypermetric articulation. The Andante's more flexible metric character correlates with the reprieve it provides from the unyielding rhythmic/expressive disposition of the first two movements. Its opening arpeggiation leads downward to the G♯ at the beginning of m. 2, which rivals the opening G♯ as a point of gravity. This antimetric anacrusis character emerges even more decisively at the return of the material in mm. 17–18, as highlighted in Example 6.12b. The finale's main theme exhibits notably less rhythmic-metric flexibility. Agogic accents occur on each odd-numbered measure, with only mm. 6 and 14 providing similar long-note emphasis on weak hyperbeats. The persistent phenomenal emphasis on hypermetric downbeats signals a return to a despondency that will prove inescapable.

The character transformation across the main themes is part of a more all-embracing shift from conventional formal characteristics in the Andante back to what we will see are ominous imbalances in the finale. Part of the calm of the Andante's A section derives from its straightforward tonal organization. The A section's opening phrase or [a] section departs from a stable tonic, one that is neither undercut by quasi-introductory character nor excessively emphasized, like so many other tonics in the cycle. It then modulates in a straightforward manner to the dominant at m. 8, which initiates a [b] section in mm. 9–16.1. As is the norm for small ternary form, this [b] material continues to expand V but in the process transforms it from a tonicized chord into a home dominant. The entrance of the [a′] section at m. 17 is similarly conventional with the retransitional V leading to a simultaneous return of main theme and structural I chord. A codetta beginning in m. 27 emphasizes the stability of E♭ major, yet avoids excessive closure by merging into a transition to the dominant key for the B section.

Even the proportions between the phrases of the A section are straightforward. The [a] and [b] phrases each span eight measures. And although the [a′] section departs from this strict periodicity, it stretches the phrase rhythm in a conventional manner. The two "extra" measures that extend the phrase—mm. 25–26—arise through cadential evasion, to create yet more emphatic closure at m. 27. This is, of

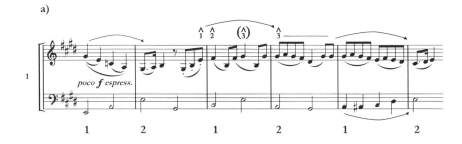

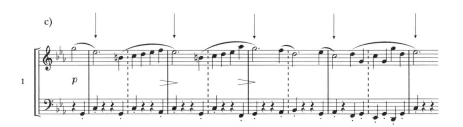

Example 6.12. Shift in Hypermetric Character from Andante to Finale
(a) Main Theme of Andante
(b) Return of Main Theme in Andante
(c) Main Theme of Finale

course, a standard procedure for the end of a reprise section in a small ternary form.

All of these conventional characteristics of the Andante's tonic material stand in stark contrast to the eccentricities of formal organization in the other three movements—another way in which the solace of the E♭-major theme stands apart from the *unheimlich* reality of what surrounds it. It would appear that it is only in the dream world of E♭ major that the quartet can present less disturbingly idiosyncratic music with its expressive corollary of consolation. The straightforward or-

Example 6.13. Metric Dissonance in B Section of Andante

ganization of the A section also contrasts sharply with eccentricities of the Andante's own B material. The sense in which Brahms holds E♮-major solace at a distance is thus manifest not only via tension between the Andante and the surrounding movements but also within the Andante itself.

Chapter 5 explored many of the B section's unusual characteristics from the perspective of structural analysis. Now it is time to zero in on expressive correlations
for this remarkable passage. Recall that the material is marked by circularity and
tense stasis in both the tonal and thematic dimensions. The entire passage remains
stuck on its local dominant harmony and preoccupied with two thematic ideas. We
also saw that the ideas themselves are noteworthy for both their resistance to development and their high degree of internal repetition. The accompaniment likewise either clings to a dominant pedal or moves back and forth from dominant to
embellishing tonic in an obsessive pattern of contrary motion. Following the serenity of the A section, these unusual elements of tonal fixation correlate with a
return to the *Unheimliches.* The combination of a continuously unresolved dominant and a seemingly endless thematic loop engenders anxiety from which Brahms
again offers no escape. This dramatic character shift even penetrates into aspects
of metric structure. In the calm A section, complete metric stability is unsettled
only by a gently rocking accompanimental syncopation. In the B section, the multiple strands of metric conflict highlighted in Example 6.13 join the tonal instability to heighten the sense of anxiety.

It seems fairly uncontroversial to map the sharp contrast of structural orientation for the A and B sections onto the kind of generalized expressive opposition
represented by solace and disquiet. Is it possible, however, to pursue the expressive
interpretation of this crucial passage to a level of more specific correlation, that is,
to move further down the ladder from Cone's notion of expressive potential to the
question of what the passage might have signified for Brahms himself? Up to this
point I have avoided any attempt to draw parallels between my interpretation and
events in either the fictional world of Goethe's *Werther* or Brahms's real-life experiences with the Schumanns. I instead have followed Brahms's own advice to imag-

Toward an Expressive Interpretation 219

ine a generic image of suicide and from there have explored how a composer might create musical correlations for the extreme despair associated with such an image. I will defer fuller discussion of the larger and notoriously problematic issue of the relationship between musical expression, literary expression, and biography until Chapter 7. I would, however, like to steer my analysis here briefly toward the possibility for more specific connections with Brahms's life experiences, if only because I find such possible connections to be a useful means to engage the special poignancy of the Andante.

I would like to propose an interpretation in which the Andante's three main thematic ideas correlate with the three protagonists of the family romance played out in the Schumann household during the mid-1850s. The solidity and consoling character of the main theme join the tessitura and timbre of the cello to endow the material not merely with masculine attributes, but also with a paternal tone appropriate for correlation with Robert. Robert, of course, was not only literally a father, but also a father figure for Brahms: an older man already world renowned in the younger man's chosen profession, in a position to appreciate the promise of Brahms's early achievements in a way that Brahms's own father surely could not, and indeed to proclaim that appreciation not only personally but in the most public of ways. Of the two ideas in the B section, the first, syncopated theme is both lighter and more delicate, especially compared to the more assertive dotted rhythms of the second idea. If we are to interpret these materials in terms of gender association, then the floating syncopated idea is the more obvious candidate for a feminine association and thus for correlation with Clara. This leaves the earnest dotted-rhythm idea as part of a thematic representation of the young Brahms.

To rely on gender association alone might not lead to a very convincing mapping of themes onto the dramatic personae of Robert, Clara, and Brahms. A case for these correlations is perhaps strengthened by the possibility of mapping musical relationships among the themes onto what we know about human relations among Brahms and the Schumanns. What do we in fact know of these relations? We know first of all that Clara and Brahms gradually lost Robert, first figuratively through his increasing mental illness and commitment to Endenich and then literally through his death. If the internal characteristics of the main theme correlate with the paternal figure of Robert, then the distance of this material from the *unheimlich* B section perhaps represents the gulf that separated Brahms and Clara facing the reality of their difficult circumstances with their memories of Robert in better times.

We also know that Brahms and Clara were very close in the mid-1850s, especially as Robert's illness worsened. In what to twenty-first-century eyes appears to be a classic case of a son acting out an Oedipal complex, Brahms virtually moved into the Schumann home in Robert's absence, helped Clara take care of the Schumann children, studied in Robert's musical library, and practiced on his pianos. He even stepped in to the practical yet intimate task of logging entries into Robert's journal of household expenses. Although Clara was not quite old enough to be Brahms's mother, the fact that she was fourteen years his senior manifests yet another Oedipal symptom. The age difference also created a parallelism between

Clara and Brahms's real mother, who was seventeen years older than his father. Be this as it may, scholars generally accept the notion that Brahms and Clara fell in love, even if they most likely never consummated their relationship. The very fact that Brahms later requested they destroy their correspondence—the surviving evidence of their feelings for each other during this time—provides implicit support for the conjecture.[45]

Yet I hesitate to take the approach that has tempted some critics and interpret the Andante as a secret expression of Brahms's love for Clara. Indeed, I have already indicated that I regard the main theme as a portrait of Robert.[46] Nor do I view the failure of the B section's F♯ dominant to resolve as a symbol of Brahms's and Clara's unconsummated love. Rather, I see issues of expression more complex than a simple one-to-one mapping of Goethe's *Werther* plot onto the Schumann-Brahms drama. In such a mapping we would have to see Brahms, like Werther, driven to suicidal despair due to love for a woman unavailable to him specifically because of her marriage to an admired older friend. But certainly Brahms had infinitely more profound feelings for Robert—feelings not only of deep gratitude and veneration but, indeed, also of love—compared to the rather more commonplace respect Werther has for Albert. (This is true even for the revised version of the novella in which Goethe's portrayal of Albert becomes more positive.)

Moreover it was Robert, not Brahms, who attempted suicide by throwing himself into the Rhine. Although Brahms's experience with the Schumanns was undoubtedly traumatic in the extreme, and although he may have *felt* the suicidal despair of a man trapped and for whom there is no other way out, we have no record that he even contemplated, much less attempted, suicide. What was upsetting to Brahms must not have been just his love for Clara in light of her marriage to Robert. If this were the case, Robert's death would have solved his dilemma. Rather, central to it all must have been the fact that as a relatively inexperienced man barely into his twenties and from a somewhat provincial background, he watched a man for whom he had equally intense feelings lose his sanity and waste away through self-starvation in a mental institute. We should also not forget that he watched Robert's decline while developing close relationships with the children who would be left without their father in the aftermath.

I prefer to interpret Brahms's association of the quartet with Goethe's *Werther* as means for providing clues for interpretation of the work's uncommon expressive range, rather than any more detailed correlation with a literary model. It seems significant in this regard that Brahms provided these clues only to his friends and his publisher. He never took the extra step of a public declaration that could have easily enough taken the form of, say, publication under the title *Werther Quartet*. Obviously Brahms did not feel a connection with the Goethe work was essential, even if he chose to hint at such an association with some of his friends. For if the work involved a close parallelism with Goethe's novella, then presumably knowledge of such a parallelism would be crucial to its appreciation. Absent any indication of a relationship, Brahms would have left his larger audience in the dark, without information necessary to interpret the quartet. This is not to deny the idea that some of the general parallels between the plot of *Werther* and the Brahms-

Schumann drama were a means for Brahms to clue his friends in to the quartet's personal significance. Rather, it is simply to say that we should approach with care the idea of transparent relationships among musical expression, literary expression, and biography.

To summarize my interpretation thus far, then, I hear the A section not as an expression of love for Clara, but as a portrait of Robert in memory. The idea of a disjunction from the present reality of the work—the pastness of the A section—maps onto the sharp break from what precedes the material in the first two movements, as well as the disjunction with what follows in both the B section and the finale. For its part, the reemergence of *unheimlich* characteristics in the B section correlates not only with the anxiety Brahms's and Clara's feelings for each other must have caused them. The B material's inability to actually achieve any kind of normal musical progress perhaps also correlates with the impotence they both confronted as they together suffered through Robert's decline. Here I refer not, as some critics have, to sexual impotence, but rather to the impotence a person feels when there is nothing to be done in the face of a loved one's progressive illness.[47] Brahms's and Clara's dilemma revolved not only around the question of how to deal with their feelings of love for each other. That issue would have been distressing enough, given their relationship to Robert and the circumstances of his illness. Rather, my point is that their mutual despair was more complex. It also was the result of the fact that they were losing a man whom they both loved deeply and who was moreover the central figure in the larger family relationship that was so dear to all three of them.

The biographical correlations I have suggested thus far hinge on the very different dispositions of the A and B material in their first occurrence. Yet as we have seen in previous chapters, Brahms recomposes these two sections when they return later. Just as developmental recapitulation has significant consequences for expressive relationships in the first movement, so too does it have a profound impact on meaning in the second half of the Andante. In a work with different expressive motivations, a composer might use the Andante's A material to frame off and contain the *unheimlich* B material. Such a framing would allow the Andante to provide a more thoroughgoing reprieve from the negativity of the surrounding movements. Yet the tone of disquiet in Brahms's B section not only unsettles the calm of the original A material: the *Unheimliches* also reverberates across the reprise of the main theme and, indeed, across the entire A′ section. Instead of containing the B material within the frame of two surrounding A sections, Brahms allows the A material to be transformed by its encounter with the B section.

The most obvious manifestation of the B section's impact is its participation in a process through which the A section begins to lose a significant source for its tone of solace: its rock-solid harmonic stability. This process begins as far back as the retransitional preparation for the A return. The B section's retransitional sequence based on the augmented triad forms another element of its anxiety-ridden circularity. Because of its symmetry, the motion away from the point of departure in the pattern of major-third related tonicizations simultaneously points back to that very point of departure. The sequence also sustains a tone of disquiet through major-to-minor mode shifts within its C♮ and G♯ tonicizations. Yet here circularity overflows the boundary between the B section and the A′ reprise, a part of the form that otherwise might have provided a more strongly articulated turning point, as described in Chapter 3. The A material reenters not as a decisive point of rearticulation but as the third stage in a loop that hypothetically could continue indefinitely in the manner of the anxiety-ridden B section. The local status of the E♮ tonic as part of a deceptive progression in G♯ minor joins the exotic reinstrumentation of the theme to intensify the otherworldly character of E♮ major. Brahms transforms the main theme's opening structural tonic into an apparent tonic just as he replaces the human vocal character of the cello with the incorporeal timbre of the piano's upper register. (The *pizzicato* in the accompaniment here and in the final measures of the movement recalls the *pizzicato* of the E♮'s in the first movement. The connection again highlights the fact that E♮ can find a natural home only in the dream world of its own tonality; in a C-minor context it remains alien.)

The solidity of the E♮ tonic is also undercut by the dislocation of all other recapitulatory components across the return of the A material. Indeed, as Chapter 3 indicated, a coordinated return of a structural tonic with exact restatement of A material arrives only at the codetta of m. 104. Significantly it is the triplet rhythms of the B section that become suddenly omnipresent throughout the accompaniment of the A′ reprise. Brahms exploits this component of formal overlap to allow rhythmic dissonance from the B section to penetrate into the A′ material. The characteristics of circularity, tonal delay, and rhythmic conflict from the *unheimlich* passage thus invade what had once been the peaceful repose of the A section.

Even when Brahms does return to exact restatement at the A′ section's codetta (m. 104), he immediately merges into a transition to secondary material. The focus of the B section on its dominant thus itself returns as part of a frame of instability around the A′ section. As noted in previous chapters, this part of the reprise sustains tension until the movement's closing cadence, similar to the delay of tonic return in the first movement. Yet in the first movement the delay is significantly longer, and when C♮ minor does finally arrive in the coda, Brahms articulates it emphatically. The scherzo then reinforces the strength of the Allegro's closing C tonic.

In the Andante, points of tonic return in the second half of the form are slightly more numerous—E♮ enters at mm. 94 and 104 in addition to the closing cadence—yet lighter in articulative force. And perhaps most importantly, the finale erases, rather than locks in, the presence of E♮ major—exactly the opposite of what happens in the scherzo to the long-delayed C minor at the end of the first movement. The finale's turn back to C minor, although abrupt on the face of it, has been prepared by a gradual loosening of E♮ major's stability, another way in which the Andante's dream world floats away with the clouds while tragic fate lurks on the horizon.

Although I did not underscore the point in Chapter 5, the Andante's reprise is marked by yet another peculiarity: the conspicuous absence of restatement for the dotted-rhythm idea. The B material's focus on V/E♮ emerges out of a return of the syncopated Clara theme only. How might we interpret this omission—as well as all of the above-described aspects of tonal delay and formal overlap—in light of the Brahms-Schumann drama I have mapped onto the first half of the form? In my view, the new instability of the Eⁿ-major Robert theme correlates with the effect of time on memory. What at the outset was a fresh and vivid mental image of a loved one has begun to fade. This interpretation is most cogently illustrated through comparison of the theme at the very beginning of the movement and at the reprise. The passing of time transforms the paternal voice of the solo cello singing out a warm and human structural tonic into the ephemeral piano octaves of a somewhat frozen and incorporeal apparent tonic.

For its part, the lone return of the Clara theme perhaps symbolizes the split that eventually occurred between Clara and Brahms. Although we do not know what exactly happened between the two, there is a point soon after Robert's death in which a marked change of tone occurs in their correspondence. Obviously there was some point of personal disagreement that led to a cooling of their romantic ardor. They were, of course, to remain close friends for the rest of their lives, but their relationship never regained the intimacy it had in the 1850s. In the quartet, as in life, Robert and Clara remain behind in an unrecoverable realm of Eⁿ major. Circumstances denied Brahms the luxury of remaining with his beloved Schumanns —of somehow sustaining the heady days of their early time together, which, as late as 1891, he still described as "the most beautiful experience of my life."[48] Instead, the musical persona of Brahms must face a solitary existence in the C-minor world of the finale, an existence both indelibly blessed and indelibly scarred by the experiences of youth.

As is often the case with works that deal with questions of fate, the finale of the quartet takes on heightened significance due to its role in determining the cycle's ultimate expressive outcome. From this perspective, the Romantic interest in techniques of cyclic integration and minor-to-major trajectories, in the wake of Beethoven's Fifth and Ninth symphonies, can be seen as part of a broader trend toward increased aesthetic importance for endings, both within single movements and across entire cycles. Nineteenth-century composers exploit a variety of strategies in their approach to the finale of minor-mode works. If a cycle is to fulfill a trajectory of transcendence, then its final movement might be cast entirely in the tonic major. Another possibility is for the finale itself to articulate the minor-to-major shift internally. Beethoven's Fifth provides the locus classicus of the first strategy. The long dominant expansion at the end of the symphony's C-minor scherzo famously culminates in the arrival of the almost blindingly bright C major of the finale's main theme.[49] Brahms's First Symphony follows a similar pattern, although by beginning the slow introduction of the finale in minor, Brahms incorporates an element of the second approach, in which the finale itself effects the transformation.

A work that is often mentioned in conjunction with Brahms's C-minor piano quartet—Mendelssohn's C-Minor Piano Trio, op. 66—provides a more straightforward example of a piece in which a progression to major occurs only within the finale itself. Although it may seem odd to juxtapose the trio—or for that matter the Brahms quartet—with such grand statements as the Beethoven and Brahms symphonies, all of these works form part of a larger expressive tradition. Not only do they each engage the C-minor/major topos, but they all likewise incorporate chorale material as central components of their finales. The same can be said for Brahms's *Alto Rhapsody,* another work that, genre distinctions aside, I have already suggested forms part of an intertextual context for interpretation of the quartet.

We will return to all of these works later to compare the very different ways they and the quartet exploit chorale-like passages as part of their expressive arcs. For now, it is enough to note that, in the Mendelssohn, the shift to major occurs rather late in the finale, only after a minor-mode recapitulation of secondary material. This can be seen as part of a strategy whereby Mendelssohn saves the arrival of major specifically for the return of chorale material originally heard in the movement's development. As is the case for the Beethoven and Brahms symphonies as well as for the *Alto Rhapsody,* it is through chorale material in particular that C major is able to overcome earlier C-minor struggles. Music of communal and religious connotations thus plays a crucial role in processes of transcendence in all of these compositions.

An alternative to Mendelssohn's strategy of delay is for the secondary material of a finale itself to function as the agent for major-mode transformation. Expressions of hope in the exposition of a second theme can be fulfilled by conventional recapitulatory procedures, with an expository minor-to-major trajectory returning all in the tonic and perhaps further confirmed by a coda. At first glance, this appears to be the scenario that Brahms follows in the finale of the piano quartet. As we have already seen, the C-minor/Eb-major key scheme of the exposition returns as a C-minor/C-major scheme in the recapitulation. With respect to comparison with our other C-minor works, it is significant that Brahms's secondary material culminates in a chorale. Once again it might appear that music of religious connotation plays a crucial role in a process of minor/major transformation. Strategic interpretation, however, reveals that, although Brahms recapitulates his mediant material in the tonic major, he does so specifically as part of a negation of any standard patterns of transcendence—above all, the tradition of turning to chorale material as the route to an affirmative close.

Rather than point toward a victory over minor, the exposition of the finale erodes the affirmative potential of secondary material established all the way back in the exposition of the first movement. Recall that, in the opening Allegro, the affirmative Eb of the secondary area poses an authentic challenge to the negative C-minor point of departure. It is only with the G-major tonicization of the recapitulation and its collapse into the coda's C minor that Brahms crushes the hope offered by the theme and variations. In the finale, formal processes within the exposition itself signal the impossibility for secondary material to provide any lasting solace, much less transcendence. It is as if there is a fundamental shift from mere hints of irony within the first movement's Eb material to a forthright expression of Eb's impotence in the face of an unyielding tragic C minor. Although the key plan of the finale follows the very conventions so flagrantly violated in the opening Allegro, neither its exposition nor its recapitulation function to correct earlier anomalies.

On the contrary, it is the devastation of the first movement's recapitulation that reverberates across the finale. Following the bitter close of the opening Allegro, E♭ is never able to regain the security it once afforded. Nor is C major, when it finally arrives in the finale's recapitulation, able to overcome the problems of the movement's damaged expository E♭ material.

The new relationship between C minor and E♭ major emerges from both the comparative length and character of the key areas. The first movement begins to move away from C fairly early, with a transition beginning in m. 42 and an emphatic arrival on V/III already at m. 52. Recall also that the C-minor area itself forms a preparatory gesture, leading to E♭ in the manner of a structural anacrusis. In the finale the C tonic stubbornly refuses to relinquish its grip. As we have seen in Chapter 5, the home key still asserts its influence even as late as the immediate preparation for the second part of the exposition's double second group. Moreover, the mediant of the opening Allegro is considerably more stable than the E♭ of the finale. When the mediant finally emerges more solidly as a key area at the finale's chorale, Brahms articulates the actual E♭ *Stufe* only lightly and at the very last moment. Remember the very different situation in the first movement, where the variation form ensures articulation of a controlling E♭ tonic at the outset and every eight or nine measures thereafter. The finale's exposition would seem to have reversed the relationships of the first movement: E♭ as an area of authentic reprieve from C-minor despair becomes a key barely able to assert itself in the face of the tonic's overwhelming force.

It is true that the finale's main theme is not nearly as disturbing as the opening paragraphs of the first movement. If E♭ is overrun, it is by C-minor material that has become in many respects less idiosyncratic. To a certain degree this is to be expected. At the outset of the work, tonic area suggests acute suffering; it introduces the topic to be struggled over through the course of the cycle. By the time we reach the finale, there has been at least some hope suggested by the E♭ material in the first movement and by the A section of the Andante. Nevertheless, even these two passages have been undercut by negative forces of despondency. With the onset of the finale, an outcome will have to be reached. The tone of the finale's main theme is one of sorrow and resignation as the work begins to reconcile itself to the idea that there will be no triumph over darkness.[50]

The discussion up to this point has already noted one source for this tone of resignation: the transformation that takes place between the solo-sonata openings of the Andante and the finale. We can gain further insight into the main theme's expressive potential via a comparison with another solo-sonata opening and by extension with some of Brahms's texted music that also bears a resemblance to the opening of the finale. A number of commentators have noted a relationship between the finale's main theme and the rondo refrain from the last movement of Brahms's G-Major Violin Sonata, op. 78. A further connection arises between the quartet's theme and two of Brahms's songs: *Regenlied* and *Nachklang*, op. 59, nos. 3 and 4. For, as is well known, Brahms recast the opening material from these songs as the main theme of the sonata.[51] The association of the quartet theme with all three of these works remains speculative: the musical connections are matters of similarity, and no documentary evidence has surfaced to indicate a conscious compositional modeling. The connection is nevertheless suggestive. It is worthwhile to pursue, in as much as the poetic content of the songs provides a window into possible expressive correlations for the finale's theme.

The texts for these songs focus on a narrator recalling pleasures of youth, in particular pleasures associated with water in nature. An analogy between raindrops and tears forms a central image. The first poem describes the potential for rain both to nourish foliage and to cool hot cheeks. In the second song the water imagery splits into a painful dichotomy. Although rain makes grass green, the drops of moisture on the narrator's cheeks are not the cooling precipitation of nature: rather, they are human tears that burn. The hope for recovery of the carefree pleasures of youth that the narrator recalls in the first song is dashed by the images of the second.

The split between unrecoverable youthful pleasure and bitter adulthood forms a clear parallel with interpretive points I have made about the quartet, in relation to Brahms's experiences with the Schumanns. Brahms uses the same raindrops theme at the beginning of each of the songs to enforce the connection between the water images of their respective texts. In the quartet, of course, he presents different themes for the Andante and finale. We have seen nevertheless that there is a strong parallelism of solo-sonata texture and motivic content at the openings of these movements. Recall that, in my interpretation, the E♭-major A section of the Andante represents the memory of Brahms's pleasurable early days with the Schumanns and in particular the image of Robert before his mental breakdown. The finale's main theme, like the images of *Nachklang,* reflects the fact that those times remain forever unrecoverable. Brahms moved on in life, to be sure, but he would always carry with him the burning tears he cried over both Robert's tragic end and his own fraught relationship with Clara.

The initial music for both songs—the theme that the sonata borrows for its rondo refrain—depicts the raindrops/tears image with its accompanimental pattern. Annotations in Example 6.14 highlight this and other similarities between the raindrops theme, as it appears in the sonata, and the opening material of the quartet's finale. These include not only the raindrops accompaniment, but also the durational pattern of the violin lines and the materials' overall texture/instrumentation. Both themes likewise move to the minor dominant as their first modulatory goal (m. 9 in the sonata; m. 20 in the quartet). Motion to v can be seen as a means of avoiding the mediant in favor of a darker tone of expression. In the quartet this strategy provides yet another instance of how E♭ has lost its potency in later movements, as part of a negative response to the hope it once afforded in the exposition of the opening Allegro.

In the sonata the modulation participates in a conventional tonal-formal process: the standard ternary form of the sonata's refrain articulates its middle section (mm. 10–13) by means of the motion to D minor. The quartet also begins as if it might articulate an ABA′ tonic area. The material of mm. 1–20 has the character of an A section, while mm. 21–38.1 follow the rhetoric of B material. Brahms, however, subverts the promise of a return to opening material in an ABA′ pattern. In-

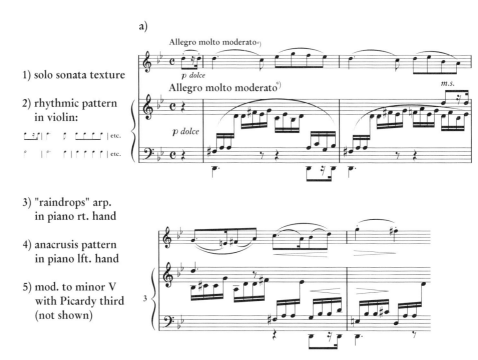

1) solo sonata texture

2) rhythmic pattern
   in violin:

3) "raindrops" arp.
   in piano rt. hand

4) anacrusis pattern
   in piano lft. hand

5) mod. to minor V
   with Picardy third
   (not shown)

Example 6.14. Similarities between Main Themes of Finales
(a) G-Major Violin Sonata

stead, the "middle" section (mm. 21–38.1) builds to an enormous climax in which the progressions of mm. 39–51 keep the exposition hopelessly mired in C minor.[52]

Although the nature imagery of the songs turns out to be part of a portrayal of the impossibility of recovering youthful pleasure and innocence, it is far more typical in Brahms's instrumental works for such images to function as sources of solace or even triumph, as we have seen in the horn trio. This is also true for evocations of religion, as manifest in the prototypical example of the First Symphony.[53] Even in the violin sonata, Brahms uses a reference to nature as part of a conciliatory ending, in contrast to the pessimistic outcome of the songs. At the end of the sonata, Brahms leaves us not with the painful image of burning tears, but with a sense of consolation through connection with the past.

The theme from the sonata's slow movement serves as the object of recovery, and this material is marked in its original form by the nature topic of horn fifths. (See the violin double stops in the return of the theme at m. 68; the fifths appear in mm. 69–70.) The final movement brings back the theme somewhat abruptly at first, without tonal or thematic preparation, as the second episode in the rondo form (m. 84). The discontinuity suggests the chronological distance of the theme from the present reality of the finale. At the end of the movement, Brahms returns to the theme yet again at mm. 142 and 149. Here, however, the material appears not only in the tonic but also as part of the transformation of the finale's minor

Example 6.14. Similarities between Main Themes of Finales
(b) C-Minor Piano Quartet

tonality into major. Moreover, Brahms integrates the melody motivically with both the material of the finale and motivic ideas recalled from the first movement.[54] In this way he brings the past fully into the present, as the means through which the finale overcomes the pain of its earlier G-minor passages.

In the quartet's finale, by contrast, musical references to both nature and religion fail to provide a means of escape from a tragic conclusion. The raindrops remain tears that burn. Indeed, the raindrop eighth notes of the tonic area freeze into the pelting hailstorm accompaniment of the restless second theme at m. 55. Although Brahms casts the theme in E♭ major, the persistence of C♭ hints at the anguish of minor, not unlike the situation in the closing section of the exposition in the first movement. Moreover, the ensuing sequential passage in mm. 61–68 centers on painful unresolved dissonance in the melody, as Brahms heightens the tension with motion into the upper register. The appassionata character reflects the difficulty of escaping tragic destiny, even as the exposition has, at least on the surface, pulled itself away from C minor.

Religion, as represented by the chorale in the second part of the second group at m. 75, is similarly undercut as a possible source of consolation. It is true that the material is calm, especially by comparison to the difficulties of the immediately prior journey through pelting hail. The strings remain in a stable middle register, and C♮ replaces C♭ in the neighbor configurations around 5̂ for a purer E♭ major. The rhythm also settles down into half notes in what is the first break from relentless eighth-note activity in the entire movement. (Prior to the chorale, the underlying anxiety of the *moto perpetuo* accompaniment has only intensified with the shift from duple eighths to the sextuplets of the hailstorm accompaniment.) Yet despite these signals of apparent calm, Brahms nevertheless holds the chorale at a distance. It is as if a suffering protagonist hears the singing of a choir, but from outside a church whose doors remain shut to him. The image is one of alienation rather than consolation, as the protagonist remains separated from the religious community.

The failure of the chorale to provide relief is a matter not only of dynamics but also of the tonal character of the material. Recall from the analysis of Chapter 5 that, rather than allow the climactic dominant of m. 73 to resolve to the tonic, Brahms cuts abruptly from the transition to the chorale. The result is a tonic with held breath—a tense prolongation of E♭ that anticipates, rather than initiates, the mediant *Stufe*. The disjunction between dominant and tonic recalls the similar disruption at the climactic entrance of the last variation of the second theme in the exposition of the first movement. Brahms even permits the agitation of the hailstorm accompaniment to impinge on the calm of the chorale, by retaining the pattern as an element of punctuation at the quasi fermatas that end each phrase. Only at the arrival of low E♭ in the piano at m. 95 does the chorale articulate a middleground resolution to the local tonic. And even there, as we saw in Chapter 5, the arrival is weakened both by its disassociation from the points of resolution in the strings—which themselves remain uncoordinated—and by the fact that it merges into a brief transition to either the exposition repeat or the development. Note in particular the clash with D♮ at m. 97, which almost immediately introduces an ominous tone into the long-delayed E♭ arrival. The adumbration of the main theme in the strings likewise keeps the resolution to E♭ in the shadow of despondent C-minor material.

The inadequacy of the chorale theme as a source of consolation becomes even more pronounced in the recapitulation. Indeed, even before Brahms arrives at the chorale, he begins to question the ability of C major to overcome the extreme anguish from which his man can find no escape. The first attempt at a C-major arrival, at the first part of the second group (m. 271), becomes more intensely integrated into an ongoing struggle than was the case with E♭ in the exposition. A glance back at Example 3.19 (p. 105) reminds us that Brahms expands the transitional passage at the end of the tonic area by adding a new *sempre crescendo* section of intensification in mm. 255–62.1. He then leads from this area of heightened agitation through a shortened version of the climactic passage that follows. The appassionata theme thus enters not only on the heels of increased turbulence, but also without even the minimal amount of slackening in pace that characterizes the continuation of the climactic passage in the exposition.

As we saw in Chapter 5, the secondary material returns in the recapitulation without significant alteration beyond tonal transposition, following Brahms's customary practice. One consequence is that the major form of the C tonic appears only in first inversion in the hailstorm passage; the appassionata theme likewise merges, at m. 277, into the same unstable and dissonant rising sequence that further delayed a solid arrival of E♭ in the exposition. The entrance of the chorale at m. 291 once again fails to provide a structural downbeat to resolve all of this agitation. In addition to the same abrupt shift in surface rhythm, dynamics, and registration at the arrival of the chorale, the material retains its muted character, hailstorm punctuations, and tonal tension until the coda (m. 311). This passage—the recapitulation of the chorale—is nevertheless the closest the entire cycle gets to a stable C major.

Finally, as we also saw in Chapter 5, the coda takes up the chorale theme one final time in a last-ditch attempt to articulate a solid C major. It falls flat on its face. The passage represents a more overt example of the kind of expressive overcompensation reflected in the excessive stability of the theme and variations of the first movement, and the outcome is even more devastating. What transpires has the character of a desperate lunge rather than anything even remotely like a satisfactory victory. The piano crashes in, *subito forte,* but is unable to provide a sustainable C major of victorious character. The brittleness of the failed climax results in part from the timbral shift from the more vocal character of the strings to the percussiveness of the piano. The expressive use of instrumentation here is reminiscent of the transformation of the Andante's main theme at the beginning of the movement's A′ section. At that point the timbre of the piano also serves to negate what had previously been the more human vocal character of the theme as it had been sung by the solo cello at the opening of the movement.

Another component of anxiety in the chorale's failed C-major climax arises through changes in the accompaniment. The hailstorm sextuplets suddenly become more aggressive: compare the markings of *piano, leggiero,* and *diminuendo* to *pianissimo* for the earlier version in the piano (mm. 294–310) to the *forte, crescendo,* and *sforzandi* of the strings. Moreover, the C tonic almost immediately loses stability. It not only shifts to first inversion but also begins to function as V/IV, with the addition of B♭ and even a painful minor ninth, D♭. Once again, these aspects of disruption have a precedent earlier in the cycle. Recall that Brahms has similarly undercut the arrival of a C tonic with a Picardy third at the end of the scherzo's A section by means of its immediate transformation into a V/iv chord.

Brahms's expressive intent seems all the more devastating in light of the tradition he evokes through his use of chorale material. The final failed attempt at a C-major climax does not provide merely a self-referential negative response to earlier suggestions for the possibility of transcendence. C major fails specifically through negation of a time-honored means of triumph in tragic works, and especially C-minor works, in the nineteenth century. If in his First Symphony Brahms wrestled with the C-minor/major topos on Beethoven's terms, then the quartet reflects an entirely more personal arena of struggle. This makes perfect sense, given the connection Brahms hinted at between the work and his experiences with the Schumanns.

An example closer to home in the chamber repertoire—the conclusion of Mendelssohn's C-minor piano trio mentioned earlier—provides a striking counter-example to Brahms's strategy. As I have already noted, its chorale material solidly articulates a victorious C major that comes to dominate the close of the cycle. The force of religion is all the more powerful because the chorale follows recapitulation of secondary material in the tonic minor, despite the fact that the second theme appears in E♭ major in the exposition. Mendelssohn thus uses *chiaroscuro* shading of the second theme to intensify the brightness of the C-major chorale when it finally arrives.[55]

Following the failed climax on the chorale, the remainder of Brahms's finale maintains the major form of the tonic. It absorbs this major tonic, however, into an otherwise minor context with a decidedly resigned character. The process results in the tragic major tonic described in earlier chapters. This tragic C major has multiple functions. With respect to the finale itself, it serves to drag into the grip of a C-minor key context, the weakly articulated C-major tonic chord of the double second group. Moreover, it does the same, on a global scale, with the work's motivic E♮ pitch class. It takes the pitch E♮, recalling the *pizzicato* motive from the first movement and the key of the Andante, and recasts it as a chromatic inflection within a passage that otherwise maintains the darkness of C minor. One need only think of the kind of pure and bright C major of the main themes in Beethoven's Fifth or Brahms's First Symphonies to appreciate the difference of strategy in the quartet.

The element of modal mixture in the coda demonstrates an obvious but important point: it is not the quality of a tonic harmony alone that determines the affective character of a passage but the entire musical context in which that tonic functions. It is true that there are instances of C-minor chords—for example, in mm. 336–40 and 343. But factors such as the prominence of A♭ and D♭ and the lament symbol of extended descending chromaticism are equally important in sustaining the dark presence of minor. For example, the major tonic in m. 346 enters, after a long chromatic descent in the piano in counterpoint with a double neighbor figure around G in the cello that emphasizes A♭. Moreover, this instance of a C-major tonic again functions as a V/iv chord, here within a minor-mode circle-of-fifths sequence. Similarly, when the sequence concludes with a return to the major tonic at m. 351, the ensuing passage contains prominent statements of A♭ and D♭, so that the character is anything but a bright C major. Instead, a tone of resigned despair arises from the *tranquillo* loss of tempo and energy, the *piano* and *pianissimo* dynamics, and the ominous C pedal heard first in the cello at m. 351 and then doubled by the violin at m. 359.

Also significant is the fact that the melodic material of mm. 351–68.1 derives from mm. 21–38.1 of the tonic key area, that section of the form that was unable to lead normally to a transition out of C minor. Following their recall of this unyielding C-minor material, the violin and viola return at m. 371 to the ascending quarter-note motive from the E♭ appassionata theme. This material was originally active and striving as it attempted to pull away from C minor. Now it appears not only at a slower tempo, but also in fragmentary form, and in combination with both a long chromatic descent in the piano and a continuation of the ominous C pedal in the cello. This is the final stage in the process by which the work defeats the potential of secondary material to pull away from C minor and thereby suggest an escape from utter hopelessness.

Brahms has carried us from the genuine hope of the theme and variations in the first movement, to the extreme irony of the recapitulation of this material, to the diminished potency of E♭ major and C major in the exposition and recapitulation of the finale, and finally to the last gasps of life for secondary material in the coda. The feeling of defeat is heightened when the appassionata motive appears one last time in rhythmic augmentation in mm. 374–76, before the abrupt final chords. The concluding punctuation on C major fails to communicate a sense of attainment. It is prepared not by a dominant, but instead by a five-octave chromatic descent that culminates with D♭ sinking down to C, as the vanishing point for a decrescendo to *pianissimo*. The shift to *forte* for the last two chords enters without preparation. Rather, the chords cut off the suffering without ending it, in a gesture of surrender—or perhaps even sarcasm—with Brahms's man declaring: "If this is my fate, then there is no use in trying to fight it any longer. I've tried my best, now just leave me alone in my misery."

7 Intertextual Resonances: Tragic Expression, Dimensional Counterpoint, and the Great C-Minor Tradition

For the conclusion of this study of Brahms's C-minor piano quartet, it seems only appropriate to develop and recapitulate several of the expository ideas introduced at the outset of my analytical odyssey. The main animating point for much that has transpired has been the notion that the quartet holds a unique and paradoxical position within Brahms's oeuvre. It is in so many respects unmatched for both structural idiosyncrasy as well as expressive intensity. Yet as we have had occasion to observe again and again, the quartet achieves this special status through intensification of compositional strategies that permeate Brahms's works. Although the focus with respect to this paradox has been largely on matters of structure, it is also the case that the quartet's unusual affective status allows it to function as a springboard into discussion of archetypes of Brahmsian expression. The idea of a work that expresses the agony of an individual about to commit suicide obviously sets the quartet apart. But this absolutely hopeless form of despondency can also be viewed as an extreme that nevertheless resides not on an island but on the outer edges of a continuum of tragic expression.

The strategy for the first part of this chapter will be to zoom out from the close-range perspective of Chapter 6 and provide a wide-angle view of approaches to meaning in Brahms's minor-mode compositions. The second part will broaden even further to explore relationships between Brahms's strategies and the approaches found in two representative examples drawn from the C-minor works of his Viennese precursors. The survey of part one will involve four main categories: compositions that create correlations with dramatic actions of classical tragedy, those that make a turn away from the tragic and culminate in passages of victorious transcendence, those that similarly turn away from darkness but end in quiet consolation or ethereal transcendence, and finally a small group of pieces that approach the extreme despair of the piano quartet. Throughout I will highlight the role of dimensional counterpoint as a means toward construction of meaning. What is to be gained from a broader perspective will, of course, come at a cost. In contrast to the time lavished on strategic interpretation of the quartet, this chapter will focus primarily on matters of stylistic correlation. Although I will attempt to individualize my readings through attention to characteristic features, the analyses presented here represent only the first steps of a process by which observations about archetypal patterns can be refined into more individualized interpretations.

A good place to begin is with some of Tovey's ideas about expression in the piano quartet. Tovey interprets meaning in the quartet not in terms of the work's connection with Goethe's *Werther*. Instead he views the quartet through the prism of classical theories of tragedy, in particular Aristotle's notion that pity and fear inspired by the demise of a tragic hero will lead an audience to catharsis.[1] He finds the cool critical response of his contemporaries to the quartet to be the result of a misguided focus on human sympathy, without an ability "to admire and assent to the destiny that brings the catastrophe to pass" (203). The devastating conclusion of the quartet suggests to Tovey the grandeur of the larger world, which dictates the conditions under which a tragic hero lives. Rather than seek artistic depictions of this world as "wholly bad and the catastrophe wholly unjustifiable" (203), Tovey implores us to appreciate the crisis as an "inevitable working of the design [that] leaves us, not miserable with impotent vexation, but strengthened by the conviction of its own supreme grandeur and truth" (204).

For Tovey, the moment of catastrophe coincides with the failed climax on the chorale theme at the beginning of the finale's coda. What follows in the coda causes us to realize what lies beneath the "mystery" of the movement. His idea is that the catastrophic moment corresponds with the demise of a tragic hero; the bleak passages that follow reflect the fact that the dramatic action has taken place within a world that has existed and will continue to exist beyond the narrow confines of the hero's life. It is here that Tovey locates the problem that he claims the work poses for many listeners: we are denied the easy emotional escape of assuming that the object of our sympathy has been treated unfairly. Rather, we are faced with a more challenging notion, the idea that there is more pathos in "the tragedy of a noble mortal whose error brings his own and others' fall in a world that would itself crash to ruin if its course were stopped to save him" (204). The audience can find solace only in the restoration of the moral order that the remainder of the coda represents for Tovey.

This interpretation along classical lines is both suggestive and problematic. Tovey no doubt identifies a central reason why the C-minor quartet might not be as popular as, say, a work like the G-minor piano quartet with its crowd-pleasing *alla Zingarese* finale. Moreover, although Werther is hardly a tragic hero, Brahms's relationship with Robert and Clara might itself be construed as classically tragic: from the vantage point of hindsight, it seems to have been destined to fail. There simply was no way for Brahms to reconcile his feelings for Clara in light of his relationship with Robert, other than to distance himself from her. To push the analogy further, we might say that Brahms's tragic flaw was his uncommon sincerity of feeling. The depth of his regard for Robert as a father figure made his similarly honest love for Clara a taboo. The personality trait that motivated his heroic deeds in the Schumann household during Robert's illness and in the wake of his demise also prevented him from sustaining an intimate relationship with Clara.

These connections with classical concepts of tragedy notwithstanding, Tovey's expressive interpretation has one serious shortcoming: it lacks specificity as it relates to musical details of the quartet. His interpretation turns out to be a mere frame around what is otherwise a characteristically blow-by-blow description of the quartet's thematic and tonal outlines. Beyond identifying the climax on the chorale as the "final tragic irony . . . [that] brings about the catastrophe" (214), he fails to engage the work in dramatic terms. This does not mean that his interpretive perspective is unenlightening. What it does indicate is that his ideas are best understood as part of an *analogy* to drama that has the potential to illuminate a work like the C-minor quartet. As Tovey himself puts it elsewhere, in his analysis of Brahms's *Tragic Overture,* the piece "is certainly not written at the dictation of any one tragedy . . . and any tragic characters of which it may remind us can be safely regarded only as our own illustrations of its meaning. On this understanding, we may legitimately compare Brahms's energetic but severely formal conclusion with Shakespeare's Fortinbras, not as a course of events, but as an esthetic fact."[2]

In my view, however, it is not the C-minor quartet that best fits Tovey's model for interpretation along Aristotelian lines. Rather, it is in the *Tragic Overture* and in several other works that Brahms creates a culmination for the whole that suggests a denouement along classical lines. One definitive feature for these works is an emphatic minor-mode close akin to Tovey's "severely formal conclusion." Such a conclusion suggests a restoration of the moral order, as represented by Tovey's reference to the triumph of Fortinbras following Hamlet's demise. The material that Brahms sometimes uses to close his minor-mode cycles can suggest the grandeur of a larger design—the real world in which actions, heroic or otherwise, have and will continue to take place long after a tragic hero meets his fate.

James Webster follows Tovey in interpreting the closing passage of the *Tragic Overture* in this way, noting its "formal" character, "quotidian busyness," and "lack of emotional resonance."[3] These are the very qualities Tovey claims his contemporaries found unsatisfying, as evidence of what they took to be Brahms's "academic coldness." Taken on its own, Webster's description might suggest nothing more than the liquidation of characteristic features associated with closure in pieces of various expressive character. What makes Tovey's and Webster's assertions compelling is not the generic quality of the closing phrase per se, but its position within a larger process in which it is possible to hear correlations for a tragic denouement.

What, then, are some of the features we might listen for to hear a closing phrase as a restoration of the moral order, rather than material characterized by conventional motivic liquidation? First, the music might build to a climax in order to create a correlation for the central moment of crisis in a drama. Second, the process that comes to a head at this climax would likely resolve, possibly creating an analogue for a dramatic action in which a hero's fate is sealed. Finally, the character of the music that follows might suggest something akin to Aristotelian pity and fear, before the final cadential material pushes on with the inexorable continuity of time.

Webster identifies all of these components in the coda of the *Tragic Overture.* His interpretation of the work centers around the idea of personification, specifically the notion that the overture's motto can be taken to represent a tragic hero.

The motto's tragic flaw is its inability to articulate the tonic, that is, to function normally in the real world of D minor. Although this flaw resonates throughout much of the overture, it reaches its apotheosis in the coda. For it is in the coda, given the conventional requirement for closure, that the conflict between the motto's harmonic problem and exigencies of tonal form comes to a head. As Webster has it, the motto as tragic hero returns in a "last defiant gesture" (115) in m. 379, as the coda pushes inexorably toward closure. It is in the passage that follows (mm. 395–402) that the music builds to a climax, which takes on the character of a catastrophic culmination of all of the struggles that have come before.

The augmentation of the main theme that caps off this climactic buildup forces the hero finally to submit to tonal convention. As Example 7.1 shows, the climax transforms the motto into a stereotypical $\hat{2}$–$\hat{1}$ motion over a standard V–i cadential bass. The multiple repetitions of this cadential gesture and the breaking off on the dominant rather than resolution to the tonic at the end of the passage (m. 403) symbolize the intensity of the struggle, as the hero resists his fate. As the augmentation nevertheless brings about the motto's demise, it also recalls two earlier passages based on similar half-note rhythms: the retransition to the recapitulation of the second theme in the major tonic (mm. 291–99) and the A♭ transition theme from the exposition (m. 84). In the case of the approach to the recapitulation, Webster hears an expression of pathos: "As the hero presumably attempts to accept the world's law as his own, he acknowledges his tragic flaw; the poignancy is the emotional upwelling that accompanies admission of error, renunciation of pride, heightened consciousness of one's humanity" (115). In the case of the A♭ theme, he hears the hero's "vision of an ideal world," in contrast to Tovey's idea of a "message of peace" (113).

According to Webster, the recall at the climax of these two passages reveals their tragic irony. "The solemn augmentation in the trombones explodes the illusion of [the retransition] and perhaps also signifies that [the hero's] idealistic vision [in A♭] harboured, ironically, the seeds of his own destruction." What is left in the motivically fragmented passage that follows in mm. 409–23 is "the equivalent of the hushed shock and mourning onstage that accompany" the demise of a tragic hero (116). Crucial to this correlation with Aristotelian pity and fear is not just the motivic fragmentation, but also the softer dynamic level, *espressivo* markings, and *un poco sostenuto* slackening of the tempo. The music seems suddenly unsure of how to proceed following the assertive cadential motions of the previous passage. Finally, the entrance of the less characteristic closing material at m. 423, *in tempo,* correlates with the restoration of the moral order. D minor presses on in generic assertions of the tonic via repeated V–i gestures. In Tovey's analogy, even as fate has crushed Hamlet—the object of our sympathy—the larger world must continue, with Fortinbras as king.

This summary should suffice to illustrate the case Webster makes for Tovey's ideas about musical tragedy as they apply to the *Tragic Overture.* But what of the C-minor piano quartet, the focus of Tovey's application of Aristotelian concepts? Certainly the failed climax on the chorale can be taken to represent a final tragic irony, as Tovey suggests. It might also be possible to interpret the gradual slackening

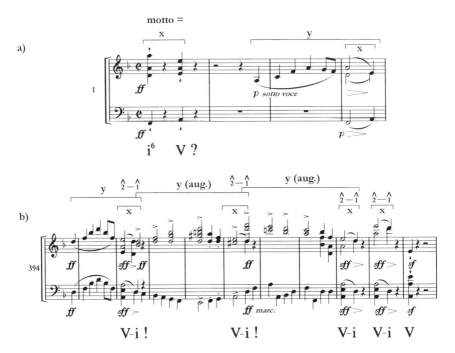

Example 7.1. Transformation of Motto in the *Tragic Overture*

of the pace that follows, along with the strange turn to the major tonic throughout the coda's otherwise minor-mode context, as correlations for shock and awe. Yet one searches in vain for anything equivalent to a restoration of the moral order following these passages of disorientation. Indeed, the closing tonic simply cuts off the music following the coda's descent into despair, as described in Chapter 6. This abrupt conclusion is altogether too ambivalent and idiosyncratically personal to represent the grandeur of the larger world. Indeed, its very abruptness suggests just the opposite of the continuity of time extending beyond the dramatic frame of a particular tragic course of events.

Rather, it is in another group of pieces that we find codas whose processes correlate more closely with Aristotelian concepts. At least in their set of closing gestures, the final movements of the D-minor violin sonata, C-minor string quartet, B-major piano trio (revised version), and Fourth Symphony follow a similar pattern as the *Tragic Overture*. Our focus here will be on the sonata and quartet. In both of these works, a sense of tragic culmination in the final movements arises through processes of extensive tonal delay. Thus, as with the C-minor piano quartet, issues of dimensional counterpoint prove crucial to expressive interpretation. Another striking characteristic of the finales is their uncommon tendency toward rhythmic *moto perpetuo* and motivic concentration. The obsessive urgency of the thematic materials joins the tension of tonal delay to create the feeling of crisis appropriate for the final movement of a cycle devoted to tragic themes.

The other side of the coin of this catastrophic motivic obsessiveness is the inability of the movements to maintain lyrical stability as a break from the relentlessness of their thematic materials. In the somewhat different context of the *Tragic Overture,* Arno Mitschka attributes tragic expression to the failure of the work's lyrical second theme to sustain itself in the face of the devastation that surrounds it. The human voice of melody is overwhelmed by the corrupting forces of the world.[4] For its part, the string quartet's finale represents an extreme approach to thematicism in which lyrical melody is never even allowed to enter the equation. The movement eschews a second theme in favor of conventions of continuous exposition. As we shall see, extremes of both tonal delay and motivic redundancy join these continuous procedures to create the kind of tragic sweep that Mitschka associates with forces of chaos and destruction.

In the violin sonata we find more of a middle ground. The movement does at least present lyrical material at m. 39 following a medial caesura at m. 37. Yet this cantabile theme lacks both the tonal stability and conventional key of the secondary idea in the *Tragic Overture.* In other words, the violin sonata's attempts to escape forces of disquiet are even more tenuous than the overture's. The lyrical passage turns out to be the first part of a double second group, and, as is common for this type of formal area, the material proves to be highly unstable. Its initial tonicization of C at m. 39 enters without preparation following a transitional arrival on V/A, and its antecedent and consequent phrases both fail to close in C. Instead they lead to dominant harmonies in E minor and A minor, respectively (mm. 54 and 66–76). The consequent's arrival back on V/A reactivates the same E dominant first articulated by the transition, and it is this *Stufe* that Brahms prolongs across both parts of the double second group. Thus, in both surface tonal character and deeper-level structure, the lyrical interlude falls under the shadow of the chaotic *moto perpetuo* material. As Mitschka would have it, the human voice of melody remains unable to hold fast within the amoral world of the finale.

In addition to a failure of cantabile melody, the movements from the sonata and quartet share with the *Tragic Overture* conventions of a special type of Mozartean sonata-rondo form that Brahms favored for the finales of his multimovement cycles. The definitive characteristics of this hybrid form are (1) a recapitulation of at least part of the main theme in the tonic immediately following the exposition, (2) a subsequent section that functions as either a quasi-independent development or a conflation of development and further recapitulation of main theme material, and (3) the reemergence of recapitulatory restatement leading into the transposed return of secondary material.[5] Examples 7.2a and b summarize the outlines of the hybrid form in the finales of the sonata and quartet. Notice that in each movement Brahms withholds the opening structural tonic until the beginning of the transition. In the sonata he likewise delays the arrival of the exposition's harmonic goal—the tonicized minor dominant—until the very end of the secondary area. In the quartet he goes a step further and avoids articulation of a secondary tonic entirely.

Brahms builds on these tonal idiosyncrasies in the movements' recapitulations. As Example 7.2 illustrates, both finales exemplify the composer's tendency to counterbalance the thematic parallelism of sonata form with large-scale tonal con-

Example 7.2. Formal Outline of Finales

(a) D-Minor Violin Sonata

Exposition	Recapitulation
Tonic Key Area	*Tonic Key Area*
mm. 1–16.1: Main theme in D but on V	mm. 114–33: Main theme in D but on V
	Development
	mm. 134–93.1: On ideas from main theme
Transition	*Transition*
mm. 17–38: Delayed articulation of opening structural tonic followed by modulation to A minor via arrival on V/A	mm. 194–217: In D but on V. *No rearticulation of structural tonic.*
Double Second Group	*Double Second Group*
Part 1	*Part 1*
mm. 39–54: Lyrical theme antecedent. Begins in C major but cadences on V/E minor.	mm. 218–33: Lyrical theme antecedent. Begins in F major but cadences on V/A minor.
mm. 55–72: Lyrical theme consequent. Begins in C major but cadences on V/A minor.	mm. 234–51: Lyrical theme consequent. Begins in F major but cadences on V/D minor.
mm. 73–76.1: Transitional link to	mm. 252–55.1: Transitional link to
Part 2	*Part 2*
mm. 77–107: In A minor but on V/A. Arrival of A tonic only in mm. 104–107.	mm. 256–86: In D minor but on V. Arrival of D tonic only in mm. 283–86.
mm. 108–13: Transitional link to return of main theme	mm. 287–92: Transitional link to return of main theme
	Coda
	mm. 293–310.1: Main theme in D but on V until delayed structural downbeat at m. 311
	mm. 311–37: Expansion of closing tonic

Continued on the next page

Example 7.2. *Continued*

(b) C-Minor String Quartet

Exposition	Recapitulation
Tonic Key Area	*Conflation of Development and Recap. of Tonic Area*
mm. 1–32.1: Main theme in C but on V	mm. 94–101.1: Main theme material in C but on VI reinterpreted as V/♭II
	mm. 102–23.1: Based on main theme material. Modulates from D♭/C♯ to A♮ minor.
Transition	*Transition*
mm. 33–41: Delayed articulation of opening structural tonic followed by modulation to E♭ via arrival on V/E♭	mm. 124–32: Starts in A minor and modulates to C but *no rearticulation of structural tonic*
Secondary Area of Continuous Exposition	*Secondary Area of Continuous Exposition*
mm. 42–70: In E♭ but on V/E♭	mm. 133–61: In C but on V
mm. 70–80.1: *poco tranquillo* but still on V/E♭. *No ultimate arrival of E♭ tonic.*	mm. 161–71: Still on V. *No ultimate arrival of C tonic.*
mm. 81–93: Transitional link to return of main theme	mm. 172–91: New transitional link
	Coda
	mm. 192–230.1: Main theme in C but still on V until delayed structural downbeat at m. 231
	mm. 231–48: Expansion of closing tonic

tinuity, as discussed in Chapters 3 and 4. He withholds the tonic at the beginning of the reprise through an overlap of development and recapitulation and exploits the end-orientation of the secondary material to delay tonic arrival until the end of the recapitulation. It is in the process of approaching this long-delayed tonic articulation that Brahms creates correlations for a tragic denouement along the lines of the process we have observed in the *Tragic Overture*.

In the violin sonata, the first point to note is the way the end of the recapitulation rushes past the potential points of closure in mm. 283–86. The material is exactly parallel to the close of the exposition. In both locations it is possible to hear the arrival of a structural tonic, as suggested in Example 7.2a. Given the passages' hectic character, however, it would be more accurate to say that Brahms evokes the idea of closure, yet withholds the sense of rhythmic arrival that normally coincides with such a formal moment. In expressive terms, these failed tonic articulations have a function similar to the repeated cadential gestures in the climactic augmentation of the *Tragic Overture*. If the material of the movement has a tragic flaw, it is felt in its refusal to acquiesce to everyday demands for tonic articulation. The heroic will strives for a more independent existence in which it need not conform to the conventional behavior expected of commonplace themes, even as the form tries to force tonic articulation upon it.

As the recapitulation merges into the coda, this conflict comes to a head. On the one hand, the recapitulation avoids the fate of closure and leads to a final statement of the refrain with its characteristic dominant prolongation and wild eighth-note activity—the hero's last act of defiance, as it were. This time, however, the sense of crisis intensifies. The material is still stuck on the dominant, but now the harmonic tension stands as the culmination for all of the various forms of tonal delay that have characterized the entire movement. Moreover, Brahms interjects a disquieting C♯ suspension into the V/iv chord of m. 302 and heightens the relentlessness of the violin line by switching from legato slurs to detached eighth notes. He likewise creates a sense of urgency by increasing the dynamic level to *fortissimo* at m. 307. In each previous statement of the refrain, the material has remained at the *forte* level throughout. Indeed, this is only the second time in the entire movement that Brahms has allowed the dynamic level to expand beyond *forte*. (The other *fortissimo* passage occurs in mm. 171–75 of the development.)

Finally, in place of the gossamer-like tonic that enters belatedly at the beginning of the transition in the exposition (m. 17), Brahms lands on a D-minor structural downbeat at m. 311 that is visceral in its articulative force. As if to emphasize this point—the moment at which the hero's fate is sealed—Brahms states the articulation not once, but twice. The *agitato* tempo and the emphatic character of the tonics at mm. 311 and 315 together embody the sense of catastrophe appropriate for the demise of a tragic hero. The further agitation of the passage that ensues finally hits a wall of D minor at m. 325, as the shock of what has just occurred begins to sink in. The return to legato and longer durational patterns in mm. 325–30, as well as the eventual *diminuendo* and slackening of the tempo, correlates with the pity and fear that accompanies the tragic hero's fall. Just as in the *Tragic Overture*, this *sostenuto* passage is followed by a restoration of the moral order in the form of a *subito forte* and *in tempo* expansion of the closing tonic via generic cadential material.

The finale of the string quartet builds to a similar climax as its thematic materials also finally submit to tonal closure. As already mentioned, the quartet's secondary area is remarkable not only for its extensive tonal delay. Even as it reaches its endpoint, it eschews articulation of a middleground mediant *Stufe* but instead remains poised on V/III. Although the form unfolds according to conventions of continuous exposition, it lacks the eventual arrival of a stable harmonic goal that characterizes this type of exposition in Haydn and other composers. The most Brahms allows in the way of stasis is the spent energy of the *poco tranquillo* passage of mm. 70–80.1, which nevertheless retains the tension of the prolonged B♭ dominant.

In the recapitulation this passage returns as part of a prolongation of the home dominant that extends across the entire recapitulation. The strategy is similar to the dimensional counterpoint in the violin sonata as well as in the string quartet's first movement, as discussed in Chapter 2. Brahms avoids tonic rearticulation at the beginning of the reprise through an overlap of development and recapitulation. He then redirects the transition to lead in m. 131 to the home dominant rather than V/III. Following the pattern of the exposition, this transitional dominant *Stufe* remains the tonal focus for the secondary material, which now returns in the tonic key.

In the recapitulation Brahms adds a new passage that emerges out of the phrase repetition at m. 172. In formal terms, this new material functions as a transition from the secondary material to the final refrain. In expressive terms, it correlates with the final struggle the hero mounts against the fate of C-minor articulation. By the time the final phrase of the secondary area has arrived, the dominant prolongation has lost considerable energy in its fight to resist tonic resolution. The *poco a poco crescendo* that soars into the upper register for the new material of mm. 172–91 embodies the hero's last attempt to rouse his energy in order to continue the fight.

At first, this attempt appears to succeed when the struggle resumes with the return of the refrain's dominant prolongation and *moto perpetuo* eighth notes. Yet as is inevitable for a Brahmsian form, fate has doomed our hero from the outset: the coda must arrive at closure. This does indeed occur as the tonal struggle reaches its apotheosis: the eighth-note motion hits a wall of double- and triple-stop chords at m. 224 that finally lead to a rock-solid tonic at m. 231. Here again we see another example of the kind of passage that Tovey interprets as a representation of the larger world to whose grandeur we must assent following a hero's demise. Just as in the *Tragic Overture* and violin sonata, the final tonic expansion spins forth less characteristic material, *forte,* and in a faster tempo—in this case *stringendo*—following the broadening that is almost inevitable in the multiple-stop climax.

In their shared conventions of tragic expression, the *Tragic Overture,* D-minor violin sonata, and C-minor string quartet provide a useful foil for the C-minor piano quartet. Although the denouement of the piano quartet shares some features with these other works, it distinguishes itself through the very absence of those essential characteristics—the suggestion of the continuity of historical time and restoration of the moral order—that Tovey emphasizes. The sonata and string quartet also highlight the special status of the piano quartet in other ways as well. For although they are each remarkable works, neither quite achieves the unique standing of the quartet. It is true that the sonata contains many striking features, including a first-movement development that unfolds entirely over a dominant pedal. This pedal in turn is answered by a tonic pedal in the coda, and the parallel quarter-note tolling on A and D provides an ominous signal with unquestionable tragic significance.

Yet in other ways the sonata lacks the strategic extravagance that characterizes the piano quartet. Although it is a work that comes to a tragic close, its overall character is not nearly as unyielding. Indeed, if a correlation with Aristotelian concepts rings true, then the sonata must allow an audience both to purge itself and to move on, as it were, via a musical restoration of the moral order. The piano quartet, by contrast, serves up a catastrophic climax but then fails to set things right. The finale ends, but it does not resolve.

The sonata also lacks the relentlessness of the quartet—the excessive formal procedures necessary to put us face-to-face with a crisis that allows for no escape. To cite just a few points along these lines, note that the sonata's first movement presents a conventional second theme in the mediant and recapitulates this material in the major tonic. In a similar vein, the slow movement sings out calm and consoling D-major material, as a marked break from the disquiet that surrounds it. Unlike the piano quartet, the violin sonata is able to achieve these areas of peace and contentment, in the home key and through conventional formal procedures.

The situation in the string quartet is similar, although it is a composition that more nearly approximates the degree of eccentricity of the piano quartet. Certainly its motivic concentration is remarkable, not only within the first movement but also in the slow movement and finale. The structure-design conflicts in the first and last movements also approach the extremes of tonal delay found in the piano quartet, as discussed here and in Chapters 2 and 4. Yet despite residual tensions, the string quartet's slow movement is able to achieve at least some tranquility in the closely related key of A♭ major. Likewise, in stark contrast to the relentless C minor of the piano quartet's scherzo, the third movement incorporates a conventional pattern of relaxation for its middle section. Its folklike trio provides an effective break from the mournful Allegretto material, and it does so again in a closely related key, in this case the major subdominant.

A still stronger contrast with the piano quartet emerges with the compositions of our second category of Brahmsian minor-mode expression. Although these works wrestle with various forms of conflict, in the final analysis they cannot be described as tragic per se. Rather, they are characterized by large-scale processes in which anguish ultimately gives way to reconciliation. Broadly speaking, this reconciliation comes in two forms: a denouement of quiet consolation or one of victorious transcendence. Both subcategories reflect the well-known interest of nineteenth-century composers in the *per aspera ad astra* plot archetype, especially as a basis for symphonic works. This archetype is most famously represented in Brahms's oeuvre by the First Symphony.

The essence of the darkness-to-the-stars archetype is straightforward. Reinhold Brinkmann has described it as "the resolution of a conflict of ideas through an inner formal process aimed toward a liberating ending—in a nutshell, the 'positive' overcoming of a 'negative' principle."[6] Brinkmann goes further, however, to delve into more specific aspects of meaning that Brahms communicates in his First Symphony via this archetypal progression. He lavishes considerable attention on the finale and its relationship to Beethoven's Ninth. Following a time-honored tradition, Brinkmann interprets formal procedures in the finale as symbolic of Brahms's efforts to escape Beethoven's long and imposing shadow. It is almost a cliché to observe that Brahms's main theme alludes to Beethoven's *Freude* theme. Yet Brahms reimagines the symphonic context for this material in order to carve out his own creative space. For Brinkmann, this act of liberation centers on Brahms's treatment of his alphorn and chorale themes, both first heard in the finale's introduction.

His interpretation focuses on the fact that these two themes substitute for restatement of the main theme at the beginning of the recapitulation and the coda, respectively. Brinkmann views these substitutions as a means for Brahms symbolically to excise Beethoven and reconceive the symphonic turn to major on his own terms. Beethoven's symphony, as a product of the Enlightenment, reflects an idealistic vision in which man himself, as referenced by the *Freude* theme, is capable of bringing about transcendence. Brahms, by contrast, expresses a more skeptical late nineteenth-century view. In Brinkmann's words, "it is no longer the humanistic fervor of freedom and brotherliness but nature [in the form of the alphorn theme] and religion [in the form of the chorale] that resolve the issue for Brahms" (45). Brinkmann argues that the idea of nature for Brahms specifically "denotes an anti-historical, anti-civilizing force," a reference to something external to man "and also a reference to man's 'inner' nature, his true self, visualized as being 'natural' in origin" (48). Beethoven retains faith in the potential for down-to-earth societal progress expressed in the form of a utopian vision. Brahms by contrast turns somewhat pessimistically to forces that stand outside history and human volition.

Viewed through Brinkmann's hermeneutic window, the failed climax on the chorale in the piano quartet is devastating on two levels. In the symphony, Brahms's pessimistic stance at least allows for the possibility of transcendence through spiritual realms, even if not through the more human route of freedom and brotherhood. In the piano quartet, even the cosmic forces of nature and religion—pastoral religiosity, as Brinkmann calls it—provide no path to salvation.

Given the differences of genre and expressive intent—and to a certain degree the two are inseparable—it is not at all surprising that the symphony and quartet stand at opposite ends of Brahms's expressive universe. Brahms nevertheless does embrace the *per aspera ad astra* plot archetype in other chamber works. Chapter 6 has already touched briefly on one piece, the G-major violin sonata, that falls into a subcategory of this archetypal umbrella: compositions that overcome negativity through conclusions of quiet consolation. As we have seen, the sonata also engages pastoral elements as a component of its positive expressive transformation. Indeed, pastoral and religious themes play a crucial role in numerous works in which Brahms presents some form of progression from darkness to light. The consistency of the practice is significant because it highlights the unique status of the piano quartet as a work that evokes pastoral religiosity only to crush it as a potential source of solace.

One example of Brahms's more typical approach, on the level of a single movement, is the variation set from the G-major sextet. Up to this point I have focused attention mainly on structural/expressive correlations in sonata contexts. A brief look at the sextet variations will allow us to observe ways in which Brahms incorporates similar dynamic strategies of expression for an additive rather than developmental form. In some respects the sextet movement follows a standard pattern of formal progress in a variation context. Following presentation of a haunting theme and icy first variation, each successive section increases the rhythmic activity and contrapuntal complexity. This gradual intensification even includes an acceleration of tempo initiated by variation 3 (m. 37). Also conventional is the fact that the process of intensification leads to a climax at approximately the two-thirds point of the movement, with variation 4's final cadential progression (m. 60).

Yet even with respect to global features, the movement evolves according to its own prerogatives. Although Brahms sets the theme and variations 1–4 all in minor, each of these sections, with the exception of variation 4, closes with a Picardy third. The sustained minor mode at the end of the fourth variation (m. 60) prepares for the definitive shift to major that Brahms introduces in the final variation and coda. The final variation stands apart as the single formal unit that resolves a preparatory dominant; each of the previous sections commences without a lead-in from what precedes it, while Brahms composes a brief transitional bridge following variation 4 (mm. 61–65). Thus, although the variations are sectionalized, Brahms highlights the shift to major by letting it resolve, rather than merely follow, the tensions that have built across a large-scale process.

In addition to this immediate aspect of resolution, the shift to major also participates in a global transformation of thematic characteristics. The coda, with its almost exclusively diatonic progressions and long E pedal, ameliorates two of the main sources for the movement's initial anxiety: the prevalence of descending chromatic motion in the theme and variation 1 and the absence of tonic articulation until the final cadences of these two sections (mm. 12 and 24, respectively). With respect to Brinkmann's ideas about nature and religion, what is noteworthy here is the role that pastoral gestures play in the final transcendent passages. Brahms takes pains to heighten the expressive impact of the stereotypical, horn-fifths material of both variation 5 and the coda with his continual admonitions for *dolce, molto dolce, espressivo* and *molto espressivo* execution. Yet although the coda builds to a final, valedictory climax in m. 82, the movement does not end with the bombast of grandiose triumph, as does the symphony. Rather, the large-scale resolution is consolatory and personal. The movement's conclusion communicates a sense of inner peace rather than a universal, heaven-storming triumph.

It is this type of progression to transcendence that we also find in the chorale conclusion of the *Alto Rhapsody,* first mentioned in Chapter 6. In most accounts of Brahms's artistic development, emphasis tends to fall on the completion of the First Symphony as the central turning point in the period following his first maturity. James Webster, however, has recently argued that it was the *Alto Rhapsody* that was perhaps more significant for Brahms's development as a composer.[7] Finally completing the symphony, as well as the C-minor piano quartet and the op. 51 string quartets, was an important step before Brahms was able to move ahead as a composer of instrumental music. But in Webster's opinion, the significance of this step was specifically that it allowed Brahms to put to rest his aspirations for Beethovenian progressions leading to grandiose triumph. His treatment of the C-minor/major topos in the *Alto Rhapsody* moves into the forefront as a model for later compositions. Webster emphasizes the *innig* character of the final C-major section, and he also highlights characteristics of pastoral religiosity in the work's choral conclusion. The *Alto Rhapsody,* in other words, provides yet another example in which forces of nature and religion function as the means through which a large-scale musical process achieves, in this case quiet, transcendence.

Webster cites the aforementioned G-major violin sonata and Third Symphony as examples that similarly transcend minor-mode difficulties without the undue strain of the First Symphony.[8] Yet the idea that Brahms struggled with the C-minor/major topos in his earlier years only to abandon aspirations for heaven-storming conclusions is only partly borne out by two other C-minor works, in this case pieces that stand on either side of the divide marked by the First Symphony. As an alternative to the idea of quiet consolation in a work like the G-major violin sonata, Brahms also occasionally fulfills trajectories of grandiose triumph in chamber contexts. The scherzo he wrote for the *FAE* Sonata in 1853, well before the works of the first maturity, and his C-minor piano trio, a mature composition published in 1887, both project large-scale progressions from dark C minor to a victorious C major. Although the modest instrumental forces of these compositions limit the expansiveness of their codas, they nevertheless share something of the bombast we find in the ending of the First Symphony. (Here I do not fully agree with Webster's view that the trio joins other late works in achieving a minor-to-major progression "with a sense neither of undue strain nor of unearned triumph.")[9]

The scherzo might appear to be a less-than-perfect choice for our survey, given the fact that it is but one movement and was written as part of a collaborative cycle with Schumann and Albert Dietrich. Yet its function within the *FAE* Sonata is only one context in which to assess its meaning. Indeed, modern audiences most often hear the scherzo as an independent concert piece, whether in live performance or on recording.

The movement's form falls into the normative compound ternary alternation of scherzo and trio sections, within which Brahms introduces a number of striking characteristics. Example 7.3 outlines the main key centers and prolonged harmonies that unfold in counterpoint with the movement's tripartite design. Perhaps the most striking feature, and a main source of the scherzo's expressive tension, is the orientation of its key areas around dominant harmonies. The scherzo also focuses on a small number of driving rhythmic gestures, which further contributes to its overall character of disquiet. A summary of these gestures appears in Example 7.4. Another source of angst is the prevalence of A♭ neighbor figures, especially in the context of painful dominant ninth harmonies, as highlighted in Example 7.4. Finally, notice that the harmonic goal of the scherzo's [a] section is E♭ minor rather than the more conventional major mediant. Similar to the first movement of the First Symphony, Brahms refuses to allow the subordinate key to provide expressive relief. Indeed, given the more modest proportions of the scherzo's form and its characteristic driving rhythmic continuity, there is no opportunity for Brahms to flirt with the relative major the way he does in the first part of the symphony's double second group, as described in Chapters 2 and 5.

There is, however, some relief provided by the contrasting theme that enters at the beginning of the scherzo's [b] section (m. 28).[10] The theme even appears in C major in the phrase repetition of mm. 39–48. This new idea nevertheless fails to break out of the overriding tensions of the movement, in part because of the har-

Example 7.3. Formal Outline of *FAE* Scherzo

A/Scherzo (mm. 1–98)	B/Trio (mm. 99–135)	A'/Scherzo (mm. 136–230)
a	*a*	*a*
mm. 1–9: In C minor but on V	mm. 99–112: In G major but no structural G $^5_3$ until closing cadence	mm. 136–44: In C but on V
mm. 10–27.1: In E♭ minor but on V/E♭ until closing cadence		mm. 145–62.1: In E♭ minor but on V/E♭ until closing cadence
b	*b*	*b*
mm. 28–69.1: Third-related tonicizations on contrasting idea moving through A♭, C, and E before arrival back on V/C	mm. 113–21.1: Tonicization of E♭ and C via return of ideas from scherzo	mm. 163–204.1: Third-related tonicizations on contrasting idea moving through A♭, C, and E before arrival back on V/C
a'	*a'*	*a'*
mm. 70–78: In C minor but on V	mm. 122–35: In G major but no structural G $^5_3$ until closing cadence	mm. 205–13: In C but on V
mm. 79–98: Transposed return of E♭-minor material from [a] now in C minor. Still nevertheless on V until closing cadence.		mm. 214–30: Transposed return of E♭-minor material from [a] now in C minor. Still nevertheless on V until closing cadence.
		Coda
		mm. 230–33.1: Transitional link
		mm. 234–55: Restatement of theme from trio transposed to C major

monic instability of its two statements. The two *fortissimo* phrases have the character of manic outbursts as opposed to confident assertions of resilience in the face of emotional difficulties. Indeed, the outbursts quickly lose strength as they each fade to *piano* for a return of the [a] section's ominous eighth-note rhythms in mm. 37 and 48. Moreover, the two statements of the theme fall within a larger pattern of third-related tonicizations that culminates in a retransition back to C minor. The reprise itself follows through on the negative implications of the [a] section's E♭-minor tonicization. It redirects the tonal motion so that the E♭-minor material can return transposed into C minor in mm. 87–95.

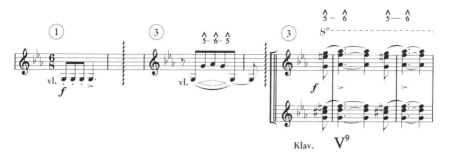

Example 7.4. Rhythmic Motives in *FAE* Scherzo

The lack of a more forthright break from expressive intensity is not so surprising, given the tendency toward formal continuity in small-scale aba′ forms of the type found in the scherzo's A section. The conventions of scherzo-trio form dictate that a more dramatic contrast should fall between the large-scale A and B sections. Even in major-mode movements, the trio section usually provides an area of relaxation following greater drive and intensity in the scherzo proper. Compared to the scherzo's [b] section, Brahms's trio does indeed establish a somewhat more thoroughgoing break from the overall agitation of the movement. Yet it sits in the key of the major dominant, an unusual choice for any minor-mode movement, but especially striking for the middle section of a compound ternary form. We have already seen, in the C-minor piano quartet, the ironic potential the major dominant possesses as a key that may appear stable on the surface but that points inexorably to tonic resolution. In the *FAE* movement Brahms does indeed lead directly from the trio's final cadence on G back to the G dominant that initiates the scherzo's reprise at m. 136. The temporarily stable G major is thus unmasked as an impostor tonic immediately on the musical surface.

In addition to this foreground connection, Brahms also provides veiled hints of G's ephemeral nature within the trio itself. The bass of the G tonic at the end of the trio's [a] section immediately transforms into a recall of the foreboding eighth-note motive from the scherzo as the trio progresses into its own [b] section at m. 113. The trio's [b] section also takes up the thematic material that is part of the motion back to C minor in the scherzo's middle section (cf. mm. 113–21.1 and 50–60). Finally, Brahms solidifies these connections when he leads the trio's [b] section to a G harmony that functions locally as V/C at m. 120 and indeed resolves to C at the return of the [a] material.

Despite all of these reminders of G major's subservience to C minor, the trio does contain one important hint of the eventual expressive triumph of major. It falls at the just-mentioned C chord at the reprise of the trio's [a] material and the formally parallel moment at the beginning of the trio (mm. 122 and 99, respectively). In both locations Brahms uses a major form of a local C tonic as a pivot into G major. At the beginning of the trio, this C chord follows on the heels of the closing C-minor tonic of the scherzo, so the progression puts the minor-to-major transformation directly into our ears. For its part, the [b] section tonicizes E♭ major

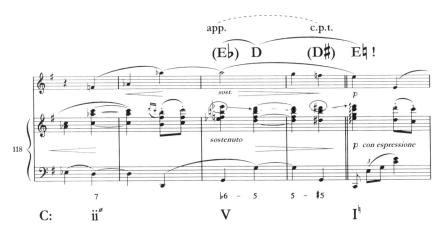

Example 7.5. E♭/D♯ Reinterpretation

before it progresses to the G dominant of mm. 120–21. The second appearance of C major thus enters as part of an implied shift from minor. Here Brahms highlights the E♭–E♮ transformation through the embellishing role he assigns E♭ within the G dominant, as shown in Example 7.5. By reinterpreting the E♭ appoggiatura as an ascending D♯ passing tone, he underscores the function of E♮ as a cancellation of E♭.

In the case of both C-major articulations, Brahms immediately reinterprets the C chord as IV in G major, so the hints of C major are ephemeral. They nevertheless foreshadow the sudden emergence of the victorious major key that arrives in the movement's coda at m. 234. The connection is strengthened by the fact that it is by means of the trio's main theme—the very material that originally hinted at C major—that Brahms brings about the conclusive arrival on the major tonic. Thus, it is through a sonata procedure—transposition of a subordinate theme into the tonic—that Brahms achieves the triumphant turn to major. Note that this is the very strategy he avoids in the piano quartet, where the secondary material *returns* in the major dominant.

The tonic transposition in the scherzo has a dual function in relation to the victory of major. Not only does it provide the most basic element of modal change, the shift from E♭ to E♮: it also highlights A♮ as a prominent melodic pitch at m. 234 in a correction of the scherzo's obsession with A♭ neighbor figures. Indeed, the two processes are intertwined in the sense that the E♮ at the head of the trio theme—the element that foreshadows the coda's turn to C major—becomes the A♮ corrective when the material returns in the tonic key.[11]

Despite this attractive aspect of motivic interconnection, the scherzo's coda is vulnerable to an obvious criticism: it projects a victory that is willed rather than earned and thus fails to provide a convincing close to the movement. The thematic reprise solves the problem of how to end the movement, but the coda's bombast nevertheless appears excessive. The seemingly unprepared return of the subordinate theme, now suddenly *sempre fortissimo* and *grandioso,* enters like an expressive deus ex machina rather than as the consequence of a process of emotional transformation. The final multiple stops in the violin, with their ringing, open E string, following the buildup of trills in the previous measures, may simply be too much for many listeners. (The emphasis on E perhaps relates poetically to Joachim's FAE motto. Yet the grandiose character of the final cadence contradicts the bittersweet notion that freedom comes only at the expense of intimacy: *Frei, aber einsam.*) The character of the coda possibly correlates with the idea of a Romantic hero capable of suddenly bursting onto the scene and saving the day. Although, from our vantage point, this mode of expression appears strikingly un-Brahmsian, it is not so surprising when viewed for what it is: the artistic outpouring of a composer who was barely twenty years old at the time of its conception, and in the thrall of literary and musical Romanticism.

Brahms achieves a more gradual and somewhat more convincing process of transformation in the finale of the C-minor piano trio, a work published over thirty years after the *FAE* scherzo. The trio's more sophisticated treatment of the progression to major resonates with Webster's idea that Brahms was able to overcome his youthful anxiety regarding the C-minor/major topos. Indeed, as Webster points out, C minor itself lost its hold over the mature composer. Following Brahms's preoccupation with C minor—as reflected by the *FAE* scherzo, the *Alto Rhapsody,* the *Song of Destiny,* the op. 51, no. 1, string quartet, the op. 60 piano quartet, and the First Symphony—he turned to the key only once more in later years, for the piano trio.[12] Yet although the trio may achieve a more effective minor-to-major progression than the *FAE* scherzo, it scarcely approaches the artistry of the piano quartet and C-minor string quartet. Moreover, despite its possible shortcomings—not least the bombast of its coda—the First Symphony dwarfs the trio as an aesthetic achievement. The *Alto Rhapsody* may have been as significant as the First Symphony in helping Brahms tame his C-minor demons. But it is with the piano quartet and string quartet, in addition to the *Alto Rhapsody*—and not in the more "mature" trio—that he approaches his highest levels of artistic achievement.

As in the piano quartet, the trio's first movement presents a sharp contrast between turbulent primary material and a lyrical second theme in the major mediant (m. 38). Yet in contrast to the quartet's recapitulatory irony, Brahms exploits the reprise to underscore the solace provided by the trio's secondary material. He focuses a spotlight on the lyrical theme by using it to rearticulate the tonic *Stufe* at m. 150, following an extended intermingling of development and (scattered) restatement of thematic ideas from the tonic area in mm. 80–149. The movement nevertheless ends in extreme darkness: the recapitulation of the second theme is followed by an extended coda (mm. 192–234) oriented around emphatic articulation of the minor tonic via main-theme material. In Tovey's terms, this final turn to minor exposes the tragic irony of the C-major recapitulation.[13] This irony, however, is not nearly as devastating as the disjunction between literal and expressed meaning in the G-major recapitulation of the piano quartet. The trio's major tonic achieves stability in a way that the major dominant never can in a minor-mode context.

Another difference between the works emerges from the ways in which their second movements respond to the catastrophe of their first movements' codas. Recall that the quartet's scherzo extends, in a thematically and harmonically confined range, the unyielding despondency of the opening Allegro. By contrast, the trio's second movement, Presto non assai, eschews a stormy character and instead functions as a distant echo of the first movement's tragic ending. Its overall mood correlates with the kind of shock and pity that we have observed on a smaller scale in the codas of the D-minor violin sonata and C-minor string quartet.

The Presto movement is noteworthy for its minor-mode focus, both within the A section (mm. 1–30), where the minor dominant functions as secondary key, and across the B section (mm. 31–94), where F minor stands as tonal center. As mentioned in Chapter 5, it is not until the third movement that Brahms introduces a movement-level expressive opposition comparable to the dramatic juxtaposition of primary and secondary material within the first movement. It is significant that, both within and across movements, Brahms allows C major itself to stand in opposition to C minor. In an approach totally at odds with the strategy in the piano quartet, he points to the potential for solace in the real world of the home tonic.

This potential for relief eventually comes to fruition in the form of an outright triumph over negative forces at the end of the finale. The finale's overall character is somewhat less oppressive than the intense darkness of the first movement. It nevertheless avoids major-mode lyricism in its secondary area of mm. 34–84. Brahms instead opts for a strategy of continuous exposition in which the secondary material hovers between the minor dominant and the key of its upper third, B♭ major. Ultimately the minor dominant wins, with closure in G finally arriving toward the end of the exposition (mm. 74, 80, and 84). One consequence of this delay is that, by the end of the recapitulation, the movement finds itself poised on a C-minor close (m. 186) that is parallel to the G-minor close at the end of the exposition. Brahms leaves the final shift to C major for a return to the main theme at the coda (m. 190). In contrast to the transposition of secondary material in the *FAE* scherzo, it is thematic transformation of primary material that effects the major-mode victory here.

The freshly warm and congenial character for the primary theme is the result of a number of factors. Example 7.6 highlights the main agents of transformation. In addition to the sudden shift to C major, Brahms replaces the theme's *staccato* articulations with slurs, increases the dynamic level from *piano* to *mezzo piano*, takes out the accent marks in the fourth and fifth measures and all other parallel places, keeps the theme within the *meno Allegro* tempo of the secondary area, and provides a more sustained harmonic underpinning. The new solidity of the tonic, both here and at the phrase repetition of m. 206, is especially significant. It participates in a broader process by which Brahms has gradually undercut the strength of C minor in favor of a suddenly more assertive C major.

The first two movements leave no doubt about the control of C minor, both at their very beginnings and at their final cadences. The finale, however, begins with

a)

minor, *staccato*, *piano*, accents in mm. 3-4 etc., *Allegro molto*, no tonic 5/3

BECOMES

major, *legato*, *mezzo piano*, no accents, *meno Allegro*, solid tonic 5/3

b)

Example 7.6. Transformation of Primary Theme

only a lightly articulated tonic in first inversion. It is not until the counterstatement at m. 21 that the root position emerges as a tonal point of departure. The return of the primary material at the recapitulation (m. 123) builds on the harmonic ambivalence of the opening, so that the thematic reprise enters without a rearticulation of the tonic *Stufe*. One compositional strategy Brahms could have opted for in these circumstances would be to delay tonic return until the arrival of material parallel to the counterstatement. He instead chose to cut the counterstatement and lead directly into the more-or-less continuously transitional material of the secondary area at m. 144. The result is that the return of the C-minor *Stufe* falls only at the point of closure at the very end of the recapitulation (m. 186). Brahms even heightens the delay by excising the cadential phrase that occurs in mm. 73–74 of the expository version. He also denies the final C-minor cadence full force as a point of closure by ending the recapitulation on a G-major question mark rather than a C-minor period (m. 189).

The freshly solid tonic at the beginning of the coda thus stands as the culmination of a process by which the overriding C minor of the cycle gradually loosens its grip and gives way to major. This process, however, does not end at the beginning of the coda. The coda itself further transforms the main theme so that the genial version at the turn to C major becomes a rousing pastoral climax of hunt material by the end of the movement. The transformation into pastoral triumph involves an extended passage of dominant expansion (mm. 213–28) in which Brahms accentuates the harmonic tension with a *crescendo* and a long-delayed acceleration back to *tempo primo,* following the *meno Allegro* of m. 159. The ever-increasing intensity culminates in the brilliant pastoral close of mm. 229–56, whose hunt characteristics include the $^6_8$ meter and stereotypical arpeggiation patterns in which third doublings alternate with perfect intervals. As in the First Symphony, Brahms evokes the idea of nature as a crucial component through which the positive forces of C major triumph over the darkness of C minor.

The categories of minor-mode expression that this survey has thus far outlined are all comprised of works that include at least some form of reconciliation if not outright triumph in their endings. This is obviously the case for pieces like the piano trio that follow the *per aspera ad astra* plot archetype and for works that end in quiet consolation like the G-major violin sonata. Brahms nevertheless seems much more at home creating the kind of warm, congenial, and nostalgic close found in the violin sonata, rather than the bright and emphatic endings of C-major works like the First Symphony, piano trio, or *FAE* scherzo. He likewise achieves greater artistic success in pieces that conclude with passages of a more ethereal character, such as the Third Symphony or *Alto Rhapsody.* Indeed, as Webster and others have suggested, Brahms's tendency toward bombast in a work like the First Symphony perhaps betrays the underlying ambivalence he felt toward emphatic versions of the *per aspera ad astra* archetype. Even taking into account the more skeptical aspects of meaning that Brinkmann reads into the symphony, Brahms simply does not seem to be at home when he engages this mode of expression.

At first glance, it might appear that the pieces I have analyzed as classically tragic come closer to the despondency of the C-minor piano quartet. Yet these works do not end in complete despair. Despite Brahms's "severely formal" conclusions, a vicarious experience of tragic events, embodied in the form of a catastrophe of tonal process and capped off by a musical restoration of the moral order, should have a cathartic effect. The question then remains: do any of Brahms's instrumental compositions approach the resignation with which the C-minor piano quartet ends? There are very few works that come to mind in this context. On the level of a single movement, the Adagio mesto of the horn trio concludes with a bleakness that finds relief only in the pastoral jocularity of the finale, as discussed previously in Chapters 5 and 6. As for a complete cycle, the large-scale expressive trajectory of the clarinet quintet culminates in a final coda that stands as one of Brahms's most intense passages of negative expression.

In the horn trio a number of exceptional characteristics contribute to the tone of sorrow that Brahms himself signals with his *Adagio mesto* tempo indication. Indeed, the tempo indication itself marks the movement as a special case: this is the one instrumental work in which he includes a *mesto* character designation. The tonality of E♭ minor is also an unusual choice for Brahms, a remote and "difficult" key through which he accentuates the expressive intensity of the movement. The timbre of the waldhorn itself contributes as decisively to the mournful tone of the Adagio as to the jocularity of the hunt material in the scherzo and finale. In addition to the contrast between the Adagio and these immediately surrounding movements, the horn's timbre helps to create a similar expressive polarity between the first two movements, as well as between the main and middle sections within the scherzo itself.

Unlike in so many of Brahms's compositions, dimensional counterpoint and extremes of formal noncongruence do not play a major role in the Adagio. The basic outline of the movement's ABA′ form are unambiguous, and no extended tonal delays blur the boundaries of the design. Rather, details such as the periodic return of the dirgelike material of mm. 1–4 endow the movement with its unusually intense tone of sorrow.[14] As Example 7.7a highlights, the material itself establishes the elegiac mood with its prominent placement of the archetypal $\hat{8}$–$\hat{5}$ lament tetrachord in the top voice. The main theme proper likewise focuses on lament figures with its combination of an initial $\hat{3}$–$\natural\hat{7}$ diminished fourth and a $\hat{6}$–$\hat{5}$ appoggiatura figure, as shown in Example 7.7b.

What is remarkable is the way Brahms reinterprets the dirge idea as a link between statements of the main theme within the A section, as well as across the larger boundaries of the ternary form. It is as if the uneven gate of the theme represents the depressed trudge of a funeral procession as it makes its way slowly onward. The individual phrases linked by the dirge idea perhaps represent a mourner's internal thought process, which periodically breaks off and refocuses on the external act of walking.

The linking function of the dirge idea achieves its most intense form of expression at the retransition to the A′ material. In what is one of the most moving passages in all of Brahms, a final statement of the fugue subject from the B section appears in contrapuntal combination with the dirge idea (mm. 43–46). The haunting and archaistic subject—a transformed version of the main theme from the first movement—prominently features the $\hat{6}$–$\hat{5}$ appoggiatura motive that has contributed to the elegiac character of the Adagio's primary theme. The fugal idea fades away to *ppp quasi niente*—another unique expressive marking for Brahms—as the funeral procession continues, with the simultaneous reemergence of the dirge idea. The intensity of the moment is underscored by the fact that it follows shortly after the middle section has reached a climax and gradually subsided into the tense an-

a) Dirge Idea

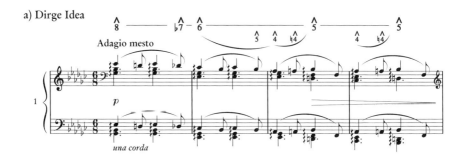

b) Main Theme

Example 7.7. Lament Figures in Horn Trio
(a) Dirge Idea
(b) Main Theme

ticipation of the retransitional dominant of mm. 40–42. Brahms heightens the mournful character of the dominant arrival by bringing back the 6̂–5̂ lament figure, now in augmentation and at the outer boundary of the horn's lowest register.

The only time the Adagio allows some light to shine occurs as the A′ section reaches what should be its final cadential dominant in m. 59. As mentioned in Chapter 5, the shift to an E♭-major horn-fifths pattern at this point foreshadows the expressive shift that will occur at the beginning of the finale. Yet this unprepared glimmer of hope cannot hold fast. Tonally the material remains unstable as part of a $^6_4$ chord, and the pastoral evocation falls within what turns out to be a larger sequential progression. The horn-fifths material also alternates, as part of the sequence, with recollections of the haunting minor-mode fugue subject from the B section. Moreover, instead of coming forth with a cadence, Brahms leaves the $^6_4$ chord hanging and uses the sequence to build to one last passionate climax on the main theme at m. 69. The movement closes in the darkness in which it began, as the climax subsides into a final phrase based on the dirge material (mm. 77–86). Brahms does not conclude this phrase with a V–i cadence. Rather, the funeral procession ends with a darkly religious and awe-inspiring plagal motion, within which Brahms creates a final stab of pain via a *sforzando* arrival on the closing E♭ tonic (m. 83).

A similar dark close caps off the coda in the finale of the clarinet quintet. Here, however, the darkness is absolute; there will be no subsequent relief like that provided by the trio's finale. The despair is heightened by the fact that the coda returns to material from the first movement and thus forms a conclusion not just for the finale but for the quintet as a whole. The finale is a variation movement in which Brahms adopts some of the same strategies we have observed in the slow movement of the G-major sextet, but now in the service of a bleak rather than transcendent ending. As in the sextet movement, Brahms links the variations through a gradual pattern of rhythmic intensification. The similarity includes Brahms's treatment of mode across the form. Both movements are set entirely in minor with the exception of one section. As we have seen, the sextet movement shifts to major for its final variation and coda. The quintet's finale does likewise, but for its penultimate or fourth variation. The modal shift helps to create a large-scale subdivision in the form at the arrival of the major-mode variation 4, following the rhythmic acceleration across variations 1–3.

One consequence of this large-scale articulation is that it allows Brahms to present the subsequent final variation and coda as a unified passage (mm. 161 and 193, respectively), similar to the strategy he follows in the sextet. Brahms heightens the continuity between the final two sections by means of their shared triple meter following the $\frac{2}{4}$ time of all that has come before. He also allows the coda to resolve the cadential dominant of the last variation. Prior to this point, all the variations have been sectional; both the pattern of sectionalization and the presence of a unique cadential continuity are additional features the quintet movement shares with the sextet variations. The difference, of course, is that the quintet is directed toward a tragic minor-mode close, in contrast to the ethereal E-major denouement of the sextet.

The sense of continuity across the quintet's final variation and coda also emerges out of a thematic process of far-reaching consequences. The final $\frac{3}{8}$ variation begins to hint at connections between the material of the finale and the theme from the tonic area of the first movement. Example 7.8 outlines the main points of contact between what until this point have appeared as disparate ideas. The veiled connections come to the fore when the two ideas interact directly in the coda. It is in the process of bringing together the main substance of the two movements that the coda provides a culmination for the entire cycle. The return of material from the first movement is crucial to the profoundly bleak tone of the finale's close. Despite all that has transpired across the work, the quintet finds itself back where it started.

But where did it in fact start? What are some of the specific expressive characteristics of this thematic recall? As Example 7.9 highlights, the first-movement material is saturated with the anguish of multiple appoggiatura figures. A further sense of angst emerges from the unyielding tonic bass that initiates the phrases at mm. 193 and 201–203. Brahms heightens the pathos of these tonic articulations with *forte piano* and *rinforzando* markings, respectively. Similar *subito forte* cries of anguish occur in mm. 208 and 210 on chords that disrupt the harmonic flow as the material breaks down into smaller units. The closest Brahms comes to a normal cadential progression is the hollowed-out octave doublings of the line that culminates on B at m. 199. It is not until the final phrase of the movement that he allows

Example 7.8. Motivic Connection of First-Movement Theme and Variation 5

for a full-fledged cadence, and, in a unique procedure for Brahms, this progression restates the closing material from the first movement.

The restatement manifests a devastating return to the extreme darkness in which the first movement ended. Following that expressive low point, Brahms continues with middle movements and a finale that are not nearly so dark. The B-minor gypsy improvisation of the Adagio's middle section is framed by A and A′ sections of ethereal D-major calm. The third movement also alternates D-major and B-minor sections, with the minor-mode material again in the subordinate position. Moreover, the passages in major are relaxed and *semplice* while the B-minor material is hardly despondent or angst-ridden. Rather, it has a *scherzando* and even at times playful character. Similarly, the finale's theme and variations avoid *Sturm und Drang* intensity. It is not until the coda that Brahms returns to the bleakness

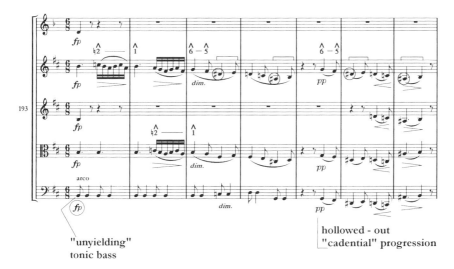

Example 7.9. Correlations for Anguish in Coda

of the opening movement. The effect is so powerful partly because of the very break from despair provided by the middle movements. The coda and especially the final cadential progression suddenly strip away any feelings of security that have built across the interior movements and reveal that no authentic recovery has been achieved. This irony is all the more powerful for the fact that it surfaces only in the final measures of the cycle and through an exact parallelism with the close of the first movement.

Although the previous survey has dealt with compositions set in a variety of keys, readers will no doubt have noticed that special emphasis has fallen on C-minor works. This is no coincidence. It is a matter, first of all, of simple percentages. Brahms turned to C more than any other key when he chose to set a symphonic or chamber work in the minor mode, as Example 7.10 illustrates. More importantly, a focus on C minor grows from the conviction that the key had a special expressive significance for Brahms, as well as for other composers in the Viennese tradition.[15] We have seen that three crucial works that Brahms completed in the 1870s after long compositional gestation are set in C minor: the First Symphony, the op. 51, no. 1, string quartet, and our op. 60 piano quartet. Moreover, two choral masterpieces from this period also engage the C-minor/major topos: the *Alto Rhapsody* and the *Song of Destiny*.

For Beethoven, the significance of C minor has long been recognized, above all in the prototypical example of the Fifth Symphony.[16] But it also seems to be the case that the key was a vehicle for a striking intensity of expression for other composers as well. In the case of Mozart, I would cite, in addition to the Piano Concerto in C Minor, K. 491, the famous (or even notorious) introduction to the *Dissonant Quartet*, K. 465. The significance of the quartet's introduction is not merely its

Example 7.10. Brahms's Key Choices for Minor-Mode Instrumental Works

C Minor

1. String Quartet, op. 51, no. 1
2. Piano Quartet, op. 60
3. First Symphony, op. 68
4. Piano Trio, op. 101

5. *Academic Festival Overture,* op. 80 (comic work, very little time actually in C minor)
6. *FAE* Scherzo (one mvt. of collaborative cycle in A minor, with Schumann and Dietrich)

D Minor

1. Piano Concerto, op. 15
2. *Tragic Overture,* op. 81
3. Violin Sonata, op. 108

A Minor

1. String Quartet, op. 51, no. 2
2. Double Concerto, op. 102
3. Clarinet Trio, op. 114

F Minor

1. Piano Quintet, op. 34
2. Clarinet Sonata, op. 120, no. 1

3. Third Symphony, op. 90 (mvt. III in C minor, finale articulates F minor/major progression)

E Minor

1. Cello Sonata, op. 38
2. Fourth Symphony, op. 98

G Minor

1. Piano Quartet, op. 25

2. Violin Sonata, op. 78 (mvt. II in E♭, finale articulates G minor/major progression)

B Minor

1. Clarinet Quintet, op. 115

2. Piano Trio, op. 8, both versions (mvt. II in B minor, finale in B minor including conclusion)

nearly chaotic chromaticism, but the fact that this chromaticism prepares for a shift to the diatonic C major of the exposition. The quartet thus exemplifies not only the dark intensity of C minor, but also the contrasting brightness and purity that C major seems to have symbolized for the Viennese masters. Along with the entrance of the finale in Beethoven's Fifth, the famous C-major "Let there be light" in Haydn's *Creation* provides perhaps the most famous example of this extreme affective polarity between major and minor forms of the key. Thus, although the introduction to the *Dissonant* Quartet represents just one brief passage, it seems more than a matter of chance that Mozart chose to create such an extraordinary—indeed, bizarre—invention to begin a work in C, as opposed to any other key.

The same might be said of the two works that will be the focus of the next section of this chapter: Haydn's Symphony in C Minor, no. 95, and Schubert's *Quartettsatz*, D. 703. A shift of emphasis to Haydn and Schubert at this late stage is not intended to suggest that Brahms modeled his approach to C-minor expression specifically on these two works. Rather, the point is to demonstrate that Brahms was engaged in the same C-minor tradition of which the Haydn and Schubert compositions both form a part. In addition to providing a sharper perspective on this continuity of compositional practice—which, after all, has long been a mainstay of Brahms scholarship—the analyses will illustrate that the interpretive strategies that I have developed for Brahms also have relevance for a wide range of works in the Viennese tradition. Although other compositions (and, indeed, other tonalities—D minor, for instance) might have been chosen, these two pieces attract attention due to their high degree of structural idiosyncrasy and expressive intensity. Neither of them feature anything quite as bizarre as what occurs in the introduction to the *Dissonant* Quartet. They nevertheless present profound stylistic deviations that not only provide further evidence of the affective significance of C minor, but also invite close interpretive scrutiny.

In particular, the symphony and *Quartettsatz* both manifest a tendency toward the kinds of extremes of dimensional noncongruence that we have observed in Brahms. Among the issues that we have dealt with over the course of this book, we will see that tonal delays, recapitulatory overlaps, ambiguities of two- and three-key expository articulation, mode shifts on multiple structural levels, and motivic figures of age-old rhetorical significance emerge as core components of the Haydn and Schubert works. Let us begin with the Haydn symphony and one of the central points developed in Chapter 3: the notion that the initial appearance of a main theme often predicts its recapitulatory reinterpretation. In the case of the Haydn as well as the Schubert, it will be necessary to spend some time untangling this and other structural complexities before a move can be made toward expressive interpretation.

Haydn's theme appears in Example 7.11. One of its most striking features is the difficulty it has articulating C minor. In a deep structural sense—and here emphasis must fall on deep—it is possible to infer a C-minor *Stufe* from the motto-like outbursts of mm. 1–2 and 10–11. An interpretation along these lines appears in Example 7.12a, along with two alternatives whose significance will become clear momentarily.[17] The outbursts, however, are far too abrupt to provide the kind of

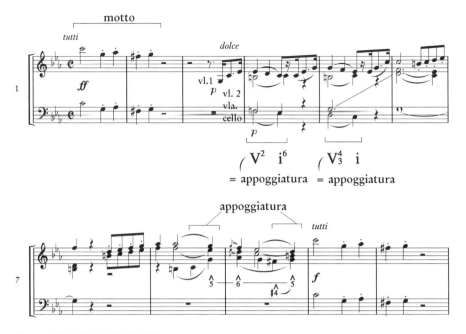

Example 7.11. Haydn's Main Theme

straightforward tonic anchor we listen for as a point of departure for a sonata exposition. The problematic status of the tonic arises from the absence of explicit harmonization and the fact that the motto emphasizes a dominant-oriented $\hat{5}$ rather than a tonic-oriented $\hat{1}$. If the statement and return of the motto do articulate a structural tonic, then it is a tonic filled with tension and anxiety. Indeed, the entire tonic area teeters precariously between emphasis on i and V.[18]

The two alternative interpretations of Example 7.12 reflect this lack of harmonic clarity. In the case of Example 7.12b, I have highlighted the potential to hear tonic expansion throughout the beginning of the phrase. If it is possible to attribute tonic function to the off-balance motto statements, then might it not also be possible to assign structural status to the tonics that receive emphasis as resolutions of the appoggiatura dominants in mm. 4 and 5? On the other hand, the V of mm. 6–7 forms a temporary harmonic goal for the first part of the phrase, perhaps absorbing the previous tonic expansion under its control, as shown in Examples 7.12a and c. Similarly, although the tonic reenters in m. 8, this i chord also falls within a directed motion to the dominant of m. 9. Finally, this last V does not actually resolve but rather is interrupted by a return of the outburst, whose emphasis on $\hat{5}$ takes on heightened significance in relation to the previous dominant focus.

In the end, the important interpretive point is not that one and only one of these graphic interpretations is correct. Rather, the crucial issue is that, regardless of where one's interpretation falls along the range of possible readings of the passage, there seems no doubt that the material raises questions about prolongational con-

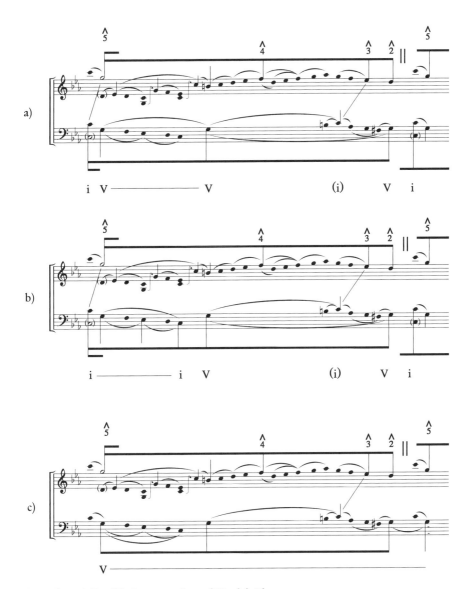

Example 7.12. Possible Interpretations of Haydn's Theme

trol. It does not speak to a single, unambiguous interpretation, but rather articulates a problem that Haydn will need to address at the recapitulation.

How does Haydn reconcile the idiosyncrasies of his theme with recapitulatory exigencies of sonata form? The analytical tools of dimensional counterpoint reveal that he fashions an overlap between the end of the development and the onset of the recapitulation. Example 7.13a summarizes the main events as they unfold in the dimensions of theme, key, and tonal structure. The graph in Example 7.13b

Example 7.13. Haydn's Recapitulatory Overlap

(a) Formal Outline

Exposition	Recapitulatory Overlap
	mm. 104–9: Tonicization of G minor, on motto
Tonic Key Area	
mm. 1–2: Motto	mm. 110–19: Motto at tonic pitch level initiates circle-of-fifths sequence. *No structural tonic rearticulation.* Culminates on V as middleground *Stufe* instead.
mm. 3–9: Main theme, in C but wavers between prolongation of tonic or dominant *Stufe*	mm. 120–28.1: Main theme subsumed within prolongation of retransitional home dominant. *Still no structural tonic.*
Transition	—
mm. 10–11 and 12–15.1: Motto with fragmentary extension, moves to mediant key	—
mm. 16–28: Sequence on motto leads to standing on V/E♭ as main structural harmony for transition	—
Second Key Area	*Resolution of Overlap/Secondary Area*
mm. 29–43.1: Second theme, statement and repetition. In E♭ with E♭ tonic *Stufe* in control throughout.	mm. 129–44.1: Second theme in C major, statement and repetition. *Delayed rearticulation of C tonic* Stufe *but now major.*

b) Graph

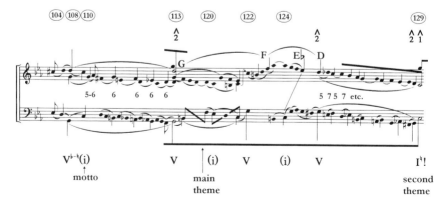

clarifies salient aspects of harmony and counterpoint that undergird this remarkable passage.[19] The main point to note is that Haydn absorbs both the opening outburst and his main theme proper within an expansion of the retransitional dominant. If recapitulation can be understood as a form of self-analysis, then Haydn's recomposition posits the dominant as the governing harmony for his opening material. When sonata form offers Haydn the opportunity to recontextualize his theme within a broader continuity, he does not try to force it to rearticulate the tonic. Rather, he chooses to build on those elements of instability highlighted by the graphs of Examples 7.12a and c.

As interesting as issues of dimensional counterpoint may be on their own terms, the recapitulatory overlap in the Haydn symphony—like so many other examples of dimensional noncongruence we have explored previously—also has a decisive impact on expressive interpretation. For as Example 7.13b indicates, it is only with the shift to C major for the return of secondary material that Haydn allows the overlap between retransition and recapitulation to resolve. What effect does this delayed structural downbeat have in the expressive realm? For an answer, we first need to explore stylistic correlations and strategic interpretations for the C-minor and Eb-major sections of the exposition. It will then be possible to interpret the expressive significance of the new relationship Haydn creates between these sections in the recapitulation.

On a generic stylistic level, the opposition between the C-minor and Eb-major themes maps onto the same kind of opposition of tragic and nontragic expression that Brahms creates in the exposition of the first movement of the piano quartet. Although strategic interpretation reveals some additional similarities between the movements, there are, as we would expect, major differences as well. With respect to similarities, one main point of contact is the tonal instability of the openings of the two expositions. (Recall that Brahms begins with a tonic area and transition that function as structural anacrusis to his Eb variations.) In addition, Haydn's main theme is noteworthy for its appoggiatura sigh motives, the same kind of angst-ridden gestures found in Brahms's opening paragraph. As Example 7.11 highlights (p. 262), these appoggiaturas occur not only in mm. 4–5, as noted above, but also in the syncopated violin lines of mm. 8–9. Note also the emphasis Haydn, like Brahms, places on $\hat{6}$–$\hat{5}$ neighbor gestures as well as $\sharp\hat{4}$–$\hat{5}$ embellishment, additional rhetorical figures of tragic connotation. Finally, Haydn includes the same type of abrupt shifts in texture and dynamics that Brahms does, elements of discontinuity that contribute to an overall character of anxiety and foreboding.

Despite this recourse to similar rhetorical gestures, the openings of the two movements are nevertheless highly distinct. This is only to be expected for a comparison between an eighteenth-century symphony and a late nineteenth-century chamber work, notwithstanding the profound influence the Viennese masters had on Brahms. Most obviously, the opening phrase of Haydn's tonic area unfolds within the rhythmic flow of the exposition. Unlike Brahms, he does not embed elements of a slow introduction within his main theme. Nor does Haydn incorporate anything nearly as idiosyncratic as Brahms's *pizzicato* E♮'s, his B♭-minor phrase repetition, or the relentless C-minor pedal of his counterstatement. In short, al-

Example 7.14. 6̂–5̂ Neighbor Motive in Second Theme

though both composers draw on gestures from the same storehouse of traditional rhetorical figures, Brahms pushes the expressive envelope further as befits his unusual expressive aims.

A comparison of the opposition between tonic and mediant material in the two movements reveals a similar mix of stylistic similarity and strategic difference. Haydn, like Brahms, juxtaposes an angst-filled opening with a marked shift in expressive orientation for his secondary material. Yet in the symphony, Haydn eschews any contrary impulses like the subcutaneous disquiet or ironic overcompensation that we found in Brahms's variations. In striking contrast to the tensions of C minor in the tonic area, Haydn's second theme articulates the mediant as an unambiguous point of departure at m. 29. The prolongation of this E♭ *Stufe* is similarly untroubled. Haydn expands it with a straightforward I–(V–I⁶)–ii⁶–V–I progression as the underpinning for a standard Schoenbergian sentence in mm. 29–35.1. He then repeats the sentence in mm. 37–43.1 before he moves on to the kind of looser-knit push toward closure (mm. 44–61) that typically caps off an exposition.

The sustained texture and undisturbed piano dynamics of the sentence form another point of contrast with the opening. The *Sturm und Drang* main theme has given way to a phrase of gracious and elegant eighteenth-century simplicity. As Example 7.14 shows, the sentence even includes a prominent articulation of a major form of the 6̂–5̂ motive, with its pastoral connotations, as a contrast to the angst of the minor 6̂–5̂ version prominent in the main theme. In expressive terms, Haydn has lifted away the gloom of the opening and let the sun shine in without even a hint of a storm cloud on the horizon.

Even more than was the case in the Brahms quartet, then, Haydn's secondary material points toward the very real possibility that C-minor angst can be overcome in the recapitulation. The difference, of course, is that Haydn fulfills this tra-

Example 7.15. Liquidation of Main-Theme Head Motive

jectory of consolation, whereas Brahms crushes it in a most devastating fashion. Indeed, by absorbing the primary material into an overlap with the development, Haydn heightens the impact of the C-major resolution at the entrance of the secondary material. The primary material loses the problematic potential it once had to articulate C minor. One might even say that Haydn's dimensional counterpoint reverses the roles of his expository themes. The primary theme becomes further attenuated and assumes a secondary status in relation to the tonic transposition of the E♭ idea, which moves into the spotlight as resolution of the recapitulatory overlap. This reversal is confirmed when Haydn liquidates the main theme's head motive as part of the *galant* expansion of his closing major tonic in mm. 151–65, as highlighted in Example 7.15. What once was part of an expression of disquiet and foreboding dissolves into triumphant C major.

Although the motion to C major in the first movement represents perhaps the single most important turning point in the cycle, the remaining three movements continue to play out the drama of mode shift and expression. Because a thorough treatment of expressive issues would require extensive analysis, I will limit myself only to the most salient points. In particular, the concept of framing that emerged as a crucial component for interpretation of the piano quartet also plays a central role in the symphony. What is striking is the way Haydn engages techniques of enclosure both within and across movements, so that framing becomes a primary means of integration for the cycle.[20]

Both middle movements—the Andante theme and variations and the minuet and trio—exhibit internal strategies of enclosure through which Haydn sustains the tension between minor and major. The E♭-major Andante unfolds in a conventional manner with a harmonically closed binary theme followed by four variations. The element of framing comes into play with the shift to E♭ minor for the

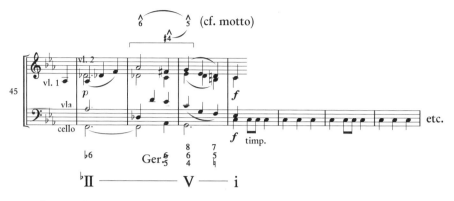

Example 7.16. Closing Progression of Minuet

second variation at m. 25. Haydn reins in the dark intensity of this *Minore* variation not simply by enclosing it within the surrounding E♭-major variations: he also refuses to allow the *Minore* section to close on its tonic. It is the one variation that leads from its final cadential dominant into the tonic that initiates the following section (m. 41). As in Brahms's variation movements discussed previously, this unique cadential continuity allows for a more active resolution of minor into major than framing alone could achieve.

The consolatory reemergence of the major mode recalls the resolution of the first movement's recapitulatory overlap into the bright C major of the secondary material. In the Andante Haydn intensifies the sense of expressive release through the addition of a painful minor ninth in the dominant at the very end of the *Minore* section (m. 39). The process also recalls the first movement in its shift from violent *fortissimo* outbursts and tentative *piano* responses in mm. 29–37 of the *Minore* variation, to sustained dynamics in the following sections.

Yet despite the emphasis on major-mode consolation, the Andante's E♭ key nevertheless sustains the shadow of C minor. The character of the theme and its major-mode variations calls to mind late eighteenth-century grace and elegance, similar to the second theme in the first movement. It would be hard to argue for some form of underlying tragic resonance or ironic expression for this material. The beginning of the variation movement nevertheless articulates a somewhat jarring chromatic shift following the closing C-major section of the first movement.[21] Moreover, although the point is obvious, it is nevertheless worth stressing that E♭ finds its place in the cycle as relative major of C minor. Indeed, the E♭ tonality of the variation movement prepares the large-scale shift back to C minor for the minuet and trio.

The third movement's return to C minor temporarily reverses the C-major triumph of the first movement. The frame here is again a conventional one: the C-minor minuet encloses the C-major trio. An especially moving passage in this process of reversal occurs in the minuet's coda. First observe the expressive intensity of the cadential ♭II⁶–(Ger.⁵)–V–i closing progression shown in Example 7.16, in particular its emphasis on the disquieting diminished-third motion around G. It seems no coincidence that this chromatic double neighbor is the same figure that embellishes $\hat{5}$ in the first movement's motto. Yet this is not all. Following his dark approach to closure, Haydn creates a stunning effect of orchestration. He supports a final ascending arpeggiation of his minor tonic in mm. 48–53.1 with an awe-inspiring tolling on C in the timpani. The result is perhaps the most ominous passage in the entire cycle. The grip of despair applied by this unrelenting C pedal underscores the minuet's expressive regression following the first movement's progression to C major.

By assigning such a crucial role to the third movement, Haydn elevates a part of the Classical symphony that tends to be lighter and less idiosyncratic, as opposed to structurally complex opening sonata forms and expressively sublime slow movements. The closing passage demonstrates Haydn's commitment to producing musical materials adequate to the task of performing under the glare of this spotlight. Haydn likewise exploits the reemergence of minor in the minuet to heighten the significance of the finale, to which falls the task of determining the cycle's expressive outcome. Haydn answers the dark C minor of the minuet's close with a relentlessly bright C-major finale. In the final analysis, the motion back to C minor in the middle movements itself proves to be part of a larger pattern of enclosure. The first movement articulates the cycle's fundamental shift from C minor to C major. This C major then returns to dominate the finale, joining with the close of the first movement to create a frame around the E♭ major/C minor of the middle movements.

Two noteworthy features of the finale stand out within its function as conclusive rearticulation of C major. First, there is a single passage in which Haydn returns to the minor version of the tonic, but only in such a way as to confirm C minor's demise. This brief shift to minor occurs toward the end of the recapitulation at m. 152. There are no real progressions in C minor, however—just the sudden intrusion of the minor tonic, with linear elaboration over a C pedal. When the bass finally pushes up chromatically to $\hat{5}$, the dominant arrives at m. 168 in the form of a *major* version of the cadential $^{6}_{4}$. C minor, in other words, disappears as suddenly as it had reemerged. The remainder of the movement is devoted to expansion of the conclusive major tonic via material of *galant* character. The liquidation of C minor into this *galant* coda harkens back to the end of the first movement. Recall that Haydn similarly puts C minor to rest there through dissolution of the main theme's head motive as part of a *galant* culmination on C major.

The second noteworthy feature of the finale is the fact that, with the exception of the main theme, the movement is consumed with passages of imitative counterpoint and, in particular, species-style writing. This type of contrapuntal finale is not at all unusual in the eighteenth century. Many of Haydn's early string quartets close with fugal finales, as does Mozart's *Jupiter* Symphony, perhaps the most famous example of the practice. (Mozart's casting of the *Jupiter* in C major makes for a suggestive connection with the Haydn symphony.)[22] The idea of a fugal finale, however, does acquire special significance in a work that articulates a minor-to-major trajectory. The associations of imitative writing in general and species counterpoint in particular with the church, learned style, and Palestrina lend the victory

of C major an air of both authority and transcendence—that is, absolute and unquestionable transcendence—that it might not otherwise have if achieved with
music without these topical associations.[23] Haydn's fugal finale thus reflects an
eighteenth-century alternative to the focus among nineteenth-century composers
on chorale writing in the finales of works that engage the minor-to-major topos.
Our knowledge of the influence this topos was to acquire in the nineteenth century
should not cause us to lose sight of the remarkable achievement Haydn's symphony
represents.

Haydn's symphony forms an interesting foil for Brahms's quartet in part because
of the crucial role the first movement's recapitulatory overlap plays in the work's
expressive trajectory. Schubert's *Quartettsatz* also articulates an overlap between
development and recapitulation, with important consequences for expressive interpretation. The *Quartettsatz,* however, also raises additional issues of dimensional counterpoint as they relate to double second groups, a topic that Chapter 5
has identified as centrally important for Brahms in general and for the finale of the
piano quartet in particular. Structural analysis of Schubert's double second group
and other aspects of dimensional counterpoint will once again necessarily precede
expressive interpretation of this complex work.

Example 7.17 summarizes the main outlines of the *Quartettsatz*'s form. The
three main sections of the exposition each eschew the kind of harmonic ambivalence that characterizes the opening theme of the Haydn symphony. The challenge
for harmonic interpretation instead arises with respect to prolongational relationships among the expanded C, A♭, and G expository tonics. In terms of traditional
formal analysis, the second group begins at the arrival of the A♭ lyrical theme in
m. 27, as Example 7.17 indicates. Attention to dimensional counterpoint, however,
reveals that the C *Stufe* remains in effect well past the point that the dimensions
of theme and key indicate a shift to secondary material.

The idea that A♭ represents a less-than-decisive move away from the tonic grows
in part from the fact that Schubert does not prepare the lyrical theme with a
sonata-style transition. Rather, he opts for an abrupt pivot-chord modulation in
mm. 23–26. He launches a more forthright transitional passage only after the A♭
section closes at m. 60. Moreover, in a paradox typical for Schubert, this displaced
transition touches back on the tonic before it moves onward to the exposition's ultimate harmonic goal.[24] The means of reference is not a C tonic itself, but rather
the G harmony of mm. 77, which functions as dominant by virtue of the C iv⁶–V
progression in mm. 76–77. Only following articulation of this back-relating dominant does Schubert move, in mm. 81–92, to the dominant of the up-and-coming
G tonicization. It is here that he finally provides the kind of transitional preparation
absent from the earlier modulation to A♭. His expansion of the D dominant creates
the buildup of tension necessary to allow the subsequent resolution to G at m. 93
to articulate a middleground harmonic shift.

Where, then, does the tonic *Stufe* give way? The answer emerges out of attention
to two of the factors just enumerated—the absence of proper transitional prepa-

Example 7.17. Formal Outline of *Quartettsatz*

Exposition	Development	Recapitulation
Tonic Area	*Part 1*	
mm. 1–12.1: Imitative entrances on lament tetrachord, anacrusis to C *Stufe*	mm. 141–56.1: A♭ major expanded through B♭ neighbor, then becomes V/D♭	—
mm. 13–18.1: Homophonic phrase also based on lament tetrachord, expansion of C *Stufe*		—
	Part 2	
mm. 19–26.1: Phrase repetition merges into abrupt pivot-chord modulation to A♭	mm. 157–90.1: D♭ tonicization leads to ascending circle-of-fifths sequence, B♭–F–C–G–D, and expansion of D as V/G minor	—
Double Second Group	mm. 191–94.1: Common tone modulation from V/G to B♭ major	*Double Second Group*
Part 1		*Part 1*
mm. 27–60: Lyrical theme in A♭ major, antecedent/consequent but no harmonic closure		mm. 195–228: Lyrical theme, antecedent in B♭ major, consequent in E♭ major
Transition		*Transition*
mm. 61–92.1: Begins in A♭ minor but leads to G as V/C. Then modulates to G major via arrival on D as V/G.		mm. 229–56.1: Begins in E♭ minor but leads to G as V/C
Part 2		*Part 2*
mm. 93–104.1: Phrase 1, statement and repetition with G-major *Stufe* in control throughout		mm. 257–68.1: Phrase 1, statement and repetition with C-major *Stufe* in control throughout

Continued on the next page

Example 7.17. *Continued*

Exposition	Development	Recapitulation
mm. 105–24.1: Phrase 2, statement and expanded repetition. Arrives at closure in G major.		mm. 269–88.1: Phrase 2, statement and expanded repetition. Arrives at closure in C major.
mm. 125–40: Closing material, further expansion of closing G-major tonic		mm. 289–304: Closing material, further expansion of closing C-major tonic
		Tonic Area/Coda
		mm. 305–15: Abrupt shift back to C minor, imitative entrances on lament tetrachord as anacrusis to final cadence

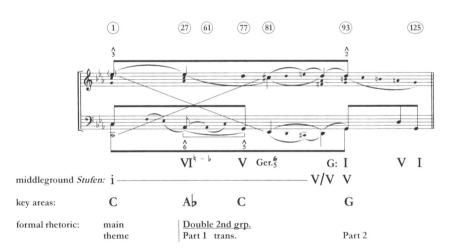

Example 7.18. Middleground Graph of Exposition

ration for the A♭ material and the return of G as dominant in m. 77—as well as the arrival on an E♭/C♯ augmented-sixth chord at mm. 83 and 87–88. The G dominant and augmented sixth together reactivate the tonic *Stufe*, following the apparent progression away to A♭. The augmented sixth, in particular, is decisive: it enters as part of a chromatic voice exchange with the overriding 3̂/i of the tonic area. Example 7.18 depicts this middleground voice leading, in counterpoint with the for-

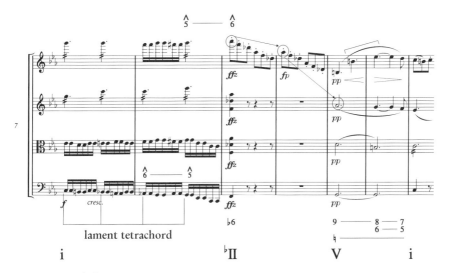

Example 7.19. $\hat{5}$–$\hat{6}$ Neighbor Motive

mal parsing that emerges from the thematic and key scheme dimensions.[25] Schubert presents us with a dimensional counterpoint similar to the formal unfolding in the finale of Brahms's piano quartet. Recall that in the quartet, Brahms also holds an apparent motion to secondary material under the grip of the tonic *Stufe*. Not until the arrival of his chorale theme does he articulate a middleground move away from C. The difference, of course, is that Brahms works with only two keys—C and E♭—whereas Schubert engages three.[26]

The consequences for expressive interpretation are also similar in the two works. In the piano quartet we have seen that the finale's attenuation of E♭ is part of a strategy whereby Brahms eliminates the potential of secondary material to point toward the possibility for escape from suicidal despair. In the *Quartettsatz* the relegation of A♭ to a subsidiary role likewise participates in a process through which Schubert expresses the inevitability of a tragic outcome.

The *Quartettsatz*'s main expressive opposition arises between the C-minor material and the A♭-major lyrical theme. The tonic area establishes a state of anxiety and foreboding by virtue of some of the same rhetorical gestures we have observed in Brahms and Haydn. Its primary motive is the lament tetrachord, a figure that Schubert repeats obsessively throughout virtually every measure of the tonic area. A sense of inescapable angst also arises from the rhythmic agitation of sixteenth-note motion in the imitative opening (mm. 1–12.1), as well as the constantly repeated eighth-note pattern in the first violin in the two phrases that follow (mm. 13–18.1 and 19–26.1). A $\hat{5}$–$\hat{6}$ neighbor motive—itself a fragment from the lament tetrachord—also contributes to the material's disquiet. As Example 7.19 shows, Schubert heightens the tension of the neighbor by introducing it at the apex of the opening phrase at the climactic *ffz* arrival on the Neapolitan harmony. He then absorbs A♭ into the harrowing V[9] chord of m. 11, whose expansion includes a dis-

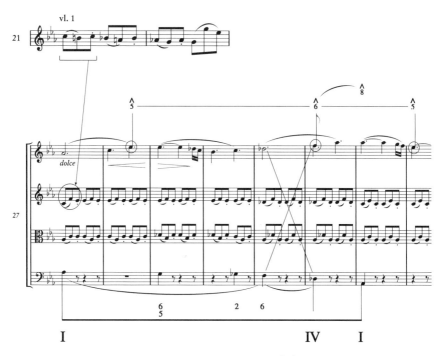

Example 7.20. Transformation of Lament Tetrachord and 5̂–6̂ Neighbor

quieting B♮–E♭ diminished fourth familiar to us from the main theme of Brahms's finale.

The character of the A♭ theme stands in direct opposition to the anxiety of the tonic area. The melody itself is the kind of sweet, simple, tuneful outpouring characteristic for Schubert in the middle areas of his three-key expositions. The phrase of mm. 27–38 abandons the obsessive repetitions of the opening in favor of a conventional sentential design, within which Schubert presents a normal diversity of durational patterns. As part of this shift, Schubert transforms both the lament tetrachord and 5̂–6̂ neighbor, seemingly stripping them of their tragic connotations, illustrated by Example 7.20. The lament idea—last heard in the form of the first violin's eighth-note pattern in mm. 19–22—dissolves into the gently rocking eighth notes of the accompaniment. For its part, the 5̂–6̂ neighbor returns at the E♭–F pitch level, as part of a I–IV–I tonic expansion. Schubert thus abandons the tension of the minor neighbor in favor of a comforting whole-step motion within a progression of pastoral-religious connotation. Indeed, the foreground continuation of F up to A♭ (6̂–8̂), as top voice for the plagal IV–I resolution in mm. 32–33, might even be thought to bless the escape from C minor with a relieved "amen."

Nevertheless, as we have already seen, the A♭ material provides only apparent relief from the angst of the opening. Viewed from a broader perspective, it remains stuck within the middleground grip of C-minor despair. The motion away from

C-minor anxiety is not real, in other words. Rather, the prolongational role of the A♭ section correlates with the idea of a fantasy—a dreamlike vision of a sudden and miraculous escape from emotional torment. The fact that the dramatic shift in character has occurred without a proper transition is crucial to this interpretation. There has been no real process of emotional transformation comparable to the fully prepared arrival of secondary material in the first movements of the Brahms quartet and Haydn symphony. There is instead merely an abrupt leap to a different expressive world.

Further strategic interpretation confirms the notion that the relief offered by the A♭ section is otherworldly. The first point to consider is the fact that the A♭ section fails to achieve harmonic closure. Not only does A♭ enter too quickly, but it never subsequently establishes its own emotional force with an authentic cadence. In place of the tonic close that should answer the antecedent's half cadence in m. 38, Schubert interjects one of the most violent moments in the movement. He allows the transition to brusquely interrupt the cadential dominant of m. 60 with the sudden and brutal entrance of A♭ minor. It seems no mistake that it is with a return to the main-theme's sixteenth-note rhythms, in particular, that the movement abruptly awakens from its dream of escape to the disquieting realities of minor.

Finally, when this transitional passage carries the A♭ bass onward, A♭ sinks down to the G that supports the back-relating dominant of m. 77, as highlighted in Example 7.18 (p. 272). Not only is the A♭ key area trapped within a prolongation of an overriding C-minor *Stufe*, but it also turns out that the A♭ bass pitch itself forms part of an enlargement of the neighbor motive that contributed to the anxiety of the tonic area. The entire A♭ passage is, from both tonal and motivic perspectives, a foreground dream that remains unable to transcend the middleground angst of C minor.

The G-major section that follows would appear to be an entirely different matter. On the scale of the exposition, at least, it articulates a more forthright motion away from the opening C *Stufe*. It is prepared by a proper transition, as noted above, and closes at m. 125 on a solid G tonic that Schubert expands for no less than fifteen measures. Yet when viewed from the perspective of the entire movement, it turns out that even the G-major *Stufe* fails to achieve a middleground status on a par with C. The unusual tonal structure of the *Quartettsatz*'s recapitulation denies the expository dominant its standard role as divider within the conventional i–V‖ i–V–i interruption scheme of sonata form.

Crucial to this denial is the fact that Schubert does not lead the development to an arrival back on G major reinterpreted as retransitional home dominant. Rather, as Example 7.17 makes clear (p. 271), he makes his way to V/G minor at m. 191 and then abruptly moves down a major third for a recapitulation of the lyrical theme in B♭ major (m. 195). No doubt the status of this B♭ articulation as the beginning of the reprise emerges only retrospectively. Nevertheless, as Example 7.17 outlines, the subtonic arrival does indeed initiate a thematically parallel restatement of the second and third sections of the exposition. Schubert saves a reprise of the opening, anxiety-filled theme for the very end of the movement, where it returns as coda (m. 305).

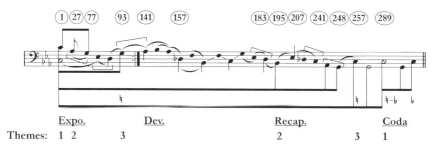

Example 7.21. Middleground Bass for *Quartettsatz*

Example 7.17 also indicates that the only conventional aspect of Schubert's tonal reinterpretation of his secondary material is his restatement of the G-major section in C major. From the perspective of the sonata principle, this tonic transposition might be thought to reconcile an expository polarity between i and V. The return of the lyrical theme, by contrast, introduces rather than resolves tonal complications. Not only does Schubert restate the lyrical material in the unusual recapitulatory key of the subtonic, but he also leads from the expanded subtonic to a tonicization of the mediant in the consequent phrase of mm. 207–28.

The connection of this modulatory motion with the idea of a recapitulatory formal overlap emerges from four main factors. First and most obviously, the off-tonic return allows Schubert to delay rearticulation of the tonic *Stufe* until the return of the third part of the exposition. Indeed, the delay extends even further in the sense that the minor tonic reemerges only when the main theme reenters as coda. Second, the modulatory pattern within the lyrical theme provides an additional element of developmental instability, above and beyond the tonic delay. Third, Schubert's reversal of the order of his primary and secondary material erases the conventional recapitulatory parallelism. Finally, the end of the development proper merges into the thematic restatement of m. 195 without a proper retransition. The result is that the B♭ entrance initially sounds like another developmental episode rather than a turning point in the form.

To return to our earlier question, however: What does this all say about the status of the expository G-major *Stufe?* Despite the *Quartettsatz's* unconventional tonal organization, a consensus has emerged in several recent Schenkerian accounts of the work's large-scale tonal relations. My bass-line graph of Example 7.21 outlines some of the main points of convergence in these interpretations.[27] The graph depicts the expository V as a relatively shallow middleground event, a striking feature when one considers the deep-level function expository dominants usually achieve in more conventional sonata forms. In this interpretation the stepwise connection between the opening C tonic and the B♭ *Stufe* at the reprise takes precedence over the motion to G at the end of the exposition.

Two interrelated aspects of the graph are likely to be controversial and therefore require clarification. The first point of concern is indeed the deep-level status of B♭. The graph assigns B♭ this function despite the fact that it receives no dominant preparation and itself turns out to function as V of the mediant that enters at the consequent. Support for the structural significance for B♭ comes in two forms. First, as we have seen, the subtonic enters at what turns out to be a crucial turning point in the form. This location helps to mark B♭ for the consciousness associated with a middleground event. Similarly, the very fact that the subtonic is so unusual as a recapitulatory harmony draws attention to B♭ and helps it to reverberate on a deep structural level.

The other possibly controversial aspect of the graph is the significance it assigns to the A♭–G bass motion at the end of the transition (mm. 245–56). Critics of Schenker's approach might take exception to the fact that the movement's middleground bypasses tonicized harmonies that govern thematic sections—the G major of the exposition and the E♭ of the recapitulation—in favor of a cadential German sixth–V progression. Yet to return to a point defended at length in Chapter 2, Schenkerian analysis requires neither tonicization for all middleground harmonies nor that all tonicized harmonies reach the middleground. The stepwise C–B♭–A♭–G motion takes precedence over the local resolution to E♭, even despite the subsequent expansion of E♭ across the consequent.

The analytic point here is similar to the idea that the G major of the exposition has a prolongational function in relation to a C–B♭ stepwise connection. The rationale behind the interpretation, however, is not merely the idea that stepwise melodic fluency can sometimes trump harmonic hierarchy and thematic articulation. The structural bass is also motivated by motivic considerations: the main bass motion turns out to be an enormous enlargement of the lament tetrachord that dominates the material of the tonic area. And this point leads finally to the observation that a deep-level dominant arrives not at the end of the exposition, but only as preparation for the C-major recapitulation of the exposition's third part at m. 257. Although the exposition's G major reaches somewhat deeper into the structural hierarchy than A♭, the initial dominant nevertheless also winds up falling under the long shadow cast by the opening C-minor *Stufe*. What this means in terms of expression is that the only substantial challenge to the angst of the tonic area arrives with the C-major material of the recapitulation.

On its face, the C-major material would appear finally to provide the release from torment that Schubert problematizes in all other major-mode areas. The form has finally followed through with a section of major-mode solace that resides on the same middleground level as the opening tonic. A tragic connotation for the C-major section emerges only with the turn to minor that follows when the main theme returns as coda. This is another example of the kind of conventional recapitulatory tragic irony we observed in the first movement of Brahms's C-minor piano trio. In the *Quartettsatz,* however, it is not merely a matter of a generic shift back to minor. The main theme also brings back the obsessive repetitions of the lament tetrachord and agitated sixteenth-note motion that created the tone of anxiety at the outset. Despite all attempts in the various statements of the lyrical theme and in the material of the exposition's third part, the movement finds itself unable to transcend its original state of angst.[28]

Some commentators have found this anxiety-filled ending less than satisfactory.

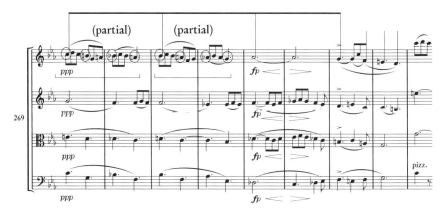

Example 7.22. Lament Tetrachord in Theme 3

David Beach, for example, describes it as "too abrupt to be totally successful."[29] I view this abruptness, however, not as a liability, but rather as an integral aspect of the work's expressive character. The abrupt conclusion articulates a final and ultimate manifestation of the kind of violent expressive shift that has occurred with the sudden intrusion of minor at the beginning of the transition in both the exposition and recapitulation. In those two spots the brusque entrance of the sixteenth-note motive from the main theme provides a rude awakening from the lyrical idea's dream of solace. The beginning of the coda lacks the violence of these two earlier articulations. It does, however, similarly drag the heavenly calm of the C-major closing passage into the grim minor mode of the main theme. Schubert cuts off the dream of transcendence expressed by his ethereal C-major closing material with a sudden and jarring return to reality.[30]

Moreover, the coda culminates in a gruff and violent gesture of its own. In the exposition the enormous *crescendo* and registral expansion of the opening imitative passage settle down at least somewhat into the tense continuation of the tonic area at m. 13. In the recapitulation Schubert simply cuts off the theme following the buildup with a blunt ♭II[6]–V–i progression. The agitated sixteenth notes hit a wall of grim downbeat hammer blows, and the movement ends in a state of bitter *fortissimo* anger without any dissipation of the main theme's angst.

The new proximity of the third and main themes at the end of the movement also highlights a motivic connection that further contributes to the negativity of the close. As Example 7.22 indicates, Schubert embeds the lament tetrachord within the third theme. If the movement were to end in major, this motivic connection might function as part of a transformation of minor-mode angst into C-major transcendence. Instead the return of the main theme as coda wrenches the lament tetrachord out of C major and back into the grip of the negative minor mode.[31]

Some of the movement's anomalous characteristics take on newfound significance when viewed from the perspective of this despondent ending. Schubert denies both of the major-mode sections of the exposition their potential to challenge the emotional angst of C minor. As we have seen, the A♭ and G areas fall under the long prolongational shadow cast by the opening tonic *Stufe*. The unusual structure of the recapitulation has a similar negative effect. The B♭ return of the lyrical theme and its prolongation via E♭ have a twofold expressive significance. Not only are they crucial to the process by which Schubert cancels any possible deep-level role for the exposition's G-major *Stufe*. They also simultaneously deny the potential for the A♭ lyrical theme to return in C major. The return of the G-major material provides the recapitulation its only hope to achieve major-mode solace in the real world, where C functions as tonic. Yet, as we have seen, this last attempt is doomed by the framing of the movement within the initial and long-delayed final statements of the main theme. Finally, the motivic parallelism, between the movement's unusual middleground bass and the main theme's lament tetrachord, indicates that C-minor despair dominates not only the work's left-to-right temporal unfolding but also the deepest levels of its top-down structural derivation.

Even in the context of Schubertian sonata innovations, the *Quartettsatz* stands out as a piece characterized by a high degree of structural idiosyncrasy. It is a work very much like Brahms's piano quartet in that it reflects core Schubertian concerns even as it carries many of these compositional strategies to extremes not found in other sonata forms. Up to this point, I have interpreted this strategic extravagance as a means for Schubert to express an inescapable angst, set forth at the outset of the movement and retained as a backdrop for all that transpires before the coda's final crushing blows. The question remains whether it is possible to further specify meaning in the *Quartettsatz*. What is the source of the angst, for instance, and why should its impact be so devastating? These questions bring us to a central challenge for expressive interpretation: how to find a middle ground between the generic expressive potential of a work—Cone's "wide but not unrestricted range of possible expression"—and the kind of highly specific hermeneutic interpretations that often feel arbitrary.[32]

The *Quartettsatz* obviously does not present the interjection of a disquieting element into an otherwise innocent context the way the A♭ *Moment Musical* does, as described by Cone and discussed in Chapter 6.[33] (To the degree that the action of many of Schubert's compositions *is* motivated by this type of promissory note, the *Quartettsatz* once again stands out as a special case.) The angst, rather, is both all consuming and present from the outset. The continual imitative entrances on the lament tetrachord perhaps suggest that this anxiety is a consequence of thoughts of death. Because the anxiety is intense and unrelenting within the tonic area, we can further specify that the prospect of death must be imminent. The tension of the tonic area correlates not with contemplation of abstract concepts of mortality but rather with its immediate possibility, perhaps manifesting itself in the form of the later stages of a terminal illness.

What the rest of the movement symbolizes, then, is the failure of any attempts to overcome the fate of this illness. The A♭ material provides relief but only in the form of a dream of escape or memory of earlier untroubled times. Following the rude awakening from this fantasy manifested by the entrance of the transition, the form makes its way to a seemingly more substantial area of recovery. The G-major section might at first appear to correlate with the idea of a remission or perhaps even the promise of a cure, the latter implied by the idea that this material should return in the tonic in the recapitulation. Yet as we have seen, the G-major *Stufe* also winds up having a relatively shallow structural significance. Likewise, it remains preoccupied with the lament tetrachord despite the apparent contentment of its thematic materials. Rather than remission, therefore, in retrospect it turns out to correlate more closely with the temporary experiences of relief and even pleasure that terminally ill people sometimes can find, despite an awareness of the ultimate hopelessness of their circumstances.

As the movement progresses, the possibility for relief becomes more tenuous. The material of the A♭ dream loses, in the recapitulation, the ability it once had to provide at least a fantasy of escape. It once again enters too abruptly to provide authentic security, but in addition, it no longer can remain in a single key. Moreover, the B♭ bass participates in the enlargement of the lament tetrachord, which itself indicates that all activity up to the arrival of C major falls under the shadow of death. The possibility for a more authentic experience of relief apparently comes to fruition with the recapitulation's C-major section. But this seemingly more genuine reprieve—whether in the form of an actual remission or a willful experience of pleasure—proves all the more poignant when it fails to hold fast in the face of the return to the anxiety of death in the coda.

Having further specified expressive correlations for the *Quartettsatz,* we might ask whether it is possible, following Cone, to deduce yet more specific human situations that correlate with its structure. Indeed, might it be possible to speculate about what the *Quartettsatz* signified for Schubert himself? Can we move from the notion of deathly anxiety—an interpretation roughly parallel to the idea that Brahms's quartet expresses suicidal despair—to a biographically significant interpretation analogous to a reading of Brahms's work as a response to his experiences with the Schumanns?

I do not discount the possibility that further strategic interpretation could lead to a more individualized expressive interpretation. This, however, will not be my charge here. Rather, I would like to conclude by engaging issues raised by Cone's speculation about the relationship between Schubert's personal experiences and the expressive significance of his compositions.[34] The topic is relevant, of course, not just for Schubert and the *Quartettsatz,* but for discussions of musical expression in general and above all for a study that has dealt specifically with a work of seemingly deep personal significance for Brahms.

The *Quartettsatz* was written in 1820, two years before scholars have suggested that Schubert most likely contracted syphilis.[35] It therefore is not feasible to connect the movement's expression of deathly anxiety with "the sense of desolation, even dread, that penetrates much of his music from [1822] on" and which Cone suggests may have been a consequence of Schubert's awareness of his illness.[36] My expressive interpretation undoubtedly could be tied to some other aspect of Schubert's life. Such an endeavor would likely add dramatic weight to the correlations

I have proposed; certainly I do not wish to deny the influence of a composer's life on the character of his works, nor the relevance of biography for interpretation. Indeed, I have argued that the unique status of Brahms's quartet at least in part reflects the great personal significance it seems to have had for the composer. Yet at the same time, issues of biography and expression must be dealt with cautiously.

If we briefly allow ourselves to step out of the realm of music analysis and consider parallels with literary interpretation, then the need for caution becomes all the more obvious. It is certainly possible for novelists, like composers, to write about their lives, either loosely or even strictly speaking. But it is also often a mistake to assume too close a correspondence between a writer's biography and his work. Although the characters in a novel may bear some similarity with people a writer knows, they are nonetheless fictional creations. This is the case even when a writer self-consciously attempts to paint a portrait of a friend or relative in a fictional context, much less in those circumstances in which a writer merely initiates the creative process with a real person as inspiration for a fictional flight of fancy. The portrait will still be rendered through the artist's eyes. Moreover, the narrative voice of a novel is not synonymous with the writer himself. It, too, is a fictional creation, the veracity of whose statements is not always to be trusted. The best writers can create characters and explore cultures and contexts that extend well beyond the confines of their personal experience. This is the imaginative power of literature. Although it is certainly true that knowledge about an author's life can illuminate literary interpretation, it would be a foolish literary critic indeed who would insist that interpretation must, as a matter of course, culminate with speculation on the correlation between the work's course of events and incidents in the writer's life. Many books simply are not about an author's life in this literal sense.

Yet such a mode of interpretation would be the literary parallel for a hermeneutic of music that attempts to hear pieces as expressions of a composer's personal experiences and emotions. In the case of Cone, I do not mean to suggest that he advocates such a dogmatic approach. Indeed, he describes the final stage of his hermeneutic exercise as "only the most tentative of hypotheses" about a relationship that he hears in the particular case of the *Moment Musical*. He does not present it as some type of universal principle for expressive interpretation, but rather as a mere attempt to answer "possibly a forbidden question."[37]

On the other hand, the recent trend in Brahms scholarship that focuses on ciphers and allusions appears to be based on the idea that interpretation should center around correlations between a composer's life and works. In the case of the piano quartet, for example, the opening of the main theme has been interpreted as a transposed version of a Clara cipher that Brahms supposedly learned from Robert, as outlined in Example 7.23. Recent critical examination of the very notion of ciphers in Schumann and Brahms, however, has raised serious doubts about the extent of the practice by either composer. The situations in which they may have incorporated ciphers appear to be far more narrowly circumscribed than previously believed.[38] And as I have just suggested, even if ciphers do occasionally occur, it seems exceedingly simplistic to pursue, as a general principle of expressive inter-

Example 7.23. Reputed Clara Cipher in Brahms's Main Theme

pretation, relationships between artistic expression and biography in such a direct manner.

Put otherwise, the kind of relationship I have sought, and that Brahms appears to have hinted at, between the piano quartet and his experiences with the Schumanns is the exception rather than the rule. Moreover, my approach has for the most part avoided attempts to trace narrative correlations between the work and Brahms's life. The furthest I have gone in that direction has been my identification of the three themes in the Andante with Robert, Clara, and Brahms. Otherwise, I have simply followed Brahms's own advice and explored how it is possible for the quartet to express suicidal despair, as an abstract psychological state.

As a general rule, it is more reasonable to aspire to a middle ground of interpretation between highly specific biographical readings, on the one hand, and the broad and generic expressive potential all compositions possess, on the other. Few of us have been driven to the brink of suicide, much less found ourselves in a situation parallel to the one Brahms stumbled into in the Schumann household of the 1850s. Yet most listeners have experienced deep despondency at some point in their lives and therefore, despite diverse sources for the emotion, can respond viscerally to the expressive power of the quartet. (This is not to say that listeners will become despondent—much less suicidal—while listening, although Brahms's communicative powers certainly allow the quartet to have a profound emotional impact if we are willing to submit to it.) In the end, to focus too much attention on the idea that the quartet is about the particulars of Brahms's experience would be to limit its expressive force. Although the composition may have been inspired by Brahms's real-life struggles, it speaks to us on a more universal emotional level.

A desire to engage the work broadly has also steered me away from too much attention to the connection with Goethe's *Werther*. As mentioned in Chapter 6, I interpret Brahms's statements associating the quartet with the novella as a means of hinting at the work's unusual expressive motivations to his friends and associates, not as any sort of suggestion of even a loose program. First of all, as I mentioned earlier, Brahms's relationship with Robert was fundamentally different from Werther's with Albert. That it was Robert, not Brahms, who attempted suicide further undercuts the parallelism. Moreover, Brahms had anything but a Werther-like personality. Rather than wallow in suicidal self-pity, Brahms picked himself up from the emotional difficulties he faced in his relationship with the Schumanns and, among other activities, embarked on an intensive study of counterpoint that his friend Joachim was barely able to keep up with. I mention this study merely as one piece of evidence of Brahms's more all-embracing determination to succeed as a composer. Brahms's dedication to his craft and the hard work he exerted on its behalf are scarcely surpassed in music history. His work ethic and the artistic achievement that flowed from it are testament to the gulf that separates his personality from Werther's.

More specific correlations with *Werther* also seem unlikely on purely technical grounds. Given Brahms's commitment to traditional musical forms, with their own patterns of repetition, development, and contrast, it is hard to imagine how he could have created a corollary for Goethe's epistolary unfolding of events. Moreover, it would be fatuous to attribute, to specific moments in the quartet, correlations for actions in the novella—"Werther watches Charlotte with the children" or "Werther pulls the trigger." Rather than force notions of narrativity of this sort onto Brahms, I have endeavored to treat his musical expression as a progression of psychological states, as experienced by an abstract consciousness. Within this proposed plot of free association, what has been paramount has been an exploration not only of *what* is being expressed through conventional forms, but *how* those very forms can be bent to accommodate the particularities of expression.

And this is where my focus on structure receives its strongest justification. My analytical bent arises not out of a desire to replace other routes toward hermeneutic interpretation, such as historical and biographical approaches. Rather, it is inspired by the theorist's desire to stay close to the notes, to avoid leaps of faith and imaginative flights of fancy—simply put, to ground interpretation of meaning in musical relationships. Just about all modes of expressive interpretation will involve some form of analysis. The point here has been to illustrate the benefits of a particular *style* of analysis: close technical scrutiny undertaken from the perspective of highly developed theoretical systems. I have attempted to demonstrate that theoretically based analysis—and what other kind is there, after all—is not something that we need to move beyond in the pursuit of critical insight. Rather, theory should be exploited as the solid foundation upon which edifices of expressive interpretation can be constructed.

Despite the current disciplinary polarization of new musicology and analytical theory, there is no reason why theory cannot work in conjunction with biographical, historical, critical, literary, or hermeneutic modes of engagement. What I have presented, with its focus on analysis, is but one perspective, a demonstration of an approach that I hope will ultimately be absorbed into more all-embracing methods of expressive interpretation. And here my message is intended not just for those skeptical of theory but also for theorists themselves. While it is my conviction that theory has much to offer contemporary musicology, I also believe that music theorists would do well to take seriously those who have urged us to engage meaning and expression.

Some of the advantages of a theoretical perspective nevertheless reside in those very characteristics that have formed the target of theory's fiercest critics. Postmodern criticism, for example, has called into question the organicist principles that underlie so much music-theoretic discourse. Yet among other attributes, the very attention to relationships of whole to part and part to whole in a theory like Schenker's is precisely what makes it a useful tool for expressive interpretation. For it is my conviction that a focus on fragments, phrases, or small sections in isolation, on the one hand, or merely on the broad outlines of a work, on the other, will lead to impoverished hermeneutic interpretations. Without question, the approach I have outlined in this book has eschewed the idea of a totalizing Schenkerian model, in which all relationships of the foreground find their origin in the *Ursatz*. But in the process of combining Schenkerian insights with attention to quasi-independent musical forces in other dimensions, I have nevertheless held to an organicist emphasis on integration and process, as well as to more specific Schenkerian concepts of tonal structure. To repeat a point made in Chapter 2, we should embrace the insights that Schenkerian analysis affords even as we turn our backs on the less palatable aspects of Schenker's ideology.

Ultimately the success of any analytical endeavor rests on the interpretive fruit it bears. The test is not whether there is 100 percent agreement on expressive conclusions drawn from structural analysis, nor even that there is 100 percent agreement on the structural analysis itself, which is also interpretive in nature. In the case of the C-minor piano quartet, attention to dimensional counterpoint has allowed me to demonstrate ways in which Brahms's image of suicide finds its expression in the musical processes of this extraordinary work. More broadly, by exploring the expressive meanings that can be grounded in close analysis, I have not only bridged discourses in music theory, but also offered an alternative to some of the less-well-grounded interpretive forays of new musicology.

The result is but one contribution toward what is ultimately an unachievable goal: an understanding of the expressive powers of music. Like physicists pursuing the origins of the universe, musicians have made great strides recently in confronting this age-old mystery. Yet just as physical evidence of the big bang raises new questions even as it tentatively confirms existing hypotheses, so too do advances in expressive interpretation lead to additional challenges with which to wrestle. Through it all, we nevertheless find ourselves confronted by a venture that should not drive us to despair—much less Werther-like despondency—but instead should inspire us with its wonder and mystery.

Notes

I. Quintessential Brahms and the Paradox of the C-Minor Piano Quartet

1. Max Kalbeck, *Johannes Brahms,* rev. ed., 4 vols. in 8 (Berlin: Deutsche Brahms-Gesellschaft, 1913–22), vol. 1, 232.

2. Ibid., vol. 3, 12.

3. Other references to a relationship between the quartet and Goethe's *Werther* appear in Otto Billroth, *Billroth und Brahms im Briefwechsel,* ed. Otto Billroth (Berlin: Urban und Schwarzenberg, 1935), 211; *Johannes Brahms Briefwechsel,* vols. IX–X: *Johannes Brahms: Briefe an P. J. Simrock und Fritz Simrock,* ed. Max Kalbeck, 2 vols. (Berlin: Deutsche Brahms-Gesellschaft, 1917), vol. IX, 200–201; and *Johannes Brahms Briefwechsel,* vol. XIII: *Johannes Brahms im Briefwechsel mit Th. Wilhelm Engelmann,* ed. Julius Röntgen (Berlin: Deutsche Brahms-Gesellschaft, 1918), 22–25.

4. Forte's seminal 1959 article on Schenkerian theory reflects these concerns: "Schenker's Conception of Musical Structure," *Journal of Music Theory* 3 (1959): 1–30. See especially the concluding section of the article, where Forte suggests ways in which a Schenkerian approach might contribute to research in five areas of music scholarship. For a representative statement of Babbitt's views, see "The Structure and Function of Music Theory," in *Perspectives on Contemporary Music Theory,* ed. Benjamin Boretz and Edward T. Cone (New York: W. W. Norton, 1972), 10–21.

5. See, for example, Joseph Kerman, *Contemplating Music: Challenges to Musicology* (Cambridge, Mass.: Harvard University Press, 1985), 60–112.

6. Edward T. Cone, *The Composer's Voice* (Berkeley: University of California Press, 1974); Leonard B. Meyer, *Emotion and Meaning in Music* (Chicago: University of Chicago Press, 1956).

7. For a summary of the main criticisms leveled against music theory with references to some of the most prominent of the critics, see Pieter C. van den Toorn, *Music, Politics, and the Academy* (Berkeley: University of California Press, 1995), 11–43.

8. V. Kofi Agawu, *Playing with Signs: A Semiotic Interpretation of Classic Music* (Princeton, N.J.: Princeton University Press, 1991); Robert S. Hatten, *Musical Meaning in Beethoven: Markedness, Correlation, and Interpretation* (Bloomington: Indiana University Press, 1994).

9. The idea that the chamber works for piano and strings of the early 1860s represent the flowering of a first maturity originates with Tovey: "Brahms's Chamber Music," in his *Essays and Lectures on Music* (London: Oxford University Press, 1949), 220–70. Brahms's artistic development has customarily been subdivided into this first maturity followed by a period (ca. 1866–71) in which he turned to

vocal music, only then to enter into a new stage of instrumental composition in the years of 1871–76. For a critique of the notion that the ten-year span from 1866 to 1876 divides into two distinct subperiods based primarily on genre distinctions, see James Webster, "The *Alto Rhapsody:* Psychology, Intertextuality, and Brahms's Artistic Development," in *Brahms Studies,* vol. 3, ed. David Brodbeck (Lincoln: University of Nebraska Press, 2001), 19–45.

10.   James Webster, "Schubert's Sonata Form and Brahms's First Maturity," parts 1 and 2, *19th-Century Music* 2 (1978): 18–35, and 3 (1979): 52–71. The specific reference to the C-minor quartet appears on p. 54 of part 2. Webster's discussion of Brahms's engagement with the C-major/minor topos in "The *Alto Rhapsody*" also barely mentions the C-minor quartet. He does, however, explore the relationship between the two versions of the work in "The C Sharp Minor Version of Brahms's Op. 60," *Musical Times* 121 (1980): 89–93.

11.   Walter Frisch, *Brahms and the Principle of Developing Variation* (Berkeley: University of California Press, 1984).

12.   On the concept of noncongruence, see Leonard B. Meyer, *Explaining Music: Essays and Explorations* (Chicago: University of Chicago Press, 1973).

13.   Some examples of this trend include David Brodbeck, *Brahms Symphony No. 1* (Cambridge: Cambridge University Press, 1997) and "Medium and Meaning: New Aspects of the Chamber Music," in *The Cambridge Companion to Brahms,* ed. Michael Musgrave (Cambridge: Cambridge University Press, 1999), 98–132; Robert Fink, "Desire, Repression and Brahms's First Symphony," *Repercussions* 2 (1993): 75–103; and Dillon Parmer, "Brahms the Programmatic" (Ph.D. diss., University of Rochester, 1995) and "Brahms, Song Quotation, and Secret Programs," *19th-Century Music* 19 (1995): 161–90.

14.   On the special significance of C minor for Beethoven, see Michael C. Tusa, "Beethoven's 'C-Minor Mood': Some Thoughts on the Structural Implications of Key Choice," in *Beethoven Forum* 2, ed. Lewis Lockwood and James Webster (Lincoln: University of Nebraska Press, 1993), 1–27.

15.   The closest precedent I have come across for Brahms's casting of the recapitulation of secondary material in the major dominant in the context of a minor-mode sonata form is the finale of his own E-Minor Cello Sonata, op. 38. The sonata's G-major secondary idea of m. 53 returns in B major in m. 123. There are, however, a number of crucial distinctions between the two movements that make the contexts for the formal procedure decidedly different. Not only is the cello movement a finale but it also articulates its sonata component within the context of an overarching fugal design. Moreover, Brahms reverses the order of his thematic materials in the recapitulation so that the B-major expansion of the secondary idea is more easily assimilated into an extension of the retransition. In the piano quartet the dominant recapitulation is more disruptive of sonata conventions in the sense that the retransition and return of the main theme have already restored the home key to immediate consciousness, while they have likewise fulfilled expectations for thematic ordering. For an analysis of the cello sonata movement with attention to the impact of the B-major return on the large-scale form, see Timothy L. Jackson, "The Tragic Reversed Recapitulation in the German Classical Tradition," *Journal of Music Theory* 40 (1996): 76–77.

16. Another is the B-major Piano Trio, op. 8. Chorale-style material appears as the opening theme in the slow movement of both versions.

17. For a discussion of the consolatory resolution in the *Alto Rhapsody* and its significance for Brahms's approach to expression in his later works, see Webster, "The *Alto Rhapsody*."

18. Brodbeck traces the long gestation of the symphony in *Brahms Symphony No. 1*, 1–30. He cites a mid-1860s date for an earlier completed version of the quartet, with reference to evidence in letters of members of the Brahms circle, in "Medium and Meaning: New Aspects of the Chamber Music," 104–105.

19. Webster, "The *Alto Rhapsody*," 41–45.

20. *Johannes Brahms Briefwechsel*, vols. V–VI: *Johannes Brahms im Briefwechsel mit Joseph Joachim*, ed. Andreas Moser (Berlin: Deutsche Brahms-Gesellschaft, 1908), vol. V, 124–27. All subsequent references in this chapter to discussion of op. 60 between Joachim and Brahms are from these two letters.

21. Webster, "The C Sharp Minor Version." Webster includes translations of the relevant portions of both letters.

22. Brodbeck, "Medium and Meaning: New Aspects of the Chamber Music," 118–19. Clara's letter appears in Renate Hofmann, "Johannes Brahms im Spiegel der Korrespondenz Clara Schumanns," in *Brahms und seine Zeit: Symposion Hamburg 1983*, ed. Constantin Floros, Hans Joachim Marx, and Peter Petersen (Laaber: Laaber Verlag, 1984), 48. Kalbeck transmits Dietrich's recollection in "Fragebogen für Herrn Hofkapellmeister Albert Dietrich," ed. Max Kalbeck, transcribed in *Katalog 100: Johannes Brahms* (Tutzing: Hans Schneider, 1964), 12.

23. Webster, "The C Sharp Minor Version," 90–91.

24. A transcribed version of the catalog appears in Alfred Orel, "Ein eigenhändiges Werkverzeichnis von Johannes Brahms: Ein wichtiger Beitrag zur Brahmsforschung," *Die Musik* 29 (1937): 529–41. The reference to op. 60 occurs on p. 539.

25. Kalbeck, *Brahms*, vol. 3, 14. For similar conclusions see Karl Geiringer, *Brahms: His Life and Work*, 3rd enlarged ed. (New York: Da Capo Press, 1981, 1982), 233–34; Ivor Keys, *Brahms Chamber Music* (Seattle: University of Washington Press, 1974), 20; and Altmann's preface to the Eulenberg miniature score. All of these references are cited by Webster.

26. Quoted in Kalbeck, *Brahms*, vol. 3, 12–13; translated in Webster, "The C Sharp Minor Version," 91.

27. Kalbeck attributes this idea to Joachim; see ibid., vol. 1, 129–30 and 231–33, and vol. 3, 13. Tovey does likewise in "Brahms's Chamber Music," 253–55.

28. Webster, "The C Sharp Minor Version," 91–92.

29. Ibid., 92.

2. Analytical Preliminaries

1. I borrow the concept of *dimensional counterpoint* from Milton Babbitt, *Words about Music*, ed. Stephen Dembski and Joseph N. Straus (Madison: University of Wisconsin Press, 1987).

2.   Carl Schachter makes this point in "Analysis by Key: Another Look at Modulation," *Music Analysis* 6 (1987): 298.

3.   Schachter clarifies the issues involved, ibid., 299–304. See also his discussion of the distinction between key scheme and structural harmonic progression in "The First Movement of Brahms's Second Symphony: The Opening Theme and Its Consequences," *Music Analysis* 2 (1983): 62–65.

4.   The most important discussion of the concept of a three-key exposition remains Webster's "Schubert's Sonata Form." Further insight into Brahms's three-key strategies appears in Roger C. Graybill, "Brahms's Three-Key Expositions: Their Place within the Classical Tradition" (Ph.D. diss., Yale University, 1983). Although the finale of the piano quartet and the movements from the symphony and string quartet do not articulate three keys in their expositions, they do each present a two-part or double second group. I will explore the relationship between this kind of double second group and the idea of a three-key exposition in Chapter 5.

5.   See Webster, "Schubert's Sonata Form."

6.   Here I develop further the idea of noncongruence put forward by Meyer, *Explaining Music: Essays and Explorations*.

7.   Leonard B. Meyer explores ways in which nineteenth-century composers reanimated Classical style conventions in *Style and Music: Theory, History, and Ideology* (Philadelphia: University of Pennsylvania Press, 1989), 218–71.

8.   Heinrich Schenker, *Free Composition,* trans. and ed. Ernst Oster (New York: Longman, 1979), 88–90. Examples of sonata forms that initiate their secondary areas with $^6_3$ chords as part of auxiliary cadence structures include the first movement of Mozart's C-Major Piano Sonata, K. 545, and the first movement of Beethoven's E♭-Major Piano Sonata, op. 31, no. 3. For a thorough exploration of the topic of auxiliary cadence, see L. Poundie Burstein, "The Non-tonic Opening in Classical and Romantic Music" (Ph.D. diss., City University of New York, 1988).

9.   See Raymond Knapp, "A Review of Norrington's Brahms," *American Brahms Society Newsletter* 11 (1993): 6; and David Brodbeck, *Brahms Symphony No. 1,* 33–34; Brodbeck also acknowledges formal ambiguity regarding the beginning of the secondary area.

10. My emphasis on temporality and multivalence is inspired by Edward T. Cone's and David Lewin's critiques of the tendency for music theorists to regard as definitive analytic statements that are rendered from a synoptic perspective. See Cone, "Three Ways of Reading a Detective Story—Or a Brahms Intermezzo," in *Music: A View from Delft,* ed. Robert P. Morgan (Chicago: University of Chicago Press, 1989), 77–93; and Lewin, "Music Theory, Phenomenology, and Modes of Perception," *Music Perception* 3 (1986): 327–92. I apply the analytic methodology that Lewin develops to counter this tendency in my "Structural Tonic or Apparent Tonic? Parametric Conflict, Temporal Perspective, and a Continuum of Articulative Possibilities," *Journal of Music Theory* 39 (1995): 245–83.

11. Edward T. Cone coined the term *structural downbeat* in *Musical Form and Musical Performance* (New York: W. W. Norton, 1968), 24–25. Fred Lerdahl and Ray Jackendoff provide a technical definition of the phenomenon in *A Generative Theory of Tonal Music* (Cambridge, Mass.: MIT Press, 1983), 33–35.

12. The term *sonata principle* is Cone's, from *Musical Form and Musical Performance*, 76–77.

13. Schenker introduces the concept of interruption in *Free Composition*, 36–40. He identifies it as a defining characteristic of sonata form in the final chapter, 133–41.

14. Carl Schachter provides a stimulating discussion of apparent tonics in "Either/ Or," in *Schenker Studies*, ed. Hedi Siegel (Cambridge: Cambridge University Press, 1990), 171–75.

15. In this practice he joins a trend among nineteenth-century composers. Robert P. Morgan focuses on the proclivity for delay across the recapitulation in the Romantic era in "The Delayed Structural Downbeat and Its Effect on the Tonal and Rhythmic Structure of Sonata Form Recapitulation" (Ph.D. diss., Princeton University, 1969).

16. See, for example, the first movement of Beethoven's D-Minor Piano Sonata, op. 31, no. 2, mm. 143–85.

17. Charles J. Smith, "Musical Form and Fundamental Structure: An Investigation of Schenker's *Formenlehre*," *Music Analysis* 15 (1996): 191–297. See also Arthur J. Komar, "The Pedagogy of Tonal Hierarchy," *In Theory Only* 10 (1988): 23–28; and Suzannah Clark, "Schenker's Mysterious Five," *19th-Century Music* 23 (1999): 96–102. Clark's article is noteworthy not only for its acceptance of Smith's argument that form and fundamental structure should be regarded as one and the same. She accuses Smith of getting "cold feet" in his failure to carry his assertions to their logical conclusion and argues for an even more thoroughgoing application of the concept that functional harmonic relationships on the phrase level are not necessarily in effect on larger levels of form (Clark, "Schenker's Mysterious Five," 100–101).

18. Smith, "Musical Form and Fundamental Structure," 215 and 263.

19. Ibid., 235 and 246–49.

20. Ibid., 263.

21. The latter is a possibility even for the tonic key area at the opening of a sonata form. See mm. 1–16 of the first movement of Beethoven's A-Major Piano Sonata, op. 101.

22. Smith, "Musical Form and Fundamental Structure," 263.

23. Ibid., 235 and 246–49.

24. David Beach discusses these motivic parallelisms and traces their impact on the tonal structure of the movement's development section in "A Recurring Pattern in Mozart's Music," *Journal of Music Theory* 27 (1983): 1–29. My interpretation of the main theme is consonant in all essential details with the graph that Beach presents. Other major mode sonata forms of Mozart that unambiguously articulate $\hat{5}$ as *Kopfton* include the first movements of the piano sonatas in E♭ major, K. 282, G major, K. 283, and C major, K. 330, as well as the first movement of the E♭-Major *Symphonie Concertante*, K. 364. The slow movement of the *Symphonie Concertante* provides a straightforward example of a minor-mode open form designed around $\hat{3}$ as *Kopfton*.

25. For a somewhat different interpretation of this theme, see David Gagné, "The

Compositional Use of Register in Three Piano Sonatas by Mozart," in *Trends in Schenkerian Research*, ed. Allen Cadwallader (New York: Schirmer Books, 1990), 32. Note in particular that Gagné hears a prolongation of ii in mm. 27–29, whereas I hear a tonic orientation. My interpretation is based on hearing the top-voice D in m. 27 as part of a complete $\hat{5}$–$\hat{6}$–$\hat{5}$ neighbor and thus as a diminution within an expanded tonic. Gagné by contrast reads the C in m. 28 not as a return to the local *Kopfton* but as a passing tone that connects an incomplete D neighbor of m. 27 to B♭ (m. 29) within his prolonged ii. Both the parallelism between mm. 27 and 28 and the change in melodic design at m. 29 help me to hear the C–D–C as a unit, only then to be followed by descending motion to G for the half cadence.

26. Schenker, *Free Composition*, 139.

27. Smith, "Musical Form and Fundamental Structure," 276–78.

28. Schenker, *Free Composition*, 128–45.

29. Smith discusses Schenker's graphs of this Mozart movement in "Musical Form and Fundamental Structure," 216–19, 227–31, and 245. In sharp contrast to my view, he asserts that the reprise in the trio "corresponds closely to the opening, and so is misrepresented by an upper-voice $\hat{5}$ where the original has $\hat{8}$" (245). He responds by reinterpreting the movement as an example of an interruption form with $\hat{3}$ as *Kopfton*, similar to the minuet (229). Because both minuet and trio are three-part open forms, they must, in Smith's view, have the same middleground structure.

30. David Beach, "Schubert's Experiments with Sonata Form: Formal-Tonal Design versus Underlying Structure," *Music Theory Spectrum* 15 (1993): 1–18.

31. Eric McKee, "Auxiliary Progressions as a Source of Conflict between Tonal Structure and Phrase Structure," *Music Theory Spectrum* 18 (1996): 51–76. Inner form is analogous to what I have been referring to as tonal structure; outer form corresponds to patterns of articulation provided by thematic design and key scheme; see William Rothstein, *Phrase Rhythm in Tonal Music* (New York: Schirmer Books, 1989), 104.

32. Lauri Suurpää, "Continuous Exposition and Tonal Structure in Three Late Haydn Works," *Music Theory Spectrum* 21 (1999): 174–99.

33. Schachter, "The First Movement of Brahms's Second Symphony."

34. Examples 5 and 7, ibid., 62 and 64.

35. Though Brahms was interested in Wagner's music, he regarded Liszt as a mediocre composer, advised the young Wolf that he first had to study counterpoint before his potential as a composer could be evaluated, and after reviewing the score of his Second Symphony, dismissed Mahler as "king of the revolutionaries." On Brahms's attitude toward Liszt and the New German School, see Geiringer, *Brahms: His Life and Work*, 30–32, 84, and 340–41. Wolf's interview with Brahms is reconstructed in Frank Walker, *Hugo Wolf: A Biography* (Princeton, N.J.: Princeton University Press, 1992), 83–87. Brahms's reaction to Mahler's Second Symphony is quoted in David Brodbeck, "Mahler's Brahms," *American Brahms Society Newsletter* 10 (1992): 1–5. The enthusiasm for Wagner in the second half of the nineteenth-century had a strong influence on Schenker's theoretical work

even though his major writings did not appear until the early decades of the twentieth century. See, for example, his historical sketch of the supposed decline of musical culture in his essay "Organic Structure in Sonata Form," trans. Orin Grossman, in *Readings in Schenker Analysis and Other Approaches,* ed. Maury Yeston (New Haven, Conn.: Yale University Press, 1977), 38–53. For Schenker's reaction to modernism in music, see his comments on Stravinsky's Piano Concerto in *Das Meisterwerk in der Musik,* vol. 2 (Munich: Drei Masken Verlag, 1926), 37–40.

36. Heinrich Schenker, *Beethoven's Ninth Symphony: A Portrayal of Its Musical Content, with Running Commentary on Performance and Literature as Well,* trans. and ed. John Rothgeb (New Haven, Conn.: Yale University Press, 1992), v.

37. Gustav Jenner, *Johannes Brahms als Mensch, Lehrer und Künstler: Studien und Erlebnisse* (Marburg in Hessen: N. G. Elwert'sche Verlagsbuchhandlung, 1905), 6.

3. A Schoenbergian Perspective

1. Allen Cadwallader and William Pastille, "Schenker's Unpublished Work with the Music of Johannes Brahms," in *Schenker Studies 2,* ed. Carl Schachter and Hedi Siegel (Cambridge: Cambridge University Press, 1999), 26–46.

2. Arnold Schoenberg, "Brahms the Progressive," in *Style and Idea: Selected Writings of Arnold Schoenberg,* ed. Leonard Stein, trans. Leo Black (New York: St. Martin's Press, 1975; reprint, Berkeley: University of California Press, 1975), 398–441.

3. See, for example, John Rothgeb, review of *Brahms and the Principle of Developing Variation,* by Walter Frisch, *Music Theory Spectrum* 9 (1987): 204–15.

4. Arnold Schoenberg, *Fundamentals of Musical Composition,* ed. Gerald Strang and Leonard Stein (London: Faber and Faber, 1967), 20–81.

5. As John Daverio points out, just under half of the musical examples in Schoenberg's essay come from Brahms himself, but second place goes to Mozart, with about twice as many citations as Beethoven, Wagner, Mahler, or Strauss: see John Daverio, "From 'Concertante Rondo' to 'Lyric Sonata': A Commentary on Brahms's Reception of Mozart," in *Brahms Studies,* vol. 1, ed. David Brodbeck (Lincoln: University of Nebraska Press, 1994), 111–38.

6. Frisch views aspects of development in Brahms's large-scale formal repetitions as an extension of the Schoenbergian principle of developing variation in *Brahms and the Principle of Developing Variation.*

7. My strategy of analyzing movements as pairs is similar to Lawrence Kramer's attention to what he calls "expressive doubling" in Beethoven; see his *Music as Cultural Practice, 1800–1900* (Berkeley: University of California Press, 1990), 21–71. For Kramer, "expressive doubling is a form of repetition in which alternative versions of the same pattern define a cardinal difference in perspective" (22). By contrast, in the case of the Brahms quartet, I am arguing for an intensification that serves to pair the first two movements, not an opposition per se.

8. In Brahms, as with his Viennese forebears, reconciliation is often a matter of simple restatement in the tonic key. In the case of third-related key areas, Brahms sometimes transposes by fifth: the result is that a motion through a third-related

key toward the dominant becomes a motion through another (usually third-related) key toward the tonic. This is sometimes the case both in traditional two-key expositions as well as in expositions with three key areas. In the three-key context of the Second Symphony, for example, a I–iii–V key scheme in the exposition returns as a I–vi–I scheme in the recapitulation. Similarly the i–vi$^{\flat-\sharp}$ two key-layout in the first movement of the piano quintet becomes a i–$\flat$ii$^{\flat}$–i pattern of keys in the recapitulation. Beethoven and Schubert also sometimes transpose third-related material by fifth, rather than restate in the tonic. Another option is to do both, as Beethoven chooses to in the *Waldstein* Sonata.

9.   For a more detailed discussion of the quintet's tonic area and its recapitulation see my "Structural Tonic or Apparent Tonic?"

10.   Webster in "Schubert's Sonata Form," part 2, 65–68, and Frisch in *Brahms and the Principle of Developing Variation,* 83–86, discuss this and various other formal consequences of the neighbor motive.

11.   For an insightful discussion of the main theme in the symphony see Schachter, "The First Movement of Brahms's Second Symphony."

12.   The compositional concern to avoid redundancy forms the basis for what Ethan Haimo generalizes as a "redundancy principle," one of five basic premises that he sees governing Haydn's formal thought. Although Haimo's focus is Haydn, he also suggests that the redundancy and his other formal principles play an important role in the compositional strategies of Mozart and Beethoven; see his *Haydn's Symphonic Forms: Essays in Compositional Logic* (Oxford: Oxford University Press, 1995), 5–7 and 270–74.

13.   James Webster notes this dichotomy of treatment between primary and secondary material in Brahms's recapitulations in "The General and the Particular in Brahms's Later Sonata Forms," in *Brahms Studies: Analytical and Historical Perspectives,* ed. George S. Bozarth (Oxford: Oxford University Press, 1990), 49–78.

14.   I explore Brahms's tendency to develop the harmonic potential of this type of $^6_4$ chord in "Brahms and Motivic $^6_4$ Chords," *Music Analysis* 16 (1997): 175–217.

15.   Donald F. Tovey, *Essays in Musical Analysis,* vol. 2 (London: Oxford University Press, 1935), 19.

16.   Donald F. Tovey, "Brahms," in *Essays in Musical Analysis: Chamber Music* (London: Oxford University Press, 1944), 209–10.

17.   Elaine R. Sisman explores issues of formal bivalence in Brahms's slow movements in "Brahms's Slow Movements: Reinventing the 'Closed' Forms," in *Brahms Studies: Analytical and Historical Perspectives,* ed. George S. Bozarth (Oxford: Oxford University Press, 1990), 79–103.

18.   The practice of articulating structural tonic return with an embellished version of the main theme is common in Brahms's slow movements. The varied return may follow several earlier references to the opening idea that are more straightforward thematically, but that prove false due to their inability to articulate a structural tonic. The variation, in turn, disguises the true moment of recapitulation. A characteristic example is the return of the A section in the slow movement of the G-minor piano quartet. The Adagio from the Second Symphony includes a similar strategy for recapitulation, but the situation is complicated by the dominant prolongation at the outset of the opening phrase. Sisman discusses Brahms's pro-

clivity for false reprise in these and other slow movements in "Brahms's Slow Movements."

19. In graphic terms this function can be expressed by use of a closed note head for the quasi articulation while an open note head can be reserved for the later unequivocal point of arrival. In a paper titled "Quasi-auxiliary Cadences: Some Preliminary Observations" delivered at the Third International Schenker Symposium at the Mannes College of Music (1999), Roger Kamien discussed these types of tonics in relation to Schenker's concept of the auxiliary cadence, rather than the idea of an apparent tonic.

20. The seminal work with respect to Schubert's influence on Brahms is Webster, "Schubert's Sonata Form." Graybill discusses eighteenth-century precedents for Brahms's approach to issues of second-key organization in "Brahms's Three-Key Expositions."

4. Brahms and Schenker

1. See, for example, the first movements of Haydn's *Farewell* Symphony, Mozart's Piano Sonata in C Major, K. 545, Beethoven's Piano Sonata in D Minor, op. 31, no. 2 (*Tempest*), and Schubert's *Trout* Quintet and *Quartettsatz*. For a highly stimulating analysis of the Haydn see James Webster, *Haydn's "Farewell" Symphony and the Idea of Classical Style* (Cambridge: Cambridge University Press, 1991), 30–57. Beach analyzes the *Trout* Quintet movement and several other one-part Schubert sonata forms in "Schubert's Experiments with Sonata Form." Although Schenker reads the K. 545 sonata as an interruption form in *Free Composition* (supplementary vol.: Fig. 47,1), its subdominant reprise of the main theme can be interpreted as part of a continuous middleground structure. John L. Snyder argues for an interpretation along these lines in "Schenker and the First Movement of Mozart's Sonata, K. 545: An Uninterrupted Sonata-Form Movement?" *Theory and Practice* 16 (1991): 51–78.

2. Nor is the reverse inevitable: thematic parallelism need not always articulate an interruption.

3. In Schenker's words, "the conventional technical term *semicadence,* used to describe the first $\hat{2}/V$ . . . too easily suggests the concept of 'cadence' in the sense of closure, which contradicts the true meaning of interruption. . . . The interruption not only creates more content; it also has the effect of a delay, or retardation, on the way to the ultimate goal, $\hat{1}/I$. The interruption is able to produce this effect only because it carries within it the fundamental structure, which must achieve its fulfillment despite all detours"; see Schenker, *Free Composition,* 37.

4. See Rosen's *Sonata Forms,* rev. ed. (New York: W. W. Norton, 1988). As Roger Graybill states, "Rosen's model is more static [than Schenker's], insofar as resolution is brought about by the transposed restatement of a block of material"; Roger Graybill, "Harmonic Circularity in Brahms's F Major Cello Sonata: An Alternative to Schenker's Reading in *Free Composition,*" *Music Theory Spectrum* 10 (1988): 52, n. 14.

5. Allan Keiler, "On Some Properties of Schenker's Pitch Derivations," *Music Perception* 1 (1983–84): 200–228. See also Komar, "The Pedagogy of Tonal Hierarchy."

6. For a more detailed examination of Schenker's discussion of interruption, as well

as illuminating insight into his analysis of the theme of Brahms's *Variations on a Theme of Haydn,* op. 56, see Keiler, "On Some Properties," 215–27.

7.   Schenker, *Free Composition,* 36 and 38.

8.   Keiler, "On Some Properties," 211. See also Allan Keiler, "Two Views of Musical Semiotics," in *The Sign in Word and Language,* ed. W. Steiner (Austin: University of Texas Press, 1981), 138–68, esp. 151–64; and "The Syntax of Prolongation (Part I)," *In Theory Only* 3 (1977): 3–27, esp. 13–27.

9.   Schenker, *Free Composition,* 36–37.

10.   Ibid., 37.

11.   Ibid., supplementary vol.: Fig. 21b.

12.   Joseph Lubben pointed out this contradiction with species principles to me in a personal communication.

13.   Schenker, *Free Composition,* supplementary vol.: Fig. 24–26.

14.   Schenker supports this assessment of the dotted slur in the text where he comments, first in reference to interruption in the case of $\hat{3}$, that "the primary tone combines within itself a mental retention, that is, a motionless state, and an actual motion of the linear progression," and later, in the case of $\hat{5}$, that "[b]esides resting on $\hat{2}$/V, the interruption of $\hat{5}$–$\hat{1}$ rests also on the first $\hat{5}$ as the primary tone of the linear progression $\hat{5}$–$\hat{2}$, just as though the line of a fourth were not present between these two points" (ibid., 38–39).

15.   This is the crux of the problem, as I see it, with Schenker's graphic analysis of the theme from Brahms's *Variations on a Theme by Haydn,* discussed with attention to these issues in Keiler, "On Some Properties," 211–28.

16.   For example, Larry Laskowski suggests in a recent article on formal issues and Schenkerian analysis that Schenker's "dogmatic emphasis on background structure is in many cases not to be taken quite literally"; see Laskowski, "J. S. Bach's 'Binary' Dance Movements: Form and Voice Leading," in *Schenker Studies,* ed. Hedi Siegel (Cambridge: Cambridge University Press, 1990), 90.

17.   For an extensive discussion of both the contradictions between Schenkerian theoretical claims and Schenkerian analytic practice and the problems that arise when music theorists argue on an ad hoc basis for an informal interpretation of Schenker's theoretical assertions, see Richard Cohn, "The Autonomy of Motives in Schenkerian Accounts of Tonal Music," *Music Theory Spectrum* 14 (1992): 150–70; and "Schenker's Theory, Schenkerian Theory: Pure Unity or Constructive Conflict?," *Indiana Theory Review* 13 (1992): 1–20.

18.   Charles J. Smith suggests a similar acceptance of the inability to reconcile interruption with a continuous background. He argues instead that it is best to view the divided middleground as a case of "two distinct but equally weighted descents, neither of which can be subordinated to the other"; see Smith, "Musical Form and Fundamental Structure," 267–69. He acknowledges that my discussion of interruption in an earlier published version of the present chapter anticipates his: see my "Brahms and Schenker: A Mutual Response to Sonata Form," *Music Theory Spectrum* 16 (1994): 77–103. Yet he also claims that I did not, in that article, recognize the possibility for a third alternative—his notion of equally weighted descents—in addition to my type 1 and 2 derivations. I did explicitly

state, however, that questioning the idea that Schenker's theory "requires a literal derivation of interruption from a single *Ursatz*... only further supports this ultimate point: that if we attend to the implications of Schenker's theory, *we are left with a two-part structure for sonata form.* ... In the spirit of analytic pragmatism, however, we can accept the fact that *the interruption paradigm is not satisfactorily reconcilable on an earlier level* and conceive of the *Ursatz* as a metaphysical connection between Schenker's chord of nature and a specific parallel construction" (83–84, italics added).

19. Oster cites the first movements of Beethoven's piano sonatas op. 109, op. 2, no. 3, and op. 14, no. 2, as well as the first movements of the op. 24 violin sonata and the Sixth Symphony as examples. See Schenker, *Free Composition,* 138, n. 16.

20. Ibid., 138. Oster clarifies Schenker's meaning in note 16.

21. Ibid., 43–45 and 73–82.

22. On at least one occasion Schenker reconciles these problems by interpreting the recapitulation of the transition as a prolongation of the $\hat{2}$/V, with the second theme expanding only the terminal $\hat{1}$/I (ibid., supplementary vol.: Fig. 35-1). Though this interpretation conforms to Schenker's criteria for linear progressions, it shows the structural close too early given Schenker's normal analytic practice. In formal terms it has the unfortunate effect of attributing a coda-like function to the recapitulation of the second theme.

23. In a major-mode movement in which both theme groups articulate fifth progressions, Schenker is able to derive the recapitulation from a single replica *Ursatz.* He graphs the first group as a prolongation of $\hat{5}$ and elevates the entire second group to the earlier level so that its linear progression provides the descent from $\hat{5}$ to $\hat{1}$. Though one might argue therefore that major-mode sonata forms with $\hat{3}$ as their *Kopfton* represent a special category, the logical conclusion of this argument is highly un-Schenkerian: that these movements are less organically unified than those with $\hat{5}$ as their *Kopfton.* Indeed, many of the sonata forms that Schenker discusses throughout *Free Composition* take $\hat{3}$ as their *Kopfton,* as discussed in Chapter 2. Moreover, the harmonic problems in the reconciliation of the two-part middleground with a single *Ursatz* remain regardless of the identity of the *Kopfton.*

24. *Free Composition,* 138, n. 16.

25. Keiler, "On Some Properties," 221.

26. See Morgan, "The Delayed Structural Downbeat."

27. Beach describes a similar reconciliation of sonata-form design with continuous middleground structures in several Schubert movements in "Schubert's Experiments." The examples Beach cites involve a reorientation of the main theme around the subdominant in the recapitulation and a return to the structural dominant at the end of the bridge material. The restatement of the second group, however, prolongs the tonic similar to late eighteenth-century sonata forms. As Beach demonstrates, the status of the tonic in the second group allows for an alternate interpretation of the movements as interruption forms. In contrast, Brahms's emphasis on the dominant throughout the recapitulation in the op. 60 quartet forces the issue, so that the location of a middleground interruption is not possible. Given Brahms's well-known admiration for Schubert, we can view

his approach as an alternative to the procedures of his predecessor, rather than an outright innovation.

28. For other examples, see my "Brahms and Schenker: A Mutual Response to Sonata Form," 93–103.

29. See, for example, Rosen, *Sonata Forms,* and Leonard Ratner, *Classic Music: Expression, Form, and Style* (New York: Schirmer, 1980). Rosen states that "we must not assume that the eighteenth-century composer was required to begin at the head with the first theme, or that he had to go over the whole of the exposition. Indeed, it was possible to begin anywhere in the first group." He later adds that "[w]hat must reappear in the recapitulation—and this is a rule that holds true from the very beginnings of anything that can be called sonata style—is the second group, at least any part of it that has an individual and characteristic aspect, and that does not already have its analogue in the first group" (Rosen, *Sonata Forms,* 285, 287).

5. Brahms's Expository Strategies

1. Rosen, *Sonata Forms,* 25.

2. James Hepokoski and Warren Darcy suggest the idea of a de-energizing transition as a nineteenth-century alternative to Classical precedent in "The Medial Caesura and Its Role in the Eighteenth-Century Sonata Exposition," *Music Theory Spectrum* 19 (1997): 123.

3. William E. Caplin develops the idea of a dichotomy between tight-knit and looser organization as a basis for Classical expositions in *Classical Form: A Theory of Formal Functions for the Instrumental Music of Haydn, Mozart, and Beethoven* (Oxford: Oxford University Press, 1998).

4. On the concept of rhythmic dissonance, see Harald Krebs, *Fantasy Pieces: Metrical Dissonance in the Music of Robert Schumann* (Oxford: Oxford University Press, 1999); and "Some Extensions of the Concepts of Metrical Consonance and Dissonance," *Journal of Music Theory* 31 (1987): 99–120.

5. Morgan explores the prevalence of this type of recapitulatory pattern in nineteenth-century music and traces its roots back to the Classical era in "The Delayed Structural Downbeat."

6. As described in Sisman, "Brahms's Slow Movements," 86 and 101.

7. As noted by Margaret Notley in "Brahms's Cello Sonata in F Major and Its Genesis: A Study in Half-Step Relations," in *Brahms Studies,* vol. 1, ed. David Brodbeck (Lincoln: University of Nebraska Press, 1994), 139–60. Notley's perceptive analysis also demonstrates ways in which the A′ section "resolves" harmonic issues introduced by the A and B sections and thus contains an additional sonata component. She nevertheless describes the movement as "a binary/ternary hybrid," uses letter designations rather than the descriptive labels of sonata theory to identify its formal parts, and like me therefore presents an interpretation in which sonata components function as secondary attributes.

8. The situation is nevertheless complicated by the fact that Brahms conflates developmental and recapitulatory formal functions in his treatment of the return of main-theme material. The result is a special type of sonata-rondo hybrid un-

common for Brahms in a slow movement, but characteristic for many of his finales and some first movements. Brahms likely learned this form from Mozart, as Daverio argues in "From 'Concertante Rondo' to 'Lyric Sonata'."

9. Another orchestral slow movement that falls in the same category as the movements from the Second and Third Symphonies (but with secondary material in ♯VII (!) rather than the dominant) is the Adagio non troppo from the A-Major Serenade, op. 16. Webster provides an analysis of the movement's sonata/ternary hybrid form in "Schubert's Sonata Form," part 2, 60. Sisman likewise has many insightful things to say about Brahms's synthesis of sonata and ABA conventions in "Brahms's Slow Movements."

10. Caplin provides a detailed exploration of sentence conventions in *Classical Form,* 9–12 and 35–48.

11. There are exceptions, of course. See, for example, the end of the exposition of the finale of the Third Symphony.

12. Webster, "Schubert's Sonata Form."

13. Ibid., 19 and 26.

14. Rosen lays out his polarity model in *Sonata Forms.*

15. The "hailstorm" characterization is Tovey's. See his *Essays in Musical Analysis: Chamber Music,* 212.

16. Graybill, "Brahms's Three-Key Expositions."

17. Webster also identifies a fourth, intermediate category: secondary areas that begin with a new theme in a key that initially seems firmly established, but that nevertheless remains unable to close without modulating to the dominant. He cites Schubert's *Great* Symphony, F-Major Octet, D. 803, and *Reliquie* Sonata as examples; see Webster, "Schubert's Sonata Form," part 1, 29.

18. Rey M. Longyear and Kate R. Covington nevertheless explore some possible eighteenth-century precedents for Schubert's innovations in "Sources of the Three-Key Exposition," *Journal of Musicology* 6 (1988): 448–70.

19. The finale of Schubert's C-Minor Piano Sonata, D. 958, provides another example of the mode-shift type. Like the *Death and the Maiden* movement, it articulates two main keys in its secondary area, C♯ minor and E♭. It is within the E♭ material that Schubert presents a shift from minor to major.

20. Tovey develops the concept of a first maturity in "Brahms's Chamber Music," 220–45. Webster notes that his own notion of first maturity expands Tovey's focus on piano and strings chamber music to include all of Brahms's chamber works from 1859 to 1865; see Webster, "Schubert's Sonata Form," part 2, 53, note 2.

21. This dual function for V^7/F originates in the quartet's slow movement. For a stimulating discussion of its crucial role in a network of Neapolitan relationships, see Christopher Wintle, "The 'Sceptred Pall': Brahms's Progressive Harmony," in *Brahms 2: Biographical, Documentary, and Analytical Studies,* ed. Michael Musgrave (Cambridge: Cambridge University Press, 1987), 197–222.

22. It is also interesting to note that a hint of three-key organization informs the exposition of Brahms's F-Minor Piano Sonata, op. 5, a work published before the first maturity, in 1854. The sonata's secondary area tonicizes A♭ beginning at

m. 39. Yet toward the very end of the exposition, Brahms transforms A♭ into a dominant and closes with an authentic cadence in D♭ in m. 68. Although the move to D♭ does not blossom into a formal area of its own, the key scheme does provide evidence of Brahms's interest in expanded tonal resources at a time prior to his immersion in Schubert's works. Recall that the Tovey/Webster argument is that the Schubert influence emerges only later with the works of the first maturity. The point here is not that Brahms developed a three-key approach independent of his studies of Schubert. Rather, it is that Brahms may have been inspired by Schubert's three-key expositions in part because in them Schubert had realized more extensive compositional ramifications for a strategy that Brahms had already experimented with, however tentatively. Graybill includes the F-minor piano sonata and even the C-Major Piano Sonata, op. 1, of 1853, in his list of three-key expositions (Graybill, "Brahms's Three-Key Expositions," 69).

23. Hepokoski and Darcy, "The Medial Caesura," 115–54.

24. Webster and Walter Frisch both note similarities between the quintet and the *Appassionata,* although neither includes the mode shift in the second group of the Beethoven as a link: see Webster, "Schubert's Sonata Form," part 2, 68; Frisch, *Brahms and the Principle of Developing Variation,* 83–86.

25. Several of these special cases—exceptions that prove the rule—include the expositions from Haydn's *Farewell* Symphony and Beethoven's piano sonatas in D major (op. 10, no. 3, mvt. II), C♯ minor (op. 27, no. 2, mvt. III), D minor (op. 31, no. 2), and E minor (op. 90).

26. Ernst Oster, "Register and the Large-Scale Connection," in *Readings in Schenker Analysis and Other Approaches,* ed. Maury Yeston (New Haven, Conn.: Yale University Press, 1977), 67.

27. Hepokoski and Darcy label the type of secondary area found in the *Pathétique* a *mid-expositional trimodular block;* see Hepokoski and Darcy, "The Medial Caesura," 145–50. In brief, a trimodular block consists of (1) a section that appears to initiate second-theme rhetoric following a medial caesura, (2) the dissolution of this second-theme rhetoric into an unstable transition-like passage that culminates in another big arrival on a dominant, and (3) the statement of a new theme that now achieves the stability and harmonic closure that failed to materialize at the earlier aborted second theme.

28. Oster, "Register and the Large-Scale Connection," 68.

29. Of the trio, Webster writes: "Brahms continues [in the works of the late first maturity] to cultivate the double second group of the type in which the two sections stand in the major and minor modes of a single tonic. The Cello Sonata is an unusually clear case. . . . In the Horn Trio, only the finale is in sonata form . . . it also has an unmistakable double second group in the dominant" (Webster, "Schubert's Sonata Form," part 2, 69).

30. Ibid., part 2, 62–68. The third is the B♭ sextet, where Webster's case for a Schubertian influence is strongest.

31. Graybill, "Brahms's Three-Key Expositions," 355–58.

32. Robert S. Winter explores the role this type of medial articulation plays in eighteenth-century music in "The Bifocal Close and the Evolution of the Vien-

nese Classical Style," *Journal of the American Musicological Society* 42 (1989): 275–337.

33.   Hepokoski and Darcy, "The Medial Caesura," 133–38.

34.   For a description of principles of continuous exposition see Jens Peter Larsen, "Sonata Form Problems," in *Handel, Haydn, and the Viennese Classical Style,* trans. Ulrich Krämer (Ann Arbor, Mich.: UMI Research Press, 1988), 269–79; and Hepokoski and Darcy, "The Medial Caesura," 117–21. Specific evidence of Brahms's appreciation for techniques of continuous exposition appears in a letter to Joachim of October 1871. Brahms describes the sonata-form Andante of Haydn's Symphony no. 16 in B♭ as "a paragon of beauty," and adds that he knows "of no better example of the newly invented 'unending melody.'" As Margaret Notley has pointed out, the only exceptional aspect of continuity in the movement involves the absence of a clear articulation of the second key area. In other words, the movement provides an example of a continuous as opposed to two-part exposition. The letter appears in *Johannes Brahms: Life and Letters,* trans. Josef Eisinger and Styra Avins (Oxford: Oxford University Press, 1997), 427. Notley's discussion of it can be found in "Late-Nineteenth-Century Chamber Music and the Cult of the Classical Adagio," *19th-Century Music* 23 (1999): 42.

35.   The secondary areas in the piano sonatas by Mozart in C Major, K. 545, and Beethoven in E♭ Major, op. 31, no. 3, are just two of many examples.

36.   Hepokoski and Darcy, "The Medial Caesura," 127–33.

37.   The multivalence of the appassionata theme is reflected in conflicting interpretations of its formal function in the scholarly literature. Tovey and Brodbeck, for instance, both refer to it as a second theme. Malcolm MacDonald by contrast labels it a transition theme and assigns second-theme status to the chorale instead. Michael Musgrave shares MacDonald's view of the chorale, implying a similar interpretation of the appassionata theme as transitional material. As a corollary to their interpretation of the appassionata theme, Tovey and Brodbeck describe the chorale as closing material. Their overall interpretation, in other words, is the exact opposite of the view expressed by Musgrave and MacDonald; see Tovey, *Essays in Musical Analysis: Chamber Music,* 212–13; Brodbeck, "Medium and Meaning," 119–20; Malcolm MacDonald, *Brahms* (London: Dent, 1990), 228; Michael Musgrave, *The Music of Brahms* (London: Routledge and Kegan Paul, 1985), 117–19.

38.   Lauri Suurpää discusses a similar situation in the exposition of Haydn's G-Minor String Quartet, op. 74, no. 3. The material in mm. 55–78 of the quartet has the formal rhetoric of a closing theme. Yet it is only with the closing cadence of the passage that the top voice makes its way down from the active melodic pitch of D to closure on B♭. See Suurpää, "Continuous Exposition and Tonal Structure in Three Late Haydn Works," 185–90.

39.   Noted by both Geiringer and Musgrave: Geiringer, *Brahms: His Life and Work,* 231; Musgrave, *The Music of Brahms,* 110.

40.   In the horn trio, an idiosyncrasy marks the resolution. The progression moves directly from a dominant $^6_4$ chord to the tonic $^5_3$, with an elision of the dominant $^5_3$.

41.   One recent analysis ties this passage explicitly to Brahms's relationship to the Schumanns: see Brodbeck, *Brahms Symphony No. 1,* 31–50.

42. The first movement of Brahms's F-Major Cello Sonata, op. 99, provides another example of this type. For an insightful analysis of its exposition see Graybill, "Harmonic Circularity in Brahms's F Major Cello Sonata."

43. As discussed by Reinhold Brinkmann in *Late Idyll: The Second Symphony of Johannes Brahms,* trans. Peter Palmer (Cambridge, Mass.: Harvard University Press, 1995), 32–53.

44. Brodbeck suggests that the return of the chorale in the coda "represents a transcendence that Brahms cannot finally embrace," in *Brahms Symphony No. 1,* 78.

6. Toward an Expressive Interpretation

1. Nicholas Cook, "Theorizing Musical Meaning," *Music Theory Spectrum* 23 (2001): 170–95.

2. McClary's analysis addresses the entrance of the reprise in the first movement of Beethoven's Ninth Symphony. See Susan McClary, *Feminine Endings: Music, Gender, and Sexuality* (Minneapolis: University of Minnesota Press, 1991), 128–29.

3. Treitler's critique of Schenker appears in *Music and the Historical Imagination* (Cambridge, Mass.: Harvard University Press, 1989), 19–45.

4. Of the two, Cook expends more critical energy on Hatten via discussion of his *Musical Meaning in Beethoven.* For Cook's representative list of formalists, which includes Cone as well as Treitler and Newcomb among many others, see "Theorizing Musical Meaning," 174.

5. Ibid., 190.

6. Edward T. Cone, "Schubert's Promissory Note: An Exercise in Musical Hermeneutics," in *Schubert: Critical and Analytical Studies,* ed. Walter Frisch (Lincoln: University of Nebraska Press, 1986), 13–30.

7. Ibid., 16.

8. For a discussion of Peirce's concepts of type and token, see Hatten, *Musical Meaning in Beethoven,* 44–50.

9. Cone, "Schubert's Promissory Note," 16.

10. Ibid.

11. Ibid., 25. Cone adopts both the term *expressive potential* and his definition of it from his book *The Composer's Voice,* 166.

12. Ibid., 28.

13. Maynard Solomon, "Franz Schubert and the Peacocks of Benvenuto Cellini," *19th-Century Music* 12 (1989): 193–206.

14. For a lucid argument in favor of striving to choose the more "artistically true" alternative among multiple plausible analyses, see Schachter, "Either/Or." While Schachter argues that analysis should aspire to perceive "clear and distinct shapes," he nevertheless notes that ambiguity and multiple meaning "certainly do exist [in tonal music]." In his view, however, their function is "more narrowly circumscribed than some analysts, perhaps misled by false analogies to language, seem to believe" (169).

15. Kofi Agawu has made this point, as has Pieter van den Toorn, in much greater

detail and specifically in defense of Schenkerian theory. See Agawu, "Analyzing Music under the New Musicological Regime," *Journal of Musicology* 15 (1997): 302; and van den Toorn, *Music, Politics, and the Academy,* 75–100.

16. Here again Agawu (more succinctly) and van den Toorn (at much greater length) provide compelling arguments: Agawu, ibid., 297–307; and van den Toorn, ibid., 75–100.

17. As I read them, neither Agawu (ibid.) nor van den Toorn (ibid.) defend Schenkerian theory as an alternative mode of engagement that is superior yet somehow inherently at odds with the reputedly more humanistic approach of New Musicology. On the contrary, they see Schenkerian analysis as a tool that could well serve the needs of scholars grappling with questions of musical meaning.

18. Cook, "Theorizing Musical Meaning," 176.

19. Ibid., 175.

20. Ibid.

21. Ibid., 170. The approach Cook refers to as scatter-gun appears in van den Toorn's *Music, Politics, and the Academy.* It is curious in this regard that Cook notes with approval Agawu's rebuttals of New Musicological critiques of theory, even though many of Agawu's arguments are virtually identical to van den Toorn's. Why van den Toorn's approach is "scatter-gun" while Agawu's represents "persistent probing" is never explained. Cook's characterization is especially curious given the fact that van den Toorn's views are both considerably more extensively elaborated and considerably more tightly argued than Agawu's. If either theorist's work on the topic could be described as persistent, it would seem to be van den Toorn's.

22. Hatten, *Musical Meaning in Beethoven,* 9–28.

23. Treitler, for example, sees "a *permanent* difference between analysis and criticism" (*Music and the Historical Imagination,* 32, italics added). In his view, Schenker's analysis of Beethoven's Ninth was intended to "demonstrate the unity of the work and the necessity of its constituent moments, and to display it as exemplification of a theory." Treitler's intention in engaging the Ninth, by contrast, is "the illumination of the work in its individuality." Regardless of whether Treitler's characterization of Schenker's aims is accurate, the idea that either theoretical exemplification or the pursuit of unity represent permanent differences between analysis and criticism is highly questionable. Why does theory have to exist as Treitler describes it? Quite the contrary, it seems obvious that theory can function as a tool for illumination of individuality.

24. Cone highlights the influence of expressive interpretation on his structural analysis when he notes that his "analysis has not been wholly objective. I have insinuated a few leading phrases to suggest [to the reader] the kind of expression I find in the work, and to encourage [the reader] to hear it in the same way"; see Cone, "Schubert's Promissory Note," 26.

25. This is my understanding of Schenker's approach as well: the foreground is not a level that enters analysis trivially, but as the fruit that has ripened into a meaningful whole through its connection to the middleground and background.

26. Cook, "Theorizing Musical Meaning," 190.

27. Heinrich Schenker, "Beethoven's Third Symphony: Its True Content Described for the First Time," in *The Masterwork in Music: A Yearbook,* vol. 3, ed. William Drabkin, trans. Derrick Puffett and Alfred Clayton (Cambridge: Cambridge University Press, 1997), 10–34.

28. Hatten, *Musical Meaning in Beethoven,* 29–66.

29. Examples of this trend include Brodbeck, "Medium and Meaning," and his *Brahms Symphony No. 1.* For a thorough-going critique of the notion that musical ciphers are pervasive in Brahms's works or even in Schumann's, see John Daverio, *Crossing Paths* (Oxford: Oxford University Press, 2002), 65–152.

30. Gregory Karl also emphasizes the role binary oppositions can play in expressive interpretation in "Structuralism and Musical Plot," *Music Theory Spectrum* 19 (1997): 13–34. Karl focuses his discussion of opposition on the notions of *roles* and *plot functions* or *functional sequences,* concepts he borrows from structuralist literary theory. Out of these categories he develops useful tools for analysis and applies them insightfully to interpretation of extra-musical meaning in the first movement of Beethoven's *Appassionata* Sonata. His ideas about expressive interpretation in general and the function of binary opposition in particular have had an important influence on my own approach to meaning in the Brahms quartet. Hatten nevertheless extends the concept of opposition to embrace a wider range of musical and interpretive categories and thus provides a fuller realization of the analytical potential of this structuralist construct.

31. Hatten, *Musical Meaning in Beethoven,* 30.

32. Ibid.

33. Ibid., 34.

34. Kalbeck, *Brahms,* vol. 1, 232.

35. Cook, "Theorizing Musical Meaning," 190.

36. Massenet, of course, wrote an opera based on Goethe's *Werther.* An exploration of intersections of structure and meaning in this work would be fascinating on its own terms. The fact that he and his librettist, Georges Hartmann, first turned to the novella more than a decade after Brahms published his piano quartet (the opera was not actually premiered until 1892)—not to mention that compositional structure and expression in Massenet's operas are worlds apart from Brahms's musical language—nevertheless make any possible intertextual connections between the two works highly unlikely.

37. On the concept of large-scale dissonance, see Rosen, *Sonata Forms.*

38. My concept of framing is analogous to Karl's notion of "enclosure," one of a number of categories of "functional sequence" that he develops for analysis of musical plot in "Structuralism and Musical Plot," 20–22.

39. James Hepokoski and Warren Darcy label this type of repetition of a large-scale thematic pattern a "rotation"; see their *Elements of Sonata Theory: Norms, Types, and Deformations in the Late 18th-Century Sonata* (Oxford: Oxford University Press, forthcoming). In their terms the Brahms movement, like many sonata forms, articulates three rotations. The first consists of the thematic pattern of the exposition, which is followed not only by the standard retraversal of primary

and secondary material in the recapitulation but also by an outline of the same thematic pattern in the development.

40. On the motivic significance of the augmented triad in the *Rhapsody*, see Wallace Berry, "Text and Music in the Alto Rhapsody," *Journal of Music Theory* 27 (1983): 249–52; and Allen Forte, "Motive and Rhythmic Contour in the Alto Rhapsody," *Journal of Music Theory* 27 (1983): 255–71. Webster provides structural and expressive interpretation of the C-minor/major trajectory of the *Rhapsody*, as well as an argument about the work's importance for Brahms's subsequent compositional development, in "The *Alto Rhapsody.*"

41. Cone, "Schubert's Promissory Note," 27.

42. Webster argues for the special expressive significance of C minor/major for Brahms and many of his predecessors in "The *Alto Rhapsody.*"

43. Many critics have found this turn to transcendence at odds with the work's text. A more sympathetic account of the C-major close is provided in John Daverio, "The *Wechsel der Töne* in Brahms's *Schicksalslied,*" *Journal of the American Musicological Society* 46 (1993): 84–113.

44. A similar use of the diminished fourth in a $\hat{3}$–$\natural\hat{7}$–$\hat{1}$ motive occurs at the beginning of the main theme (mm. 5–6) of the Adagio mesto movement from the horn trio. The *mesto* designation supports the idea that the interval contributes to a correlation for despair in the finale of the quartet.

45. He first asked that they each return the letters of the other; then they were to destroy them. Initially Clara agreed, but fortunately she held on to some of the letters Brahms had written and in the end decided not to destroy the ones he had returned to her. He, on the other hand, upheld his end of the arrangement. Nancy B. Reich describes the fate of the correspondence with reference to the documentary evidence in the letters themselves in "Clara Schumann and Johannes Brahms," in *Brahms and His World*, ed. Walter Frisch (Princeton, N.J.: Princeton University Press, 1990), 43.

46. Kalbeck views the Andante as a declaration of Brahms's love for Clara, an interpretation bound up with his (unsubstantiated) notion that Brahms recast the original slow movement of the C♯-minor version of the quartet as the Andante of the published work; see *Brahms*, vol. 3, 14. Similar to my interpretation of the Andante, Daverio hears homage to Robert in the slow movement of Brahms's D-minor piano concerto; see *Crossing Paths*, 148–52. While not denying that, as Brahms himself put it, the movement was conceived as a "gentle portrait" of Clara, Daverio argues for a more complex view in which the composer alternates passages oriented around Clara with others that suggest requiem music for Robert.

47. Robert Fink develops a hermeneutic interpretation of Brahms's First Symphony that centers around issues of sexuality and the composer's relationship with the Schumanns in "Desire, Repression, and Brahms's First Symphony," *Repercussions* 2 (1993): 75–103. Toward the end of the article (96–102), he ties his ideas about expression specifically to his notion that Brahms may well have suffered from what Freud termed *psychical impotence.*

48. Quoted by Reich, "Clara Schumann and Johannes Brahms," 47.

49. Beethoven replicates, within the movement, this progression from darkness to light via the return of scherzo material as preparation for the reprise of the main theme. For an insightful discussion of how these passages have been received by Beethoven's critics as well as for original interpretive insights, see Scott Burnham, "How Music Matters: Poetic Content Revisited," in *Rethinking Music,* ed. Nicholas Cook and Mark Everist (Oxford: Oxford University Press, 1999), 193–216.

50. The idea that the main theme should have a tone of sorrow and resignation perhaps motivated Brahms's change of heart regarding the proper tempo indication for the finale. In the manuscript he marked the movement first *Presto* and then *Tempo giusto* and *Un poco presto*. In the published version he slowed it down to *Allegro commodo*.

51. Authors who suggest a putative relationship between quartet and sonata include Brodbeck, "Medium and Meaning," 119–20; and Basil Smallman, *The Piano Quartet and Quintet: Style, Structure, and Scoring* (Oxford: Oxford University Press, 1994), 94–95. Parmer provides a stimulating analysis of the relationship between songs and sonata in "Brahms, Song Quotation, and Secret Programs," 167–77. A connection between songs and sonata is unquestionable: the musical material is virtually identical, and Brahms himself drew attention to the borrowing in a letter to Theodor Billroth, cited by Parmer; see *Johannes Brahms and Theodor Billroth: Letters from a Musical Friendship,* trans. and ed. Hans Barkan (Norman: University of Oklahoma Press, 1957), 80.

52. Advocates of the idea that "allusive webs" are a core component of Brahms's musical language might also assert a relationship between the rhythmic motive that dominates the climax and the rhythmic germ from Beethoven's Fifth Symphony. This would be a case of "allusive irony" since the quartet's finale resists the kind of victorious outcome projected by the symphony. For a discussion of allusive irony in Brahms, see Kenneth Hull, "Allusive Irony in Brahms's Fourth Symphony," in *Brahms Studies,* vol. 2, ed. David Brodbeck (Lincoln: University of Nebraska Press, 1998), 135–68. Brodbeck suggests a connection between the opening of Brahms's finale, with its pickup figure and melodic G–E♭, and the head motive of Beethoven's Fifth in "Medium and Meaning," 120.

53. Brinkmann discusses the crucial role of images of nature and religion in the turn to light in the First Symphony in *Late Idyll,* 33–53.

54. My view of expressive content in the sonata has many points of contact with the interpretation offered in Parmer, "Brahms, Song Quotation, and Secret Programs," 167–77.

55. Brodbeck similarly contrasts the expressive outcome of Mendelssohn's trio and Brahms's quartet in "Medium and Meaning," 120–22.

7. Intertextual Resonances

1. Tovey, *Essays in Musical Analysis: Chamber Music,* 203–14. Page numbers for all subsequent citations from this essay appear in the text.

2. Tovey, *Essays in Musical Analysis,* 152. Page numbers for all subsequent citations from this essay appear in the text.

3. James Webster, "Brahms's *Tragic Overture:* The Form of Tragedy," in *Brahms: Biographical, Documentary, and Analytical Studies,* ed. Robert Pascall (Cambridge: Cambridge University Press, 1983), 99–124. Page numbers for all subsequent citations from this essay appear in the text.

4. Arno Mitschka, *Der Sonatensatz in den Werken von Johannes Brahms* (Gütersloh, 1961), 287–91.

5. For a recent discussion of this formal type, see John Daverio, "From 'Concertante Rondo' to 'Lyric Sonata.'"

6. Brinkmann, *Late Idyll,* 34. Page numbers for all subsequent citations from Brinkmann's book appear in the text.

7. Webster, "The *Alto Rhapsody.*"

8. In the case of the Third Symphony, Brahms again turns to music of religious connotation in the service of a quiet denouement. The symphony's conclusion transforms the dirgelike theme from both the second movement and the finale's tonic area into an otherworldly funeral hymn for the brass and winds (m. 281). This solemn funeral processional ushers in the famous final statement of the main theme from the first movement, which itself derives from Schumann. The ethereal reverie of the Schumann quotation—its veiled appearance within sixteenth-note figuration—transports its original impassioned character, which remained earthbound due to internal conflicts (the A♭–A♮ cross-relation, syncopated accompaniment, etc.), into a celestial and shimmering F-major triad. Also noteworthy for the expressive impact of this heavenly close is the fact that the progression to major occurs in conjunction with yet another Brahmsian delay of tonic return. The final bars of the symphony are programmatically the ultimate resting place for Schumann and structurally the only stable statement of the tonic in the recapitulation. For more detailed discussion of this recapitulatory tonal delay, see my "Brahms and Schenker," 95–100. For an analysis of the symphony as a whole, see Robert Bailey, "Musical Language and Structure in the Third Symphony," in *Brahms Studies: Analytical and Historical Perspectives,* ed. George S. Bozarth (Oxford: Oxford University Press, 1990), 405–21.

9. Webster, "The *Alto Rhapsody,*" 44.

10. This theme provides a motivic recall of the theme that Albert Dietrich composed for the very opening of his contribution to the *FAE* Sonata, the *Allegro* first movement.

11. The final choral section of the *Alto Rhapsody* also places special emphasis on the major form of 6̂, as described by Webster in "The *Alto Rhapsody,*" 34–41.

12. In addition to the trio, one might also cite the *Academic Festival Overture.* The unique generic status of the overture, however—the fact that it shows Brahms able to incorporate C minor into a comic work (not to mention the minimal amount of time the piece actually spends in C minor)—supports rather than contradicts the notion that Brahms had tamed his C-minor demons. Moreover, the contrast between the overture's murky C-minor opening and blindingly bright C-major conclusion provides further evidence of Brahms's fidelity to traditional affective associations for the key.

13. *Essays in Musical Analysis,* 19.

14. Notley discusses the crucial role the refrain material of mm. 1–4 plays in the movement in "Late-Nineteenth-Century Chamber Music," 53–56.

15. On this point and especially the significance of C-minor-to-major transformations, see Webster, "The *Alto Rhapsody*."

16. For a recent discussion see Tusa, "Beethoven's 'C-Minor Mood.'"

17. The first graph is based on an interpretation that Lauri Suurpää presented as example 8b in the handout for his lecture "The Undivided *Ursatz* and the Omission of the Tonic *Stufe* at the Beginning of the Recapitulation," which he delivered at the 2000 Annual Meeting of the Society for Music Theory in Toronto.

18. The topic of sonata forms that open with unharmonized main themes that emphasize $\hat{5}$ is a broad one. For discussion of some of the harmonic and formal issues involved, see my "Structural Tonic or Apparent Tonic?"

19. My graphic interpretation corresponds in almost all essential details with Suurpää's reading in examples 7 and 9 of his SMT lecture. The main difference centers on the point at which we each locate the arrival of the retransitional G *Stufe*. As my graph shows, I hear the arrival of the structural dominant at m. 108, a point at which G enters as a tonicized harmony. Suurpää, by contrast, subsumes this G arrival within a broader prolongational motion that connects the B♭ tonicization of mm. 88 with the C harmony that enters along with the return of the motto at m. 110. He hears the middleground G *Stufe* enter only at m. 113, following the sequential progression initiated by the return of the head motive.

20. Cyclic integration is an aspect of Haydn's art that has drawn considerable attention in recent years. Studies that focus attention on the topic include Webster, *Haydn's "Farewell" Symphony and the Idea of Classical Style;* and Haimo, *Haydn's Symphonic Forms.*

21. Webster discusses this type of juxtaposition of remote keys across movements in *Haydn's "Farewell" Symphony and the Idea of Classical Style,* 219–20.

22. For a discussion of contrapuntal traditions in eighteenth-century music, see Warren Kirkendale, *Fugue and Fugato in Rococo and Classical Chamber Music* (Durham, N.C.: Duke University Press, 1979). A recent discussion of the contrapuntal finale of the *Jupiter* Symphony can be found in Elaine R. Sisman, *Mozart, The "Jupiter" Symphony, No. 41 in C Major, K. 551* (Cambridge: Cambridge University Press, 1993).

23. Robert S. Hatten proposes the correlation of "authoritative" for the markedness of fugal writing in *Musical Meaning in Beethoven,* 87.

24. The seminal exploration of these and other Schubertian sonata-form innovations remains Webster, "Schubert's Sonata Form," part 1.

25. My graph is similar to the Schenkerian interpretations found in Webster, "Schubert's Sonata Form," part 1, 27; David Beach, "Harmony and Linear Progression in Schubert's Music," *Journal of Music Theory* 38 (1994): 13–17; and Jackson, "The Tragic Reversed Recapitulation in the German Classical Tradition," 80–83. As I have, Webster, Beach, and Jackson all graph the A♭ tonicization as subsidiary to the i–V progression. Webster and Beach, however, hear the main arrival of G at m. 77, while Jackson agrees with me that V enters on the middleground only at m. 93. None of these writers attends to the chromatic voice exchange I hear connecting the opening tonic to the augmented-sixth chord on E♭ at m. 81.

26. The three-key exposition of the first movement of Brahms's Second Symphony provides an example whose middleground is even more closely related to the voice leading in the *Quartettsatz*. As Carl Schachter has persuasively argued, the symphony's tonicization of the mediant at the beginning of its double second group falls within a chromatic voice exchange that connects the opening tonic to an augmented-sixth chord. Just as in the *Quartettsatz*, this augmented-sixth chord prepares the arrival of V/V, which in turn eventually resolves to the tonicized dominant of the third key area (Schachter, "The First Movement of Brahms's Second Symphony").

27. Beach ("Harmony and Linear Progression in Schubert's Music," 15) and Jackson ("The Tragic Reversed Recapitulation in the German Classical Tradition," 84) both provide graphic interpretations of the *Quartettsatz*. Like me, Beach focuses on the structural bass, while Jackson includes both bass and *Urlinie* in his analysis.

28. Jackson focuses attention on the very act of recapitulatory thematic reordering as a central component of tragic expression in the *Quartettsatz* as well as a host of other movements. He relates the idea of a "reversed recapitulation" to the rhetorical figure *hyperbaton*, "a class of figures in which normal word order and semantic logic are abrogated, the dislocation reflecting violent or disordered feelings" ("The Tragic Reversed Recapitulation in the German Classical Tradition," 64).

29. Beach, "Harmony and Linear Progression in Schubert's Music," 17.

30. Beach notes the parallelism of the major-to-minor shift between the second theme and transition, on the one hand, and the C-major section and coda, on the other (ibid.).

31. Beach suggests that theme three's tonic transposition joins its new proximity with theme one to solidify the connection by shifting its descending-fourth motions to the tonic pitch level (ibid.).

32. Cone, *The Composer's Voice*, 166.

33. Cone, "Schubert's Promissory Note."

34. Ibid., 27–28.

35. Eric Sams, "Schubert's Illness Re-examined," *Musical Times* 121 (1980): 15–22.

36. Cone, "Schubert's Promissory Note," 28.

37. Ibid., 27.

38. This long-overdue reassessment of the topic appears in Daverio, *Crossing Paths*, 65–152.

Bibliography

Adrian, Jack. "The Ternary Sonata Form." *Journal of Music Theory* 34 (1990): 57–80.

Agawu, V. Kofi. "Analyzing Music under the New Musicological Regime." *Journal of Musicology* 15 (1997): 297–307.

———. "Does Music Theory Need Musicology?" *Current Musicology* 53 (1993): 89–98.

———. *Playing with Signs: A Semiotic Interpretation of Classic Music.* Princeton, N.J.: Princeton University Press, 1991.

Babbitt, Milton. "The Structure and Function of Music Theory." In *Perspectives on Contemporary Music Theory,* edited by Benjamin Boretz and Edward T. Cone, 10–21. New York: W. W. Norton, 1972.

———. *Words about Music.* Edited by Stephen Dembski and Joseph N. Straus. Madison: University of Wisconsin Press, 1987.

Bailey, Robert. "Musical Language and Structure in the Third Symphony." In *Brahms Studies: Analytical and Historical Perspectives,* edited by George S. Bozarth, 405–21. Oxford: Oxford University Press, 1990.

Beach, David. "Harmony and Linear Progression in Schubert's Music." *Journal of Music Theory* 38 (1994): 1–20.

———. "A Recurring Pattern in Mozart's Music." *Journal of Music Theory* 27 (1983): 1–29.

———. "Schubert's Experiments with Sonata Form: Formal-Tonal Design versus Underlying Structure." *Music Theory Spectrum* 15 (1993): 1–18.

Berry, Wallace. "Text and Music in the Alto Rhapsody." *Journal of Music Theory* 27 (1983): 249–52.

Brahms, Johannes. *Billroth und Brahms im Briefwechsel.* Edited by Otto Billroth. Berlin: Urban und Schwarzenberg, 1935.

———. *Johannes Brahms Briefwechsel.* 16 vols. Berlin: Deutsches Brahms-Gesellschaft, 1906–22.

———. *Johannes Brahms: The Herzogenberg Correspondence.* Edited by Max Kalbeck. Translated by Hannah Bryant. New York: Da Capo Press, 1987.

———. *Johannes Brahms: Life and Letters.* Translated by Josef Eisinger and Styra Avins. Oxford: Oxford University Press, 1997.

———. *Letters of Clara Schumann and Johannes Brahms, 1853–1896.* Edited by Berthold Litzmann. 2 vols. New York: Vienna House, 1973.

Brinkmann, Reinhold. *Late Idyll: The Second Symphony of Johannes Brahms.* Translated by Peter Palmer. Cambridge, Mass.: Harvard University Press, 1995.

Brodbeck, David. *Brahms Symphony No. 1.* Cambridge: Cambridge University Press, 1997.

———. "Brahms, the Third Symphony, and the New German School." In *Brahms and His World,* edited by Walter Frisch, 65–80. Princeton, N.J.: Princeton University Press, 1990.

———. "Mahler's Brahms." *American Brahms Society Newsletter* 10 (1992): 1–5.

———. "Medium and Meaning: New Aspects of the Chamber Music." In *The Cambridge*

Companion to Brahms, ed. Michael Musgrave, 98–132. Cambridge: Cambridge University Press, 1999.

Burkholder, J. Peter. "Brahms and Twentieth-Century Classical Music." *19th-Century Music* 8 (1984): 75–83.

Burnham, Scott. "How Music Matters: Poetic Content Revisited." In *Rethinking Music,* edited by Nicholas Cook and Mark Everist, 193–216. Oxford: Oxford University Press, 1999.

———. "The Role of Sonata Form in A. B. Marx's Theory of Form." *Journal of Music Theory* 33 (1989): 247–71.

Burstein, L. Poundie. "The Non-tonic Opening in Classical and Romantic Music." Ph.D. dissertation, City University of New York, 1988.

Cadwallader, Allen. "Foreground Motivic Ambiguity and Its Clarification at Middleground Levels in Selected Late Piano Pieces of Johannes Brahms." *Music Analysis* 7 (1988): 59–91.

———. "Form and Tonal Process: The Design of Different Structural Levels." In *Trends in Schenkerian Research,* edited by Allen Cadwallader, 1–21. New York: Schirmer, 1990.

———. "Schenker's Unpublished Graphic Analysis of Brahms's Intermezzo Op. 117, No. 2: Tonal Structure and Concealed Motivic Repetition." *Music Theory Spectrum* 6 (1984): 1–13.

Cadwallader, Allen, and William Pastille. "Schenker's Unpublished Work with the Music of Johannes Brahms." In *Schenker Studies 2,* edited by Carl Schachter and Hedi Siegel, 26–46. Cambridge: Cambridge University Press, 1999.

Caplin, William E. *Classical Form: A Theory of Formal Functions for the Instrumental Music of Haydn, Mozart, and Beethoven.* Oxford: Oxford University Press, 1998.

Clark, Suzannah. "Schenker's Mysterious Five." *19th-Century Music* 23 (1999): 84–102.

Cohn, Richard. "The Autonomy of Motives in Schenkerian Accounts of Tonal Music." *Music Theory Spectrum* 14 (1992): 150–70.

———. "The Dramatization of Hypermetric Conflicts in the Scherzo of Beethoven's Ninth Symphony." *19th-Century Music* 15 (1992): 188–206.

———. "Metric and Hypermetric Dissonance in the *Menuetto* of Mozart's Symphony in G Minor, K. 550." *Intégral* 6 (1992): 1–33.

———. "Schenker's Theory, Schenkerian Theory: Pure Unity or Constructive Conflict?" *Indiana Theory Review* 13 (1992): 1–20.

Cohn, Richard, and Douglas Dempster. "Hierarchical Unity, Plural Unities: Toward a Reconciliation." In *Disciplining Music: Musicology and Its Canons,* edited by Katherine Bergeron and Philip V. Bohlman, 156–81. Chicago: University of Chicago Press, 1992.

Cone, Edward T. *The Composer's Voice.* Berkeley: University of California Press, 1974.

———. *Musical Form and Musical Performance.* New York: W. W. Norton, 1968.

———. "Schubert's Promissory Note: An Exercise in Musical Hermeneutics." In *Schubert: Critical and Analytical Studies,* edited by Walter Frisch, 13–30. Lincoln: University of Nebraska Press, 1986.

———. "Schubert's Unfinished Business." *19th-Century Music* 7 (1984): 222–32.

———. "Three Ways of Reading a Detective Story—Or a Brahms Intermezzo." In *Music: A View from Delft,* edited by Robert P. Morgan, 77–93. Chicago: University of Chicago Press, 1989.

Cook, Nicholas. "Theorizing Musical Meaning." *Music Theory Spectrum* 23 (2001): 170–95.

Cooper, Grosvenor, and Leonard B. Meyer. *The Rhythmic Structure of Music.* Chicago: University of Chicago Press, 1960.

Czerny, Carl. *School of Practical Composition.* Translated by John Bishop. 3 vols. London: Robert Cocks, ca. 1848. Reprint (3 vols. in 2), New York: Da Capo Press, 1979.

Dahlhaus, Carl. *Between Romanticism and Modernism: Four Studies in the Music of the Late Nineteenth Century.* Translated by Mary Whittall. Berkeley: University of California Press, 1980.

———. *The Idea of Absolute Music.* Translated by Roger Lustig. Chicago: University of Chicago Press, 1989.

———. *Nineteenth-Century Music.* Translated by J. Bradford Robinson. Berkeley: University of California Press, 1989.

Daverio, John. *Crossing Paths: Schubert, Schumann, and Brahms.* Oxford: Oxford University Press, 2002.

———. "From 'Concertante Rondo' to 'Lyric Sonata': A Commentary on Brahms's Reception of Mozart." In *Brahms Studies,* vol. 1, edited by David Brodbeck, 111–38. Lincoln: University of Nebraska Press, 1994.

———. "The *Wechsel der Töne* in Brahms's *Schicksalslied.*" *Journal of the American Musicological Society* 46 (1993): 84–113.

Denny, Thomas. "Articulation, Elision, and Ambiguity in Schubert's Mature Sonata Forms: The Opus 99 Trio Finale in Its Context." *Journal of Musicology* 6 (1988): 340–66.

Dunsby, Jonathan. *Structural Ambiguity in Brahms: Analytical Approaches to Four Works.* Ann Arbor, Mich.: UMI Research Press, 1981.

Epstein, David. *Beyond Orpheus: Studies in Musical Structure.* Cambridge, Mass.: MIT Press, 1979.

———. "Brahms and the Mechanisms of Motion: The Composition of Performance." In *Brahms Studies: Analytical and Historical Perspectives,* edited by George S. Bozarth, 191–226. Oxford: Oxford University Press, 1990.

Fink, Robert. "Desire, Repression and Brahms's First Symphony." *Repercussions* 2 (1993): 75–103.

Fischer, Wilhelm. "Zur Entwicklungsgeschichte des Wiener klassischen Stils." *Studien zur Musikwissenschaft* 3 (1915): 24–84.

Forte, Allen. "Motive and Rhythmic Contour in the Alto Rhapsody." *Journal of Music Theory* 27 (1983): 255–71.

———. "Motive and Structural Levels in the First Movement of Brahms's C-Minor String Quartet." *Musical Quarterly* 69 (1983): 471–502.

———. "Schenker's Conception of Musical Structure." *Journal of Music Theory* 3 (1959): 1–30.

Frisch, Walter. *Brahms and the Principle of Developing Variation.* Berkeley: University of California Press, 1984.

———. *Brahms: The Four Symphonies.* New York: Schirmer, 1996.

———. "The Shifting Barline: Metrical Displacement in Brahms." In *Brahms Studies: Analytical and Historical Perspectives,* edited by George S. Bozarth, 139–63. Oxford: Oxford University Press, 1990.

Gagné, David. "The Compositional Use of Register in Three Piano Sonatas by Mozart." In *Trends in Schenkerian Research,* edited by Allen Cadwallader, 23–39. New York: Schirmer Books, 1990.

Gal, Hans. *Johannes Brahms: His Work and Personality.* Translated by Joseph Stein. New York: Knopf, 1963.

Geiringer, Karl. *Brahms: His Life and Work.* 3rd enlarged ed. New York: Da Capo Press, 1981, 1982.

Graybill, Roger C. "Brahms's Three-Key Expositions: Their Place within the Classical Tradition." Ph.D. dissertation, Yale University, 1983.

———. "Harmonic Circularity in Brahms's F Major Cello Sonata: An Alternative to Schenker's Reading in *Free Composition.*" *Music Theory Spectrum* 10 (1988): 43–55.

Haimo, Ethan T. *Haydn's Symphonic Forms: Essays in Compositional Logic.* Oxford: Oxford University Press, 1995.

Halm, August. *Von zwei Kulturen der Musik.* 3rd ed. Stuttgart: Klett, 1947.

Handschin, Jaques. *Musikgeschichte im Überblick.* Lucerne: Rüber, 1948.

Hanslick, Edward. *The Beautiful in Music: A Contribution to the Revival of Musical Aesthetics.* Translated by Gustav Cohen. New York: Da Capo Press, 1974.

Hatten, Robert S. *Musical Meaning in Beethoven: Markedness, Correlation, and Interpretation.* Bloomington: Indiana University Press, 1994.

Henschel, George. *Personal Recollections of Johannes Brahms: Some of His Letters to and Pages from a Journal Kept by George Henschel.* Boston: Badger, 1907.

Hepokoski, James, and Warren Darcy. *Elements of Sonata Theory: Norms, Types, and Deformations in the Late 18th-Century Sonata.* Oxford: Oxford University Press, forthcoming.

———. "The Medial Caesura and Its Role in the Eighteenth-Century Sonata Exposition." *Music Theory Spectrum* 19 (1997): 115–54.

Hofmann, Renate. "Johannes Brahms im Spiegel der Korrespondenz Clara Schumanns." In *Brahms und seine Zeit: Symposion Hamburg 1983,* edited by Constantin Floros, Hans Joachim Marx, and Peter Petersen, 45–58. Laaber: Laaber Verlag, 1984.

Hull, Kenneth. "Allusive Irony in Brahms's Fourth Symphony." In *Brahms Studies,* vol. 2, edited by David Brodbeck, 135–68. Lincoln: University of Nebraska Press, 1998.

Imbrie, Andrew. "'Extra' Measures and Metrical Ambiguity in Beethoven." In *Beethoven Studies,* edited by Alan Tyson, 45–66. New York: W. W. Norton, 1973.

Jackson, Timothy L. "Aspects of Sexuality and Structure in the Later Symphonies of Tchaikovsky." *Music Analysis* 14 (1995): 3–26.

———. *Tchaikovsky, Symphony No. 6 (Pathétique).* Cambridge: Cambridge University Press, 1999.

———. "The Tragic Reversed Recapitulation in the German Classical Tradition." *Journal of Music Theory* 40 (1996): 61–111.

Jenner, Gustav. *Johannes Brahms als Mensch, Lehrer, und Künstler: Studien und Erlebnisse.* Marburg in Hessen: N. G. Elwert'sche Verlagsbuchhandlung, 1905.

Jonas, Oswald. *Introduction to the Theory of Heinrich Schenker: The Nature of the Musical Work of Art.* Translated and edited by John Rothgeb. New York: Longman, 1982.

Kalbeck, Max. *Johannes Brahms.* Rev. ed. 4 vols. in 8. Berlin: Deutsche Brahms-Gesellschaft, 1913–22.

———, ed. *Katalog 100: Johannes Brahms.* Tutzing: Hans Schneider, 1964.

Kamien, Roger. "Quasi-auxiliary Cadences: Some Preliminary Observations." Paper delivered at the Third International Schenker Symposium, Mannes College of Music, March 12, 1999.

Karl, Gregory. "Structuralism and Musical Plot." *Music Theory Spectrum* 19 (1997): 13–34.

Karl, Gregory, and Jenefer Robinson. "Shostakovich's Tenth Symphony and the Musical

Expression of Cognitively Complex Emotions." In *Music and Meaning,* edited by Jenefer Robinson, 154–78. Ithaca, N.Y.: Cornell University Press, 1997.

Keiler, Allan. "The Empiricist Illusion." *Perspectives of New Music* 17 (1978): 161–95.

———. "On Some Properties of Schenker's Pitch Derivations." *Music Perception* 1 (1984): 200–28.

———. "The Syntax of Prolongation (Part I)." *In Theory Only* 3 (1977): 3–27.

———. "Two Views of Musical Semiotics." In *The Sign in Word and Language,* edited by W. Steiner, 138–68. Austin: University of Texas Press, 1981.

Kerman, Joseph. *Contemplating Music: Challenges to Musicology.* Cambridge, Mass.: Harvard University Press, 1985.

Keys, Ivor. *Brahms Chamber Music.* Seattle: University of Washington Press, 1974.

Kirkendale, Warren. *Fugue and Fugato in Rococo and Classical Chamber Music.* Durham, N.C.: Duke University Press, 1979.

Kivy, Peter. *The Corded Shell.* Princeton, N.J.: Princeton University Press, 1980.

———. *Music Alone.* Ithaca, N.Y.: Cornell University Press, 1990.

———. *Sound and Semblance.* Princeton, N.J.: Princeton University Press, 1984.

Knapp, Raymond. "A Review of Norrington's Brahms." *American Brahms Society Newsletter* 11 (1993): 4–7.

Komar, Arthur J. "The Pedagogy of Tonal Hierarchy." *In Theory Only* 10 (1988): 23–28.

Kramer, Lawrence. "Haydn's Chaos, Schenker's Order, or Hermeneutics and Musical Analysis: Can They Mix?" *19th-Century Music* 16 (1992): 3–17.

———. *Music as Cultural Practice, 1800–1900.* Berkeley: University of California Press, 1990.

———. *Music and Poetry: The Nineteenth Century and After.* Berkeley: University of California Press, 1984.

Kraus, Joseph. "Tonal Plan and Narrative Plot in Tchaikovsky's Symphony No. 5 in E Minor." *Music Theory Spectrum* 13 (1991): 21–47.

Krebs, Harald. *Fantasy Pieces: Metrical Dissonance in the Music of Robert Schumann.* Oxford: Oxford University Press, 1999.

———. "Some Extensions of the Concepts of Metrical Consonance and Dissonance." *Journal of Music Theory* 31 (1987): 99–120.

Langer, Suzanne K. *Feeling and Form.* New York: Charles Scribner's Sons, 1953.

Larsen, Jens Peter. "Sonata Form Problems." In *Handel, Haydn, and the Viennese Classical Style,* translated by Ulrich Krämer, 269–79. Ann Arbor, Mich.: UMI Research Press, 1988.

Laskowski, Larry. "J. S. Bach's 'Binary' Dance Movements: Form and Voice Leading." In *Schenker Studies,* edited by Hedi Siegel, 84–93. Cambridge: Cambridge University Press, 1990.

Leppert, Richard, and Susan McClary. *Music and Society: The Politics of Composition, Performance, and Reception.* Cambridge: Cambridge University Press, 1987.

Lerdahl, Fred, and Ray Jackendoff. *A Generative Theory of Tonal Music.* Cambridge, Mass.: MIT Press, 1983.

Levinson, Jerrold. *Music, Art, and Metaphysics.* Ithaca, N.Y.: Cornell University Press, 1990.

Lewin, David. "Music Theory, Phenomenology, and Modes of Perception." *Music Perception* 3 (1986): 327–92.

———. "On Harmony and Meter in Brahms's Op. 76, No. 8." *19th-Century Music* 4 (1981): 261–65.

———. "Vocal Meter in Schoenberg's Atonal Music, with a Note on a Serial Haupstimme." *In Theory Only* 6 (1982): 12–36.

Litterick, Louise. "Brahms the Indecisive: Notes on the First Movement of the Fourth Symphony." In *Brahms 2: Biographical, Documentary, and Analytic Studies,* edited by Michael Musgrave, 223–35. Cambridge: Cambridge University Press, 1987.

Littlefield, Richard, and David Neumeyer. "Rewriting Schenker: Narrative—History—Ideology." *Music Theory Spectrum* 14 (1992): 38–65.

Litzmann, Berthold. *Clara Schumann: Ein Künstlerleben nach Tagebüchern und Briefen.* Rev. ed. 3 vols. Leipzig: Breitkopf & Härtel, 1920.

Longyear, Rey M., and Kate R. Covington. "Sources of the Three-Key Exposition." *Journal of Musicology* 6 (1988): 448–70.

Lubben, Joseph. "Schenker the Progressive: Analytic Practice in *Der Tonwille.*" *Music Theory Spectrum* 15 (1993): 59–75.

MacDonald, Malcolm. *Brahms.* London: Dent, 1990.

Marx, Adolph Bernhard. *Die Lehre von der musikalischen Komposition.* 4 vols. Leipzig: Breitkopf & Härtel, 1837–1847.

Maus, Fred Everett. "Music as Drama." *Music Theory Spectrum* 10 (1988): 56–73.

———. "Music as Narrative." *Indiana Theory Review* 12 (1991): 1–34.

May, Florence. *The Life of Johannes Brahms.* 2nd ed. 2 vols. London: Reeves, 1948.

McClary, Susan. *Conventional Wisdom: The Content of Musical Form.* Berkeley: University of California Press, 2000.

———. *Feminine Endings: Music, Gender, and Sexuality.* Minneapolis: University of Minnesota Press, 1991.

McCreless, Patrick. "Contemporary Music Theory and the New Musicology: An Introduction." *Journal of Musicology* 15 (1997): 291–96.

———. "Schenker and Chromatic Tonicization: A Reappraisal." In *Schenker Studies,* edited by Hedi Siegel, 125–45. Cambridge: Cambridge University Press, 1990.

———. "Syntagmatics and Paradigmatics: Some Implications for the Analysis of Chromaticism in Tonal Music." *Music Theory Spectrum* 13 (1991): 147–78.

McKee, Eric. "Auxiliary Progressions as a Source of Conflict between Tonal Structure and Phrase Structure." *Music Theory Spectrum* 18 (1996): 51–76.

Meyer, Leonard B. *Emotion and Meaning in Music.* Chicago: University of Chicago Press, 1956.

———. *Explaining Music: Essays and Explorations.* Chicago: University of Chicago Press, 1973.

———. *Music, the Arts, and Ideas.* Chicago: University of Chicago Press, 1967.

———. *Style and Music: Theory, History, and Ideology.* Philadelphia: University of Pennsylvania Press, 1989.

Mitschka, Arno. *Der Sonatensatz in den Werken von Johannes Brahms.* Gütersloh, 1961.

Morgan, Robert P. "The Delayed Structural Downbeat and Its Effect on the Tonal and Rhythmic Structure of Sonata Form Recapitulation." Ph.D. dissertation, Princeton University, 1969.

Moyer, Brigitte. "Concepts of Form in the Nineteenth Century with Special Reference to A. B. Marx and Sonata Form." Ph.D. dissertation, Stanford University, 1969.

Musgrave, Michael. *A Brahms Reader.* New Haven, Conn.: Yale University Press, 2000.

———. "The Cultural World of Brahms." In *Brahms: Bibliographic, Documentary, and Analytical Studies,* edited by Robert Pascall, 1–26. Cambridge: Cambridge University Press, 1983.

————. *The Music of Brahms.* London: Routledge and Kegan Paul, 1985.

Narmour, Eugene. *Beyond Schenkerism.* Chicago: University of Chicago Press, 1977.

Newcomb, Anthony. "Once More 'Between Absolute and Program Music': Schumann's Second Symphony." *19th-Century Music* 7 (1984): 233–50.

————. "Schumann and Late-Eighteenth-Century Narrative Strategies." *19th-Century Music* 11 (1987): 164–74.

————. "Sound and Feeling." *Critical Inquiry* 10 (1984): 614–43.

Notley, Margaret. "Brahms's Cello Sonata in F Major and Its Genesis: A Study in Half-Step Relations." In *Brahms Studies,* vol. 1, edited by David Brodbeck, 139–60. Lincoln: University of Nebraska Press, 1994.

————. "Late-Nineteenth-Century Chamber Music and the Cult of the Classical Adagio." *19th-Century Music* 23 (1999): 33–61.

Nüll, Edwin von der. "Strukturelle Grundbedingungen der Brahmsschen Sonatenexposition im Vergleich zur Klassik." *Die Musik* 22 (1929): 32–37.

Orel, Alfred. "Ein eigenhändiges Werkverzeichnis von Johannes Brahms: Ein wichtiger Beitrag zur Brahmsforschung." *Die Musik* 29 (1937): 529–41.

Oster, Ernst. "Register and the Large-Scale Connection." In *Readings in Schenker Analysis and Other Approaches,* edited by Maury Yeston, 54–71. New Haven, Conn.: Yale University Press, 1977.

Parmer, Dillon. "Brahms the Programmatic." Ph.D. dissertation, University of Rochester, 1995.

————. "Brahms, Song Quotation, and Secret Programs." *19th-Century Music* 19 (1995): 161–90.

Pascall, Robert J. "Formal Principles in the Music of Brahms." Ph.D. dissertation, Oxford University, 1973.

————. "Some Special Uses of Sonata Form by Brahms." *Soundings* 4 (1974): 58–63.

Ratner, Leonard. *Classic Music: Expression, Form, and Style.* New York: Schirmer, 1980.

————. "Harmonic Aspects of Classical Form." *Journal of the American Musicological Society* 2 (1949): 159–68.

Reich, Nancy B. "Clara Schumann and Johannes Brahms." In *Brahms and His World,* edited by Walter Frisch, 37–47. Princeton, N.J.: Princeton University Press, 1990.

Reicha, Anton. *Cours de composition musicale. Vollständiges Lehrbuch der musikalischen Composition.* Edited and translated by Carl Czerny. Vienna: Anton Diabelli, preface dated 1832.

Rosen, Charles. *The Classical Style: Haydn, Mozart, Beethoven.* New York: W. W. Norton, 1971.

————. *Sonata Forms.* Rev. ed. New York: W. W. Norton, 1988.

Rothgeb, John. "Design as a Key to Structure in Tonal Music." In *Readings in Schenker Analysis and Other Approaches,* edited by Maury Yeston, 72–93. New Haven, Conn.: Yale University Press, 1977.

————. Review of *Brahms and the Principle of Developing Variation,* by Walter Frisch. *Music Theory Spectrum* 9 (1987): 204–15.

————. "Thematic Content: A Schenkerian View." In *Aspects of Schenkerian Theory,* edited by David Beach, 39–60. New Haven, Conn.: Yale University Press, 1983.

Rothstein, William. *Phrase Rhythm in Tonal Music.* New York: Schirmer Books, 1989.

————. Review of *Brahms and the Principle of Developing Variation,* by Walter Frisch. *Journal of Music Theory* 30 (1986): 285–95.

Salzer, Felix. *Structural Hearing: Tonal Coherence in Music.* 2 vols. New York: Dover, 1962.

Sams, Eric. "Schubert's Illness Re-examined." *Musical Times* 121 (1980): 15–22.

Schachter, Carl. "Analysis by Key: Another Look at Modulation." *Music Analysis* 6 (1987): 289–318.

——. "Either/Or." In *Schenker Studies,* edited by Hedi Siegel, 165–79. Cambridge: Cambridge University Press, 1990.

——. "The First Movement of Brahms's Second Symphony: The First Theme and Its Consequences." *Music Analysis* 2 (1983): 55–68.

——. "Rhythm and Linear Analysis: Aspects of Meter." *Music Forum* 6 (1987): 1–59.

——. "Rhythm and Linear Analysis: Durational Reduction." *Music Forum* 5 (1980): 197–232.

——. "Rhythm and Linear Analysis: A Preliminary Study." *Music Forum* 4 (1976): 281–334.

Schauffler, Robert H. *The Unknown Brahms, His Life, Character, and Works; Based on New Material.* New York: Crown, 1933.

Schenker, Heinrich. *Beethoven's Ninth Symphony: A Portrayal of Its Musical Content, with Running Commentary on Performance and Literature as Well.* Translated and edited by John Rothgeb. New Haven, Conn.: Yale University Press, 1992.

——. *Five Graphic Music Analyses.* New York: Dover, 1969.

——. *Free Composition.* Translated and edited by Ernst Oster. New York: Longman, 1979.

——. *Der freie Satz.* Vienna: Universal Edition, 1935.

——. *Fünf Urlinie-Tafeln.* New York: David Mannes School, 1932.

——. *The Masterwork in Music: A Yearbook.* Vols. 1–3. Edited by William Drabkin. Translated by Ian Bent et al. Cambridge: Cambridge University Press, 1994–97.

——. *Das Meisterwerk in der Musik.* Vols. 1–3. Munich: Drei Masken Verlag, 1925–30.

——. "Organic Structure in Sonata Form." Translated by Orin Grossman in *Readings in Schenkerian Analysis and Other Approaches,* edited by Maury Yeston, 38–53. New Haven, Conn.: Yale University Press, 1977.

——. *Der Tonwille.* Ten issues. Vienna: A. Gutmann Verlag, 1921–24. Reprint in 1 vol., Hildesheim and New York: George Olms, 1990.

Schoenberg, Arnold. "Brahms the Progressive." In Schoenberg, *Style and Idea,* edited by Leonard Stein, translated by Leo Black, 398–441. New York: St. Martin's Press, 1975. Reprint, Berkeley: University of California Press, 1984.

——. *Fundamentals of Musical Composition.* Edited by Gerald Strang and Leonard Stein. London: Faber and Faber, 1967.

Sisman, Elaine R. "Brahms's Slow Movements: Reinventing the 'Closed' Forms." In *Brahms Studies: Analytical and Historical Perspectives,* edited by George S. Bozarth, 79–103. Oxford: Oxford University Press, 1990.

——. *Mozart, The "Jupiter" Symphony, No. 41 in C Major, K. 551.* Cambridge: Cambridge University Press, 1993.

Smallman, Basil. *The Piano Quartet and Quintet: Style, Structure, and Scoring.* Oxford: Oxford University Press, 1994.

Smith, Charles J. "Musical Form and Fundamental Structure: An Investigation of Schenker's *Formenlehre.*" *Music Analysis* 15 (1996): 191–297.

Smith, Peter H. "Brahms and Motivic $^6_3$ Chords." *Music Analysis* 16 (1997): 175–217.

——. "Brahms and the Neapolitan Complex: ♭II, ♭VI, and Their Multiple Functions in the First Movement of the F-Minor Clarinet Sonata." In *Brahms Studies,* vol. 2, edited by David Brodbeck, 169–208. Lincoln: University of Nebraska Press, 1998.

———. "Brahms and Schenker: A Mutual Response to Sonata Form." *Music Theory Spectrum* 16 (1994): 77–103.

———. "Brahms and the Shifting Barline: Metric Displacement and Formal Process in the Trios with Wind Instruments." In *Brahms Studies*, vol. 3, edited by David Brodbeck, 191–229. Lincoln and London: University of Nebraska Press, 2001.

———. "Liquidation, Augmentation, and Brahms's Recapitulatory Overlaps." *19th-Century Music* 17 (1994): 237–61.

———. "Structural Tonic or Apparent Tonic?: Parametric Conflict, Temporal Perspective, and a Continuum of Articulative Possibilities." *Journal of Music Theory* 39 (1995): 245–83.

Snarrenberg, Robert. *Schenker's Interpretive Practice.* Cambridge: Cambridge University Press, 1997.

Snyder, John L. "Schenker and the First Movement of Mozart's Sonata, K. 545: An Uninterrupted Sonata-Form Movement?" *Theory and Practice* 16 (1991): 51–78.

Solie, Ruth A. "The Living Work: Organicism and Musical Analysis." *19th-Century Music* 4 (1980): 147–56.

Solomon, Maynard. "Franz Schubert and the Peacocks of Benvenuto Cellini." *19th-Century Music* 12 (1989): 193–206.

Steblin, Rita. *A History of Key Characteristics in the Eighteenth and Early Nineteenth Centuries.* Ann Arbor, Mich.: UMI Research Press, 1983.

Subotnik, Rose Rosengard. *Developing Variations: Style and Ideology in Western Music.* Minneapolis: University of Minnesota Press, 1991.

Suurpää, Lauri. "Continuous Exposition and Tonal Structure in Three Late Haydn Works." *Music Theory Spectrum* 21 (1999): 174–99.

———. "The Undivided *Ursatz* and the Omission of the Tonic *Stufe* at the Beginning of the Recapitulation." Paper delivered at the annual meeting of the Society for Music Theory, November 4, 2000, Toronto.

Tovey, Donald F. "Brahms." In *Essays in Musical Analysis: Chamber Music.* London: Oxford University Press, 1944.

———. "Brahms's Chamber Music." In *Essays and Lectures on Music*, 220–70. London: Oxford University Press, 1949.

———. *Essays in Musical Analysis.* Vol. 2. London: Oxford University Press, 1935.

Treitler, Leo. "Language and the Interpretation of Music." In *Music and Meaning*, edited by Jenefer Robinson, 23–56. Ithaca, N.Y.: Cornell University Press, 1997.

———. *Music and the Historical Imagination.* Cambridge, Mass.: Harvard University Press, 1989.

Tusa, Michael C. "Beethoven's 'C-Minor Mood': Some Thoughts on the Structural Implications of Key Choice." In *Beethoven Forum* 2, edited by Lewis Lockwood and James Webster, 1–27. Lincoln: University of Nebraska Press, 1993.

Urbantschitsch, Viktor. "Die Entwicklung der Sonatenform bei Brahms." *Studien zur Musikwissenschaft* 14 (1927): 265–85.

van den Toorn, Pieter C. *Music, Politics, and the Academy.* Berkeley: University of California Press, 1995.

Walker, Frank. *Hugo Wolf: A Biography.* Princeton, N.J.: Princeton University Press, 1992.

Webster, James. "The *Alto Rhapsody:* Psychology, Intertextuality, and Brahms's Artistic Development." In *Brahms Studies*, vol. 3, edited by David Brodbeck, 19–45. Lincoln: University of Nebraska Press, 2001.

———. "Brahms's *Tragic Overture:* The Form of Tragedy." In *Brahms: Bibliographic,*

Documentary, and Analytical Studies, edited by Robert Pascall, 99–124. Cambridge: Cambridge University Press, 1983.

———. "The C Sharp Minor Version of Brahms's Op. 60." *Musical Times* 121 (1980): 89–93.

———. "The General and the Particular in Brahms's Later Sonata Forms." In *Brahms Studies: Analytical and Historical Perspectives,* edited by George S. Bozarth, 49–78. Oxford: Oxford University Press, 1990.

———. *Haydn's "Farewell" Symphony and the Idea of Classical Style.* Cambridge: Cambridge University Press, 1991.

———. "Schubert's Sonata Form and Brahms's First Maturity." Parts 1 and 2. *19th-Century Music* 2 (1978): 18–35, and 3 (1979): 52–71.

———. "Sonata Form." In *The New Grove Dictionary of Music and Musicians,* 2nd ed., ed. Stanley Sadie, vol. 23, 687–701. London: Macmillan, 2001.

Winter, Robert S. "The Bifocal Close and the Evolution of the Viennese Classical Style." *Journal of the American Musicological Society* 42 (1989): 275–337.

Wintle, Christopher. "The 'Sceptred Pall': Brahms's Progressive Harmony." In *Brahms 2: Biographical, Documentary, and Analytical Studies,* edited by Michael Musgrave, 197–222. Cambridge: Cambridge University Press, 1987.

Index of Brahms's Works

Page numbers in italics indicate musical examples and illustrations.

General Index

Page numbers in italics indicate musical examples and illustrations.

Adorno, Theodor, 183
Agawu, V. Kofi, 4, 300n15, 301nn16,17,21
allusive irony, 304n52
anxiety, 219, 222, 231, 246, 262, 265, 273–275, 277–280. *see also* deathly anxiety
Aristotle, 235–238, 243. *see also* classical tragedy
augmented-triad, expressive use of, 17–18, 204–205, *204, 205,* 214, 216–217, *216,* 222, 303n40
auxiliary cadence, 38–40, 62, 288n8, 293n19

Babbitt, Milton, 4, 287n1
bait-and-switch strategy, 160, 176–177
Bassbrechung, 33, 44, 84
Beach, David, 62, 64, 278, 289n24, 293n1, 295n27, 306n25, 307nn27,29,30,31
Beethoven, Ludwig Von, 9, 22, 36, 49, 65, 84, 90, 107, 109, 116, 130, 135, 143, 147, 149–151, 153, 158, 160–161, 172, 178, 183–184, 190–191, 232, 244–245, 259, 286n14, 291n5, 292n8, 292n12, 295n19, 304n49; A-Major Piano Sonata, op.101, 289n21; A-Major String Quartet, op. 18, no. 5, 147; Appassionata Sonata, 60, *61,* 143, *150–151,* 298n24, 302n30; Archduke Trio, 147; B flat-Major String Quartet, op. 130, 147; C-Major Piano Sonata, op. 2, no. 3, 147; C#-Minor Piano Sonata, op.27, no. 2, 298n25; C#-Minor String Quartet, op. 131, 10; D-Major Piano Sonata, op.10, no. 3, 298n25; D-Minor Piano Sonata, op. 31, no. 2, 289n16, 293n1, 298n25; E flat-Major Piano Sonata, op. 31, no. 3, 288n8, 299n35; G-Major String Trio, op. 9, no. 1, 147; Hammerklavier Sonata, 147, 189; Moonlight Sonata, 10; Pathétique Sonata, 143, *148–149,* 149–151, 153, *154,* 160–161, 167, 170, 176–177, 298n27; Piano Concerto No. 3, 15; Symphony No. 3 "Eroica" in E-Major, 190; Symphony No. 5, 10, 224–225, 232, 259, 261, 304n52; Symphony No. 9, 224–225, 244–245, 300n2, 301n23; Waldstein Sonata, 147
bifocal close, 160–161

Billroth, Theodore, 3
Brahms, Johannes. *see also* Index of Brahms's Works; Arnold Schoenberg's view of Brahms, 66–71, 85, 89, 108–109; composition of the C-Minor Piano Quintet, op. 60, 3, 8–10, 22–27, 193; correspondence with Joseph Joachim, 22–26, 287n20, 299n34; death of his mother, 174–175, 192; expressive significance of C-Minor to Brahms, 259; first maturity, 5, 21, 137, 147, 153, 158, 285n9, 297n20; Heinrich Schenker's view of Brahms, 64–66, 108–109; relationship with the Schumans, 3, 5, 8, 21–25, 193, 219–224, 227, 232, 235, 280–282, 299n41, 303n47; strategies of expository articulation 37–42, 122–137, *138–140,* 140, 143, 147–149, 151, 153–154, 158, 160–164, 167–180; strategies of recapitulatory articulation 42–49, 68–89, 99–106, 116–121, 126–127; use of ciphers, 281–282, *282*
"Brahms the Progressive." *See* Schoenberg, Arnold
Brinkmann, Reinhold, 244–246, 254, 304n53
Brodbeck, David, 23, 287n18, 288n9, 299n37, 300n44, 304n55

C-Major expression, 10–14, 106, 197, 206–207, 212–216, 224, 226, 230–232, 249–254, 259, 261, 267–269, 277–278. *see also* C-Minor/Major topos
C-Minor expression, 10–17, 22, 89–90, 95–96, 106, 195–199, 201–202, 206–216, *209,* 224, 226, 228, 230, 232, 247–254, 261–280, 286n14. *see also* C-Minor/Major topos, minor-mode expression
C-Minor/Major topos, 22, 213–215, 225, 232, 246–247, 251, 259, 286n10, 303n40, 303n42. *see also* C-Major expression, C-Minor expression, minor-mode expression, mode-mixture expression
caesura-fill 167, 170
cadential evasion. *see* evaded cadence
chiaroscuro, 232

ironic expression, 83–84, 101, 198, 210–211, 225, 233, 249, 251, 266, 268

Jenner, Gustav, 65
Joachim, Joseph, 22–26, 251, 282; Frei, aber einsam, 251

Kalbeck, Max, 23–24, 178, 303n46
Karl, Gregory, 302nn30,38
Keiler, Allan, 111
key scheme, 31–36, 40, 43–44, 49, 53, 59, 62–64, 108, 123, 128, 135, 151, 176, 270, 273. *see also* dimensional counterpoint
Koch, Heinrich, 122
Kopfton, 44, 50, 53–54, 56, 58, 60, 110–111, 113–117, 190, 289n24, 290n25, 295n23
Kramer, Lawrence, 291n7

lament tetrachord, 89, *196*, 255–256, *256*, 273–274, *274, 277–280, 278*
lament topics, 173–174, 191–192, 195, *196–197*, 207, 232. *see also* lament tetrachord
Laskowski, Larry, 294n16
Lewin, David, 288n10
linear progression, 115, 117, 294n14, 295nn22,23
liquidation, 40–41, 82, 94, 130, 167, 267, *267*, 269
Liszt, Franz, 290n35
literary parallels, 281
Longyear, Rey M., 297n18

MacDonald, Malcolm, 299n37
Mahler, Gustav, 290n35, 291n5
markedness, 190–192, 198–199, 206, 306n23
Massenet, Jules, 302n36
McClary, Susan, 183, 300n2
McKee, Eric, 62, 64
medial caesura, 123, *139,* 140, 147–150, *155–156,* 160–161, 167–169, *168,* 176–177, 239, 296n2, 299n34
mediant relationships, 32, *34, 35,* 36–45, *39, 46,* 107. *see also* medial caesura
Mendelssohn, Felix: C-Minor Piano Trio, op. 66, 224–225, 232, 304n55
metric dissonance, *219*
metric expression, 18–20, 203–204, *203,* 206, 217–219, *218, 219*
Meyer, Leonard B., 4, 288nn6,7
mid-expositional trimodular block, 298n27
Mitschka, Arno, 239
minor-mode expression, 84, 234–280. *see also* C-minor expression, darkness-to-the-stars

archetype, mode-mixture expression, tragic expression
minor-to-major topos, 10–13, 270, 306n15. *see also* darkness-to-stars archetype
mode-mixture expression, 84, 150, 178–180, 191–192, 194–202, *200,* 207–210, 213–216, 223, 232, 250–251, 257, 261, 267. *see also* C-major expression, C-minor expression, C minor/major topos, minor-mode expression
mode shift in expository design, 107, 123, 135–137, 143, *146–147,* 147–150, *148–149, 150–151, 152–153,* 154, 158, 175–180, 297n18, 298n24
Morgan, Robert P., 289n15
Moser, Andreas, 23
motivic parallelism, 279
Mozart, W. A., 9, 37, 49, 65, 67, 80, 107, 109, 116, 135, 147, 153, 161, 172, 239, 259, 269, 289n24, 290n29, 291n5, 292n12, 297n8; A Major Piano Sonata, K. 331, 61–62, *62;* B-flat Major Piano Sonata, K. 333, 54–60, *56–57, 58;* C-Major Piano Concerto, K. 545, 288n8; C-Major Piano Sonata, K. 330, 289n24; C-Major Piano Sonata, K. 545, 293n1, 299n35; C-Minor Piano Concerto, K. 491, 10, 259; Dissonant Quartet, K. 465, 259–261; E flat-Major Piano Sonata, K. 282, 289n24; E flat-Major Symphonie Concertante, K. 364, 289n24; F-Major Piano Sonata, K. 280, 32–36, *33, 34, 35;* F-Major Piano Sonata, K. 332, 143, *146–147,* 149–150, *154;* G-Major Piano Sonata, K. 283, 289n24; Jupiter Symphony in C-Major, 269, 306n22
Musgrave, Michael, 299n37
musical ciphers, 281–282, *282,* 302n29
musical hermeneutics. *see* musical meaning, expressive interpretation
musical meaning, 183–186. *see also* expressive interpretation
music theory, general discussion, 4–6

Nachlass. *see* Schenker, Heinrich
nature imagery, 160, 175, 191–192, 226–229, 245–247, 304n52
Newcomb, Anthony, 183–184
New German School, 64, 290n35
New Musicology, 183–184, 186, 188–190, 283–284, 301n17
Notley, Margaret, 296n7, 299n32

Oedipal complex, 220
open form, 50, *52, 62*

PETER H. SMITH is Associate Professor of Music Theory at the University of Notre Dame. He has also taught as a Visiting Associate Professor at the University of Chicago and is a member of the Board of Directors of the American Brahms Society.